THE LAKE SHORE ELECTRIC RAILWAY STORY

Railroads Past and Present
Series editor: George M. Smerk

THE LAKE SHORE ELECTRIC RAILWAY STORY

by Herbert H. Harwood, Jr.
and Robert S. Korach

INDIANA UNIVERSITY PRESS
Bloomington and Indianapolis

This book is a publication of

INDIANA UNIVERSITY PRESS
Office of Scholarly Publishing
Herman B Wells Library 350
1320 East 10th Street
Bloomington, Indiana 47405 USA

iupress.indiana.edu

First paperback edition 2016

The paper used in this publication meets the minimum requirements of the American National Standard
for Information Sciences—Permanence of Paper for Printed Library Materials, ANSI Z39.48-1992.

Manufactured in the United States of America

The Library of Congress cataloged the original edition as follows:

Harwood, Herbert H., Jr.
    The Lake Shore Electric Railway story / by Herbert H. Harwood, Jr. and Robert S. Korach.
        p. cm. – (Railroads past and present)
    Includes bibliographical references and index.
    ISBN 0-253-33797-6 (cl : alk. paper)
        1. Lake Shore Electric Railway Company. 2. Electric railroads—
Ohio—History. I. Korach, Robert S. II. Title. III. Series.
TF1025.L35 H37 2000
385'.09771—dc21

                                                                00-039646

ISBN 978-0-253-33797-9 (cl.)
ISBN 978-0-253-01766-6 (pbk.)
ISBN 978-0-253-01770-3 (eb)

2 3 4 5 6   21 20 19 18 17 16

CONTENTS

LIST OF MAPS

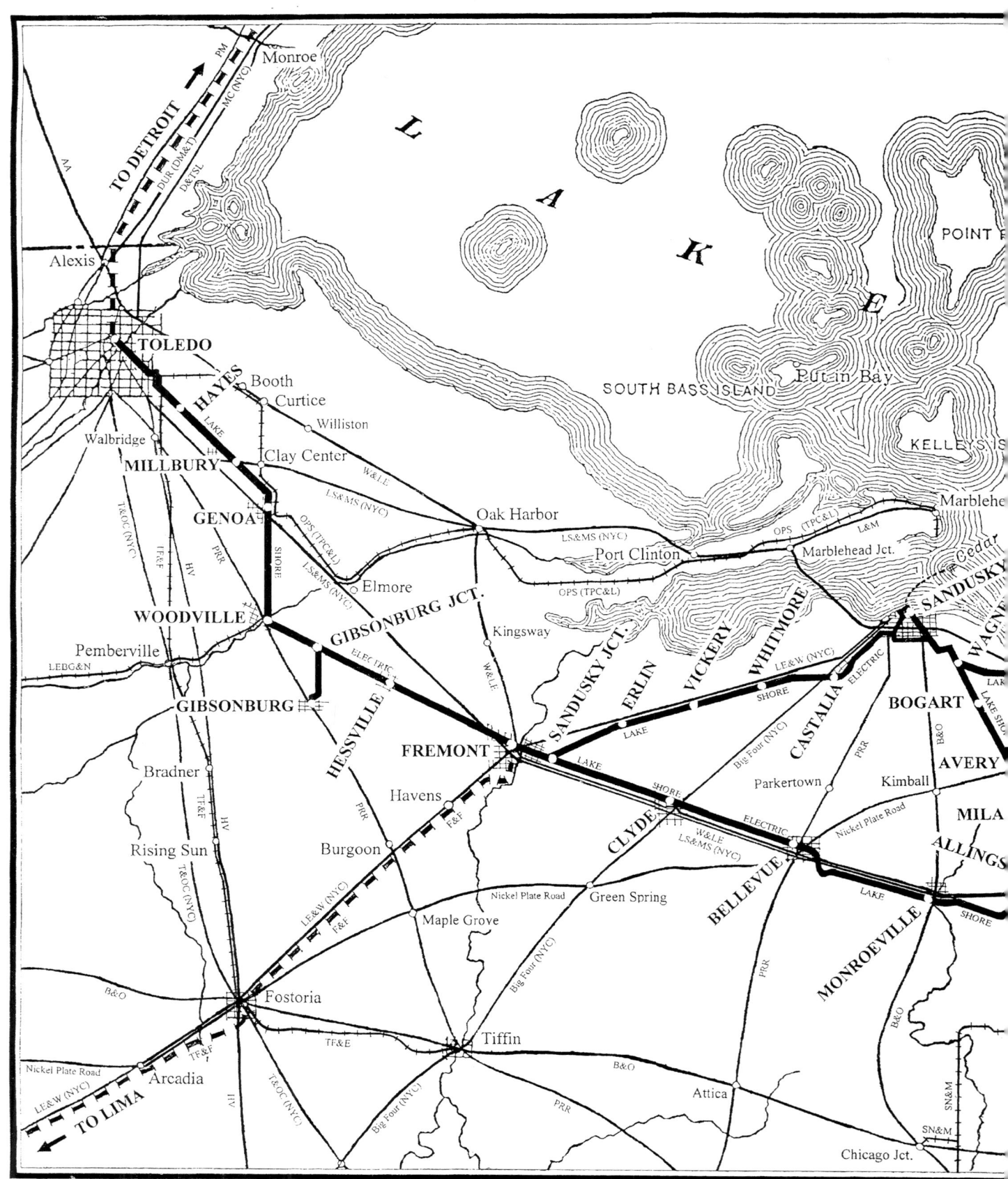

Lake Shore Electric Railway—System Map.

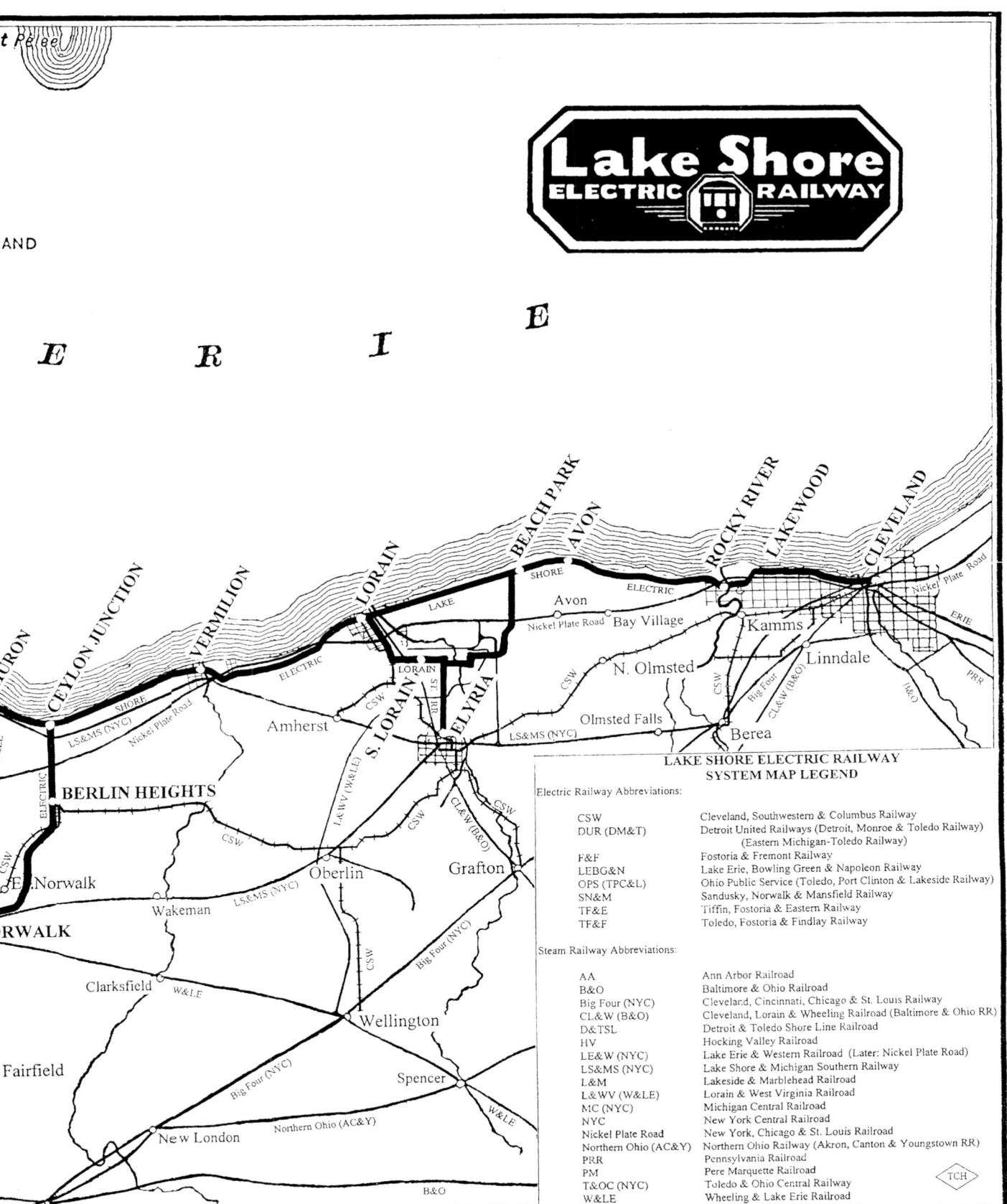

Lake Shore ELECTRIC RAILWAY

ERIE

LAKE SHORE ELECTRIC RAILWAY
SYSTEM MAP LEGEND

Electric Railway Abbreviations:

CSW	Cleveland, Southwestern & Columbus Railway
DUR (DM&T)	Detroit United Railways (Detroit, Monroe & Toledo Railway) (Eastern Michigan-Toledo Railway)
F&F	Fostoria & Fremont Railway
LEBG&N	Lake Erie, Bowling Green & Napoleon Railway
OPS (TPC&L)	Ohio Public Service (Toledo, Port Clinton & Lakeside Railway)
SN&M	Sandusky, Norwalk & Mansfield Railway
TF&E	Tiffin, Fostoria & Eastern Railway
TF&F	Toledo, Fostoria & Findlay Railway

Steam Railway Abbreviations:

AA	Ann Arbor Railroad
B&O	Baltimore & Ohio Railroad
Big Four (NYC)	Cleveland, Cincinnati, Chicago & St. Louis Railway
CL&W (B&O)	Cleveland, Lorain & Wheeling Railroad (Baltimore & Ohio RR)
D&TSL	Detroit & Toledo Shore Line Railroad
HV	Hocking Valley Railroad
LE&W (NYC)	Lake Erie & Western Railroad (Later: Nickel Plate Road)
LS&MS (NYC)	Lake Shore & Michigan Southern Railway
L&M	Lakeside & Marblehead Railroad
L&WV (W&LE)	Lorain & West Virginia Railroad
MC (NYC)	Michigan Central Railroad
NYC	New York Central Railroad
Nickel Plate Road	New York, Chicago & St. Louis Railroad
Northern Ohio (AC&Y)	Northern Ohio Railway (Akron, Canton & Youngstown RR)
PRR	Pennsylvania Railroad
PM	Pere Marquette Railroad
T&OC (NYC)	Toledo & Ohio Central Railway
W&LE	Wheeling & Lake Erie Railroad

ACKNOWLEDGMENTS

As told in the Preface, this book was begun and much of its raw material was put together by the late John A. Rehor and Willis A. McCaleb, and no expression of acknowledgments can begin without recognizing the enormous amount of work that they did. Whatever the contributions of the present authors, they rest on the awesomely huge base built by these two. Clearly, nothing would have been possible without them. Nor would it have been possible without the help and encouragement of John's widow, Phyllis, who preserved all of the material and made it available to the authors.

But this book is also the product of many other generous hands — as will be quickly seen from what follows here. Not only did numerous members of the historical and railroad enthusiast communities contribute, but many former LSE employees and their relatives were interviewed, answered many questions, and gave extensive reminiscences. Unfortunately the project's long, complex, and sometimes sad history has caused problems for the present authors in recognizing some of this help. While we have carefully pored through the innumerable records and notes left by Messrs. Rehor and McCaleb, we are all too aware that the names of some have been lost, and to them we sincerely apologize.

For this reason too, photo credits may not always be accurate. The present authors have worked from John Rehor's carefully documented photo records, but there may be cases where there is either no record of a photographer or donor, or an attribution may be incorrect. Again, we apologize for any such lapses.

Special thanks must go to George Krambles, LeRoy O. King, Jr., J. William Vigrass, James M. Semon, Bruce M. Dicken, Bob Lorenz, Robert T. Hess, Ralph A. Perkin, and Richard A. Egen, who struggled through all or parts of the manuscript draft and made numerous corrections and suggestions. Most of them also supplied information and/or photographs during the research process. In addition, Mr. Vigrass contributed several parts of the text relating to technology, and Mr. King produced the equipment rosters. Tom Heinrich did a masterful job of producing the professional mapwork while juggling the demands of an engineering job with Norfolk Southern and his family. Gilbert Gonzales of the Rutherford B. Hayes Presidential Center in Fremont was especially patient, helpful, and generous in providing early photographs. And finally, the daughterly devotion of Marcia Slattery must be recognized in translating the barely intelligible dictation tapes of co-author Korach into beautifully wordprocessed drafts.

Other individuals — many of them now gone — who have given of their time and materials over the years: Eli Bail, Roy G. Benedict, Mrs. Walter J. Bishop (daughter of

F. W. Coen)*, Robert T. Blatt, George K. Bradley, D. Paul Brown*, Terrence Burke*, Stanley O. Chausse, Harold E. Cox, Roy Deehr*, Herb Deering*, Albert C. Doane (Black River Historical Society), Mrs. E. V. Emery*, Ray Ewers, Betty Coen Fontaine*, Albert J. Fredericks*, W. Gordon Gallup*, David Garcia, Elmer Fischer*, Charles J. Hanville*, Fritz Hardendorf, C. D. Harvey, W. Lupher Hay, David J. Haynes, William R. Heller, Kermit Hoesman (Woodville Historical Society), John D. Horachek, Peter Jedlicka, Ronald Jedlicka, Edward Jenck*, Paul Jenck*, Jack Keenan, Franklyn P. Kellogg, John Keller (Allen County Historical Society), Norman Krentel, Anthony F. Krisak, Richard Krisak, Karel Liebenauer, Norma McCaleb, Emmett Mead*, Clarence Miller*, Clifford Noe, Robert Pence*, Ralph A. Perkin, R. C. Prugh, Mrs. Bernard Reed*, Howard T. Reed*, Emery J. Reiner, Frank Rossi*, David Sayles, Ralph Sayles*, Waldo A. Sayles*, Eugene H. Schmidt, Jack E. Schramm, Frank Schroeder, James P. Shuman, Nancy Schwartz (Western Reserve Historical Society), Louis Szakacs, Charles Trapani, Jr., Martin Tuohy (National Archives–Great Lakes Region), Max Wilcox, William J. Wilkinson* (SN&M), and Mariruth C. Wright (Ohio Public Utilities Commission).

In addition to those individuals, the following institutions provided invaluable original documents and photographs: Allen County Historical Society, Lima, Ohio; Bellevue (Ohio) Public Library; Black River Historical Society, Lorain, Ohio; Firelands Museum; Fremont (Ohio) Public Library; Gibsonburg (Ohio) Public Library; Rutherford B. Hayes Presidential Center, Fremont, Ohio; Historical Society of Pennsylvania, Philadelphia, Penn. (J. G. Brill Collection); Lorain (Ohio) Public Library; Norwalk (Ohio) Public Library; Ohio Historical Society, Columbus, Ohio; Oregon Historical Society, Portland, Ore. (David Stearns Collection); Sandusky (Ohio) Public Library (Brownworth Collection); University of Oregon Library, Eugene, Ore. (Randall Mills Collection); and Woodville Historical Society, Woodville, Ohio. Our thanks to them all and, posthumously, the thanks of John Rehor and Willis McCaleb.

Herbert H. Harwood, Jr.
Robert S. Korach

[*indicates a former LSE employee or relative.]

PREFACE AND DEDICATION

The odyssey of this book has lasted longer than the legendary wanderings of Odysseus himself — longer, in fact, than the life of the Lake Shore Electric as an operating railway. It was, in effect, the lifetime project of two noted Cleveland railway historians, John A. Rehor and Willis A. McCaleb. Rehor is perhaps best known among railroad historians for his monumental history of the Nickel Plate, *The Nickel Plate Story* (Kalmbach Publishing Co., Milwaukee, Wis., 1965) and his self-published *Berkshire Era* (1967); he was also a railroader, working various operating management positions on the Nickel Plate and Norfolk & Western, and more recently was senior accident investigator for the National Transportation Safety Board in Washington. A professional photographer, McCaleb served many years as the Nickel Plate's official photographer and his work has recently been memorialized in several posthumous pictorials.

John conceived the idea of the book, acted as the project leader, and gathered a tremendous amount of information, documents, and photos himself. Willis and his wife Norma aided with extensive on-the-spot research in Ohio, including meticulous research in numerous local newspapers from 1890 to 1938, interviews with former LSE employees, and finding, copying, and printing many of the photos. Casually over 30 or more years and more intensively during the 1980s and early 1990s, John and Willis accomplished what must be the most exhaustive coverage of any interurban line. In the process many, many others contributed — as is noted in our Acknowledgments.

The book's raw material and an outline were partially complete when John died in October 1993. At that point it was decided that the work must somehow be completed and the present authors, Herbert H. Harwood, Jr., and Robert S. Korach volunteered to try to finish it. Willis continued to help as best he could until he, too, died in 1996. Harwood, a retired CSX Transportation officer, has written extensively on railroad and traction history subjects (among them *Blue Ridge Trolley: The Hagerstown and Frederick Railway* in 1970, as well as several books on the B&O Railroad and Baltimore traction) and, while not a Cleveland native, lived there for 12 years. Korach, however, not only is a native, but has worked as a professional transit manager his entire career, giving him an insider's viewpoint on how and why things happened during the railway's life. Beginning with the Cleveland Transit System, he later became assistant general manager for the Port Authority Transit Corp. (Lindenwold line) in New Jersey and assistant general manager–operations for the Los Angeles County Metropolitan Transit Authority. He is also co-author (with James M. Blower) of *The N.O.T.& L. Story* (CERA Bulletin 109, 1966).

Early in their Lake Shore
Electric project, a young
John Rehor (right) and
Willis McCaleb pay their
respects to the Lorain Street
Railroad's onetime car 85(II)
in January 1955.
(J. William Vigrass photo)

Herbert H. Harwood, Jr.
(left) and Robert S. Korach
(right)

While John and Willis provided a huge and solid base, the present authors found that more research was needed to fill in the blank spots, and this was mostly accomplished by co-author Korach between 1995 and 1997. Harwood also contributed additional research and wrote most of the final text.

Thus the book is the product of many hands over many years, and credit for specific authors is murky. Choosing a dedication, however, is far clearer: this book is dedicated to John A. Rehor (1929–1993) and Willis A. McCaleb (1920–1996). We celebrate their original inspiration and their monumental efforts to preserve an important but now almost-forgotten part of Ohio's past.

Herbert H. Harwood, Jr.
Robert S. Korach

(Stephen P. Davidson photo)

INTRODUCTION

The Lake Shore Electric —
What It Was and Where It Went

It never imposed much on the landscape and now has all but disappeared back into it.

Drive west from Cleveland along the rim of Lake Erie to the old lake port of Sandusky, once a serious competitor of Cleveland and Toledo. Then head south to Norwalk, Ohio — another charming nineteenth-century town — and keep moving west on U.S. Route 20 toward Toledo, passing through more nineteenth-century main streets at places like Monroeville, Bellevue, and Fremont. If you are particularly perceptive, along the way you will spot bits of light grading alongside the roads or crossing them; you may spot pole lines marching across fields, and here and there some strange, small, brick buildings of uncertain purpose.

What you are seeing are the dim remains of "The Greatest Electric Railway in the United States," as it proudly called itself in its earlier days — the Lake Shore Electric Railway. In the few years between the perfection of electric power for railway use and the perfection of motor vehicles and paved highways, the Lake Shore Electric was the premier carrier of people in the well-populated territory between Cleveland and Toledo, and one of the most important links in the network of interurban electric lines which once blanketed the Midwest.

And to millions of people, the big orange electric cars were an economical and comfortable means of escape from the week's toil in urban mills and shops or the humdrum boredom of rural living. In summers during the glory years there were never enough cars to handle the crowds seeking weekend pleasure at such Lake Erie beach resorts and amusement parks as Linwood, Crystal Beach, Avon Beach Park, Mitiwanga, Rye Beach, Ruggles Grove, and, of course, the "Atlantic City of the Great Lakes" — Cedar Point — still as popular in the 1990s as it was a hundred years before. To thousands of newlyweds from all over the Midwest, the Lake Shore Electric was one of the more enjoyable avenues taken on the long but not-so-tedious trip to Niagara Falls — a trip which also included the long-vanished night boat from Cleveland to Buffalo.

Born in 1901 and dead at the young age of 37 in 1938, the Lake Shore Electric nonetheless led an active, memorable, and influential life. Among other things it was the first truly long-distance interurban linking two or more major population centers. It originated high-speed, limited-stop services and was a pioneer in train operation. For many years it set the technological and operating practice pace and it was widely emulated in its industry. And thanks to its strategic location in the Cleveland–Toledo corridor, it was a key link in the Midwestern interurban network. As such it operated two major interline passenger services

Among other things, the Lake Shore Electric provided the first "rapid transit" service to Cleveland's western suburbs bordering Lake Erie. Here a Toledo-bound interurban approaches Detroit Road in Rocky River in August 1937. (Ralph A. Perkin photo)

which were among the longest interurban runs in the country; it also was the central corridor for numerous interline freight routes spreading across Ohio, Indiana, and Michigan — perhaps more than any other such line.

Furthermore its pedigree went back to the industry's pioneering days. One component was one of the country's two earliest interurban operations, and its city lines dated to the horsecar era and early days of electrification. For a time at least, it was financially one of the more profitable members of an industry never noted for lucrative returns.

During that time too, the Lake Shore did much to develop the present-day territory along and near the western part of Lake Erie, including the western Cleveland suburbs, the Lake Erie resorts, and the many towns and small cities.

Its history was one of anomalies, an uneven mixture of radical innovation and conservatism. A spectacular interurban industry pacesetter in its early days, it challenged the main line of Vanderbilt's powerful New York Central Railroad with fast, frequent limited train services and innovative promotion. And in the early 1930s it sponsored a pioneering form of trailer-on-flatcar intermodal service, over three decades ahead of the railroad industry. Yet while the Indiana Railroad and the neighboring Cincinnati & Lake Erie made industry headlines in the early 1930s with high-speed one-man lightweight cars, the Lake Shore continued to its last day depending on a fleet of fast but obsolete heavy steel two-man interurbans dating to World War I. In fact, when it died in 1938 it was virtually an operating museum of early twentieth-century interurban technology, still operating wooden cars dating as far back as the turn of the century.

Location and Routes

The Lake Shore Electric's main line roughly followed the shore of Lake Erie between Cleveland and Toledo, Ohio, a distance of 116 miles by the shortest of its two routes. Along the way it passed through such lakeside communities as Lorain, Vermilion, Huron, and Sandusky — as well as the more inland cities of Norwalk and Fremont. Roughly midway between its two terminal points — at an otherwise insignificant spot east of Huron, Ohio, called Ceylon Junc-

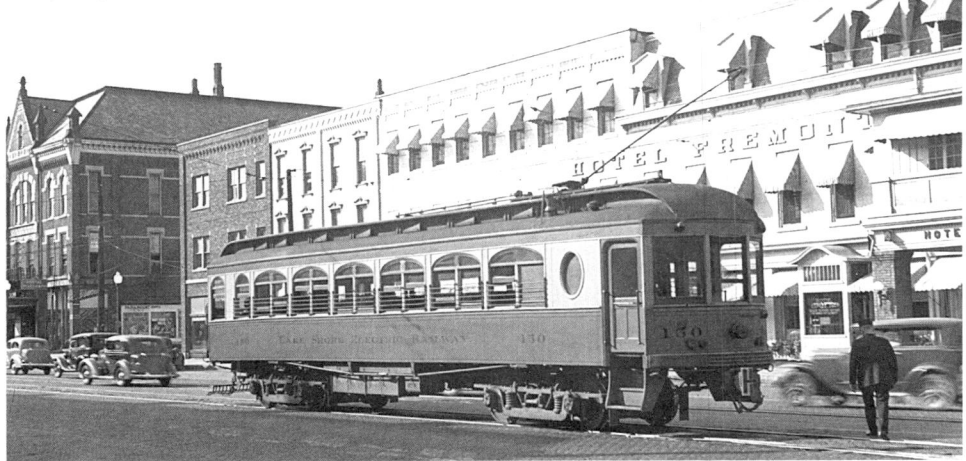

The Lake Shore Electric's classically styled, wooden Niles–built interurban cars fitted nicely with the late-nineteenth-century character of the line's principal towns. On an afternoon in August 1936, car 150 pauses on State Street at Front Street in Fremont, one of its major traffic points. (Ralph A. Perkin photo)

tion — the line divided into a pair of alternate routes which came together again at Fremont. One, considered the "main line," continued to follow the lake shore west through Huron to Sandusky, then headed southwest to Fremont via Castalia; the second route dropped southwest to serve Norwalk, Monroeville, Bellevue, and Clyde before meeting the "main line" again at Fremont. Typically, schedules were coordinated for the two routes so that passengers could make a continuous trip either way. In earlier days, multiple-car trains would split at either of the two junctions and reunite at the end of each alternate route.

There were also four branches of varying lengths and life spans. The westernmost — and shortest — was a three-mile spur to Gibsonburg, in western Ohio. From Sandusky an 18-mile-long route ran south through Avery and Milan to Norwalk. This line dated to 1893 and was one of the first interurbans in America. Ironically, it was also one of the LSE's earliest major abandonments in 1928. Another north–south branch connected Lorain with Elyria, a distance of ten miles; this busy double-track urban and suburban route was owned by an LSE subsidiary, the Lorain Street Railroad. Finally, a fourth line connected South Lorain and Beach Park (Avon Beach), eight miles apart. This unlikely route was intended as a shortcut for traffic between Elyria and Cleveland, as well as other points along the lake east of Lorain — but was ill-starred and short-lived. Yet one segment of it survives today as the only piece of the LSE still in operation.

The company's title was no advertising exaggeration. In many spots the interurban track was practically on Lake Erie's beaches. This view looks east at the aptly named Lake Siding west of Vermilion. (Ralph A. Perkin photo)

Multiple-unit trains were a Lake Shore Electric hallmark through the 1920s, and even into the 1930s for special movements. This three-car set is at Sandusky in 1936. (Bruce Triplett photo)

Genesis, Peak, and Decline

The Lake Shore Electric Railway Company was a creation of the Cleveland-based Everett-Moore syndicate, a leading promoter, builder, and manager of Midwestern interurbans. The company came into being in the fall of 1901 as an assembly of four disconnected and physically disparate properties which its promoters proceeded to weld together into a single system. Making a high-speed intercity through system out of this mongrel assortment took several years, during which it was beset by both financial and physical problems. But the end result was a premier interurban line which operated successfully for over two decades. It hit its peak of traffic and profitability in 1920, and its physical peak three years later. Through cars were run between Cleveland and Detroit and Cleveland and Lima, Ohio; for a time they even ran as far west as Fort Wayne, Indiana. Freight was handled over a vast network of connecting lines reaching east into western Pennsylvania, south to Louisville, and west to South Bend and Michigan City, Indiana.

Then, inevitably, came the decline and dissolution. Like most of its interurban brethren, the Lake Shore Electric was a victim of luckless timing. It was created as a clean, fast, and cheap method of moving people in a time of horse-powered carriages and wagons on primitive roads. But it was born less than a decade before the advent of the cheap, mass-produced automobile. By the mid-1920s its managers found themselves in a fruitless struggle as highways improved and as autos, trucks, and buses began crowding them. On one hand they had to compete with a form of transportation that was far more flexible and convenient; on the other, they were burdened with heavy fixed construction debts and the day-to-day cost of maintaining their tracks and other facilities — and paying taxes on it all. Thus even if they could devise ways of keeping ahead of this competition — and there were ways the Lake Shore could have done so, at least for a while — the economics were unpromising and the money unavailable.

Nonetheless the Lake Shore Electric hung on almost to the eve of World War II. When it finally succumbed, it was the last of Cleveland's once-extensive network of radiating interurban lines and one of the last of the "true" Midwest interurbans. In retrospect it had lived longer than it probably should have. The environment which created the company in 1901 and nurtured it into the early 1920s had disappeared; in its place was a world in which it did not fit. Its only practical alternative was to shrink its horizons and become a bus operator of more limited scope. It finally did so, and the "Greatest Electric Railway in the United States" vanished with little visible trace.

FREDERICK W. COEN
1872 – 1942

"Mister Lake Shore Electric"

The life of the Lake Shore Electric and the life of Frederick William Coen were one and the same. Fred Coen was an incorporator and an official of the railway from the day it began, effectively its chief executive from 1907 to the day rail service ended, and continued as head of the successor bus company until he retired in 1940. More than any single individual, he was responsible for the company's prosperity during its good days and its survival in the bad ones.

Coen came early to the electric railway business. In fact, he was there as a young man at the industry's dawn. Born in Rensselaer, Indiana, on June 15, 1872, he moved to Vermilion, Ohio, in 1891 with his brother Edward to go into the banking business. Their little Erie County Banking Company happened to be a major investor in one of the country's earliest interurban railways, originally called the Sandusky, Milan & Huron. The line opened in July of 1893 but that October was reorganized as the Sandusky, Milan & Norwalk. To protect its now-uncertain investment, the bank dispatched the 21-year-old Coen to Sandusky as the company's secretary. In effect, he never left.

A gifted mathematician, the young Coen caught the attention of people in Cleveland's Everett-Moore syndicate, who moved him to their newest project, the Lorain & Cleveland Railway in 1895. From there it was to Everett-Moore's Lake Shore Electric when the company was formed in 1901 — first as secretary, but with the occasional added duties of general passenger agent (between 1902 and 1904) and purchasing agent (in 1907). Upon the premature death of LSE general manager Furman J. Stout in 1907 Coen was made general manager and, three months later, vice president, general manager, and director. Until his brief and mysterious departure between 1926 and 1927, Coen ran the LSE for the Everett-Moore group; when he returned in 1927 he became the company's president under Cities Service control.

Bankruptcy in 1933 hardly changed Coen's status; the court appointed him receiver and he continued to direct the interurban's affairs until rail operations ended in 1938 and the

Frederick W. Coen (Mrs. Walter J. Bishop collection)

company itself was dissolved. In the meantime, however, he had established the subsidiary Lake Shore Coach Company and headed that until he finally retired in 1940 at age 68.

Although Coen was a quiet, reserved, and private person, he was nonetheless an outstanding handler of people and an able negotiator — as evidenced by his adroit management of the Lake Shore Electric's numerous financial, legal, and labor problems over the years. He had, according to one of his four daughters, almost total recall of people and events and was completely devoted to his work with no real outside interests. During the height of the interurban era Fred Coen was one of the industry's most respected leaders and took a prominent role in the industry's trade organization, the Central Electric Railway Association.

As is sadly true of many whose work is their life, Fred Coen lived only a short time after his retirement. He died suddenly on January 24, 1942, in Lakewood, Ohio, his long-time home. We salute Fred Coen as a man with a singular mission in life — the Lake Shore Electric Railway.

PART I

THE STORY

Homely though its face may be, this is the LSE's baby picture. As the company falteringly got into business in 1901 and 1902 it relied on a fleet of rugged Barney & Smith–built interurbans inherited from the Toledo, Fremont & Norwalk. No. 8, dating to 1900, poses in Fremont about 1903. (W. A. McCaleb collection)

CHAPTER 1

GENESIS

1901 – 1903

The year was 1901, the first year of the twentieth century. Ohio's own William McKinley was in the White House and Victoria was Queen of Great Britain and Ireland, Empress of India, and monarch of Britain's other dominions beyond the seas — including Canada. Neither would survive the year — McKinley felled by an assassin's bullet and Victoria of the more natural effects of age. She was 82, had reigned for 64 years, and had defined an entire age.

And in Ohio, reigning over a wholly different empire — which also included Canada — were Henry A. Everett and Edward W. Moore, two Cleveland entrepreneurs who were rapidly moving to exploit the latest and most promising technological development — the electric railway. By the dawn of the new century steam railroads overwhelmingly dominated American intercity transportation; virtually all overland travel and freight movement was by rail. To get anywhere beyond a few miles, there was no other way.

But a different kind of railroading had suddenly evolved during the decade just past. Electricity was applied to urban street railways beginning in 1888, radically changing their form and potential. Now no longer limited by the speed and stamina of horses, these street railways were built outwards from the cities over increasingly longer distances. By the mid-1890s some were beginning to link towns and cities and distinguishing themselves from ordinary streetcar lines with a new name — interurbans. By the turn of the century the development of high-voltage three-phase alternating current transmission made long-distance electrified lines practical, and proved the key to interurban expansion.

The interurbans were built to lighter standards than their steam railroad cousins and were cleaner, more flexible, and usually much cheaper to build and operate. Lines could be constructed quickly, often using existing rights-of-way in or alongside roads; when completed they usually had a ready-made business from established communities along the route, and could develop territories previously isolated by lack of transportation. For many people, the interurban offered the first practical means of mobility. The alternatives, after all, were horses, mules, wagons, carriages, and primitive roads — mud-bogged in the spring, snowbound in the winter, and rough and dusty in the best times. And even where steam railroads already operated, the interurbans offered lower fares and more frequent service. Furthermore they were more accessible and convenient, stopping at rural road crossings and delivering their passengers right to the middle of Main Street in town. Little wonder that shrewd turn-of-the-century investors saw interurbans as their route to riches. Motor vehicles? In 1901 they barely existed; only 14,800 autos were registered in the entire United

States, and no trucks whatsoever. What did exist was highly expensive, and, outside of cities, had few places to operate.

There were some problems, of course. Cheap to build as they were, interurbans still required a substantial sunk capital investment. This, plus the nature of the markets, usually meant that no more than one line could be established between any two points; while two could sometimes survive, that was pretty much the upper limit. Thus anyone who wanted to reap this perceived bonanza had to move quickly to stake his claim before someone else did — otherwise it was usually too late.

The Everett-Moore group had been early and fast movers; its members, in fact, were pioneers in building true interurban lines. Their first project, the Akron, Bedford & Cleveland, was launched in 1894 and opened in late 1895. Following this the syndicate incorporated the Cleveland, Painesville & Eastern in 1895, completing it in July 1896. Later in 1895 they incorporated the Lorain & Cleveland Railway — what was claimed as the first high-speed interurban, with a route entirely on private right-of-way (excluding city entries), and cars capable of over 50 mph. It began operations in October 1897. The 27-mile-long L&C linked Cleveland with the Lake Erie town of Lorain, a one-time fishing village then on the brink of transformation into an industrial center.

By 1901 the promoters had hit full stride, taking over (among other things) the Toledo street railway system, the Detroit United Railway system serving the city of Detroit and much of eastern Michigan, plus two companies which together constituted a partially completed interurban route between Detroit and Toledo. Their original Akron, Bedford & Cleveland had blossomed into the Northern Ohio Traction Company and was rapidly expanding into the industrial and population centers south and east of Akron. Along with numerous other electric railway properties, they controlled several telephone companies and had organized the Cleveland Construction Company to build interurban and railroad lines.

A Cleveland–Toledo Interurban

Not surprisingly, the Everett-Moore group quickly visualized an interurban route between Cleveland and Toledo, which would tap a lucrative territory on its own while connecting their lines radiating from Cleveland with their Toledo and Michigan systems.

It was a bold gamble. The Cleveland–Toledo territory was a well-populated and prosperous corridor with excellent passenger potential. And already it had numerous popular Lake Erie summer resorts and parks which promised excursion business — most notably Cedar Point, near Sandusky. But there also was intense and deeply entrenched competition. The territory was dominated by the Lake Shore & Michigan Southern Railway, a key component of the vast and lordly New York Central system. The LS&MS formed the western part of the Central's New York–Chicago main line and operated at very high service levels. Various other steam railroad main lines and branches also crisscrossed the area.

It was bold in another way, too. Having evolved from street railways, the turn-of-the-century interurbans typically were still primarily oriented to relatively short-distance stop-and-go local business, feeling that they could not effectively compete with the faster steam railroad trains for the more profitable long-distance passengers. Most interurban managers felt that the limit of their competitive range was about 50 miles, at best no more than 75. But Everett-Moore's planned Cleveland–Toledo line would be almost 120 miles long. The distance and nature of the competition demanded a new approach to the business, and the promoters planned to inaugurate a fast, limited-stop service with equipment capable of 60 mph.

Who were Everett and Moore, and what was "Everett-Moore" collectively? To begin with, "Everett-Moore" was a convenient shorthand term for a syndicate of what were mostly Cleveland capitalists dominated by the two principal promoters. It was not really a single monolithic entity, however; the group's composition varied from property to property, and

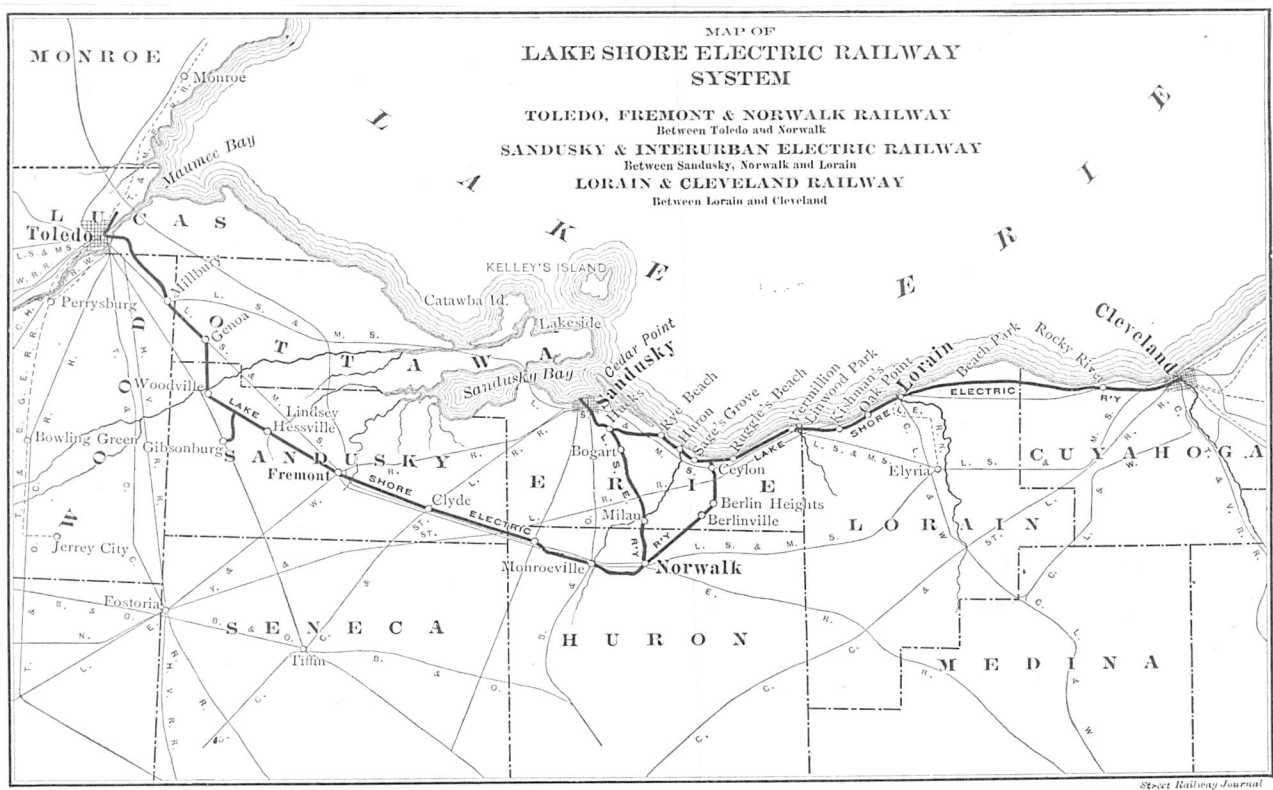

The Lake Shore Electric
Railway's original system,
1902.

Everett and Moore themselves had major investments apart from one another. Most were relatively young; Everett, the senior partner, was about 43; Moore was 37. The two came from banking backgrounds and had been associated since about 1889 when they took over and electrified the East Cleveland Railroad. Among other things, they put together the Cleveland Electric Railway in 1893. Both were the picture of the turn-of-the-century entrepreneur, prematurely balding with closely-trimmed beards, steel-rimmed glasses, and highly dignified demeanors. Everett primarily concentrated on operations while Moore was chiefly interested in the financial end of the businesses. The *Sandusky Register* of July 3, 1901, artlessly described the syndicate and its leaders thus:

> Indications are the Everett-Moore syndicate is composed of about 85 men. Everett habitually chews a quill toothpick as a substitute for a cigar. He dresses to the latest fad and is immaculately clean. Moore is also well-dressed and is an entertaining companion. He does business constantly even while dressing in the stateroom of a ship and thinks nothing of working up a million-dollar deal during lunch. He works harder than anyone else in the business. Both men have charming smiles.

Big city ways apparently counted for much in Sandusky.

A principal partner in their Cleveland–Toledo project was another Cleveland financier named Baruch Mahler, universally called "Barney." Aged 50 in 1901, Mahler began his career humbly in 1868 as a telegrapher for the Lake Shore & Michigan Southern; after associating himself with the Everett-Moore group, he helped finance the Lorain & Cleveland and served as its president from 1896 to August 1901. He was also the principal founder and president of the Electric Package Company, the Cleveland-based agency jointly created by most of the city's interurban lines in 1898 to handle their package freight business.

Mahler took a major role in launching the new company, aided by a promising young banker named Frederick W. Coen. Only 29 years old in 1901, Coen first caught the Everett-Moore group's eye when he was helping to put the faltering Sandusky, Milan & Norwalk interurban in better financial order in 1893. Two years later he was moved to its newly incorporated Lorain & Cleveland and by 1901 he was acting as the syndicate's secretary.

By early 1901 the Cleveland–Toledo corridor was beginning to fill up with electric railways, although there were still some significant gaps and those lines which existed had varying physical characteristics. But all the pieces of a through route were in place — in theory at least. Everett-Moore's own Lorain & Cleveland took the route as far west as Lorain, 27 miles. And at the west end, Michigan interests were just completing the 61-mile-long Toledo, Fremont & Norwalk between the cities in its name.

Filling the gap between Lorain and Norwalk was a company called the Sandusky & Interurban, which had grown out of Sandusky's original local streetcar system and was then trying to extend itself east along the Lake Erie shore between Sandusky and Lorain. (Legally it was spelled "Sandusky & Inter-Urban," but neither the company nor anyone else regularly used that spelling.) It had also projected a branch from a point near Ceylon to Norwalk via Berlin Heights. But the S&I consisted more of fond intentions than reality. By 1901 it was bogged down in franchise problems at Huron, Vermilion, and Berlin Heights as well as various other political troubles, and had only been able to complete a ten-mile line between Sandusky and Huron along with some work on the Norwalk branch. One of the S&I's most intractable problems was bridging the Huron River at Huron on its way east to Lorain. To save its meager capital, it wanted to use the Berlin Street highway bridge, an iron swing structure which the county commissioners felt could not carry interurban cars without being rebuilt.

Finally, there was a second Sandusky streetcar company, the Sandusky, Norwalk & Southern, which also owned a pioneering 1893 interurban route between Sandusky and Norwalk. This offered an alternate link between the S&I and the TF&N — albeit a more roundabout and generally less desirable one.

Despite this disjointed situation, the Everett-Moore group was under pressure to move quickly; there was already competition for their route. The Toledo, Fremont & Norwalk's Michigan promoters intended either to eventually reach Cleveland themselves or to form part of a connecting route to Cleveland. One plan was to connect at Norwalk with the Cleveland, Elyria & Western, which was slowly building west from Cleveland through Elyria and Oberlin. The CE&W (later part of the Cleveland Southwestern & Columbus system) was the child of the Pomeroy-Mandelbaum syndicate, a rival group of Cleveland interurban financiers headed by A. H. Pomeroy, his son Fred T. Pomeroy, and banker Maurice J. Mandelbaum. It had reached Oberlin in December 1897 but paused there for several years while it financed and built several other branches. In 1901, however, it resumed building toward Norwalk to close the 24-mile gap. Happily for Everett and Moore, a formidable crossing of the Vermilion River valley at Birmingham briefly stymied the extension.

Creating the Lake Shore Electric: 1901

In any event the Everett-Moore group already had moved in. As early as 1898 it apparently was involved in financing the Sandusky & Interurban, and in 1900 it also bought control of the Sandusky, Norwalk & Southern, effectively putting the two Sandusky interurban companies into the same family. With them came Sandusky's street railway system, which was to prove a future economic albatross but was necessary in order to operate interurbans in the city. Equally necessary but even less remunerative was a short local city operation in Norwalk, required by the franchise inherited by the Sandusky, Norwalk & Southern.

Next Everett and Moore negotiated with the Toledo, Fremont & Norwalk owners, who already were prepared to sell their yet-uncompleted line and had been dickering with the Pomeroy-Mandelbaum interests. Talks began in April 1901 or earlier, and a deal was finally formally acknowledged in July. Everett-Moore now controlled the entire Cleveland–Toledo route, and swiftly moved to consolidate their collection into a single company. Someone, in a happy inspiration, came up with one of the most memorable names in electric traction: Lake Shore Electric Railway. (Pleasant as the name was, however, it strangely gave no clue as to what cities the company served.)

No time was wasted giving it life. On August 29, 1901, the four companies entered into a joint agreement to consolidate as the Lake Shore Electric Railway Company. Its principal offices were to be in Cleveland, Everett-Moore's base of operations, with an initial organization consisting of nine directors and five corporate officers — president, two vice presidents, a secretary and a treasurer. Barney Mahler became its first president as well as a director; Fred Coen was named secretary. Besides Mahler, other directors were Everett, Moore, James B. Hanna, James B. Hoge, Charles H. Stewart, and William J. Gwane (all of Cleveland), William H. Price of Norwalk, and J. Horace Harding of Philadelphia. Hanna and Price also acted as vice presidents and Stewart as treasurer.

The new company was capitalized at $12 million, split between $4.5 million in common stock, $1.5 million in 5 percent preferred stock, and $6 million in 5 percent bonds. Lorain & Cleveland stockholders were to get $2 million of LSE stock, S&I stockholders $1.35 million, TF&N stockholders $2 million, and SN&S stockholders $270,000. The joint consolidation agreement was filed with the Ohio Secretary of State's office on September 25, 1901, and the LSE was in business. Physically the properties were combined September 30.

But physical combination was mostly an abstract concept at this point. Practically nothing was actually connected, and two large gaps existed — 32 miles between Lorain and Huron and 13 miles from Ceylon Junction to Norwalk. Before any through Cleveland–Toledo service was possible, both extensive construction and new equipment were necessary. None of the component companies had cars suitable for the high-speed, deluxe intercity services which the promoters visualized and which were needed to compete in this railroad-saturated territory. Only the Toledo, Fremont & Norwalk fleet of 22 large and rugged Barney & Smith–built interurban cars was remotely suitable for long-distance service. But they were rather Spartan and, with only two 75-hp motors per car, underpowered and slow.

As its first general manager the LSE hired Richard E. Danforth, former general superintendent of the Buffalo, New York, traction system. Otherwise, the TF&N seemed to have the best operating talent for the new company. Its 42-year-old general manager, Furman J. Stout, had come to the TF&N from the Wheeling & Lake Erie Railroad, where he had risen through the operating ranks to general superintendent. On August 12 he was appointed the LSE's general superintendent under Danforth. TF&N superintendent W. B. W. Griffin became superintendent of motive power, and its attorney, Harry Rimelspach, became the Lake Shore Electric's legal representative at Fremont. Subsequently he also served as the LSE claims agent and claims attorney until 1939. Dan H. Lavenberg, TF&N's chief dispatcher and another Wheeling & Lake Erie alumnus, was appointed superintendent at Fremont.

Danforth, Stout, Griffin, and their people had much to do and little time to do it. The Everett-Moore group's headlong 1901 acquisition binge had left it over-stretched and financially vulnerable, with huge financial obligations and several properties in an uncompleted or developmental state. Their telephone companies — which competed with the evolving Bell system — were proving particularly unstable. Thus there was intense pressure to put their new Lake Shore Electric together and begin producing profits quickly, and they were determined to operate a car over the full Cleveland-Toledo route by the end of 1901. (Their projected connecting line from Toledo to Detroit was in about the same state, an unconnected assembly of two companies — the newly opened Toledo & Monroe and the yet-unfinished Detroit & Toledo Shore Line.)

The most critical job was to bridge the crucial gap between Lorain and Norwalk, originally part of the Sandusky & Interurban's charter. A secondary priority was to complete the planned S&I route east from Huron to Ceylon Junction to create a through line between Cleveland and Sandusky. While the lake shore terrain was relatively easy and there were no major engineering problems, the route required two grade-separated crossings of the Nickel Plate Road's main line between Lorain and Vermilion, plus the strengthening of the highway bridge over the Vermilion River at Vermilion to carry interurban cars.

The work proceeded feverishly through the remainder of 1901 with construction workers pushed to the limit, often in dismal weather. For example, on December 4 the *Lorain Daily Democrat* reported: "One workman who had worked 60 hours without any sleep fell asleep under a tree and was rained on. He was taken to the hospital with convulsions and cramps." The *Lorain Times-Herald* added on December 11: "Records of employees show 121, 100, 75, and 60 hours work without sleep. . . . They were rewarded with double pay, new dry clothes, and all expenses including board and lodging. . . . 'Not a knocker, not a growler, not a quitter was among us, and we were treated right by the company.' Last night the men slept in beds for the first time in five days. Monday morning every one of them was given a big breakfast at the Franklin."

By that time the rudiments of a through Cleveland–Norwalk–Toledo route were complete, although parts were in no condition for scheduled operations. A pair of trolley wires was haphazardly strung from Lorain to Norwalk. The Sandusky & Interurban's direct-current Sandusky power plant was inadequate, so power for this section had to be transmitted from the TF&N's alternating-current Fremont powerhouse. A crude transmission line was run cross-country from the Monroeville substation to Milan and Berlin Heights; it then followed the new line to Ceylon Junction where a clapboard shack was built as a temporary substation. In another expediency, the underpass for the Nickel Plate west of Lorain (later called Undergrade) was not yet graded, so the track was simply laid on the surface of the adjoining wagon road under the railroad.

Newspapers reported that on December 11 the first test car ran from Lorain to Norwalk, and on December 16 four daily round trips were scheduled between Lorain and Vermilion using LSE car 120, a single-truck streetcar inherited from the East Lorain Street Rail-

Moving quickly to connect Everett-Moore's Lorain & Cleveland with its western lines, workers lay track on West Erie Avenue in Lorain. This 1901 view looks east toward Broadway. In the center distance an L&C car waits at its old terminal. (Photo from Albert C. Doane)

way. At the same time Everett-Moore's Toledo–Detroit line was being rushed to a similarly crude form of completion.

Finally on December 23 Everett, Moore, Mahler, Danforth, Stout, and other LSE officials took an inspection trip all the way from Cleveland to Detroit, using the Lake Shore Electric, the Toledo & Monroe, and the Detroit & Toledo Shore Line. The little ex–Sandusky & Interurban car *Alpha* carried them as far as Monroe, Michigan, where they had to transfer across a track break to the Detroit & Toledo Shore Line. The trip took all day, negotiating the Lorain–Norwalk section especially slowly and gingerly. En route the *Alpha* paused at Kishman's, east of Vermilion, ostensibly to give its riders a chance to stretch their legs. The party was delayed here reportedly because Henry Everett got lost in the woods. His "disappearance" was probably a ploy to give workmen time to lay a temporary track over the Vermilion River wagon road bridge, which was then removed when the car passed.

December 29 appears to be the first day of scheduled through Cleveland–Toledo service, although it was not really "through" and certainly not fast. Initially passengers were required to change cars at least twice along the way. The original schedules are unknown, but apparently by early 1902 cars were running every two hours. Newspapers variously reported the torpid running times as anywhere from seven to ten hours for the 119-mile

While the interurbans got the attention, city streetcars like the 106(II) plodded dutifully around Sandusky. The 1901 Brill product waits at the LS&MS railroad station on the LSE's Depot Belt Line some time after 1905. This route was the company's earliest predecessor, dating to 1883–85. (Karel Liebenauer collection)

Cleveland–Toledo trip. (Service was more frequent and faster on the established Cleveland–Lorain and Norwalk–Toledo sections.) The lumbering ex-TF&N Barney & Smith interurban coaches handled the schedules. Service between Cleveland and Sandusky, however, was still stymied by the Sandusky & Interurban's old bugbear, the Berlin Street bridge at Huron. Thus there was no immediate attempt to run cars west of Ceylon Junction, where the Cleveland–Norwalk–Toledo route branched off, although Sandusky–Huron services continued as before.

But incomplete and unimpressive as it may have been, at least the Lake Shore Electric now had a semblance of a Cleveland–Toledo line. In addition, a patchwork connecting service between Toledo and Detroit began December 28, although it too involved a transfer — this one at Monroe, Michigan. Everett and Moore's dream of linking Cleveland and Detroit with high-speed interurbans was clearly close to reality, or so it seemed.

In the meantime other projects were underway. One of the first orders of business for "The Greatest Electric Railway in the United States," as the new company immodestly called itself, was new equipment. But these were not the promised and much-needed regal high-speed interurban cars; as it turned out, those would not appear for another two years. Rather, the Lake Shore's first car order went to Brill for ten plebeian little single-truck trolleys which were required by a new Sandusky city franchise which became effective July 29, 1901.

The next new project was also a peculiarly unprepossessing sidestep. On September 2 work began on a three-mile branch to Gibsonburg, Ohio, a small town located off the former TF&N about 24 rail miles southeast of Toledo and 15 miles northwest of Fremont. Supposedly this was to be the first section of a long line running southwest into the thriving Ohio oil fields, but it was to remain stuck in Gibsonburg for the LSE's entire life.

Otherwise, the company began rebuilding the TF&N Barney & Smith cars by closing their open rear platforms and adding toilets; it also made plans to experiment with motor and control equipment to be used for its future high-speed equipment. And on November 30th it announced that it would paint all its cars in what was called "Big Four Orange" and build a new state-of-the-art paint shop in Fremont.

Although Everett and Moore had effectively pre-empted the Cleveland–Toledo route and blocked their Pomeroy-Mandelbaum rivals, the Cleveland, Elyria & Western nonetheless continued work on its Oberlin-Norwalk extension. On September 2 the *Fremont Daily News* quoted Fred Pomeroy as saying "We might as well acknowledge now . . . that we intend to extend our line to Toledo. . . . It is only natural that we should want to connect with the Cincinnati–Toledo line at that point." Ultimately he did get to Norwalk, but no farther.

The Gibsonburg branch shuttle car rests at its Main Street terminal in a quiet Gibsonburg about 1905. The car is LSE's first No. 42, a rebuilt 1893 veteran from the Sandusky, Milan & Norwalk. (Karel Liebenauer collection)

Receivership

Unhappily the first working day of the new year of 1902 brought disaster for the Everett-Moore syndicate. Overexpanded and caught short with too many large new financial obligations in a tight money market, the group found it could not raise the capital needed to nurse its properties over the immediate hump. Obligations to 30 Cleveland banks fell due on January 1st, and the next day a seven-man banker committee took charge of all Everett-Moore companies.

A typical early LSE run, using one of the former Toledo, Fremont & Norwalk's Barney & Smith interurban cars, enters downtown Toledo over the old Cherry Street Bridge. (Toledo–Lucas County Public Library Collection)

The situation was generally deemed a temporary "embarrassment" which would eventually right itself after some financial housecleaning; thus the banks remained as friendly as possible and, together with Everett and Moore, worked toward restoring as many companies as possible to their control. Somewhat ironically from the hindsight of the early twenty-first century, most of its street railways and interurbans were considered to be in relatively sound shape but the telephone companies were candidates for disposal. The Cleveland bankers promptly issued some carefully generalized reassurances that the Everett-Moore traction investments would be kept intact.

Nonetheless the Lake Shore Electric was suddenly caught in an exposed position at the worst time. It was still barely operable as a system, a raggedy creation needing much work and new equipment. Most notably, the slapped-down section between Lorain and Norwalk had to be put in better shape. A through Cleveland–Toledo service technically existed but realistically could not be promoted. And there still was no service whatsoever between Ceylon Junction and Huron on the Sandusky line. In this state the LSE was in no position to generate enough income to support its financial obligations on its own, yet it now had no outside resources to draw from and dubious credit.

Thus on January 10, 1902, the Lake Shore — only 108 days old — was forced into bankruptcy by one of its creditors, the Valentine-Clark Company. Albion E. Lang, president of Everett-Moore's Toledo Railways & Light Company, was appointed receiver by the U.S. Circuit Court for the Northern District of Ohio. To aggravate the LSE's immediate predicament, another casualty of the Everett-Moore collapse was the Euclid Avenue Trust & Savings Company, which held $40,000 of Sandusky & Interurban funds intended for payrolls. In an incestuous relationship rather typical of the time, Everett was a director of the bank, and the bank's treasurer was also the S&I's treasurer. Thus the LSE's Sandusky and Fremont employees went unpaid until early March.

Also caught by the "embarrassment" was the just-opened Toledo–Detroit route, intended as the LSE's key connection. This line soon not only left the Everett-Moore fold but partly disintegrated. In January 1902 the Detroit & Toledo Shore Line went into receivership and the Toledo & Monroe was turned back to its original owners. Toledo–Detroit interurban service, which had haltingly begun December 28, 1901, abruptly ended January 5 — having existed all of nine days. While the Toledo & Monroe still ran between those cities, the D&TSL — which completed the route between Monroe and Detroit — was shut down completely. Not only was it lost to Everett-Moore forever but it ceased being an interurban. Eventually completed as a steam railroad, it was sold jointly to the Grand Trunk and the Toledo, St. Louis & Western ("Clover Leaf") railroads in December 1902. Diesel-powered freights continued to run over its rails in the 1990s.

Uncertain Progress: 1902

Despite the receivership, business continued more or less as usual on the LSE as the line struggled to finish its construction work and achieve its service goals with minimal funds. There were some good days and some bad days. The first bad one was January 13, when a steam locomotive used for construction damaged the Vermilion River bridge at Vermilion, halting service. The old highway bridge had been rebuilt with an outrigger structure to carry the electric cars, and the locomotive was too much for it. Some management defections then followed. On February 24 Fremont superintendent Dan Lavenburg resigned to become general manager of the North Texas Traction Company in Fort Worth. (He later returned to Ohio as general manager of the Toledo & Indiana.) General Manager Danforth departed in April, returning to New York State as general manager of the Rochester & Eastern.

The LSE owed its early form and services primarily to Furman J. Stout (1859–1907), its chief operating officer from 1902 until his untimely death. (W. A. McCaleb collection)

With Danforth gone, Furman Stout became the LSE's top operating manager and forcefully shaped the company's early form, operating procedures, and innovative technology. Among other things, he was credited with being the first to install steam railroad rules and procedures on an interurban line, and proved to be creative and aggressive in developing new business. As Everett-Moore's inside man, secretary Fred Coen was the other major power in the company's management.

In happier news, the ten new Brill-built Sandusky city cars arrived February 15, although the receivership temporarily complicated their financing and use. On March 4th it was revealed that they still had not been put into service. Brill finally released the cars to Sandusky's streets after a complex temporary settlement in which Brill received a chattel mortgage on the car bodies while the LSE rented their Brill 21E trucks from Brill for $13,020 under a lease expiring August 3, 1903.

Much more exciting was the beginning of the testing program to determine the design of the anticipated high-speed interurban cars. At least three of the TF&N Barney & Smith coaches were outfitted with various combinations of motors and controls from the two principal electrical equipment manufacturers, Westinghouse and General Electric. Beginning in February 1902 they were put through their paces, sometimes with dramatic results.

First to emerge from the shop was the former TF&N No. 13, which was repainted a dark red and renumbered 8000 in what was supposed to be a new common paint and numbering scheme for the entire Everett-Moore system. (Like many traction companies at the time, the new LSE had no desire to court bad luck with a No. 13. As it turned out, that made no difference.) The "new" No. 8000 carried four 75-hp Westinghouse motors, double its original power. The most sensational, however, was No. 18, turned out about February 13. Four GE 125-hp motors had been installed, making it one of the hottest interurban cars in existence at the time — capable of at least 75 mph, so it was advertised. Still wearing its original TF&N yellow paint, it was variously dubbed the "Yellow Flyer" and "Yellow Demon" by the local press and followed breathlessly. In one typical performance on February 22, it reportedly reached 69 mph carrying a special theater party of Fremonters home

from Toledo. Ultimately, however, the company decided that the power was more than necessary, and for its new standard it settled on the four 75-hp Westinghouse motors carried by No. 8000. That combination was capable of at least 60 mph — fast enough.

Life on the Lake Shore Electric was exciting in other ways too. On May 27 the *Fremont Daily News* carried this story, more appropriate to Dodge City:

> Exciting free-for-all on the late eastbound LSE car, Saturday midnight, in the charge of conductor McKennon. A fight started west of Bellevue and continued to the substation. A number of young Bellevue fellows assaulted two farmers living east of town. Blows were freely exchanged and knockdowns were frequent. The farmers got the best of their assailants. Night operator Roscoe Stewart fired his revolver to get the attention of the night police.

With a money transfusion from the sale of receiver certificates, work began on the improvements promised in the 1901 Sandusky city franchise, which coordinated routes and operations of the two predecessor companies, eliminated some unneeded trackage, and added new services. This included extending the Monroe Street line west to Superior Street and east to Hancock Street, creating a new (but short-lived) crosstown route. Another improvement was the routing of all Camp Street cars off Washington Street and onto Water Street and the creation of a downtown loop by building new track on Market Street between Columbus and Wayne. A block of track on West Park Street was to be abandoned, as were some tracks on Washington Street, Washington Row, West Market Street, and Pearl Street. When the dust settled, the LSE operated four local city routes: Tiffin Avenue, Depot Belt, Soldiers Home Belt, and First–Monroe Street Crosstown. (See map, p. 204.)

In its first summer season, the company did its best to exploit the resorts bordering its main line along the lake. It operated its own resort on 30 acres of shoreline property at Beach Park, or Avon Beach, about 20 miles west of Cleveland on the old Lorain & Cleveland line, which included a dancing pavilion and summer cottages; it also owned 52 undeveloped acres at Sage's Grove, ten miles west of Vermilion. It promoted trolley parties to its own properties as well as the multitude of others in the area — Hans Grove, Dover Bay Park, Mulberry Park, Randalls Grove, Linwood Park, Ruggles Grove, Rye Beach, and the like.

On an August 1902 inspection trip, LSE General Superintendent Furman Stout (center) and Secretary Fred Coen (second from left) pause at the Monroeville station–substation with agent Williams. They are riding ex-TF&N No. 18. (Gilbert Hodges photo, Bob Lorenz collection)

But the crown traffic jewel was Cedar Point, the famous and long-lived Lake Erie resort and amusement park near Sandusky operated by Sanduskian George Boeckling with backing from the Kuebeler brewing family. Close to a million people visited "The Atlantic City of the Great Lakes" in 1901, many of them arriving in Sandusky on long excursion trains hauled in by Sandusky's five steam railroads. From there they took a short steamboat ride to "The Point," where they frolicked in Lake Erie and visited a large vaudeville casino, ten bowling alleys, several dancing pavilions, and numerous other attractions. Three hotels accommodated those staying more than a day. Despite its immediate limitations, the Lake Shore Electric wasted no time injecting itself into that lucrative market; for the July 4th holiday it attracted passengers by advertising that Maude Beal Price would give a monologue, Schrock and Rice would ride bicycles and unicycles, the Gasper Brothers of Mexico would juggle, and a spectacular performance of "Red Riding Hood" would be presented at the Kinodrome.

The LSE's already disjointed services were disrupted further in early August by a smallpox outbreak in Norwalk and Berlin Township. Nearby Sandusky, Huron, Milan, and Bellevue all panicked and tried to quarantine themselves. Milan refused to allow the Sandusky–Norwalk cars through town and Bellevue forbade the Norwalk–Toledo interurbans to take or discharge passengers within its limits. Comic-opera warfare broke out in Milan on August 4 as LSE Sandusky Division superintendent Ed K. Owen tried to run cars through town over the heated opposition of the inhabitants. A hostile crowd estimated at 500 people gathered, blockades were set up, several boisterous young men waved revolvers, and Owen was ostentatiously arrested. After refusing bond he was jailed, but was then allowed to return to his job in Sandusky under the watchful guard of Milan's marshal. The town soon relented, but the hapless LSE was forbidden to sell tickets to the dreaded Norwalkers for travel to Milan, Bellevue, Sandusky, and various other communities in the area. By August 19 the crisis had passed and the last quarantines lifted.

In the meantime the rival Cleveland, Elyria & Western was still doggedly fighting its way toward Norwalk from Oberlin. It finally overcame its Vermilion River gorge problem with an impressive double-span arched truss bridge at Birmingham which measured 423 feet long and 63 feet high — and was one of the most aesthetic interurban bridges anywhere. The CE&W and the LSE's Ceylon Junction–Norwalk line crossed one another at grade near Berlinville, about seven miles northeast of Norwalk, and closely paralleled one another into the city. Back in mid-1901 when both lines were under construction, abortive efforts were made to build this section jointly. Although no agreement could be reached, the LSE eventually allowed its competitor trackage rights to enter Norwalk over its East Main Street route. The first CE&W cars arrived in town August 30, 1902, and regular service began September 2nd. For the next 21 years it and its successor, the Cleveland Southwestern, tried to battle the LSE for the Cleveland–Norwalk business. But being the latecomer it had really lost the fight before it started.

By autumn of 1902 the LSE's physical plant was in good enough shape for substantially improved services. On August 26 Cleveland–Toledo cars began running on a six-hour schedule, and on September 8th the service frequency was doubled, from every two hours to hourly. As before, all runs were locals and, according to newspaper references, through passengers had to change at Norwalk.

While the hoped-for limited services were still a year away, the railway was anxious to show what might be possible. On November 12 it dispatched newly rebuilt ex-TF&N car No. 4 to carry 55 members of the Fraternal Order of Eagles from Toledo to Cleveland. Propelled by its four 75-hp motors, No. 4 covered the distance in three hours and 28 minutes. Then in the wee hours of the night on the 13th, "Yellow Flyer" No. 18 whisked the group home in a spectacular three hours and 15 minutes, hitting 73 mph between Cleveland and Lorain. Needless to say the now publicity-conscious company made certain that the event was duly celebrated in the press, and indeed it was.

The LSE and part-competitor Cleveland Southwestern shared a terminal in Lorain on West Erie Avenue just west of Broadway. Here the joint station is framed between LSE No. 14 at the right and Southwestern 101 at the left. (Lieler photo, Karel Liebenauer collection)

At the same time the LSE did its best with the still-unresolved Huron bridge situation. On November 15 it began a scheduled service between Ceylon Junction and Sandusky, although passengers had to debark at the Huron River and hike across the still-trackless highway bridge. The line west of Lorain was further improved on November 29 by the completion of the LSE's own grading through the Nickel Plate Road underpass at Undergrade, eliminating the difficult shared use of the highway. The site was still to prove an operating menace, however, as would soon be demonstrated.

The Lake Shore Electric had been created primarily as a passenger carrier, and originally had neither the desire nor facilities to solicit and handle general freight. From the start, however, it carried express (or "package") shipments in combines and freight motors — although not in its own name. The business was handled for the Electric Package Company, an agency organized by Barney Mahler in 1898 and jointly owned by the LSE and most of the other interurban lines entering Cleveland. This company solicited the business, handled the revenue and accounting plus any necessary pickup and delivery, and shipped it over the various owner lines under contract. Some LSE station agents also acted as Electric Package agents. The business was small when the LSE was formed but grew quickly. By 1903 the agency had outgrown its storefront terminal on Cleveland's Public Square and moved into a commodious new off-street freight house between Eagle Avenue and Bolivar Road near East 9th Street.

As the LSE was painfully pulling itself together, the Toledo–Detroit connecting route was reconstituting itself, this time under independent auspices. On December 4, 1902, a new company called the Detroit, Monroe & Toledo Short Line was incorporated to take over the old Toledo & Monroe and extend it to Detroit. It would be almost two years before the line was fully completed and, for the time being, Everett-Moore had no direct involvement. But at least the hope of Cleveland–Detroit service was revived.

Among the other negative events of 1902 were numerous accidents which, while not severe, were to signal what would be a frequent and sometimes lethal LSE habit. On October 3, interurban car No. 1 hit the side of a passing Nickel Plate freight train at the Berlin Heights crossing on the Ceylon Junction–Norwalk line, ditching the car and injuring four passengers. On December 13, cars 4 and 57 collided head-on near Sheffield siding and both were destroyed by fire. (Recall that No. 4 had just been fully rebuilt and had achieved the record run with the Eagles party exactly one month earlier. Its demise inaugurated another unhappy LSE tradition — demolishing brand-new equipment.) Two days after that disaster ex–Lorain & Cleveland car 52 rear-ended sister car 54 just west of Beach Park.

The loss of the two cars in the Sheffield wreck left the cash-strapped LSE short of equipment. Forced to find cheap and expedient replacements, it went to Cleveland's Kuhlman Car Company, which happened to have six rather light cars originally built for the Cleveland, Elyria & Western but rejected by them. The Lake Shore hurriedly bought two, which became oddballs in its fleet.

The New Era Begins: 1903

The Lake Shore was all too ready to forget 1902 and move into what was mostly a much happier 1903. At last things began to come together, beginning early in the year with an uneasy resolution of the long-nagging Huron bridge problem. The Berlin Street bridge was finally strengthened to allow electric cars across and through service between eastern points and Sandusky began late in January or early February. But everyone recognized that the arrangement was temporary; the bridge was still deemed untrustworthy and the LSE's route through Huron itself involved several sharp curves and use of the village's streets. The company immediately began talking about a cutoff route across the south side of town using a new bridge — which it finally accomplished 15 years later.

And at last the company was ready to buy new equipment to fulfill its vision of fast and luxurious intercity service. On February 19 it signed an order to the J. G. Brill Company for ten custom-designed interurban passenger-baggage combines to inaugurate the long-anticipated Cleveland–Toledo limited schedules. Numbered 60–69, they were fitted with the "standard" four 75-hp motors and were capable of 60 mph. General Superintendent Furman Stout took a personal hand in their design, which was the epitome of Edwardian interurban elegance. They included unique five-section front and rear windows with curved glass corners, leather-upholstered seats, footrests, and a curving glassed-in smoking section.

In the meantime the service improvements of late 1902 began to pay off with increased revenues; gross earnings for the year were 30 percent ahead of 1901. At the same time the Everett-Moore group was straightening out its own situation. As early as July 1902 it was reported that the Cleveland bankers' committee was easing its control over the syndicate's affairs, and a month later local newspapers were carrying statements that Everett and Moore were arranging new financing for the LSE. The process was slower than predicted, but firm details were worked out by March 1903. The keystone of the reorganization was two new bond issues totaling $3.9 million, one dated January 1, 1903, for $2,160,000 and the second for $1,750,000 effective February 1st. Heavy enough itself, this debt load was added to the already-existing bonds from two LSE predecessors, the TF&N and Lorain & Cleveland, producing a total funded debt of almost $4.9 million. That amount demanded a substantial and steady earnings growth to cover the interest and eventually retire the bonds. But optimism reigned in 1903.

(*Facing page, top*) Sandusky's shop crew poses rather glumly, albeit probably proudly, by newly delivered Brill combine 62 in June 1903. The LSE's first custom-built cars, the Brills featured unusual curved glass front-end windows — a Furman Stout touch. (W. A. McCaleb collection)

(*Facing page, bottom*) Inside, the new Brills contained a smoking section enclosed by a curving, glassed-in partition, seen here in Car 61 ahead of the leather-upholstered seats. (Ralph A. Perkin photo)

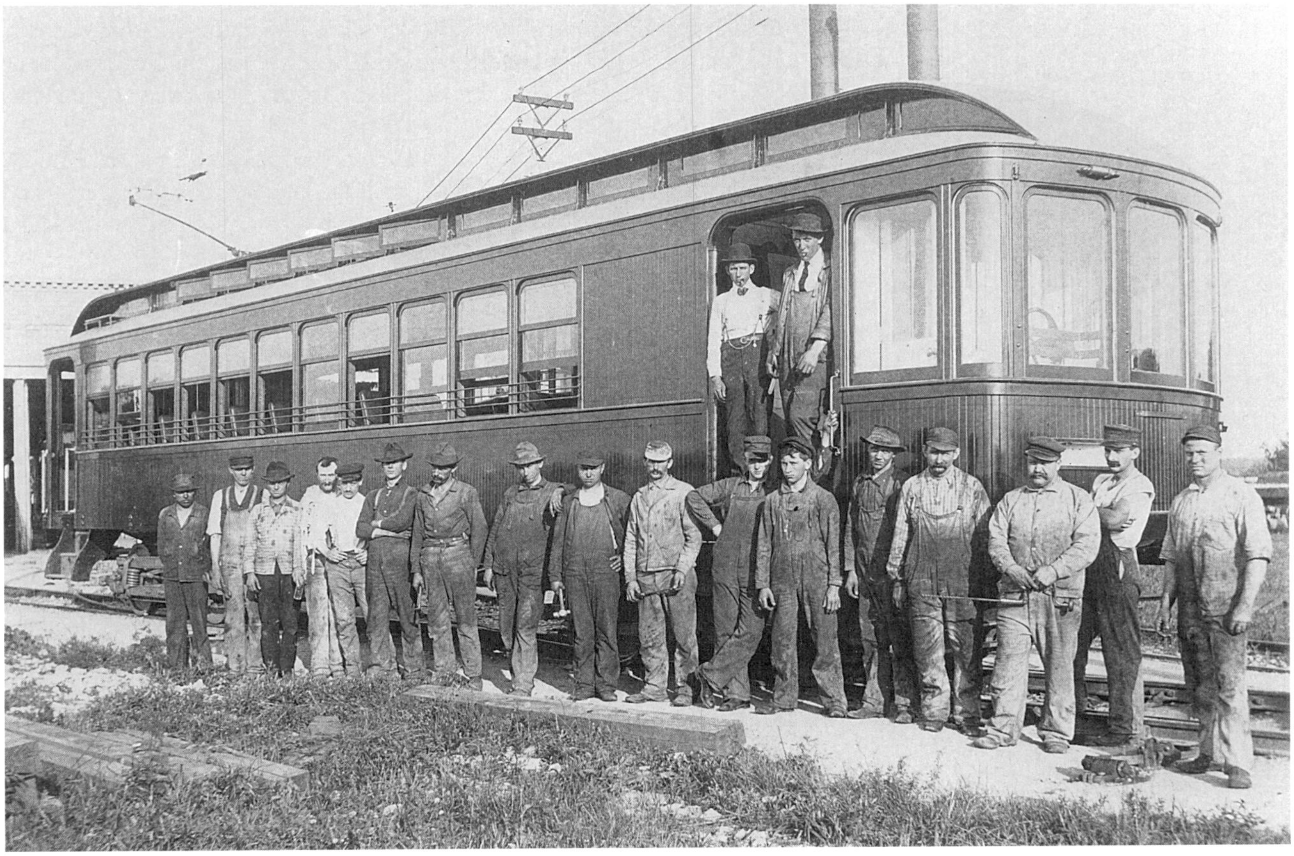

TO FLAG TRAINS
LOCAL STOPS
EXCURSION RATES

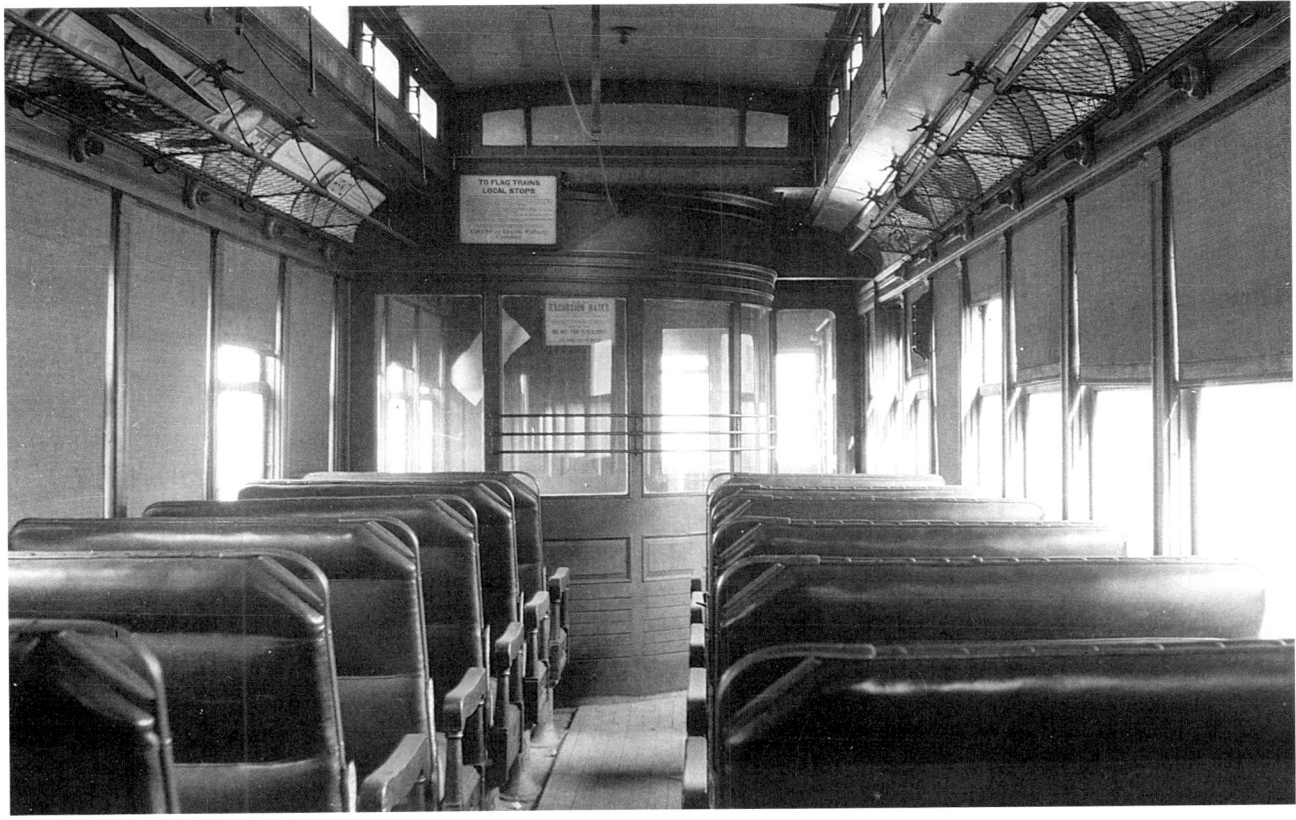

At last on April 1 the Lake Shore Electric emerged from its bankruptcy and the company nominally returned to its old owners. Actually, however, it was not quite yet out of the financial woods; it was specified that for the next five years its stock was to remain in a voting trust controlled by a group of banks representing the bondholders. As a result, bank representatives replaced most of the old Everett-Moore syndicate directors; only Everett, Moore, and Barney Mahler remained on the board from the old regime. Mahler, who had served as the line's first president and Everett-Moore's primary representative, relinquished his presidency, although he remained a director and a large stockholder.

To replace Mahler it was decided to bring in an outside professional manager not associated with the Everett-Moore group. The job went to Warren Bicknell, who moved into his new office in Cleveland on August 1. A onetime Clevelander and graduate of Adelbert College (now part of Case Western Reserve University), the 35-year-old Bicknell had made a reputation managing several of the Pomeroy-Mandelbaum lines, most recently Mandelbaum's Aurora, Elgin & Chicago. Bicknell was to oversee the company's financial and operational rehabilitation for both the banks and the Everett-Moore interests during the trusteeship period — which he proceeded to do with singular success.

Also on April 1 Furman Stout was named the LSE's top on-site manager, formally recognizing the responsibilities he had held since Danforth had left a year before. A month later Lewis K. Burge arrived from the Detroit & Monroe to become superintendent at Sandusky. He replaced Ed Owen — he of the Milan Smallpox Blockade Battle — who had resigned; eventually Burge became the LSE's chief operating officer, retiring in 1940. Fred Coen remained as secretary and was effectively the next highest power after Stout.

In a move to speed service, the LSE changed its routing into Cleveland. Since the Lorain & Cleveland days, the cars had entered the city over the Cleveland Electric Railway's Detroit Avenue line, 7.7 miles of slow running in the center of a busy main thoroughfare. On June 28, 1903, the LSE started using the Clifton Boulevard line, a newly opened paralleling route through a developing residential area. Although slightly over half a mile longer than the more direct Detroit Avenue entry, the Clifton line offered a lengthy stretch of off-street right-of-way — with tracks aesthetically laid on each side of the roadway — and considerably less congestion.

The ten new deluxe Brill interurban cars began arriving in July and were tested in August. In the meantime the company carefully fanned public interest in its forthcoming limited services with several fast special runs in July. A Cleveland–Toledo trip was made on July 1st in three hours and 15 minutes, with Stout and Coen aboard. On the 8th Everett and Stout covered the distance in a more tepid three hours 40 minutes running time, and in addition were delayed a total of 59 minutes at Rocky River and Bellevue by power failures. Finally on July 21 the *Norwalk Herald* reported that rebuilt Barney & Smith car 24 carrying Everett and Stout left the Cleveland Public Square at 12:05 p.m. and reached Toledo at 2:40 — an incredible two hours and 35 minutes, if correctly reported.

The intently awaited new Cleveland–Toledo limited-stop schedules finally went into effect in mid-October. Not surprisingly they were considerably tamer than the well-publicized special runs, making the trip in four hours and 45 minutes — but still an hour and 15 minutes better than the existing local service and very fast by interurban industry standards. The new Brills operated three daily trips each way, making only 13 scheduled

---

(Facing page, top) Beginning in 1903 the LSE used the Cleveland Railway's new Clifton Boulevard line as its entry to the city. This view looks west along the unusual divided track through suburban Lakewood, with the open double-track line in the tree lawn on each side of the roadway. (Doc Rollins photo, Cleveland Railway)

(Facing page, bottom) Shortly after delivery, an eastbound Brill limited car passes the combination station-substation at Berlin Heights. (W. A. McCaleb collection)

One of the 1903 Brill combines hurdles the Lake Shore & Michigan Southern main line at Slate Cut, east of Sandusky, on its way to Cleveland. Note that the eastbound railroad train is running on the left-hand track, a standard LS&MS practice at the time. (Reinhardt photo, W. A. McCaleb collection)

passenger stops on the 119-mile run. A caterer sold box lunches during the stop in Norwalk, and president Bicknell was quoted as saying that he was considering serving buffet lunches on the cars. But the LSE never stretched its luxury that far, and for the line's life passengers either carried their own sustenance or bought from vendors who boarded the cars at key spots like Ceylon Junction.

The limited-stop operation was the first of several significant interurban innovations introduced by the Lake Shore Electric, and perhaps the most important for the new industry. Not only was the concept itself new for an interurban line, but its competition was the most severe anyone could find. Between Cleveland and Toledo the LSE was up against one of the country's premier main line steam railroads, the New York Central's Lake Shore & Michigan Southern — among other things, the route of the newly established *Twentieth Century Limited*. But the reward was higher per-trip earnings compared to the locals with their short-distance riders — and the prestige of being a contender in the big leagues.

The Lake Shore Electric knew it could not match the LS&MS's time between Cleveland and Toledo, but with its limited stops and 60 mph running wherever possible it could offer a reasonably fast running time. That, plus lower fares and greater convenience might crack the market. It and the entire interurban industry awaited the results.

While 1903 was certainly the most promising in the line's short life, it also continued the tradition of wrecking equipment with some regularity. Things got off to an early start when the ex-S&I car *Gamma* was hit by a Lake Shore & Michigan Southern train at the Columbus Avenue grade crossing in Sandusky on February 18. Six passengers were injured and the car itself was destroyed. Then on April 7th, an LS&MS engine hit car No. 6 at Fremont, injuring three passengers. Aboard was LSE claims agent Harry Rimelspach, who got a first-hand view of claims creation.

Next, on June 3 a westbound car lost its motorman at Undergrade, the Nickel Plate underpass west of Lorain, when Warren Gregg fainted and fell from the car. The conductor managed to stop the car and walked back to find Gregg only slightly injured but dazed. The incident apparently did not hurt Gregg's promotion possibilities as he eventually served for 32 years as assistant superintendent and superintendent at Beach Park. Twelve passengers were injured on September 3rd when an unqualified conductor ran car 8 through an open switch into some parked coal cars at Sheffield Lake.

Undergrade's list of mishaps began to lengthen when on September 21 brand-new Brill interurban No. 66 came through the "S" curve too fast and derailed. Three passengers and the crew were injured and the car was demolished beyond repair — the second loss of a newly built or rebuilt car in less than a year. That tradition would continue too. Finally, two collisions came in October, one of which wiped ex–Lorain & Cleveland combine No. 40 off the roster.

This was the competition the LSE faced between Cleveland and Toledo. The New York Central's Lake Shore & Michigan Southern subsidiary was a first-class piece of railroad, as demonstrated by LS&MS 4721 storming west through Gypsum, Ohio, about 1909. The unusual high-speed 2-6-2 was built by Brooks in 1905. (E. Niebergal photo, Frohman Collection, Hayes Presidential Center)

In the category of pure humiliation, Sandusky's police chief, "in the interest of public safety," pulled Tiffin Avenue shuttle car 19 out of service in early December because of no springs, rotting windows, and a roof that threatened to separate itself from the car sides. But the LSE had no spares, so the offending car — probably a relic from the old Sandusky Street Railway — immediately reappeared on the streets. This prompted the enraged chief to dispatch a patrolman to chase it and take possession by confiscating the controller handle. The problem was resolved when superintendent Burge promised it would be quickly replaced by another car being repaired at Fremont.

All of that aside, Messrs. Everett, Moore, and Bicknell could well be heartened by their company's performance. Gross income for 1903 was 32 percent ahead of the previous year and 72 percent over 1901. The LSE still showed a modest deficit after bond interest, but it was narrowing substantially.

Indeed, the Everett-Moore syndicate itself had every reason to be confident. It was back in control of the majority of its most promising properties — mostly interurbans and street railways — and these seemed sound and solid. And it was expanding again, building an extension of its Cleveland, Painesville & Eastern to Ashtabula among other things. So Henry Everett wasted no time in treating himself to the best, a luxurious private interurban car which he and his associates could use to tour their empire and entertain customers, bankers, and politicians. On September 3, 1903, the Brill company delivered the *Josephine*, named for Everett's wife, and inspection trips were never the same again. The regal *Josephine* had large curtained picture windows and was painted dark green with gold letters and scrollwork; inside was a sleeping compartment, a kitchen and dining section, a private office, and rear observation lounge. A Vanderbilt or a Gould hardly had much better. *Josephine* would visit the Lake Shore Electric often before her untimely demise in a 1909 carbarn fire near Akron.

Collisions and other mishaps bedeviled the LSE in its early years. On October 18, 1903, misunderstood orders resulted in newly delivered Brill Limited Car 68 (left) meeting combine 40 (I) head-on west of Barnes siding. The 68 was repaired but No. 40 went to scrap. (W. A. McCaleb collection)

Yes, 1903 had been a fine year for the Lake Shore Electric — 32 percent more gross income than 1902. But that year produced another interesting statistic. National automobile registrations had climbed 43 percent in the same period and 127 percent since 1901. The gross numbers were still inconsequential, however; there were only 32,950 automobiles in the entire country, owned mostly by rich people who would never ride an interurban anyway. There was little concern there. There was even less concern with the news of an even braver new world that arrived in December — the Wright brothers of Dayton had managed to get a flying machine into the air at Kitty Hawk, North Carolina.

Henry Everett could hold court in comfort aboard his private interurban car *Josephine*, built in 1903. She was a regular visitor to the Lake Shore Electric. (Brill photo, George Krambles collection)

CHAPTER 2

PUTTING IT ALL TOGETHER

1904 – 1907

The year 1903 had been happily hectic — the receivership ended, the new high-speed Brill cars arrived, and Cleveland–Toledo limited services started. A brief breather was now necessary as President Warren Bicknell put the company's house in more firm order while the banker committee watched over and the Everett-Moore syndicate waited to reassume full control. Thus the years 1904 and 1905 were comparatively quiescent, but they built toward a final expansive burst the next year.

Unfortunately 1904 got off to a disorderly start with another rash of wrecks. In the space of a month, between January 4 and February 7, there were four separate mishaps which ran the gamut of collision classifications — a head-on, a rear-ender, a sideswiping, and the broadsiding of a Pennsylvania Railroad train at the grade crossing in Bellevue. The total toll was the loss of ex–Lorain & Cleveland car 54, six other cars damaged, and some injuries — but thankfully no fatalities.

In between these woes, a January 23 flood washed out bridges over Mud Creek, Sugar Creek, and Cedar Creek and damaged the Portage River bridge at Woodville and Muskellunge Creek bridge at Fremont. Then on March 21 eastbound Barney & Smith No. 3 derailed at high speed near Ceylon Junction, miraculously ending up upright but crosswise to the track.

Thus far the LSE had suffered an abnormal number of operational mishaps but no passengers had been killed. That luck finally ran out on June 2, 1904. Motorman Miles Beebe had taken his fully laden Toledo–Cleveland limited car out of Norwalk at 4:35 p.m. and was swinging at full speed through a curve at Wells Corners, four miles east, when he suddenly saw westbound express motor 33 five hundred feet away and heading at him almost as fast. Beebe threw his car into emergency and jumped as the two cars crashed head-on and telescoped. Six passengers riding in the limited's unique forward smoking section never had a chance and were crushed to death; 18 other passengers and crew members were injured, many of them seriously. Ironically the car handling the limited schedule was the second No. 66, which had been delivered only three months earlier to replace the deceased first No. 66, demolished the September before.

It turned out that motor 33 was operating as an unscheduled extra, making stops to drop off and pick up express shipments at local points along the line. Its crew, motorman George Sturgeon and conductor Wilbur Koons, were running for the next siding to meet the limited — a siding which the limited had just passed. While they were blamed for not strictly following rules on meets, the real culprit seemed to be a slipshod system of dispatching.

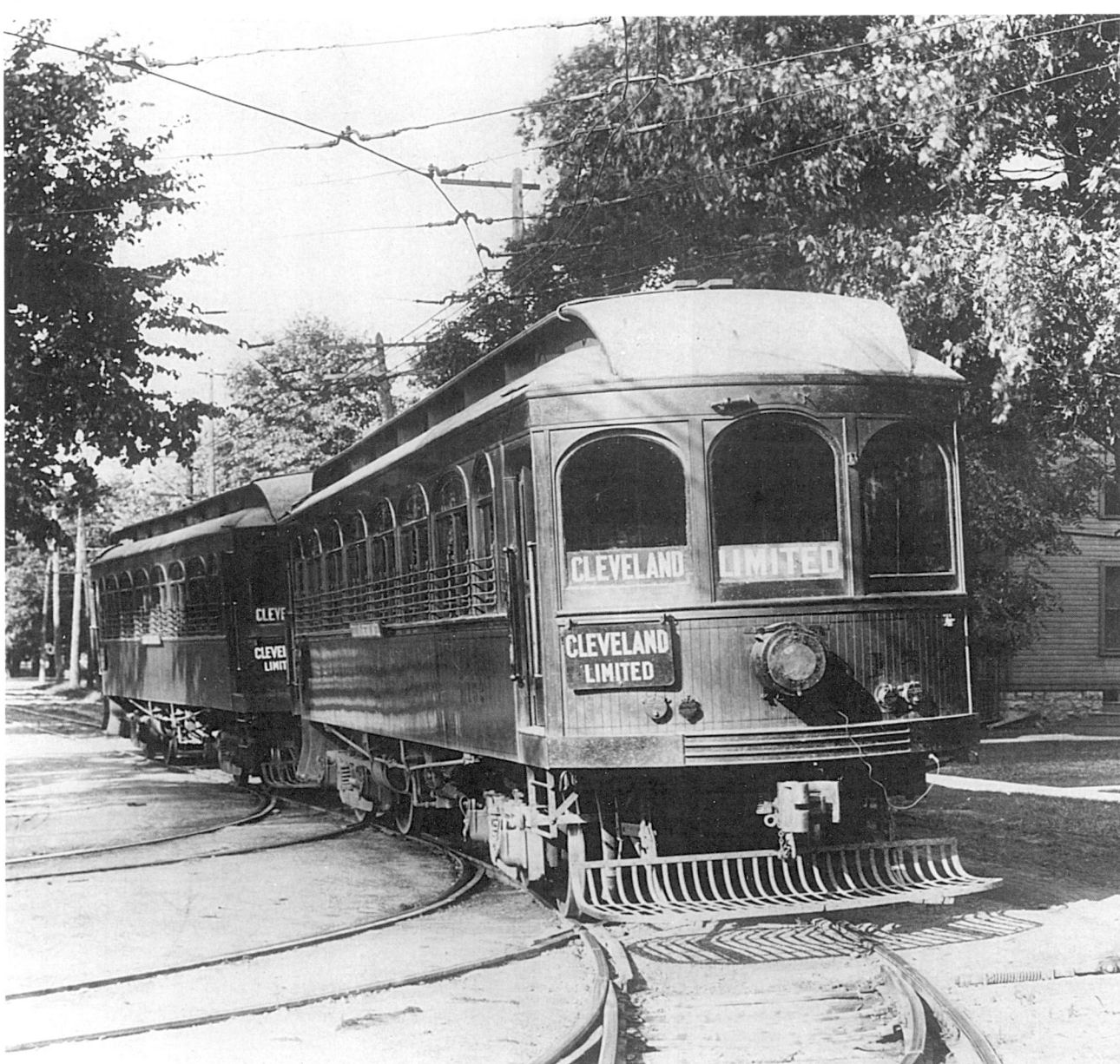

Big wooden Niles–built multiple-unit interurbans such as the 152(II) and her mate brought the LSE into its maturity. The pair is posed at Fremont Carhouse about 1915. (George Krambles collection)

The LSE's practice apparently was to run extras such as this on a single track without train orders, expecting them to keep clear of scheduled cars by watching the timetable and calculating meeting points on their own. In a final irony, the Fremont dispatcher testified that he realized what was happening when he received passing reports of the two cars, and that he had authority to shut off the power to prevent a wreck — but did not think to do so. Most likely, it would have been impossible anyway, since he would have had to telephone orders to the manual substation operators. It was to be the LSE's worst accident ever, and one of the worst in the industry at that time.

More positively, the early results of the new limited-stop services began coming in — and were very encouraging. Bicknell found an almost immediate upward trend after the limiteds were inaugurated in mid-October 1903. For the balance of October the limiteds averaged 32 cents a car mile against a system average (which included the limiteds) of 23 cents. By November 1903 the figure had risen to 35 cents vs. 22 cents. In other words the

limited cars were earning 57 percent more than their stop-and-go sisters. A month later some limited runs were earning over a dollar a car mile. The Lake Shore had found the key to its success which it would exploit for the next 30 years.

Otherwise 1904 saw mostly a plodding process of streamlining and centralizing facilities and supervisory functions. Back in October 1903, Bicknell had concentrated heavy car repair work at Sandusky and Fremont, moving machinery from the former Lorain & Cleveland Beach Park shop to Sandusky and leaving Beach Park as strictly a storage facility. By September 13, 1904, he shut down the Sandusky & Interurban's 1899 Sandusky power plant and the onetime Sandusky, Milan & Norwalk's wheezing facility at Milan. Afterward LSE's power generation was centralized at the relatively modern ex-TF&N Fremont plant and the L&C's older one at Beach Park; both were expanded and, in Beach Park's case, rebuilt in the 1906–1907 period.

Centralizing was done in the management ranks too. As the two other division superintendents left or were fired during the year, Sandusky Division superintendent Lewis K. Burge replaced them, enabling the company to handle all superintendent responsibilities for the system on a single salary.

Equipment acquisitions were minimal, mostly confined to trying to keep up with the destruction of cars in service. On March 9th a new carbody was received from the Kuhlman Car Company (a Brill subsidiary) to replace the unfortunate No. 66 destroyed in the derailment at Undergrade. The new body was similar to its predecessor and used its trucks and electrical equipment. As just related, the new No. 66 soon got its own LSE-style baptism at Wells Corners. In addition, three Stephenson-built interurban coaches with steel underframes arrived August 11, numbered 70–72. The 72 was actually only a body, replacing the wrecked *Gamma* and using equipment from ex-L&C car 50; the 50 in turn got *Gamma*'s trucks and motors.

Uncharacteristically, there were no equipment losses in 1905, but one bizarre accident made headlines. At 8 a.m. on Saturday May 13th, Brill car 64 was crossing the spindly public highway viaduct over the Rocky River gorge outside Cleveland when it derailed in mid-bridge. The single track was laid on one side of the roadway next to the bridge railing and the car lurched through the railing, its body listing toward the edge and its front end dangling precariously over

To its end, the LSE aggressively solicited excursions and special movements. A typical early example was this Lorain newsboys' outing to Cleveland the day after Christmas in 1904. A Barney & Smith coach carries the load of youngsters. (Karel Liebenauer collection)

(*Above*) The LSE had its scariest accident May 13, 1905, when westbound Brill No. 64 derailed on the Rocky River Viaduct. Everyone, including President Warren Bicknell, got out safely. (Karel Liebenauer collection)

(*Right*) A Toledo-bound Brill combine stops at the station on Genoa's Main Street. The camera looks north toward the Lake Shore & Michigan Southern crossing. (Karel Liebenauer collection)

the river 100 feet below. The terrified passengers were ushered out safely. One of them happened to be LSE president Warren Bicknell, who got a frightening firsthand glimpse of what was becoming a chronic habit for the new company.

New Connections — Strong, Weak, and Nonexistent

If things were relatively placid on the LSE in 1904, its immediate territory was churning with other interurban projects. The most tangible was the Toledo, Port Clinton & Lakeside, chartered by a group of Toledo businessmen in December 1902 to run from Toledo through Oak Harbor to Port Clinton and Lakeside, on the Marblehead peninsula north of Sandusky Bay. The TPC&L's projected route roughly paralleled the Lake Shore Electric from Toledo to Genoa, about 14 miles, then struck out east toward the peninsula and away from LSE territory. As a temporary economic expedient, the company decided to build its Genoa–Lakeside section first and arranged to use the LSE's track between Genoa and Toledo. The tracks actually joined at Holts Corners, just north of the town.

TPC&L cars began scheduled service October 22, 1904, and operated over the LSE for the next two years. The arrangement actually was an interline traffic agreement rather than a pure trackage rights contract. While on Lake Shore tracks the TPC&L cars were considered LSE trains; the LSE kept all revenues for local traffic between Toledo and Genoa, and

other revenues were divided between the two companies on a mileage basis. In turn the LSE paid its partner for car and crew mileage while on LSE rails. The contract ran until October 22, 1906, at which time the TPC&L opened its own Toledo line via Clay Center and Curtice to the north. Primarily serving different territories, the companies were never more than nominal competitors and helped one another with detour movements between Toledo and Genoa when someone's line was blocked. The TPC&L went on to become part of the Cities Service–controlled Ohio Public Service Company in 1924, and under the name of the Toledo & Eastern a portion of its line survived until 1958.

Two other projects also were taking form, albeit not too impressively. One, the Lake Erie, Bowling Green & Napoleon, was organized in 1901 to run crosswise across northwestern Ohio, starting from Port Clinton on Lake Erie and heading westward to Defiance. Along the way it would cross the LSE at Woodville and pass through Pemberville, Bowling Green, and Napoleon. Among other things, it would link Bowling Green (population 5,067 in 1900) with the Lake Shore Electric at Woodville, giving the town an eastern outlet to Norwalk and Cleveland — for whatever value that was. An ill-begotten idea from the start, the line initially managed to complete only an 11.5-mile central section between Bowling Green and Pemberville, where it stopped exhausted in 1902. But on August 22, 1904, the LSE received word that the LEBG&N had finally begun grading its "Port Clinton extension" eastward from Pemberville to Woodville.

Service to Woodville started early in May of 1905, but the imperial Pennsylvania Railroad — notoriously antagonistic to interurbans — refused to allow the electric line to cross its tracks to connect with the LSE on the east side. A court fight ensued while LEBG&N passengers trudged across on their own. On August 25 the underfed David beat Goliath when a federal judge allowed the crossing, which was completed early the next year. Theoretically the LEBG&N also could now proceed on eastward to Port Clinton, but mercifully that was not in the cards. The company went bankrupt in 1911 and operations on the Woodville extension ended in 1916 after a life of 11 years.

The second project was only slightly more promising. The Sandusky, Norwalk & Mansfield was incorporated in 1902 as one segment of a vast but vague scheme to build a north–south chain of interurban lines from Lake Erie at Sandusky to Portsmouth, Ohio, on the Ohio River. The SN&M itself would begin at a Lake Shore Electric connection at Norwalk

The Sandusky, Norwalk & Mansfield did not reach either of the terminals in its title and was generally unimpressive, both financially and physically. An exception was its elaborate station at North Fairfield, Ohio, the company's operating center. SN&M combine 4 awaits departure. (John A. Rehor collection)

A busy moment on Norwalk's Main Street in the early 1900s. The express motor at left is LSE's first No. 43, a 1907 rebuild of the Sandusky & Interurban's *Alpha*; ahead of it is an LSE Barney & Smith coach. Ahead of that may be a Cleveland Southwestern car, the LSE's competition between Norwalk and Cleveland. (Firelands Museum collection)

and run south to Plymouth and Shelby, a total of 28 miles. At Shelby it was to meet the Mansfield Railway, Light & Power Company's line to Mansfield, with the ultimate hope of operating through service between Sandusky and Mansfield.

The SN&M started grading south from Norwalk in 1903, heading through the flat countryside for its first terminal at Plymouth. Financing was anemic, and as the struggling project took shape in 1904 and early 1905, the Lake Shore Electric loaned a line car and crew to help put up wire and agreed to provide power from its Monroeville substation. Service between Norwalk and Plymouth began July 4, 1905, but the Shelby and Mansfield connections had to wait another two years. Although the LSE directly aided the SN&M in its early years and participated in periodic through services, the new line eventually became more closely allied with the Cleveland Southwestern, its other connection at Norwalk.

The arrival of the SN&M in Norwalk made that little city into an interurban hub, with no less than five radiating lines — three LSE routes (to Toledo, to Ceylon Junction and Cleveland, and to Sandusky), the Cleveland Southwestern to Oberlin and Cleveland, and the SN&M. It came close to having a sixth, too. Among the more fascinating "almost was" trolley projects in northern Ohio was a company that went by various names, but most commonly as the Sandusky, Bellevue, Monroeville & Norwalk Traction Company. Chartered December 20, 1899, it planned a group of radial lines out of Sandusky to the other three communities in its title. Although directly in the center of Lake Shore Electric territory, its planned system complemented rather than competed with the LSE. Even its Sandusky–Norwalk line lay considerably west of the LSE and was to have entered Sandusky over the Lake Shore's Hayes Avenue (Depot) line.

Work on this system was carried on intermittently in the early 1900s and by May 1903 it had actually graded a right-of-way for its Sandusky–Monroeville line which followed present Ohio Routes 4 and 99. It also received a franchise in Norwalk to build on Washington Street and Whittlesey Avenue, bought special trackwork, and installed it where necessary. Early in July of 1903 newspapers reported that the Elkins-Widener syndicate of Philadelphia was backing the project, and on July 10th work was started on a powerhouse in Monroeville. The next day the company ordered seven monitor-roofed semi-convertible suburban cars from Brill in Philadelphia. At the same time W. T. Forsythe, the company's chief engineer, announced that 800 tons of rails were being shipped and a contract for the overhead line was being let.

But all work stopped in late 1903, never to resume. By then Brill had completed the carbodies of the seven-car order and scrambled to find other buyers. Eventually two went to the Chicago & Indiana Air Line (a predecessor of the Chicago, South Shore & South Bend), two to the Schuylkill Traction in Pennsylvania, one to the Chicago & South Shore Railway (later Northern Indiana Railway) and two to the Oregon Water Power & Railway Company — almost a continent away from Lake Erie.

Very real and very vital was another connecting project, however. Dismembered by the Everett-Moore collapse, the Toledo–Detroit route crawled back to life in a somewhat different form. The loss of the Detroit & Toledo Shore Line in 1902 and its subsequent sale as a steam railroad had left the Toledo & Monroe interurban line stranded at Monroe, Michigan, 35 miles south of Detroit. But as noted in Chapter 1, a new company called the Detroit, Monroe & Toledo Short Line was incorporated in December 1902 to take over the Toledo & Monroe and fill the gap. The DM&TSL began building its Monroe–Detroit extension in 1903, gradually opening segments as they were completed. On November 5, 1904, it was able to start service over the entire line.

Although they had no direct control over the DM&TSL, Everett and Moore immediately celebrated the event. On December 15 the *Josephine* left Cleveland for Detroit carrying all the major powers of Cleveland's traction world. The 14 distinguished passengers included Henry Everett, Warren Bicknell, John J. Stanley (general manager of the Cleveland Electric Railway), Fred T. Pomeroy (president of the Cleveland Southwestern and a Pomeroy-Mandelbaum principal), C. W. Wason (president of the Cleveland, Painesville & Eastern and an Everett-Moore associate), and George T. Bishop (another leading interur-

All interurban lines entering Toledo shared a common union station facility. Over the years there were five different downtown station sites, most of them located in the 400-block of Superior Avenue near Jackson. This is one of the earlier locations, on the west side of Superior. (Karel Liebenauer collection)

ban entrepreneur and president of the Eastern Ohio Traction). *Josephine* swept over the LSE from Cleveland to Toledo in three hours and 55 minutes — not a record, but fast going considering that she ran during the daytime when the single-track line was carrying heavy traffic.

A month later DM&TSL president Matthew Slush and other officials visited the Lake Shore Electric to discuss through Cleveland–Detroit services. On January 6, 1905, the two companies announced the imminent beginning of through operations "immediately after the perfection of minor details." Those "minor details" took six years to work out, and by the time they were, the entire Cleveland–Detroit route was back under the Everett-Moore wing. But in the meantime many LSE passengers took advantage of the connecting service by transferring at the common interurban station in Toledo.

Expansion at Lorain and Elyria

The Lake Shore Electric was still under the banker trusteeship in 1905 and was restricted in taking on major new financial commitments. But a new acquisition opportunity appeared in Lorain and Everett and Moore moved to take it — temporarily on their own but ultimately for the LSE.

Lorain, a Lake Erie port 27 miles west of Cleveland, was then undergoing a spectacular metamorphosis. In 1890 it had been a small town of 4800 souls whose main industries were fishing, a brass works, and the coal transshipping facilities of the Cleveland, Lorain & Wheeling Railroad (later part of the Baltimore & Ohio). By 1905 it was a thriving industrial city of 25,500.

The agent for this transformation was Tom L. Johnson, a unique and colorful blend of successful entrepreneur and populist political reformer. A native Kentuckian, Johnson became superintendent of a Louisville street railway company at age 17; from there he rapidly moved into street railway investments in Indianapolis and Cleveland. Along the way he also became entranced with political economist Henry George's radical social and single-tax theories and entered politics. In 1890 he was elected a U. S. congressman from Cleveland and served two terms before being defeated in 1894.

That year the 40-year-old Johnson came to Lorain to establish a steel mill along the Black River on the south side of town. To transport what would clearly be a large number of workers, he bought the plodding little Lorain Street Railway, a short horsecar line which ran along Broadway from Erie Avenue to 21st Street. As his mill rapidly rose, Johnson rebuilt the horsecar line, electrified it, and extended it past the mill site in South Lorain and on south to Elyria, ten miles. By mid-September 1894 the new line was in full operation. The mill itself shipped its first steel in 1895.

Other large manufacturers quickly appeared. In the same year that Johnson's mill started up, the Thew Automatic Shovel Company began producing steam shovels and two years later what became the American Shipbuilding Company was established. By the time Everett-Moore's Lorain & Cleveland had arrived in the city in October 1897 Johnson's Lorain Street Railway was a bustling and growing operation.

But in 1901 Johnson sold his mill to J. P. Morgan's newly formed U.S. Steel Corporation. At the same time he satisfied his reformist political zeal by being elected mayor of Cleveland, where earlier he had crusaded for three-cent streetcar fares and became both the business and political enemy of the powerful conservative Republican Mark Hanna. With his Lorain mill profitably gone and plenty to do elsewhere, Johnson eventually decided to sell the Lorain Street Railway.

Acting for Everett-Moore, Warren Bicknell and E. B. Hale bought the railway on March 11, 1905, although for the time being the LSE had no direct involvement and the Lorain Street Railway's corporate structure was left unchanged. But the new owners immediately planned a new five-mile connecting line which started at South Lorain, on the Lorain Street Railway's Elyria line, and swung northeast to Beach Park (or Avon Beach), seven

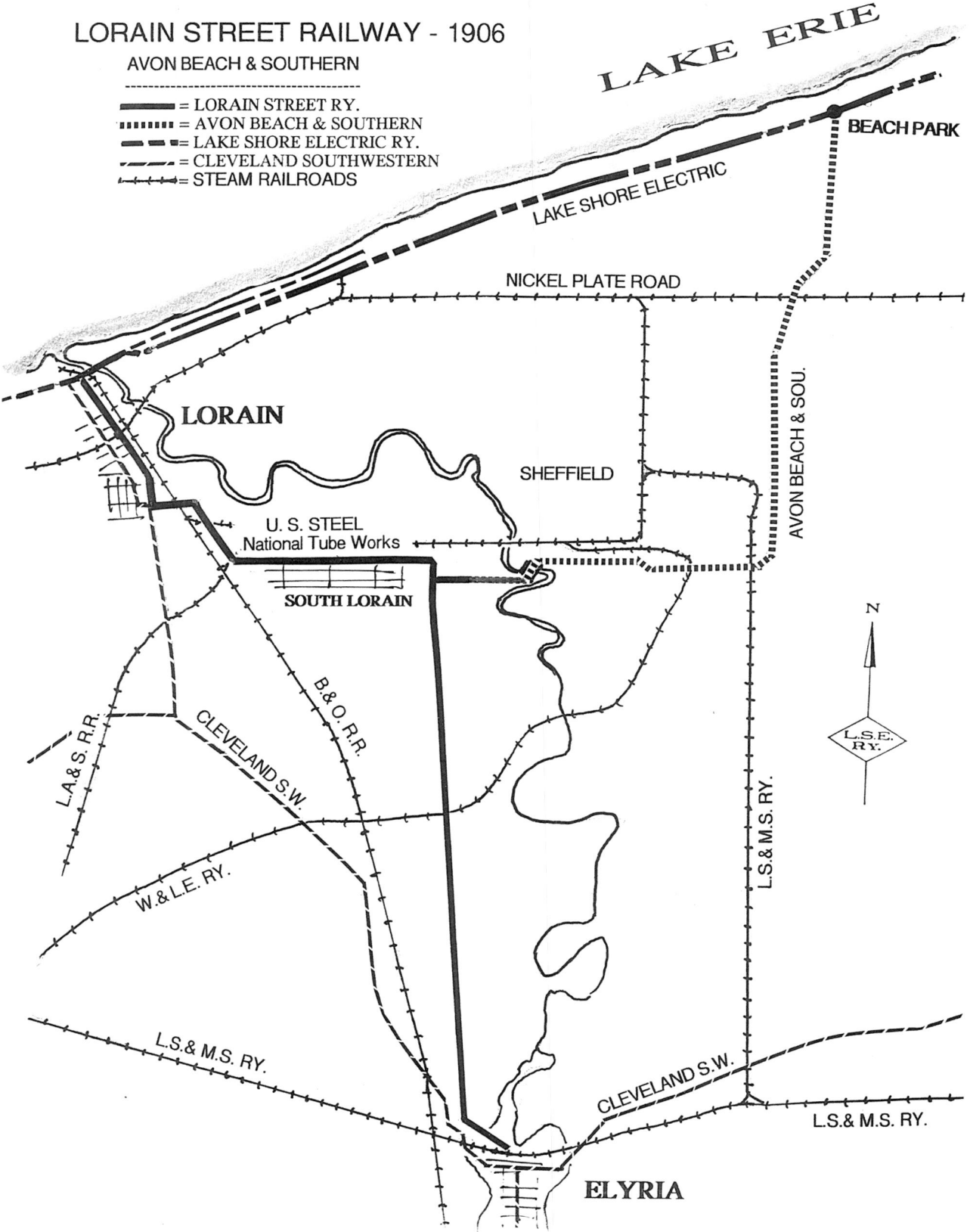

The Lorain Street Railway and Avon Beach & Southern, 1906.

miles east of Lorain on the LSE's main line. Separately incorporated as the Avon Beach & Southern, this somewhat strange route avoided anything resembling a population center. But on-line traffic was not its purpose. The Cleveland Southwestern — which by then was poaching on the LSE's territory at Norwalk — had a direct line between Elyria and Cleveland; the new AB&S was designed to create a competitive Elyria–Cleveland route, using a combination of the Lorain Street Railway and LSE main lines. For financial reasons the line was created as a Lorain Street Railway subsidiary, although it was always essentially an LSE operation using mostly LSE equipment.

By July 15th work on the single-track AB&S was well under way, although it was reported that construction in Lorain was held up by a court fight over street crossings. Actually the squabble revolved around a universal transfer arrangement in the city, which was served by three separate companies — the Lorain Street Railway, LSE, and Cleveland Southwestern. The line's most interesting engineering challenge was hurdling the wide and deep Black River valley just east of 31st Street in South Lorain; it was solved with an impressive combination of wood trestling and two-span steel truss bridge reputedly recycled from steam railroad use. On December 20, 1905, LSE's Stephenson-built interurban car 70 took officials on an inaugural trip between Elyria and Cleveland, and regular service started the next day.

Afterward, however, the Avon Beach & Southern quickly dropped into a peculiar limbo. Hourly Elyria–Cleveland schedules were maintained for less than a year when the new line was demoted to a shuttle between Beach Park and South Lorain — essentially serving no market whatever. The failure was never publicly explained and, on the surface, seems mystifying. Although the LSE's route was eight miles longer than the Southwestern's, it was generally faster, and the original schedules were competitive. And in any event, it does not appear that the business was given much time to develop; the LSE was, after all, trying to crack a new competitive market where established riding habits had to be changed. It is possible that by 1906 the owners of the LSE and the Southwestern had agreed between themselves to cut back on what was clearly wasteful competition.

In this regard it is interesting to note that on October 19, 1905, Henry Everett met with Fred Pomeroy to discuss the LSE's purchase of the Cleveland Southwestern (then actually called the Cleveland and Southwestern). Substantive or not, the negotiations clearly went no further and nothing more was heard about the idea. It was just as well; in January 1922 the Southwestern went into receivership while the Lake Shore was still prospering.

By late 1905 more expansion was brewing. Most significant was some serious thinking about building southwest from Sandusky to meet the Cleveland–Norwalk–Toledo main line at either Clyde or Fremont. Since the LSE's formation, Sandusky essentially had been a stub-end branch-line terminal from the east. While well supplied with steam railroads, including the Lake Shore & Michigan Southern's Cleveland–Toledo main line, it had no electric railway link to Toledo or other western Ohio points. Other promoters had noted this and there had been various independent proposals for lines west from the city.

By the fall of 1905 LSE management was exploring such an extension. On October 1, general superintendent Furman Stout, chief engineer John Laylin, and attorney Harry Rimelspach took a Sunday drive from Clyde to Sandusky to look over possible routes. Afterward things turned quiet for about eight months.

In addition, growing traffic now was putting heavy pressure on both the physical plant and the equipment. On September 8, 1905, the LSE vaguely announced it would begin double-tracking its system, no time or locations given. The original Lorain & Cleveland's single-track route was the clear first candidate, however; it was carrying at least 52 scheduled trains a day, and demand was growing for more service to Lorain.

More concretely, the company dispatched an order to the Niles Car Company in December for ten new interurban coaches to supplement and replace the 1903 Brills in limited service.

These, however, were not to be entirely routine designs. Thanks primarily to general superintendent Stout, they were ordered to be equipped with multiple-unit control, allowing a single motorman to operate a train of motor cars. It was a new technical innovation which already had been adopted by urban rapid transit lines and some railroad suburban operations, but not yet by any interurban lines. The Lake Shore already was having capacity problems on its limiteds and during the summers when crowds were riding to Cedar Point and the other beach resorts. "Double-headers" had to be run — that is, two cars with their full crews following each other and causing scheduling, dispatching, and safety problems on the single-track line. The application of multiple-unit control on trolley-operated equipment was another industry "first" for the Lake Shore and would become its standard for all its future interurban cars. (Actually, the 1903 Brill limited cars were delivered with GE Type M multiple-unit controls, but — while this equipment was successful elsewhere — it was apparently unsuited to the LSE's operations and never used.)

Always looking for new business, general superintendent Stout announced in July 1905 that the interurban stood ready to provide a new auto wrecking service to stranded motorists; it would furnish a flat car, planks, and block and tackle and haul disabled autos to the nearest repair shop. The rate was $15 for 15 miles, $25 for up to 50 miles, and 50 cents a mile thereafter. "It is less embarrassing than having to hire a team," he said, "although slightly more expensive." Was this just creative marketing on Stout's part — or was it a not-so-subtle warning to the LSE's clientele that this new mode of transportation was untrustworthy and potentially humiliating?

Reaching Full Form: 1906

Thanks to a combination of Bicknell's management, a growing market, and the Lake Shore's successful limited service strategy, 1905 was an excellent year. Gross income had swelled 19.5 percent over the last year and the company showed a solid profit — its first. In fact, the reported profit of $114,830 indicated that the LSE had brought 14.6 percent of its gross income down to net, an impressive performance for an interurban. (Later historians have correctly questioned some of the accounting methods commonly followed at the time, so the true profit may have been substantially less.)

The performance so heartened the LSE's banker trustees that they decided to terminate the five-year voting trust three years early. At the January 1906 directors' meeting the company was turned back to full Everett-Moore control. The changeover dictated a somewhat different top management structure. Bicknell, who had basically handled both the company's financial and operating management, resigned to head Everett-Moore's Cleveland Construction Company. Afterward his responsibilities were split. Edward Moore took his place as president, concentrating primarily on corporate and financial matters, and Furman Stout was made general manager in charge of the company's actual operation — effectively its top on-site manager. Bicknell, incidentally, went on to make a huge success of the Cleveland Construction Company and became a highly active and respected civic leader. He died in 1941 at the age of 73.

Now completely on its own, the Lake Shore proceeded to make 1906 the most active and exciting year in its history. When it was over the system had reached its physical peak; later short bits of new trackage would be added, some structures and other facilities upgraded, and two important interline services started — but by the end of 1907 the map was filled out and all major physical facilities were in place.

First off, the promised double-tracking was begun on the busy Cleveland–Lorain section. The first 2½-mile stretch out of Rocky River was finished June 21 and the work was completed through to Lorain on December 18. It was intended to continue the project as far west as Ceylon Junction, but this was deferred "temporarily." In the 1912–13 period new bridges over Beaver Creek (between Lorain and Vermilion), the Vermilion River, and

Chappelle Creek (west of Vermilion) were built to accommodate a second track, but it was never laid.

Next came the building of a new line between Sandusky and Fremont, which not only would give Sandusky its western outlet but would provide an alternate route between Cleveland and Toledo. To facilitate financing, the 23-mile extension was incorporated July 14th as a separate subsidiary, the Sandusky, Fremont & Southern Railway. While the SF&S owned the railway line and kept its own separate revenue and expense accounts, it was to be operated as an integral part of the Lake Shore Electric system with LSE employees and equipment. Ten Niles interurban cars of 1907 and eight ballast cars were assigned to SF&S ownership, but these were simply pooled with other system cars.

The Fremont route left Sandusky via the Tiffin Avenue streetcar line and was built alongside the Lake Erie & Western Railroad's Sandusky–Fremont main line for much of its distance. The LE&W — at the time a New York Central subsidiary — owned an unusually wide right-of-way with plenty of room for two paralleling single-track lines. (Unlike many large steam railroads, the New York Central's various subsidiaries in this territory generally did not oppose interurban projects and sometimes even aided them. The Central realistically recognized that many of its own local passenger services were money-losers and was happy to see the electric lines take the business.) SF&S grading was well under way by mid-August amid statements that the line eventually would be continued beyond Fremont to Tiffin and to Fostoria.

As work began on the Sandusky–Fremont line the Lake Shore also moved to legitimize its Lorain Street Railway situation. The Lorain company had been held in the name of individuals in the Everett-Moore group pending the end of the LSE voting trust and permanent financing of the purchase. On August 3 the Lake Shore created another subsidiary, the Lorain Street Rail*road*, to own the properties of the Lorain Street Rail*way* and the Avon Beach & Southern branch. Unlike the just-formed Sandusky, Fremont & Southern, the Lorain Street Railroad technically remained a separate operation, with its own supervision, employees, equipment, and facilities. But as the Lake Shore Electric added local city routes of its own in Lorain it pooled cars and employees with the Lorain Street Railroad and used the latter's South Lorain carhouse.

Electric power-generating capacity was substantially boosted by rebuilding both the Beach Park and Fremont plants. During 1906 and 1907 Beach Park's obsolete direct current equipment was replaced with high-voltage alternating current generators and the entire transmission system changed over. At about the same time a 3500 kw Westinghouse-Parsons turbine was added at Fremont to supply power for the new Sandusky–Fremont line as well as the Toledo, Fostoria & Findlay's extension from Pemberville to Toledo. A new substation also was added at Dover Bay for the growing loads on the Cleveland–Lorain section.

The heady atmosphere also produced proposals for three line relocations to allow faster operations. One was to be a direct 16-mile double-track route between Fremont and Genoa, avoiding the dogleg alignment via Woodville and saving about two miles as well as some roadside running. Similarly the roadside section between Norwalk and Monroeville would be realigned on a private right-of-way following the Wheeling & Lake Erie Railroad's main line. And finally the old Sandusky, Milan & Norwalk route between Milan and Norwalk would be relocated alongside the Wheeling & Lake Erie's Huron branch, eliminating two troublesome wood trestles and some up-and-down topography. None ever materialized,

(Facing page, top) Work motor "K" and crew work on double-tracking the Cleveland–Lorain section in 1906. (W. A. McCaleb collection)

(Facing page, bottom) A typical section of the new Sandusky–Fremont Line between Vickery and Erlin. The track was built largely on the wide right-of-way of the Lake Erie & Western, shown behind the interurban. (E. V. Emery photo, Lake Shore Electric Ry.)

although the company obtained options on land for the Fremont–Genoa cutoff and the project surfaced periodically for several years after.

Inevitably the LSE's final burst of expansion also brought a burst of new debt. The Lorain Street Railway came with a dowry of $750,000 in bonded debt and the new Lorain Street Railroad issued $500,000 in additional bonds. Also, $645,000 in new bonds were issued to build the Sandusky, Fremont & Southern — a total of $1.9 million to be added to the LSE's $4.9 million existing collection of bond obligations. Both the Lorain and SF&S bonds represented mortgages on those specific properties, not on the Lake Shore Electric itself.

As they were expanding the Lake Shore, the Everett-Moore group also recaptured the Toledo–Detroit route. Early in 1906 their Detroit United Railway completed negotiations to buy the Detroit, Monroe & Toledo Short Line, and on March 1st the deed was officially done. Afterward the DM&TSL legally remained a separate company, but was integrated into the DUR system. Planning for through Cleveland–Detroit service continued, still with no result — but at least the full route was now all in the family.

The first of the ten new Niles cars arrived May 28, with all on the property by mid-June; by July 27 most were working the limited schedules. Less distinctive than the 1903 Brills, they were more gracefully proportioned and generally more aesthetic, with arched windows glazed with what was called "cathedral art glass," cherry interiors with decorative white holly inlays, leather seats, and, it was proudly noted, "toilets furnished in white tile." With four 85-hp Westinghouse motors and their multiple-unit control — which this time was very successful — they were capable of over 70 mph and set the Lake Shore's future equipment standards. Indeed, they were the most reverently remembered of its fleet.

Stout immediately and successfully tested their multiple-unit control equipment, operating a two-car train June 15 and hitting 71 mph. Unfortunately, the 1890 iron truss highway viaduct at Rocky River precluded running trains in and out of Cleveland, so regular multiple-unit operations had to await replacement of that uncertain structure.

The gradual arrival of the new Niles cars was an event all along the line and local newspapers rhapsodized over the "rolling palaces." Said the *Fremont Daily News* of an early test

A new Niles interurban and a 1901 Brill city car meet at the picturesque Soldiers Home station outside Sandusky about 1907. The station, located on DeWitt Avenue on the north side of the Home complex (seen at far right), was an inheritance from the Sandusky Street Railway and dated to the 1890s. (Karel Liebenauer collection)

One of the line's worst accidents occurred August 4, 1906, when motorman W. D. Moody forgot his orders and collided with an eastbound local car west of Vermilion. Four people, including Moody, died. (John A. Rehor collection)

trip, "Not only beauties in looks and modern in construction, the new Niles cars are speeders. . . . One could fancy he was in a Pullman — no noise, no jarring, and none of the usual unpleasant features on an electric line. . . . Whenever the train stopped, people flocked to see it and were loud in praise." Ten identical coaches and five combines were ordered during the year, which would give the LSE a total of 25 of the Niles cars by the following year.

But the LSE's curse on newly delivered cars was still operative, this time tragically so. August 4, 1906, was a busy midsummer Saturday and schedules were disrupted. When motorman W. D. Moody left Cleveland's Public Square with his westbound limited, the car, new Niles No. 152, was fully loaded. By the time he stopped at Vermilion he was 20 minutes late and took on a contingent of 42 YMCA excursionists from Lima who were returning home from nearby Linwood Park. By then about 100 passengers were crammed in the car, leaving several others to wait for a following car. Moody had orders to meet an eastbound local at Siding 38, a mile west of town — not the normally scheduled passing point, but both were now running late.

Possibly preoccupied with his schedule problems and distracted by the crowd, Moody forgot the order and passed the siding at full speed. His conductor, Henry Remlinger, realized what had happened and tried to signal Moody; he also tried to struggle through the crowds of standing passengers to reach either the emergency brake or the trolley pole rope, but could not get there in time. Moody did slow, but too late; No. 12 running as the eastbound local met him head-on at full speed near a blind curve. He and one passenger died instantly; two others died later and 52 passengers and crew members were injured.

Both cars were taken to Fremont car shop to be repaired. But there the luckless 152 was caught in the LSE's next major disaster when the shop was partly destroyed by fire October 16. Three other cars were lost along with the 152.

Two days later the Gibsonburg branch's resident shuttle car No. 42, a combine rebuilt from a former Sandusky, Milan & Norwalk veteran, collided with a sister car at Gibsonburg Junction, destroying both. The second victim still carried its original number 11 and was serving as the junction's waiting room, placed there after passengers bemoaned "no seats, no lights, no shelter, and a rain-soaked platform at the junction." (At the same time they had complained that the 42 "was dirty and unfit for the decent traveling public to use.") Car 44, originally the Sandusky & Interurban's *Beta*, replaced the defunct 42 and faithfully plodded back and forth to Gibsonburg for the next 21 years.

Settling Everything Down: 1907

The Lake Shore spent most of 1907 finishing what it started in 1906 but otherwise marking time. It was the year of another national financial panic, and further expansion was curtailed and some employees laid off.

The primary event was the opening of the Sandusky–Fremont line less than a year after work started. A local service between Sandusky and Castalia began June 29, and the full route was opened July 21, offering local cars between Sandusky and Fremont every three hours. More importantly, the new line enabled the LSE to offer an alternate through route between Cleveland and Toledo, tapping the Sandusky market en route. Afterward schedules were redesigned so that through Cleveland–Toledo trips would alternate between the Sandusky (or "Northern") route and Norwalk ("Southern") line. Connecting shuttles on matching schedules covered whichever route was bypassed by the through train — effectively giving full service to each line. Ceylon Junction on the east and Fremont on the west became key junctions and transfer points. When regular multiple-unit train operation began in 1911, trains would normally be split and reassembled at the two junctions so that each route was covered simultaneously with a through car.

Niles completed delivery of the 25 cars ordered in 1905 and 1906. With the loss of the 152, this gave the LSE 19 coaches (Nos. 141–159) and five combines (160–164). Three of these actually used trucks and electrical equipment frugally salvaged from those burned at Fremont.

Shortly after delivery, Niles Coach 153, operating a limited schedule, pauses at the original Huron station on Main Street at Homan Street. The barrels on the baggage cart probably contain iced Lake Erie fish. In 1918 the line was relocated to the south side of town. (Frohman Collection, Hayes Presidential Center)

Construction of the Sandusky–
Fremont line also precipitated some
major track rebuilding and rear-
rangement on the west side of Sandusky's downtown area so that
interurbans could be run directly
through the city without turning or
backtracking. The net effect was to
establish a more direct through
route from Water Street to Tiffin
Avenue via Lawrence and Washington; the Tiffin Avenue city streetcar
line in turn was extended south from
its old terminal at Mills Street to
become the line to Fremont. As part
of these changes, the Tiffin Avenue
car line was partly rerouted and the
onetime People's Electric Railway
tracks on West Market and Pearl
Streets were abandoned.

Some lesser rebuilding was also
done in Norwalk in March 1907
when the LSE double-tracked its
line in East Main Street between
Townsend Avenue and the Lake
Shore & Michigan Southern Railway crossing. This stretch was now

heavily used by the three interurban routes — the Lake Shore lines to Cleveland and to
Sandusky, plus the Cleveland Southwestern — as well as the little one-car Main Street
streetcar line. (Another double-track section had been built earlier in the center of town
as far west as Hester Street.)

As it tried to set up an operating management structure to reflect its expansions the
company found itself making continuous changes during the year. As things shook down,
Milton Trueman, a onetime Wheeling & Lake Erie and TF&N conductor, was made trainmaster at Fremont. In 1910 he became Toledo Division superintendent, a job he held until
1927. When chief engineer F. B. Matthews left for another job in March, Fred Heckler
became superintendent of motive power and cars based at Fremont, combining the old jobs
of master mechanic and chief engineer. At the same time Albert Brownworth, who had
been shop foreman at Sandusky, had his responsibilities broadened to become general
foreman of car shops. On May 23 Lewis Burge was given the title of general superintendent, in charge of all day-to-day operations under general manager Stout. Both Brownworth
and Burge served as head of their respective functions through the end of rail operations
and into the bus era.

Sadly, Stout did not. On August 20 he entered a Toledo hospital for gallbladder surgery
and never came out; he died September 14th at age 48, attended by his mother who had
traveled all the way from Texas to be with him. It was a tragic loss; more than any other
single individual, Furman Stout had made the Lake Shore Electric one of the most innovative forces in the interurban industry. New Niles combine 160 carried his body back to
Norwalk, where the funeral was held at his home. It was, according to the newspapers, the
largest funeral ever held in Norwalk.

Probably not surprisingly, Moore named Fred Coen to replace Stout. On October 29
Coen — now a seasoned 35-year-old — was given Stout's general manager title, also keeping his own old job as secretary. The following January he was made vice president and a

Car 8, a 1900 Barney &
Smith product, poses with
motorman David Sayles and
conductor George Oswald
on the Whittlesey Avenue
spur in Norwalk. At the left
rear is the crossing of the
Lake Shore & Michigan
Southern's Norwalk branch.
(George Krambles collecion)

En route to Cleveland, a Brill limited car makes its stop at the LSE's storefront station in Bellevue in 1906. (Ada Baker Collection, Bellevue Public Library)

member of the board of directors, recognizing that he was in full charge of the company under Moore's general guidance. If Furman Stout had made the Lake Shore Electric a leader, Fred Coen would make it a survivor.

In between Stout's death and Coen's appointment came another tragedy. On September 19 Niles car 146, running a Cleveland–Toledo limited, hit a partly opened switch at Hayes siding east of Toledo and derailed. Conductor Frank Barnes and one passenger were killed, and motorman Sam Jones and 13 passengers were injured. Ironically, Barnes had just returned to regular duty after riding the special car carrying Stout's body from Norwalk to Detroit for burial, and had put up its black drapings.

Railroad legend says that accidents come in threes, and that was certainly so this time. Two head-on collisions followed in November but happily without fatalities. Brill interurban 65 hit Sandusky city streetcar 107 on Columbus Avenue south of Scott Street November 22, injuring 13 passengers on the city car. The next day a misunderstanding of train orders resulted in a low-speed collision between Barney & Smith cars 9 and 21 at the Nickel Plate grade crossing in Bellevue, but nobody was hurt and no real damage was done.

Less damaging but much more embarrassing was the derailment of the *Josephine* in Norwalk on August 26. While President Moore, Director Barney Mahler, Coen, Burge, and five other directors watched helplessly, the work motor "K" was summoned to pull the humiliated queen back on the track and tow it to Sandusky shop. In the meantime the party rode back to Cleveland on a regular limited train.

Moore and his friends could afford to be forgiving, however. Their LSE was still doing quite well. While revenue growth was not as spectacular as in 1905, gross income rose 9 percent between 1905 and 1906 and another 6 percent in 1907. And, accurate or not, the reported net profit continued healthy — although a combination of a somewhat higher operating ratio and the added debt interest reduced the 1907 figure slightly, but not alarmingly. Common stockholders had yet to see any dividends, but the LSE was generally commended for putting its earnings back into the property and the time would come. Indeed, the times were getting better.

Interlude A: The LSE vs. Winter

Snow and ice storms came with disagreeable regularity along Lake Erie's south shore, and between November and April the Lake Shore Electric could usually count on using its small roster of sweepers to keep its city street trackage clear. Plows were attached to work motors for other sections of the line. Thanks to their efforts, the interurban was able to provide the first regular year-round transportation for many small communities in its territory.

(*Left*) Snow sweeper "B," assisted by Stephenson-built car 72 and crew, prepares to do battle in Sandusky in 1909. (Frohman Collection, Hayes Presidential Center)

(Below) In the heat of battle, perhaps the same day, the combination rounds a curve in downtown Sandusky. Note the hardy soul on the sweeper's roof, helping to guide the trolley pole through the ice-encrusted wire. (E. Niebergal photo, Frohman Collection, Hayes Presidential Center)

In an all-too-common scene, plow-equipped work motor 401 has derailed in hard-packed snow in the center of Milan. The plow may be seen at the motor's other end. (Ralph Sayles collection)

(*Facing page, top*) Work motor 404 and a large crew seem to have things in better hand on West Erie Avenue in Lorain about 1922. The motor is well-ballasted with sets of car wheels on its open flat deck. Cleveland division superintendent Warren Gregg is in the cab and roadmaster Roy Bragdon stands at the right by the pole. (W. A. McCaleb collection)

(*Facing page, bottom*) Sometimes nothing helped. Here one of the Barney & Smith coaches sits stranded in Rocky River, crippled by fallen wires. (Photo from Albert C. Doane)

During its golden age the Lake Shore Electric was known best for two things — its Cleveland–Detroit limiteds and its summertime trains to the Lake Erie beaches. The two come together here as a two-car westbound limited passes Crystal Beach station east of Vermilion. Normally the limiteds did not stop at such intermediate spots. (John A. Rehor collection)

(Facing page) Before the Detroit–Superior High Level Bridge, LSE cars struggled in and out of downtown Cleveland over the Superior Viaduct and swing bridge, often delayed by lake freighters passing on the Cuyahoga River below. An eastbound Niles car shares the troublesome span with autos, wagons, and numerous Cleveland Railway streetcars in this 1910 view. (Carol Poh Miller collection)

CHAPTER 3

THE DEVELOPING YEARS

1908 – 1913

If the Lake Shore Electric system was within a few hairs of its full physical growth in 1908, its peak years of long-distance services and high-capacity operations were just ahead. Within three years it would be innovating again with two long-distance interline services, as well as helping sponsor a new line to make one of these operations possible.

It was a time when the Midwestern interurban industry was reaching full flower, too. As it expanded and matured, the industry was now more conscious of itself as an interconnected system instead of a collection of separate localized entities. Back in 1906 it formed the Central Electric Railway Association as a trade association, and in 1908 the Central Electric Traffic Association was created as a CERA adjunct to develop interline rate tariffs and mileage books.

The Lake Shore Electric's location was one of the most strategic in the developing interurban network, linking lines in Michigan, Indiana, and southwestern Ohio with Cleve-

land and other such northern Ohio population centers as Akron and Canton. It also connected the Midwestern lines with a somewhat tenuous route along the Lake Erie's eastern shore to Buffalo and upstate New York. That plus its pioneering of long-distance limited-stop services made the company a natural industry leader. Symbolic of both his company's stature and his own within the industry, the CERA invited Fred Coen to be the featured speaker at its 1908 annual meeting in Dayton.

By early 1908 newspapers were carrying accounts of the long trips now possible by interurban, all of which involved the Lake Shore Electric at some point. They were slow, with numerous transfers — but the point was that the interurbans were becoming intercity carriers and, if nothing else, a cheaper alternative to the steam railroads.

One could ride on Everett-Moore lines from Jackson, Michigan, to Canton, Ohio, for example, leaving Jackson on the Detroit United Railway at 7 a.m. and staggering off a Northern Ohio Traction & Light Company car in Canton at 9 p.m. A hardier traveler could go from Indianapolis to Cleveland in 16 hours and 15 minutes, leaving Indianapolis on the Union Traction of Indiana at 7:30 a.m., changing cars at Fort Wayne, Lima, and Toledo, and arriving on the LSE at Cleveland at 11:45 in the evening. Along the way one spent a total of two hours and 25 minutes waiting for connections. It was possible to get from Youngstown, Ohio, to Jackson, Michigan, in 18 hours and 45 minutes over a rather roundabout route of 365 miles via Leetonia, Salem, Canton, and Cleveland.

Marking Time: 1908 – 1910

With new equipment, greater capacity from the Cleveland–Lorain double-tracking, and its new Sandusky–Fremont route the LSE now was able to fully exploit the Lake Erie summer resort trade from both east and west. Besides the ever-popular Cedar Point, interurban cars fed crowds to such "parks" as Linwood and Crystal Beach near Vermilion, Mitiwanga, Rye Beach, and Ruggles Grove. In addition to the general public, the company actively solicited company picnics of on-line businesses, lodge and church outings, and all manner of other groups. One dramatic example came on Saturday June 17, 1909, when 22 LSE cars carried 1600 employees of Cleveland's H. Black cloak manufacturing company to Linwood Park and back — a record for a single movement at that time. Loading and departure for the affair was carried out over an hour at Public Square from 7:30 to 8:30 a.m.

Less impressive but more typical and homespun was "Gibsonburg Day" at Cedar Point on August 2 of the same year. The town and all its businesses shut down and three LSE special cars took the inhabitants to Sandusky. The annual county fair at Fremont in September also brought out the special cars in force. For the 1908 event, for example, 13 extra cars shuttled 3000 people, packed, it was said, 100 to a car. In 1912 superintendent Milt Trueman and system shop foreman Joe Brownworth decorated one special fair car with, said the *Fremont Daily News*, "corn stalks, pumpkins, cabbage, corn, beets, and everything conceivable in the agricultural line. Interwoven among the corn stalks . . . were electric lights illuminating the exterior. . . . on the front of the car ears of corn were wired in such a manner and combined with electric bulbs that the word FAIR was formed in a brilliant manner. . . . huge banners giving the date and setting forth some of [the fair's] attractions were fastened along the sides of the car." One really would need a photo to visualize this arresting display, but sadly, none have yet appeared.

Cedar Point's attractions also led to the LSE's first regularly scheduled long-distance interline service, although "regularly scheduled" may be stretching the definition. Beginning July 11, 1908, a daily summer-only schedule was run between Mansfield, Ohio, and Sandusky, operating over the Mansfield Railway, Light & Power Company to Shelby; the Sandusky, Norwalk & Mansfield to Norwalk; and the LSE's Sandusky–Norwalk branch to Sandusky. The schedule was designed so that people from Mansfield, Shelby, Plymouth, and the little towns along the SN&M could spend a day at "The Point" and return in the

evening. The Lake Shore Electric supplied the cars — usually one of the 1903 Brills or a Barney & Smith car — which were run by SN&M crews. Never shown in published time-tables, the operation ended after Labor Day but was resumed again (although perhaps not always on a regular basis) for the summers of 1909, 1910, and 1911.

On the other hand, some vague signs of doom began to appear and the interurban even found itself helping to put them into more solid form. More automobiles were now trying to navigate the primitive roads. National auto registrations stood at 194,400 in 1908 —

One of the 1903 Brill limited cars, now demoted to Sandusky–Milan–Norwalk branch service, heads south on Columbus Avenue in Sandusky. (Ralph H. Sayles collection)

Getting places by auto in the 1910 era could be a bit of a chore, as this scene near Sandusky suggests. The new contraptions were not much of a threat to the LSE's fast interurbans on smooth steel rails — not yet, at least. (Frohman Collection, Hayes Presidential Center)

The primary intermediate station on the new Sandusky–Fremont Line was Castalia. Niles car 147 stops at the station — a converted bungalow — about 1909. (E. Niebergal photo, Frohman Collection, Hayes Presidential Center)

compared to 23,000 in 1902 — and there were now also 4,000 motor trucks in use. In Ohio itself, 10,649 motor vehicles were registered. Two years later the national figures would be 458,377 autos and 10,123 trucks, with 32,941 vehicles in Ohio. Ohio became the sixth state in the country to create a highway department in 1904, and both the state and its various localities were embarking on paving projects. In May 1908 the *Fremont Daily News* reported that the highway between Gibsonburg Junction and Woodville was now macadamized and "said to be one of the best highways in Ohio."

The Lake Shore Electric helped the process, partly to bring in some revenue but partly too as a public service. LSE lines were close to stone quarries at Sandusky, Castalia, and Bellevue — and since its tracks ran in or alongside highways in many places, it could deliver right to the work sites. While the revenue was low, so was its cost since it simply used work train crews and equipment, including its existing work motors and ballast cars. A substantial traffic developed and to one degree or another continued into the 1920s. Both for this business and its own ballast needs, the LSE built a new quarry siding at Mount Pleasant, just west of Bellevue, in 1909 and a mile-long spur for the Wagner Stone Company near Castalia the next year.

Possibly the LSE saw little danger in earning a few extra dollars from roadbuilding projects anyway. At this time, autos still were mostly for the wealthy while the interurban prided itself on hauling the masses. While some cheap cars were available, they were that in all ways — light, flimsy, underpowered, and unreliable. Anything of decent quality and reliability, such as the Buick 10, cost at least $1,000 — a hefty sum in 1908, beyond the reach of working people and farmers. (And payment was expected in full — no monthly installments.) But that year Henry Ford produced his first Model T, a high-quality, practical product priced from $825. That was still a bit high, but as Ford perfected his mass production techniques the price quickly dropped. By 1916 it was $345.

A small but portentous event took place in 1908 when the Lake Shore Electric created its first commercial electric power subsidiary, The People's Light and Power Company, serving the area around Berlin Heights. Later came the Bellevue Illuminating & Power Company. The interurban was finding a small but slowly growing market for its surplus generated power in the small towns and rural territory along its lines, areas beyond the reach and the interest of the urban utilities. The market continued growing, of course, and eventually the tail wagged the dog.

New rail lines were not forgotten, but not acted upon either. During 1908 the LSE was rumored to be considering a three-mile extension of the Gibsonburg branch southeast to the tiny town of Helena, Ohio — presumably another step toward the Ohio oil fields, since there was precious little in Helena itself. The idea was never heard from again.

Concrete relief did finally come for the long-suffering Gibsonburg riders and their "rain-soaked platform" at Gibsonburg Junction. After two years of reports that "work is about to begin" the company finally spent some money to build a waiting station at the junction. Opened in early November 1909, it was a tiny, austere wooden box, but at least was a permanent structure.

Since its earliest days the LSE had based its operating headquarters at Norwalk, the most central spot on its main line. But with the opening of the Sandusky–Fremont line, Sandusky became the more logical location. It was a larger traffic-generating point, the location of the company's primary repair shops, and its local streetcar system seemed to be an endless management headache. So on April 15, 1909, the offices were moved from space in Norwalk's Case Block to the three-story Stone Block, at 202 Columbus Avenue in Sandusky. Fred Coen, however, had to split his time between the Sandusky operating headquarters and the Everett-Moore offices in the Electric Building in Cleveland; he eventually settled in a home in the Cleveland suburb of Lakewood and commuted by LSE to Sandusky.

Accidents remained a bane, but fortunately were fewer. Three collisions occurred between July 3, 1908, and July 16, 1909, which resulted in some passenger and crew injuries but no fatalities. Things were less lucky on July 30, 1909, at the now-notorious Undergrade crossing west of Lorain. Perhaps groggy at the 1 a.m. hour, motorman Daniel Howe ran his westbound car through the snaking "S" curve at full speed and derailed against the unforgiving Nickel Plate bridge abutment, killing himself instantly and injuring the conductor and the car's six passengers.

The year 1909 also included two very upscale disasters. On March 9 Henry Everett's palatial *Josephine* was lost in a fire at Silver Lake Junction, near Akron, where it was normally stored between trips. He quickly replaced it with the new Jewett-built *Northern*, every bit as luxurious. The *Northern*, however, was carried on the Northern Ohio Traction & Light roster rather than as Everett's personal property. And in a sign of the times a Sandusky-bound interurban hit a chauffeur-driven Mercedes at a grade crossing near Vermilion on July 30. Interestingly, the stricken automobile was valued at $11,000 — only $4,000 less than the imperial *Josephine*.

The vast extent of the interurban system was again dramatized in May 1910 when the Utica, New York, Chamber of Commerce chartered Oneida Railway car 502 for a 2040-mile trip entirely on electric railways. The group visited Louisville, Columbus, Dayton, Indianapolis, Fort Wayne, and Detroit, and on May 21 rolled east on the Lake Shore Electric with a stop at Fremont. The locally legendary John J. Stanley, president of the Cleveland Railway, boarded the car at Lorain for the ride into Cleveland.

This rudimentary station was built at Gibsonburg Junction in 1909 after years of complaints over lesser or nonexistent facilities. Soon after its completion Gibsonburg branch car 44 (I) (the former Sandusky & Interurban *Beta*) awaits the arrival of an eastbound main line limited. (John A. Rehor collection)

New Norwalk:- L.S.E. Interurban Cars, 1909.

(*Above*) An early auto, casually parked the wrong way, intrudes on this 1909 scene of LSE Niles cars meeting at the Norwalk station. (Note the station sign at far left.) The camera looks south. (C. S. Bateham photo, George Krambles collection)

(*Below*) In this undated but early Sandusky scene, Niles interurban 154 loads at the LSE's storefront station on the east side of Columbus Avenue while (to the left) second no. 54 heads east on Market Street. No. 54 was an oddity on the LSE's roster, acquired as an expediency from Kuhlman in 1902. The impressive Victorian building still stood in the late 1990s, although the LSE moved its station location in 1929. (Ralph H. Sayles collection)

The Fremont–Fostoria Link

When the Lake Shore committed itself to the Sandusky–Fremont line in 1906, it also announced indefinite plans to continue on southwest from Fremont to Fostoria. Other promoters had proposed the idea several years before, but this gap in the western Ohio interurban system had never been closed. It was a strategic gap. At Fostoria an interurban route reached farther southwest to Findlay and Lima, Ohio, with connections to Dayton and Cincinnati as well as Fort Wayne, Indiana. While the LSE could reach these lines through connections at Toledo, a route from Cleveland through Fremont and Fostoria would be considerably more direct.

The company most anxious to bridge the Fremont–Fostoria gap was the Western Ohio Railway, which actually did not even reach Fostoria. Originally a Pomeroy-Mandelbaum promotion, the Western Ohio had a line running southwest from Findlay through Lima to Piqua, Ohio; at Piqua the independent but allied Dayton & Troy carried the route on to Dayton. At its north end in Findlay the WO connected with the Toledo, Bowling Green & Southern's line from Findlay to Toledo, and beginning in 1906 the three companies — TBG&S, Western Ohio, and Dayton & Troy — were running a joint Toledo–Dayton passenger service advertised as the "Lima Route." Also at Findlay the Western Ohio met the Toledo, Fostoria & Findlay, reaching northeast to Fostoria. (The TF&F also got to Toledo in 1908.) By using the TF&F, the Western Ohio could get as far east as Fostoria, 22 miles from Fremont and the LSE.

Heading the Western Ohio was F. D. Carpenter, who happened to be Fred Pomeroy's brother-in-law. But in this case nepotism apparently worked out well; like Coen, Carpenter was an early leader in the CERA and was later a pioneer in developing interline freight movements. Under various titles he ran the Western Ohio for its entire life, from 1900 to the end in 1932. Carpenter approached Fred Coen about jointly building a Fostoria–Fremont line to connect their two companies and the two reached an agreement in 1909.

"Lima Route" opening advertisement.

Their ultimate goal was to create a through Cleveland–Lima limited service patterned on the LSE's highly successful Cleveland–Toledo operation.

The result was the Fostoria & Fremont Railway, which Carpenter and some associates incorporated on September 24, 1909. A latecomer in interurban history, the Fostoria & Fremont was born into a strange corporate twilight world. It existed as its own corporation, with its own property, equipment, and services — but had two masters and no operating employees of its own. In effect it was owned and operated as a joint facility, although its actual ownership is now a puzzlement. While the company was conceived and built as a joint Western Ohio–Lake Shore Electric project, the Western Ohio's management clearly controlled it and there is no evidence that the LSE had anything more than a minority investment — if that. Carpenter served as its president and other Western Ohio officials acted as the top corporate officers. The F&F's original board of directors, however, consisted of Carpenter, Fred Coen, and three Fostoria businessmen. J. D. McDonel, a Fostoria real estate operator and former banker, was a co-incorporator and the company's original secretary-treasurer; technically he also served as its general manager. Earlier,

McDonel had been involved in the Toledo, Fostoria & Findlay but disposed of that interest in 1903. Financing consisted of $250,000 in bonds, $200,000 in first preferred stock distributed among 92 stockholders, and $200,000 in common stock owned by 33 stockholders. (As with all too many interurban projects, the unfortunate common stockholders never received a dividend.)

Complicating matters further was the geography of the situation. The F&F was not connected to its primary parent, the Western Ohio. The 16-mile gap between the two was bridged by the Toledo, Fostoria & Findlay, and its cooperation was essential to the project's success. The TF&F thus became another participant, although it limited itself to granting trackage rights for the through services and was not financially involved.

On June 11, 1910, the LSE, Fostoria & Fremont, and Toledo, Fostoria & Findlay drew up a joint agreement for the F&F's operation. (Note that the parent Western Ohio was not a direct party.) It worked a bit like an occupied territory. The Lake Shore Electric had direct control of the F&F's dispatching and general day-to-day operation through its superintendent and dispatchers at Fremont. The new line also received its electric power from the LSE's Fremont powerhouse and later the Ballville plant, which was half-owned by the LSE beginning in 1918. LSE train crews operated F&F local passenger cars and all commercial freight runs; Western Ohio crews took the Cleveland–Lima limiteds as far as Fremont, and the Toledo, Fostoria & Findlay supplied both the equipment and crews for maintenance and other work needs. The F&F's own local cars were stored and serviced at the LSE's Fremont carhouse, but the Western Ohio's Wapakoneta shop handled heavy repairs.

Property acquisition and construction was the simplest part. The New York Central's Lake Erie & Western subsidiary connected Fremont and Fostoria in a straight line and had right-of-way space for the F&F's track — much as it did for the LSE's Sandusky–Fremont extension. As a struggling orphan in the Central family, it needed the money and did not seem to mind the competition. To enter Fremont and reach the LSE at Front and State Streets, the F&F bought the existing route of the tiny, half-alive Fremont Street Railway. This 2.4-mile-long line wandered from Front and State Streets to Ballville and Oakland Cemetery. Although it once had ambitions to reach Tiffin, it was no more than a submarginal small-city streetcar company with a total roster in 1910 of two open cars and a work car — and a record of erratic operations. The purchase was consummated October 25, 1909, but the line was left to operate on its own until the F&F was completed.

Surveying and property purchasing for the F&F started in July 1910 with grading work following in late August. A wye track was installed at the F&F–LSE junction at Front and State Streets in Fremont to turn F&F cars and allow direct operation of the Cleveland–Lima limiteds.

For their new through Cleveland–Lima limited services the LSE and Western Ohio dispatched a joint order to the Jewett Car Company for four interurban combines — two for each company. (Two additional similar cars went to the Western Ohio's Dayton–Toledo partner, the Dayton & Troy.) As with all LSE interurban equipment, the four new Jewetts (LSE Nos. 165–166 and WO 198–199) were equipped with multiple-unit control and could be run in trains either with one another or with the LSE's Niles cars. One Cleveland newspaper seemed mostly impressed by their supplementary facilities, reporting on February 11, 1911, that they "will have a toilet room with flush closet, lavatory mirror, and it is the intention to provide towels and a 'comb and brush' for the convenience of travelers."

To handle its own local services, the F&F itself bought three ancient wood Barney & Smith combines from the Union Traction Company of Indiana. These looked quite similar to the LSE's own "Barneys" and carried their Union Traction numbers (241, 243, and 245) with them. Already they had checkered histories; the best evidence indicates that the Union Traction picked them up from an undelivered order of 15 cars built for the Columbia & Maryland Railway, an abortive Baltimore–Washington interurban project which collapsed in 1898. Occasionally Western Ohio Kuhlman combines or LSE Brill combines also filled in on F&F local runs.

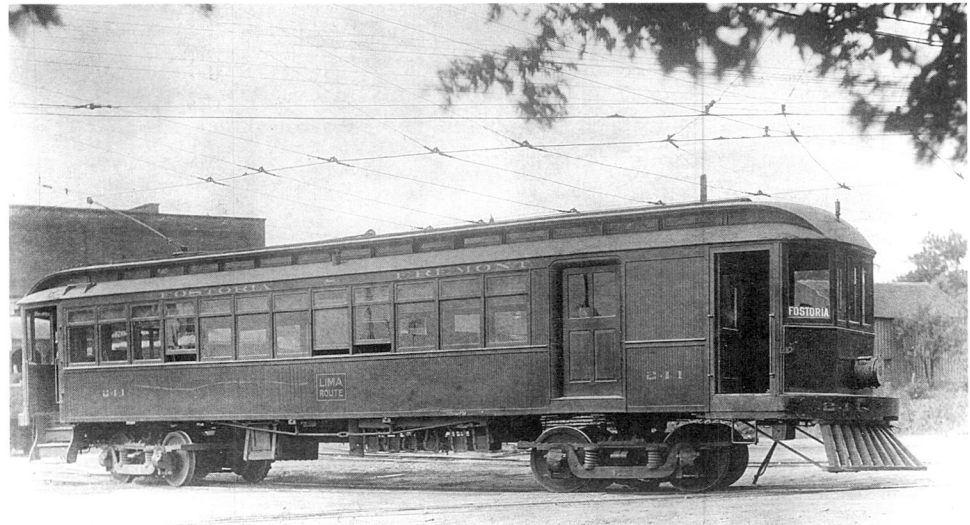

To serve its own sparsely populated local territory, the Fostoria & Fremont picked up three secondhand Barney & Smith combines from the Union Traction of Indiana. One, the 241, rests at the LSE's Fremont car-house, where it was normally stored and serviced. (John A. Rehor collection)

Over Rocky River to Detroit and Lima: 1911

If 1906 was the most active year in the Lake Shore's physical growth, 1911 marked its maturing — and, in truth, its last dramatic contributions to interurban history. Heavier traffic and better financial years were still ahead, but at this point both the geographic limits and the service and operational patterns were set.

The key to this last flowering was the viaduct over the Rocky River gorge just west of Cleveland. From the Lorain & Cleveland days, all traffic was funneled over the river on a single track laid on one side of an iron truss highway bridge built in 1890. Never designed for interurbans in the first place, it was a source of concern to its owners, the Board of Cuyahoga County Commissioners, who held the LSE to weight limitations preventing full train operations.

In addition to its increasing rail traffic, the bridge formed a primary link in the chain of roads along the Lake Erie shore. By 1908 population growth west of the river, plus heavy interurban traffic, had put severe strains on the structure and the commissioners condemned it, deeming it "dangerous to public travel." Work began late that year on a replacement, a substantial and aesthetic modern concrete arch span destined to become one of the Cleveland area's engineering landmarks. The bridge's graceful single 280-foot arch was the largest in the country at the time. It was designed to carry two interurban tracks and, at last, provide capacity for multiple cars — and also, to the LSE's later grief, a heavy flow of highway traffic.

The Rocky River bridge was formally dedicated in a grand ceremony on October 12, 1910. Prophetically a parade of 1,500 decorated automobiles marked the occasion along with the usual bands. Not on hand, however, was the Lake Shore Electric, which continued to use the old bridge until June 10, 1911 — partly because of haggling over the price for using the new one. The first multiple-unit test train crossed on June 26.

Ten years in coming, the through limited service to Detroit finally arrived June 22 — surprisingly without special ceremony. The 6½-hour, 177-mile run used the Detroit, Monroe & Toledo Short Line between Toledo and Detroit, by then a part of the Detroit United Railway. At the time the LSE was running limiteds every two hours between Cleveland and Toledo, and this two-hourly service was simply extended to Detroit. Initially LSE Niles cars operated all of the runs because of equipment incompatibilities with the DUR-DM&TSL cars of the time. The Michigan equipment used storage air tanks, which the

The new concrete highway viaduct over the Rocky River gorge west of Cleveland relieved the LSE of a troublesome bottleneck and at last allowed regular train operation. *(Top)* In this 1910 view looking east toward Lakewood, the new bridge is taking form as an LSE Barney & Smith car negotiates the single track over the 1890 iron span. *(Bottom)* The completed viaduct in 1911. Its predecessor is seen directly behind in this view looking south. (Both, W. A. McCaleb collection)

LSE's did not, and lacked compatible multiple-unit controls. But beginning in 1912 the DUR bought a group of similar Niles cars, and by 1916 it had 26 of them which could be used on the Cleveland runs. Eight wood-bodied Jewetts were added in 1917, increasing the DUR's side of the pool to 34 cars.

The Fostoria & Fremont began scheduled operations inauspiciously on June 15, 1911. The line still needed ballasting and alignment work, and a full complement of cars was not yet available. Initially local cars were operated on a three-hour headway, using a single car. One of the Lake Shore Electric's 1903 Brill interurban combines made the first trip because the F&F's only available car had suffered a burned-out armature and was being repaired at LSE's Fremont shop. A minor comedy of errors occured on the first eastbound trip when F&F president Carpenter got off the car at Burgoon to give instructions to a construction foreman and the car left without him. When it was about half a mile from the station, J. D. McDonel, also a passenger, missed Carpenter and the car backed its way to Burgoon to pick him up. It was reported that a Dayton & Troy car also filled in during the first week or two while the ailing F&F car was being patched together.

On June 25 F&F local runs were extended to Sandusky over the LSE's SF&S line to carry summer excursionists to Cedar Point. (This Sandusky service may have lasted as long as 1922.) Two-hourly local service started August 1, with a total of ten round-trips a day. This

A pairing of an LSE Niles car and Detroit United car await a meet at Reed siding on the Detroit, Monroe & Toledo Short Line. (Kirk Hise collection)

A two-car Detroit–Cleveland limited headed by Detroit United 7075 speeds through Bay Village about 1915. (Karel Liebenauer collection)

The first regular trip on the new Fostoria & Fremont on June 15, 1911, was handled by LSE Brill combine 63, shown here at State and Front Streets in Fremont. At far left, by the 63's headlight, is the F&F's founder and president, F. D. Carpenter. J. D. McDonel, the company's co-incorporator and secretary-treasurer, is at the far right. (John A. Rehor collection)

basic schedule remained in effect until October 1, 1930 — almost all of the F&F's life. Since the run took 50 minutes each way, one car still could handle an entire day's service.

The four new Jewett combines for what was branded as the "Lima Route" Cleveland–Lima limiteds left the builder's plant at Newark, Ohio, on June 25 and ran under their own power as two two-car trains to the LSE's Sandusky shop, where they were set up for service. Their leisurely 268-mile, two-day trek was made over the rails of the Ohio Electric to Columbus and Springfield, then the Springfield, Troy & Piqua to Troy, the Dayton & Troy to Piqua, the Western Ohio through Lima to Findlay, the Toledo, Fostoria & Findlay to Fostoria, the new F&F to Fremont, and LSE to Sandusky.

Although the Fostoria & Fremont was still in no condition to handle fast limiteds, the services were started as soon as the new cars were ready. The first trial run of the 157-mile Cleveland–Lima Limited left Lima at 8:15 a.m. July 31, loaded with Carpenter and other Western Ohio officials, their guests, and newspaper reporters. At Fremont a second car was coupled behind the new Jewett to accommodate Lake Shore officials, local boosters, and more newsmen. After leaving Fremont 40 minutes late and stopping briefly in Sandusky,

LSE combine 165, one of the four pooled LSE–Western Ohio cars in Cleveland–Lima limited service, poses at an unknown location soon after the run began in 1911. (John A. Rehor collection)

the train proceeded to Cleveland where a trolley pole snagged a wire. After another delay to resolve the problem, it arrived at the Public Square at 2:50 p.m., one hour and 20 minutes late. Scheduled service started three days later with two trips a day each way, a basic pattern which lasted to 1922. Interline cars were not exempt from the LSE's new car curse, however, and the Western Ohio's Jewett No. 198 had a fire at Ceylon Junction on October 3, its first day in revenue service.

An interesting announcement was carried in the Cleveland papers on March 30, 1911, which symbolized the importance of the interurbans to the city — but was also the first glimmer of something else. "During the coming year," it said, work would begin on "an immense interurban station, hotel, and office building to cost $4.5 million and occupy an entire block between Public Square and West 3rd Street." The hotel would be 12 stories high, with an adjacent twin structure to be used as an office building and "a great arcade to carry six car tracks connecting with the city lines. . . ."

Almost needless to say, nothing materialized "during the coming year." But it was no blue-sky dream. While their names were not mentioned, the project's planners were two young brothers named O. P. and M. J. Van Sweringen, a pair of real estate promoters who had bought the Public Square property in 1909. While the Square was still the city's street railway center, it had slipped into seediness as stores, theaters, and business offices gravitated eastward on Euclid Avenue. The astute brothers picked up the property cheap and hoped to create a combined transportation and commercial center which would pull business back to the city's traditional heart — their location. It was the beginning of an extended struggle during which the project would change form several times and finally emerge as the Terminal Tower–Cleveland Union Terminal complex — but which to its end would include capacious quarters for a union interurban terminal.

Also in 1911 the Lake Shore Electric took advantage of another opportunity to court its own doom. The *Sandusky Register* of March 2nd carried the news that an enterprising

Willys-Overland automobile company salesman had chartered an interurban "festooned with banners and pennants" to take 60 prospective buyers to Toledo for a tour of the Overland plant. One wonders how many of the buyers ever rode an LSE car again.

Physical improvements were few in 1911 but included a new station at Ceylon Junction, replacing a frame structure lost to fire. A key transfer point for the Sandusky and Norwalk routes, the junction received what was an elaborate building by Lake Shore standards, a masonry structure built of moulded concrete block with a decorative octagonal tower. The tower was later dismantled but the station proved to be a hardy survivor, still standing in 1998.

Solid Prosperity but a Hectic Life: 1912 – 1913

Gross revenues from the Lake Shore's interurban business grew steadily from 1908 to 1913, averaging about 5.8 percent each year. Net profits gyrated a bit, but were also reliably in the black; the Lake Shore Electric itself was producing a profit of roughly $150,000 in the 1910–13 period, but the subsidiaries — notably the Lorain Street Railroad — dragged that figure down some. Thanks to this prosperity the LSE began paying dividends to its preferred stockholders but, willingly or not, the common stockholders continued to sacrifice themselves to reinvestment in plant and equipment.

The physical improvements also continued. With regular high-speed multiple-unit train operation, the light original bridges were a particular concern. Between 1912 and 1913 four bridges were replaced on the poorly built section between Lorain and Ceylon Junction — at Beaver Creek (Oak Point), Linwood, the Vermilion River, and Chappelle Creek. The original TF&N overpass over the Wheeling & Lake Erie and Lake Shore & Michigan Southern railroad lines east of Bellevue also was rebuilt. Farther west on the former TF&N, new steel bridges replaced wooden structures at Big Muddy Creek (Hessville), Sugar Creek (west of Gibsonburg Junction), and Toussaint Creek, between Woodville and Genoa. And while the stepchild Avon Beach & Southern line was hardly concerned with heavy trains,

In 1913 the LSE replaced its old Vermilion River crossing with this steel truss bridge. At the time it still intended to extend double-track to Ceylon Junction and the bridge was designed to carry two tracks. Only one was ever laid. (LSE photo, John A. Rehor collection)

Immediately north of Milan, LSE cars crossed the Huron River on the public highway bridge. Another 60-series Brill is working the branch about 1910. (E. Niebergal photo, Frohman Collection, Hayes Presidential Center)

work also began to convert its long trestle approach to the Black River bridge to earth fill. This project proceeded slowly into 1915 using material excavated from a new underpass under the Baltimore & Ohio Railroad on 28th Street in Lorain.

In what turned out to be a longer-term project, the LSE began buying property at Huron in 1912 in preparation for a new bypass line that would finally resolve its bridge and alignment problems. The route passed in a straight line through the south edge of town and would use a new highway bridge over the river which was to replace the rickety Berlin Street structure. But progress in Huron always seemed leisurely, and consummation was six years away.

In the category of negative improvements was a temporary spur authorized in December 1912 to bring in construction materials for a new auto road into Cedar Point. By water, "The Point" is only two miles directly north of Sandusky across Sandusky Bay — but by land it was isolated at the end of a narrow, seven-mile-long strip of land jutting out into the lake. Despite the resort's huge popularity, no road or rail line had ever been built directly to it along this thin spit of land; both people and supplies had to be ferried across the bay on steamers. (At Cedar Point itself, a little narrow-gauge railroad carried freight from the steamboat dock to the Breakers Hotel and other businesses; it survived until World War II.) Back in 1909 some Cleveland promoters — with the blessings of Cedar Point's owners — incorporated an independent electric line to run from the LSE at Rye Beach directly to the resort, but the idea remained yet another "might have been." In any event, by 1912 the age of the auto was arriving, and instead of tracks a roadway was built out the long strip of land from the point where it joined the "mainland" about midway between Sandusky and Huron — aided in part by the interurban. The new road was ready for the 1914 summer season.

The year 1912 also saw the beginning of what was to be an extended construction project for a new hydroelectric power plant and dam just outside Fremont at Ballville. Built by the Sandusky River Power Company, the new high-capacity commercial plant was also intended to replace the LSE's own Fremont power house. Ballville went into partial operation October 30, 1913, and began supplying supplementary power for the LSE, but could not yet take on the interurban's full load. As it turned out, the onetime TF&N Fremont plant would continue providing most power on the western part of the LSE system until late 1916.

Lesser physical improvements included 1913 track replacements on Main Street in Genoa and East First Street in Sandusky. In Clyde the roadside line was relocated to the center of the highway as part of a repaving project to give Clyde a big city look.

With the Niles cars and new "Lima Route" Jewetts, there was little immediate need for more interurban cars. But in Sandusky the last decrepit survivors from the early predecessor streetcar companies were at the end of their lives. Looking for low-cost but higher-capacity replacements, the LSE picked up five double-truck open city cars from Atlantic City for summer use in the spring of 1912; the next year it bought five double-truck closed cars from the same source to retire the remainder of the nineteenth-century single-truckers.

One other new piece of equipment became necessary. Particularly nasty winter weather in early 1912 culminated in floods during March and April. One constant sore spot was in Fremont in the area where the State Street bridge crossed the Sandusky River. Here and at occasional other points, such as the Tiffin Avenue railroad underpass in Sandusky, high water prevented operation of the electric cars, severing service. The Lake Shore's shop came up with a creative solution: a small single-truck electric locomotive with motor mounted on the floor above the water level and a mechanical drive to the wheels. Numbered 444, this little creature was coupled to passenger trailer No. 79, a high-wheeled 1890s-era Stephenson-built car from the Lorain Street Railroad, and used to shuttle passengers from one side of the flooding to the other.

The train came just in time. In Ohio, 1913 is still remembered for its natural calamities. Winter started off badly on January 3 with a blizzard, followed by an ice storm January 7. On January 21 the weather caused the side of the Millbury tunnel under the Lake Shore & Michigan Southern (New York Central) main line to collapse. Local passengers had to walk around the problem on the adjacent highway while limited train riders were treated to a detour trip over the Toledo, Port Clinton & Lakeside line.

Then came the water. In late March the infamous 1913 Ohio floods arrived and interurban service was almost at a standstill. Tracks were washed out in Fremont and Sandusky, and even Bellevue was flooded although there was no nearby river. The LSE's Fremont power house was disabled, and Beach Park and the Toledo, Port Clinton & Lakeside plant filled in to keep both the Lake Shore and the Fostoria & Fremont going for at least two weeks. The "high water train" did its best, but full service was not completely restored over the system until April 25.

After violent electrical storms during the summer, with periodic service interruptions, the year concluded with the worst of all — the "Blizzard of '13" on November 9, 10, and

The devastating March 1913 Ohio floods brought out the LSE's "high water train," consisting of specially designed motor 444 and former Lorain Street Railroad trailer 79. The pair is gingerly wading along State Street in Fremont. (Frohman Collection, Hayes Presidential Center)

11. Snowdrifts up to ten feet high covered the tracks in many places; even the Gibsonburg shuttle stalled in a drift with passengers spending Sunday night and part of Monday on the car. Another LSE car was caught in drifts three miles west of Vermilion and its passengers were snowbound for 16 hours. Service into Cleveland was cut off by fallen wires in Lakewood and Rocky River, and all Lorain streetcars stopped running. The Lake Shore Electric could count itself lucky, though. Out on the Great Lakes 11 large lake freighters were lost through sinking or stranding and six or seven others damaged beyond repair; about 300 seamen died.

Collisions continued to be a chronic problem on the unsignaled, mostly single-track system. On June 25, 1912, a local interurban car met a limited head-on at the curve between DeWitt Avenue and Columbus Avenue near the Soldiers Home outside Sandusky. The local's motorman, Edgar Brennan, died after being extracted from the wreckage, and 13 passengers were hurt — some with crushed limbs and fractures. Four other collisions followed, including one on September 17, 1913, at Brown's Curve west of Norwalk, where the track crossed from one side of the road to the other, which injured sixteen passengers.

In another sign of the times, grade crossing accidents began to mount. One especially bad one occurred September 8, 1912, when a two-car Cleveland–Detroit limited hit a Leisy Brewing Company truck at Clague Road in Dover Bay, west of Rocky River. Both cars derailed and the train jackknifed. Thankfully there were no fatalities, but 35 people were injured including three in the demolished truck.

A happier kind of accident occurred in September 1912 when Mrs. Joseph Alten of Avon suddenly became indisposed while riding home from a shopping trip to Cleveland. When the car stopped at Beach Park she was taken into the waiting room, where Joseph Alten, Jr., was born. E. J. Burke, an extra LSE dispatcher, acted as midwife and afterward put mother and child on a special car for an express trip to Lorain. There they were met by an "invalid carriage" and taken to St. Joseph's Hospital.

During 1913 a corporate event occurred nearby which, while of small immediate consequence to the Lake Shore Electric, would eventually determine its future. After several years of financial and political turmoil, the Toledo Railways & Light Company formally changed hands on April 10. Its new owner was Henry L. Doherty & Company of New York. A native Ohioan, Doherty was a brilliant self-educated public utilities engineer and financier who was slowly assembling an electric utility, gas, and oil empire under what became the Cities Service Company. Unlike many financial speculators, Doherty brought efficiency and stability to his companies and built them up into powerful utilities. At its peak Cities Service would control 190 public utility and petroleum-producing companies, including several in northern Ohio. As part of these utilities it also inherited the Toledo & Indiana interurban and the former Toledo, Port Clinton & Lakeside as well as the Toledo streetcar system.

Despite the natural disasters and man-made mishaps, 1913 was a record-breaking year for the Lake Shore Electric, with passenger traffic and gross revenues at an all-time high. By the year's end, some limiteds were regularly running as three-car trains, splitting to cover the two alternate routes between Ceylon Junction and Fremont. Christmas Eve, traditionally the LSE's heaviest traffic day, saw three cars on all limiteds and one four-car limited out of Cleveland, which split into two-car trains at Ceylon Junction. Although early winter, it was late springtime for the Lake Shore.

Interlude B: The LSE in Summertime

During the summers, hordes heading for Cedar Point and the numerous smaller beachfront parks, resorts, and summer camps crowded on the LSE's regular cars and excursion specials. These photos sample some of the bygone pleasures.

(*Above*) Loaded down with picnic baskets and bags, a crowd from Cleveland has just disembarked at the LSE's own 30-acre Beach Park at Avon Lake. Looming behind their two special cars is the impressive onetime Lorain & Cleveland's Beach Park station and carhouse. (John A. Rehor collection)

(*Below*) Beach Park's primary landmark was its two-story pavillion which looked out onto Lake Erie. The park was an early casualty; in 1923 the LSE sold the property to the Cleveland Electric Illuminating Company for its Avon Lake power plant. (W. A. McCaleb collection)

RYE BEACH PARK ENTRANCE
RYE BEACH PARK.

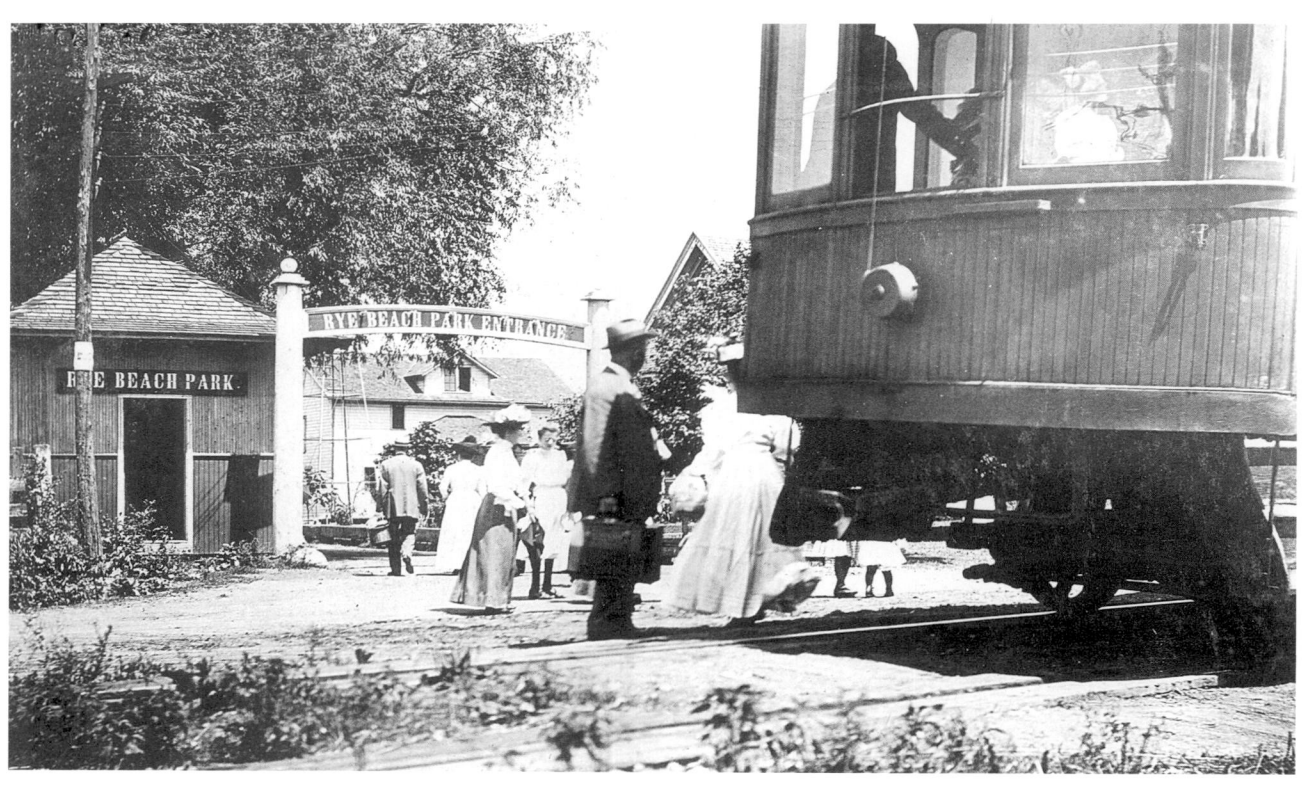

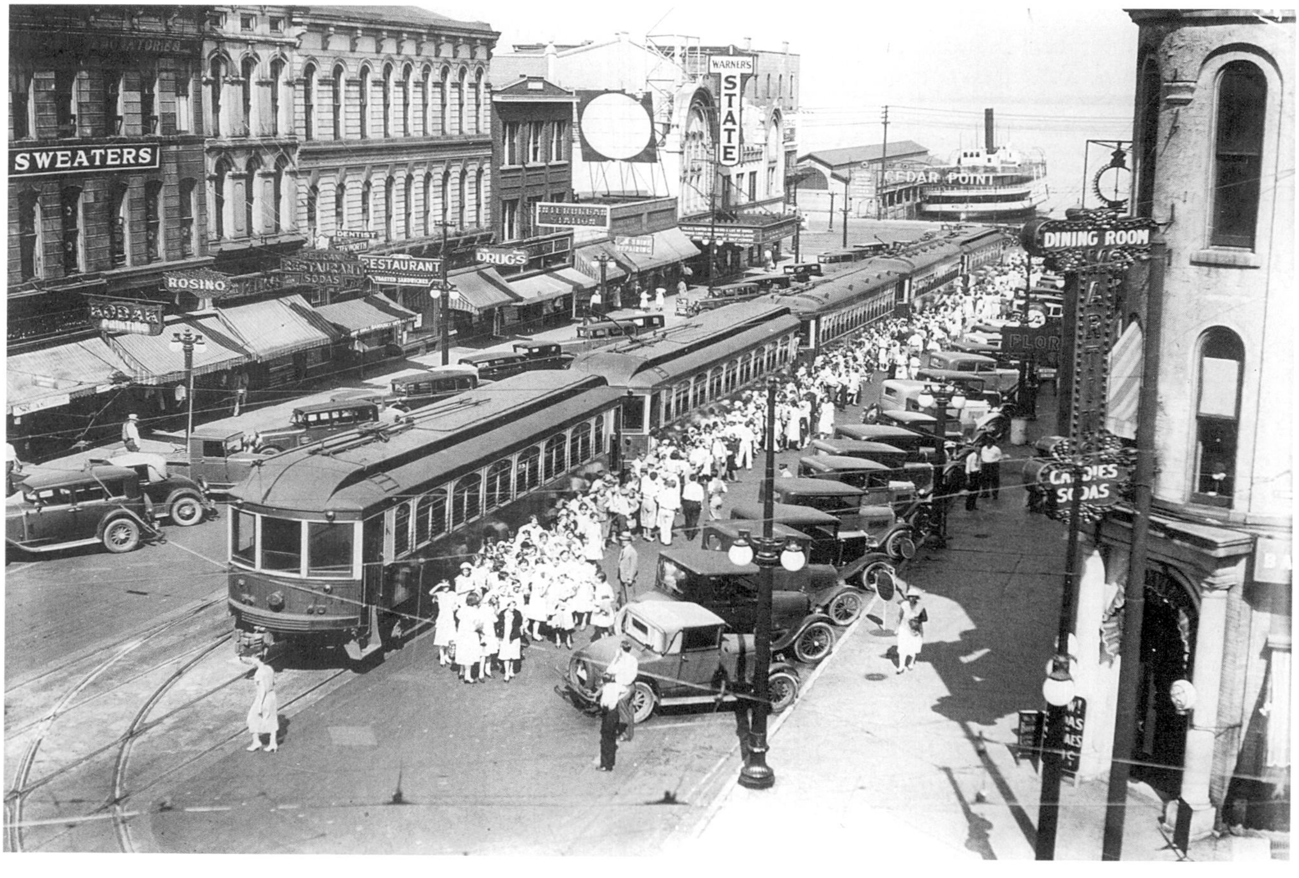
SWEATERS
WARNERS
STATE
CEDAR POINT
DINING ROOM
RESTAURANT
DRUGS
ROSINO
DENTIST
CANDIES
SODAS

Cedar Point's longtime lifeline to the mainland was its steam ferry
G. A. *Boeckling,* named by the resort's operator in honor of himself. The hardy vessel
shuttled across Sandusky Bay from 1909 to 1952. (C. E. Helms photo, 1947)

(*Facing page, top*) Rye Beach Park, west of Huron, was another popular destination.
(E. Niebergal photo, Frohman Collection, Hayes Presidential Center)

(*Facing page, bottom*) Five special cars (including two two-car trains) carrying a Huron
County 4-H contingent unloads at the foot of Columbus Avenue in Sandusky on September
12, 1930. The 4-H-ers will head to the wharf in the rear where Cedar Point's own steamer,
the G. A. *Boeckling* waits to carry them across the bay. (Bishop photo, Frohman Collection,
Hayes Presidential Center)

A tranquil and unpolluted Lake Erie brings out a large and heavily dressed crowd along Cedar Point's Boardwalk in the early 1900s. (Frohman Collection, Hayes Presidential Center)

Also feeding the crowds to Cedar Point were lake steamers and excursion trains from Sandusky's five railroad lines. Here at the Columbus Avenue and Water Street piers are the steamers A. *Wehrle, Jr.* (at left) and *Arrow* along with a train from the New York Central's "Big Four" (Cleveland, Cincinnati, Chicago & St. Louis) about 1910. (W. A. McCaleb collection)

In 1918 the LSE got sort of a semi–rapid transit entrance to Cleveland over the lower deck of the new Detroit–Superior High Level Bridge. That year it also received its last newly purchased interurban cars, typified by the 177 heading west into the viaduct's "subway." Numerous Cleveland Railway streetcar lines and the Cleveland Southwestern interurban also used this busy four-track facility. (W. A. McCaleb)

CHAPTER 4

THE GREAT WAR

1914 – 1918

The summertime of the Lake Shore Electric's life was like most summertimes — reasonably fruitful but full of annoying insects and turbulent thunderstorms. In the interurban's case, the insects took the form of more automobiles and, in the cities of Sandusky and Lorain, "jitneys" — privately-owned, unregulated motor vehicles which operated over the streetcar routes stealing passengers. As for the storms of World War I, the LSE — like most interurbans — did not see much of the huge traffic surge which eventually paralyzed the steam railroads, but it did fully experience the material and fuel shortages, the wage and price inflation, the influenza epidemic, and the first efforts at unionization. And while not yet unhealthy, the financial results began to show some instability.

On the plus side, improvements continued, with a new cutoff around Huron, extensive rebuilding in Lorain, a new fleet of steel interurbans, and (through no effort of its own) improved access to Cleveland's Public Square. The war period also saw the beginning of a new direction for LSE traffic — freight service.

An Erratic Three Years: 1914 – 1916

With ridership still climbing, the Lake Shore made more improvements to increase its handling capacity. Work on the new Huron cutoff crept along slowly between 1913 and 1918, delayed partly by the new highway bridge over the Huron River, which the cutoff would use, and by occasional property acquisition problems. In 1914, for example, a shotgun-wielding farmer and his three armed sons emphatically disputed the interurban's right to cross his land. Elsewhere it extended sidings at Maplewood, west of Fremont, and at Sandusky Junction on the east side of Fremont to store cars. Late in 1914 work began which within two years would result in a double-track line on State Street through the entire city of Fremont.

Two new steam railroad interchanges also were built in 1914 — one with the Nickel Plate Road west of Root Road on the east side of Lorain and one at Huron with the Wheeling & Lake Erie. The Root Road connection was actively used to receive coal for the Beach Park power plant, but there is no record of movements through the W&LE interchange.

A surprise visitor to the Lake Shore Electric in January 1914 was an organizer for the Brotherhood of Railroad Trainmen, who tried to unionize the Beach Park trainmen. A month later the Brotherhood of Locomotive Engineers attempted to organize the 62 trainmen at Fremont. Fred Coen actively discouraged the efforts, and there were newspaper

Car 156 on a special trip poses at Stop 274 west of Fremont about 1914. Toledo Division superintendent Milt Trueman is by the rear platform. (W. A. McCaleb collection)

stories of LSE employees being suspended for union activities. Whatever the truth of that, neither drive was successful but the LSE voluntarily raised trainmen's wages by 10 percent on March 1. There were no further major organizing efforts until the 1930s, when trainmen joined what was known as "The Amalgamated" — The Amalgamated Association of Street, Electric Railway and Motor Coach Employees, which represented many transit workers. By then the environment and attitudes were much changed.

On July 28, 1914, Austria-Hungary declared war on Serbia. Within a week their intricate webs of alliances had led every major European country into war. There was concern in the United States, but, after all, the war was another one of those regular European conflicts which was an ocean away. This country would stay out of it. And most leaders of the warring countries predicted that, one way or another, it would be over in a month or two — certainly before winter. Said Kaiser Wilhelm II to his departing troops: "You will be home before the leaves have fallen from the trees." A bit more presciently, German Chief of Staff Helmut von Moltke wrote on the eve of the first battle of "the struggle that will decide the course of history for the next hundred years."

More immediately on the Lake Shore Electric's mind was coping with the ever-growing traffic, which would reach yet another record high in 1914. The summer ended in a grand flourish. What was locally reported as the first four-car train out of Fremont ran September 7, and 14 extra cars were pressed into service for the Fremont fair the following week. Thanksgiving travel was the heaviest ever, with all limiteds running in two- and three-car trains.

Unfortunately there also was another rash of accidents, starting the year off on January 11, 1914, when LSE Niles coach 158 collided head-on with brand-new Detroit United Railway 7091 at Hooper Siding on the DUR. Niles coach 153 was then lost in a January 22 fire at Alexis, Ohio, also on the Detroit United. The now-notorious Undergrade crossing west of Lorain claimed another victim on June 26 when motorman Elias W. Hopp lost control of eastbound Barney & Smith car 7. The fast-moving car derailed on the "S" curve and turned over, killing Hopp and fatally injuring a motorcyclist passing on the adjacent road.

The following year was considerably worse. On April 28, 1915, an eastbound limited overran a meet at Flora Siding, six miles east of Fremont, and collided head-on with a westbound. Sixty passengers and crew members were injured and the two cars — wooden Niles coaches 142 and 144 — were cremated after broken overhead wires started a fire. Detouring over the Fremont–Sandusky line that day was impossible because a work train with overloaded sand cars went through the Old Woman's Creek bridge east of Huron. All of that was followed on July 11 by a sideswiping accident at Sandusky Junction in Fremont when a westbound limited from Sandusky and its corresponding westbound limited from Norwalk tried to go through the junction at the same time. The Norwalk car lost its airbrakes and ran 500 feet before derailing and striking a pole, but nobody was seriously hurt on either car.

Another head-on came September 5 at Sage's Grove, east of Huron. In a repeat of the Flora Siding incident, an eastbound limited over-ran a meet at the Sage's Grove siding and hit a westbound local. Fifty-nine people went to the hospital but, again, nobody died. October 15 fairly well wrapped up the safety year when westbound Detroit United car 7090 derailed at the New York Central grade crossing in Norwalk and was hit by a passenger train. The passengers were unloaded before the train appeared and were given a show from a safe distance as "the side of the car was smashed to pieces with splinters and glass scattered over the street. . . ."

One outcome of the mayhem was the organization of a "Safety First" association for trainmen in 1916. Every month trainmen representatives were sent from each division to general superintendent L. K. Burge's Sandusky office for discussions of various safety concerns. The representatives, who were rotated every three months, were then expected to transmit the messages back to their fellows and get suggestions for the next meeting.

On top of its "normal" accident problems, the Lake Shore also faced a highly irritating new form of competition on its local streetcar lines, particularly in Lorain. In 1914 the "jitney" concept was born in Los Angeles and almost instantly spread across the country. Enterprising owners of automobiles and other types of motor vehicles began cruising along

One of several victims of the notorious "S" curve at Undergrade, west of Lorain, was Barney & Smith car 7. On June 26, 1914, motorman Elias Hopp lost control and was killed in the wreck. Ironically, car 7 not only survived, but its body still existed in 1998. (Photo from Albert C. Doane)

Birds of a feather, more or less, steel interurban coach 172 and 60-foot steel freight motor 35 came from Jewett in 1917 and 1918 respectively and represented the peak of LSE interurban equipment development. Both photos were shot at Sandusky, the 172 when new in 1917 and the 35 in 1937. (*Above*, Frohman Collection, Hayes Presidential Center; *Below*, Bruce Triplett photo)

streetcar lines picking up passengers. By the next year jitneys had bitten so deeply into the Lorain Street Railroad's business that a 9 percent drop in LSE system ridership during 1915 was blamed almost entirely on the Lorain situation. Jitneys also appeared in Sandusky and even in Fremont.

The spring of 1915 brought gloomy international news too. Far from being over "before the leaves have fallen" in 1914, the European war had bogged down into an endless, vicious stalemate which was consuming hundreds of thousands of lives — and the United States was being slowly dragged closer to it. On May 6, 1915, a German submarine sank the British liner *Lusitania* in the North Atlantic with the loss of 1200 lives, including 189 Americans.

On June 9, 1915, the Cleveland Railway opened a line to the East 9th Street Pier, the city's brand-new terminal for Great Lakes passenger steamships. While never a regular terminal for the Lake Shore Electric, the interurban trains operated to the pier for excursions and at certain other times to meet the boats. The favorite destination for LSE passengers was Niagara Falls via the Cleveland & Buffalo Transit Company's "Great Ship *Seeandbee*," the huge 484-foot, four-stack sidewheel steamer launched in 1913 and advertised as the "fastest and most luxurious on the Great Lakes." Passengers completed their trip to the Falls on the International Railway Company's Buffalo–Niagara Falls High-Speed Line.

The loss of three Niles coaches during 1914 and 1915 led the Lake Shore into the all-steel car era — hesitantly at first, but then with full enthusiasm. The hesitant phase came in 1915 when the LSE ordered three all-steel coaches from Jewett, primarily to replace the losses — and in fact they were given the trucks from their unfortunate predecessors. They arrived in December and were numbered 167–169 — the forerunners of a 12-car fleet to be ordered exactly a year later.

Another significant arrival in 1916 was the first of two large, powerful, and fast steel freight motors. Number 34 and its sister 35, which came the next year, were the first on the LSE specifically designed to pull trains of trailers. At the time, however, the line had no trailers and no immediate plans to acquire any — nor did it apparently intend to enter the general freight market.

The year 1915 ended on a disconcerting financial note. After a steady climb through 1914, system revenues dipped by 3 percent in 1915, mostly the result of jitney competition and more automobiles. Although the gross revenue drop was not disastrous, expenses were climbing and the net profit was only a marginal $41,000 — less than half what it had been two years earlier. Dividends were paid on the senior preferred stock issue but suspended afterward. The financial picture quickly brightened again, but it would be the last dividend ever declared on any type of LSE stock.

Indeed, the climb in ridership and revenues resumed in 1916 and broke old records. In fact, it was an uncharacteristically pleasant year, with no serious wrecks and a few more physical improvements, including the long-planned switchover to commercial electric power in Fremont.

In Fremont the LSE installed a siding on Sandusky Avenue to serve the Clauss Shear Company and the Herbrand plant. (Herbrand built its own direct switch from the LSE in 1918.) This track was one of only two commercial industrial sidings on the entire Lake Shore system and was primarily used to switch steam railroad freight cars several blocks between the Wheeling & Lake Erie and the two industries.

Otherwise it was a relatively quiet year for rebuilding projects, with work still dragging along on the Huron cutoff and 2500 feet of new double-track laid in East State Street in Fremont. The major accomplishment was full modernization of electrical generation and transmission on the western half of the Lake Shore Electric system. On November 25, 1916, the company finally closed the onetime Toledo, Fremont & Norwalk power house at Fremont and switched over to commercial power supplied from the nearby Ballville plant, located on the Fostoria & Fremont. At the same time the line was changed from 25-cycle to 60-cycle power. It had been a long struggle, which began in October 1913 when Ballville first opened and fed some power to the LSE. In the meantime its operator had both tech-

(*Above*) One of the "Lima Route" Jewett combines leads a train on Clifton Boulevard near 110th Street in Cleveland. (John A. Rehor collection)

(*Right*) Beginning in 1916, the LSE obtained power for the western half of its system from the new Ballville generating plant, located alongside the Sandusky River near Fremont. As finally completed, the plant included both hydroelectric and steam generating equipment. The Fostoria & Fremont, whose track bordered the road shown in front of the plant, brought in its coal from a connection with the Lake Erie & Western. (Frohman Collection, Hayes Presidential Center)

nical and financial problems; in July 1915 the Sandusky River Power Company was reorganized as the Ohio State Power Company and subsequently a steam plant was added to the original hydroelectric facility.

An early portent of the future came on August 6, 1916, when the ill-starred Lake Erie, Bowling Green & Napoleon, in receivership since 1911, was sold to the Toledo, Fostoria & Findlay. The new owner immediately shut down all but the LEBG&N's original section between Bowling Green and Pemberville — including the Woodville extension, only eleven years old. It was one of the Midwest interurban industry's first casualties and the LSE's first lost connection.

With business climbing again after what proved to be a temporary dip in 1915, the LSE decided to take the plunge for its first major new equipment order in ten years. On December 1 it dispatched an order to the Jewett Car Company for 12 steel interurban coaches, a steel freight motor, and five steel city-suburban cars for the Lorain Street Railroad. The new steel interurbans were to replace the wood Niles cars on the limited schedules and were designed to be the fastest on the system, with four 140-hp motors and, of course, multiple-unit control.

Into the War: 1917 – 1918

Despite hopes and promises, by early 1917 it was becoming inevitable that the United States would enter the European war. On April 2 it happened and the "European war" became truly a world war.

Even before that the Lake Shore Electric began feeling the effects. Lorain's heavy industry was picking up, and, to a much lesser degree, so was Fremont's. By late February the LSE found its afternoon local out of Fremont overcrowded with workers who lived in Clyde, and put on an extra car to handle them.

The steam railroads already were beginning to experience the congestion which eventually would result in a logistics crisis and temporary government operation. Combining patriotism with marketing, the Central Electric Railway Association sent a telegram to President Woodrow Wilson in mid-March offering the Midwestern interurban system for use in handling troops and supplies.

Whether for that reason or not, the LSE found itself willy-nilly in the freight business for the first time on a regular basis — and its earliest cargo was unhappily prophetic. Beginning early in February 1917 it began hauling carloads of new Overland automobiles from Toledo to Cleveland. The *Fremont Daily News* of February 6 reported that a seven-car train passed through the city early that morning — a somewhat unbelievable train length considering the line's various physical limitations and its later freight operating practices. Whatever the volume, the movement became regular, apparently initially using freight trailers from the Toledo, Bowling Green & Southern since the LSE owned none. During 1918 and 1919 its Sandusky shop built five specialized trailer cars for this service.

The Overland movement was the harbinger of a slow entry into general freight hauling, a business that thus far the LSE had intentionally ignored except in special circumstances. As noted earlier, the company had only two industrial sidings, and these were used primarily as a means of access to Fremont industries for nearby steam railroads. Otherwise it was mostly content to concentrate on the express traffic handled for its jointly owned Electric Package Agency.

The LSE also picked up the Toledo–Fremont mail contract early in 1917 after the New York Central decided to drop it. The other competitive steam road, the Wheeling & Lake Erie, operated only one passenger train a day over the route and was not interested in bidding.

As direct American involvement in the war neared, the Lake Shore inevitably began worrying about the effect on its manpower and in early February general superintendent Burge announced contingency plans to hire women conductors. Burge went on to say that

The LSE's Toledo Division operating center was the large ex–Toledo, Fremont & Norwalk carhouse on 5th street in Fremont. In this c. 1914 view, two former TF&N cars — freight motor 32 and a Barney & Smith coach — sit alongside a Niles coach. (John A. Rehor collection)

he had planned their blue serge uniforms and that "the girls can pick their own skirts, but they must wear regulation caps." As it turned out, none needed to be hired. Glenn Burkett, a Beach Park dispatcher, became the first employee to enlist in the Army, joining the Signal Corps. Luckily he returned safely to become a Fremont dispatcher and later a power dispatcher for the LSE's Lake Erie Power & Light subsidiary until his death in 1943.

The safety campaign continued with an all-day full-force rally at the Odd Fellows Hall in Sandusky on January 9. Four special cars carried some of the 400 employees who attended. Despite the meeting a limited and a local collided head-on at Gibsonburg Junction on May 7, injuring at least 25 passengers. The local apparently had failed to clear on the junction wye.

In fact, operational and equipment frustrations characterized much of 1917, as well as some depressing management news. On August 6 the LSE lost its senior founder, Henry Everett, who died at age 60 in Pasadena, California, after several years of poor health. There was little effect on the LSE's own management; Edward Moore continued as president, handling financial and basic policy matters, and, as usual, Fred Coen ran the railway.

The new Ballville power plant still had serious teething problems, with power interruptions during October which badly disrupted service on the west end of the LSE. The result was a direct takeover of the Ohio State Power Company by its two principal customers, the LSE and American Gas & Electric, the holding company which controlled the Ohio Light & Power Company. The two companies assumed joint control in February 1918, each owning 50 percent. The new regime re-equipped the plant and expanded it. The plant provided power for the LSE and the Fostoria & Fremont and for the communities of Fremont, Fostoria, Tiffin, and Shelby.

Wartime disruptions delayed delivery of the 12 new steel Jewett coaches ordered in December 1916, and by November 1917 only three had arrived. The remaining nine filtered in during the first half of 1918 with the last delivered in July. The LSE was only comparatively luckier with the five steel suburban cars for the Lorain Street Railroad, ordered at the same time. Four finally showed up in November 1917 and the fifth three months later. Even so, its situation could have been worse; Jewett went bankrupt December 12, 1918, and ceased all production.

The tough year of 1917 ended with little mercy. A low-speed head-on collision at Sage's Grove November 14 caused little damage and no injuries, but that was merely a prelude. A blinding December 9 blizzard triggered a smashup at Beach Park when an eastbound limited, running an hour late in the storm, hit a car which was working the AB&S branch at the branch switch. Twenty-three passengers were injured in that one, and both cars — No. 154 running the limited and Barney & Smith No. 9 on the AB&S — caught fire and were destroyed. LSE Vice President and General Manager Fred Coen was riding the 154 and got to see this operational problem close up and in midair as he leaped out its front door into a snowbank.

Christmas Day, however, brought a boon at the Cleveland end of the line when the new Detroit–Superior High Level Bridge opened. The Lake Shore Electric, along with numerous Cleveland Railway streetcar routes and much motor vehicle traffic, had long endured the old Superior Avenue viaduct over the Cuyahoga River, one of the city's worst bottle-

(Above) A group boards three chartered cars alongside the well-advertised Clyde Garage in Clyde on a wintry day about 1915. (W. A. McCaleb collection)

(Below) The new Detroit–Superior High Level Bridge, opened in December 1917, was a boon to the LSE and many west side Cleveland electric lines, finally eliminating the Cuyahoga River bottleneck. This 1930s scene was shot from the old Superior Viaduct as an LSE Jewett car rumbled across on the lower deck, which was reserved exclusively for streetcars and interurbans. (Louis Szakacs photo)

necks. The 1878 structure incorporated a long swing bridge over one of the most difficult and congested sections of the river; during the Great Lakes navigation season it was constantly opening and closing for freighters bound for the upstream steel mills and bulk unloading docks. Delays of five to ten minutes were common.

The new high-level bridge not only cleared the waterway but had a completely separate lower deck for the exclusive use of streetcars and interurbans. When opened it was the longest double-deck bridge ever built — 3,112 feet, with 12 concrete arches and a single 591-foot steel arch span over the river. The lower deck, used by the LSE, carried four streetcar tracks and was designed to accommodate six. From then on, many Lake Shore Electric passengers were thrilled by the impressive views of the Cuyahoga valley as they rumbled across the viaduct in the open-sided subway.

But the spring of 1918 produced another disaster. On April 15 the Beach Park carhouse caught fire, incinerating six cars including one Detroit United interurban and two of the LSE's newest steel Jewett interurbans. The new-car curse was still operative, right down to the last large order. The two Jewetts, Nos. 173 and 174, were eventually rebuilt, as was the DUR car.

In the meantime the steam railroad system had essentially collapsed under the pressures of enormously increased wartime traffic, car shortages, plant inadequacies, and confused logistics management. In an effort to unclog them and operate them as a single coordinated system, the federal government took direct control of the railroads on December 28, 1917. Operation then passed to the U.S. Railroad Administration, headed by President Wilson's son-in-law William Gibbs McAdoo. The interurbans were exempted from USRA control, but faced with equipment shortages and increasing general congestion, the USRA encouraged them to help relieve the pressure by taking as much of the business as they could.

The steam railroads always were inherently unsuited for expeditiously handling certain types of freight traffic — particularly the labor-intensive less-than-carload shipments and relatively short-distance movements. While many lines were not yet doing so, the interurbans theoretically could move freight like this much faster and more cheaply. Furthermore, by this time the Midwestern interurban system also could be considered a single interconnected network, enabling shipments between almost all major cities between Buffalo and Chicago and south to Cincinnati and Louisville. And the Lake Shore Electric occupied one of the most strategic places within this network, linking Cleveland and other northern manufacturing Ohio centers like Akron, Canton, Massillon, and Youngstown with Michigan and Indiana.

During 1918 there were increasingly serious studies and proposals between the USRA and various interurban groups, ranging from the umbrella Central Electric Railway Association to regional Ohio interurbans to individual companies, all aimed at putting the interurbans more heavily into the general freight business.

Unfortunately most Midwestern interurbans — the Lake Shore included — were not immediately prepared to step in. The LSE was fairly typical. Having concentrated almost exclusively on the Electric Package Agency express business, its freight equipment and station facilities were adequate for that traffic but little more. In addition, considerable groundwork was needed to establish the rates, interline agreements, accounting systems, and solicitation forces needed to enter what was a completely new and complex kind of market. The process of equipment acquisition and procedures started but inevitably took time and the LSE's freight business did not begin to blossom until after the war ended. Even then it took several more years to mature fully. But a start was made in 1918 by beginning a program of building new box freight motors and trailers at its Sandusky shop.

The war continued its baneful effects on the Lake Shore's operations and economics. Coal delivery problems at its Beach Park power plant bedeviled the railway all year. And reflecting the pressures on wages, the company gave its trainmen a five-cent-an-hour raise. Concurrently, Coen's salary rose to $9,000 a year. The cost inflation also forced the LSE to increase interurban fares for the second time within a year, putting them up to two- to three-cents a mile.

The Huron cutoff became a race against time. On March 28, 1918, the chronically problematic old Berlin Street highway bridge was closed to interurbans for three days because of structural problems. Permanent relief arrived at last on November 5 when the long-awaited new line opened and work started on dismantling the twisting old route. Four years in the making, the three-mile line saved about half a mile of running, but more importantly it eliminated numerous curves, grades, and, of course, the accursed Berlin Street bridge. Included on the cutoff was a new concrete-block combination station and substation. The old bridge was promptly dismantled and even the road alignment was abandoned.

An intriguing news report from Fremont noted that on September 4 a special Navy train made up of three flatcars carrying floats depicting torpedo boats, a destroyer, submarine, and Eagle boat was to run from Detroit to Fremont and Sandusky via the Detroit United and the Lake Shore Electric. On the next day it was to continue to Lorain and Elyria. Whether it actually did and, if so, what it looked like and what equipment was used are deep in the fog of history.

On its way from Lima to Cleveland, LSE No. 166 stops at the new Huron station on the cutoff line about 1919. (E. Niebergal photo, Frohman Collection, Hayes Presidential Center)

Untangling Lorain (1914 – 1921)

Of all the Lake Shore's wartime problems and improvement needs, Lorain was the greatest. Even before the United States entered the conflict the city was rapidly outgrowing its transit facilities. In 1900, with Johnson's mill five years old, Lorain's population was 16,028. By 1910 it had climbed to 28,883, and would hit 37,295 in 1920. (Due to the lure of its heavy industry, it had become a heavily multi-ethnic community with about 35 percent of its citizens foreign-born.) Yet on the eve of the war in 1914 Lorain's entire electric railway layout still reflected the lighter turn-of-the-century traffic volumes, more casual operations, and varying heritages. By 1917 it was unlivable.

The problems were numerous and serious. For one, the Lake Shore Electric and its Lorain Street Railroad subsidiary had never been physically joined in Lorain itself. While the two lines crossed at Erie Avenue and Broadway in the city's center, there was no direct track connection; the only existing link was the roundabout Avon Beach & Southern branch, running from Beach Park on the LSE main line to 31st Street and Grove Avenue in South Lorain. Equipment transfers between the two lines were awkward, and it was impossible to pool city streetcar operations.

In addition, the Erie Avenue–Broadway intersection was a hideous tangle. Dating from Lorain's less populous and more casual earlier days, the Lorain Street Railroad's route ended in a large loop right in the center of the intersection; the LSE's double-track east–west main line crossed through the center of the loop on a curving alignment.

The Broadway–Erie chaos was compounded by the presence of two other electric railway terminals less than half a block away. Immediately west of the intersection on Erie was a "wye" terminal, jointly used by the Lake Shore Electric and the Cleveland Southwestern. The LSE originally had used it to reverse all its Cleveland–Lorain locals and it served as the Southwestern's terminal for its Elyria–Lorain services. This wye was located on the LSE's eastbound Erie Avenue track, and was laid out in such a way that cars reversing here turned east on Erie into the intersection before backing up, thus overhanging the Lorain

The Lorain Street Railroad's infamous terminal loop in the center of the Broadway–Erie Avenue intersection. The camera looks southeast at a departing LSRR 90-series car heading for Elyria. The LSE's own main line crosses the loop in its center. (Leiler photo, John A. Rehor collection)

Street Railroad's loop track; they then backed against the current of LSE traffic. The second terminal was just west of the wye, a crossover for turning the LSE's East Erie streetcar line.

The Broadway–Erie loop was only the beginning of the Lorain Street Railroad's problems. Its Lorain–Elyria route, of course, had been built to serve the now-booming steel mill as well as other heavy industry, and was handling a huge rush-hour business. But several major problems with its track layout slowed schedules and cut its capacity. Going south, there was a single-track section at the Nickel Plate Road grade crossing, a narrow-centers double-track curve near 17th Street and Broadway, and a left turn at 21st and Broadway which interfered with the Cleveland Southwestern's own left-turning movement from south to west at the same point. Then came the real agony — 12 different railroad tracks were crossed at grade on 21st Street and North Fulton, including the Baltimore & Ohio's main tracks to its coal docks and various industrial tracks into the mill area. Extensive single track followed on 28th Street and Grove Avenue, from Fulton and 28th to Grove and 36th Street, a total of about 15 blocks.

The result of all of this was that ten-minute headways were the best that the Lorain Street Railroad could operate, using four sections and some motor-trailer trains in rush hours. Had it been able to operate properly, it should have offered a two-minute headway.

The LSE made some preliminary improvements in 1914 when it moved its own wye terminal to the west end of town at Leavitt Road near the Elyria Water Works. This took some pressure off the Broadway–Erie intersection, but some LSE cars and all Cleveland Southwestern cars continued to use the awkwardly located downtown wye. At the same time, the Lorain Street Railroad's 28th Street line was double-tracked between North Fulton Road and Pearl.

But the real solutions to all the problems were deferred until the peak pressures of wartime traffic. Essentially they came in four parts: (1) The LSRR's Broadway–Erie loop was eliminated by extending the line a half block farther north on Broadway to an off-street

loop; (2) switches were built connecting LSE and LSRR lines at the Broadway–Erie intersection, allowing through-routing of streetcar lines; (3) the 21st Street–North Fulton routing to 28th Street was abandoned and replaced with a direct route on Broadway and on 28th
Street, and (4) most of the remaining single-track bottlenecks were double-tracked and
other sections realigned and rebuilt. (See p. 197 for map of this area.)

Needless to say the work was strung out over several years and was not fully completed
until 1921, but at least two major parts were in place by late summer in 1919. The longest
and most complex project was bypassing the 21st Street–North Fulton routing with a new
routing which (going southward) used Cleveland Southwestern tracks on Broadway from
21st to 28th Streets, then turned east on 28th to join the old line at Fulton. This involved
not only building about six blocks of entirely new double-track on 28th Street, but an
underpass where 28th Street crossed the Baltimore & Ohio Railroad tracks. The underpass
construction, a city project, was started in 1914 and the entire rerouting job was finally completed in the fall of 1918. Southbound cars switched to the new route on October 28 and
northbound on November 5.

During 1919, 4,000 feet of track were rebuilt on Broadway, including the Nickel Plate
railroad crossing, and on August 21 of that year the LSRR's Broadway line was extended
north of Erie to its new loop. Double-track switches were installed at the Broadway–Erie
intersection to allow movement from the LSE's east–west Erie Avenue tracks south to
Broadway from either direction. Another 1,100 feet of track were rebuilt on Broadway in
1920 and between 1920 and 1921 double-tracking was completed on 28th Street and on
Grove Avenue from Pearl to 31st Street.

In addition to all this rebuilding, the Lake Shore Electric built a new city line of its own
on Lorain's east side to reach the American Shipbuilding yard and the newly built J. C.
Cromwell Steel Company plant on Colorado Avenue west of Root Road. This route
branched south on Colorado Avenue at East Erie and followed Colorado to Root Road,
crossing the Nickel Plate main line at grade about midway. Service started as far as Colorado Avenue and Euclid August 21, 1919, and was extended to Root Road September 4.

The Trauma Ends

At eleven a.m. on the eleventh day of the eleventh month of 1918 it was over. The United
States celebrated and the world breathed a collective sigh of relief; for a war which was to
have ended quickly and decisively, ten million had died, another six million were maimed
for life, and many were later left wondering what had been accomplished. But it was ended,
with the United States now a reluctant world power — thanks in part to the industries of
Cleveland, Detroit, and Lorain and the electric railways which made them work.

At Armistice time the Lake Shore Electric could reflect on some other positive accom-
plishments. For one thing, its concerted efforts at safety consciousness seemingly had finally paid off. Despite the hectic environment no serious accidents occurred during 1918.
Late or not, it also now had a fleet of steel interurban cars which were some of the fastest
and most modern in the business. The year ended with the highest profit in the system's
history — $163,381 — even though expenses had risen and, surprisingly, system ridership
had dropped 5 percent. Actually, the interurban portion of the system performed much
better, bolstered by an increasing proportion of long-haul riding on the limited trains which
helped increase average car-mile earnings by a spectacular 25 percent over 1917. The major
problems were in the city operations.

The year also ended with some potentially exciting news from Cleveland. It will be
remembered that back in 1911 a visionary plan was announced for a combined interurban
terminal, hotel, and office development at the Public Square. Construction of the first
portion, the hotel, finally began in 1916 and in December 1918 the magnificent Hotel
Cleveland opened. In the meantime the ever-creative Van Sweringen brothers had revised

This poor but rare and fascinating view shows a three-car limited train at Cleveland's Public Square in the 1915 era. Two LSE Niles cars are trailed by a Detroit United Railway car — called a "tub" by LSE crews. (George Krambles collection)

and expanded their terminal project to include not only interurbans but steam railroads. The final product would be something radical and unique in urban planning — a single complex which would integrate all forms of urban and intercity transportation with offices, hotels, and department stores. And the Lake Shore Electric would be part of it.

In addition, the Van Sweringens — who now also controlled the Nickel Plate Road — intended to use the Nickel Plate's right-of-way as a rapid transit corridor through the city. As part of a grade crossing elimination project then under way on Cleveland's west side, they included provision for extra electric railway tracks — tracks which the Lake Shore Electric could use as a high-speed entry.

By broadening their proposal to include a union railroad terminal the Van Sweringens faced some formidable political problems, since their vision conflicted with earlier and more traditional city plans. But the brothers themselves were proving to be a formidable force, and consummation of the dream was only a matter of time. How much time was another matter.

CHAPTER 5

NOT QUITE NORMALCY

1919 – 1922

When peace returned in 1919 the Lake Shore Electric faced a mixed but mostly sunny outlook. Entry into the general freight business came too late to contribute much for the war effort, but by the early 1920s that traffic was growing as fast as equipment, physical plant, and new interline arrangements permitted. For the first two years after the war, ridership, revenues and profits rose heartily; the profit growth was especially great.

But the picture was darkening on its outer edges. The general postwar business boom masked some subtle signs of trouble which were noticeable only in certain special types of business. The interurban's managers discovered, for example, that the peak loads that they traditionally carried to fairs and on day-trip excursions were substantially smaller; many were driving autos to the events.

The two local city systems were their own special kind of problem. Unregulated jitneys continued to take passengers off the streetcar routes, some of which were economic albatrosses to begin with. Yet the cities seemed indifferent to regulating the competition and, especially Sandusky, hostile to fare increases or route adjustments.

A turning point came with the national recession in 1921. Inevitably the LSE felt it; things were bad for a while and then, as hoped, they improved to a degree — but this time the recovery was not complete. Nor would it ever be.

A Rising Tide: 1919 – 1920

Barely was the Lake Shore Electric into the postwar era when it began its first regularly scheduled interline freight operation — the type of service which originally was intended to relieve the crush on the wartime steam railroads but never did. On February 14, 1919, an overnight train started running between Massillon, Ohio, and

From 1918 onwards, the big steel Jewett cars most commonly handled the LSE's premier runs. Here eastbound 180 is approaching the Nickel Plate Road underpass in Rocky River in June 1934. (Ralph A. Perkin photo)

81

As freight traffic began developing in the late World War I period, the LSE's shops turned out six home-built freight motors, three of which were wood and three steel. The last of the steel group, No. 40(II), was completed in 1920 and posed at Fremont soon after. (John A. Rehor collection)

Detroit, originating on the Northern Ohio and using the LSE between Cleveland and Toledo. With the LSE still short of its own freight equipment, the Northern Ohio initially supplied both the freight motors and box trailers. The original service ran five nights a week and usually consisted of a motor and single trailer.

During the year, however, the Sandusky shop turned out one freight motor and six trailers, and by the time the war-initiated freight equipment program ended in 1920 it had produced a total of six motors. By that time too the company owned 21 trailers, including five specifically built for the Overland auto business. As the interline freight business and its own roster gradually grew, the LSE and its connecting interurbans worked out equipment pooling agreements similar to steam railroad practice; both motors and trailers from the Detroit United, the Northern Ohio, and various other Ohio and Indiana lines became common sights along LSE lines, piloted by LSE crews. New handling facilities also began appearing, including freight houses in Toledo and Fremont for use by the Electric Package Agency.

As the Lake Shore edged into this new and promising market, it simultaneously tried to back delicately out of an old one. Typical of many small-city streetcar operations, the Sandusky city lines always had been financially marginal; they were run primarily to preserve the franchise allowing the interurbans to use the streets and, to a degree, to keep good relationships in a key community. Here, however, the good relationship was mostly one-sided. In earlier years, Fred Coen's pleas for local fare increases to meet his costs were rebuffed, and in 1915 he had announced that the LSE was planning a new cutoff line so that the interurbans could bypass downtown Sandusky.

In May 1919 Coen was quoted as saying: "There are only two things we can do to meet the loss we are suffering in Sandusky. One of them is to curtail service . . . or raise the fares to make the returns greater." The city commission finally relented and allowed a one-cent hike. That helped but was not the entire solution — nor was the threat of a bypass route, which remained just a threat for another decade.

Coen decided to do the best he could to reduce his costs by fully re-equipping the Sandusky routes with lightweight one-man single-truck Birney cars. These could cut labor costs in half and promised substantial savings in maintenance and power consumption. In December 1919 he ordered 16 of the little cars, which were put in service the following July — allowing a mass housecleaning of old two-man cars. Virtually the entire early Sandusky fleet disappeared, including all of the happily remembered open summer cars; the secondhand Atlantic City closed cars bought in 1913 went to Lorain. Unglamorous and not too comfortable, the bouncy little Birneys at least helped resolve the economic problem for a while — although it would never disappear.

Indeed, labor costs generally were a steadily growing concern. During 1919 trainmen were given another wage increase, with interurban men now receiving up to 46 cents an hour and city men up to 34 cents. (Coen himself received a raise to $10,800 a year.) The next year the top trainman rate went to 60 cents; Coen moved up to $15,000 — a very ample reward by the standards of the time.

The heavy debt was another nagging problem. On

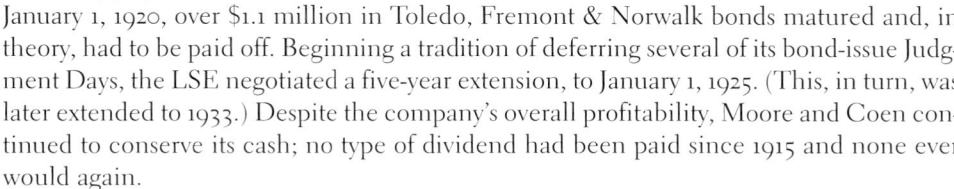

January 1, 1920, over $1.1 million in Toledo, Fremont & Norwalk bonds matured and, in theory, had to be paid off. Beginning a tradition of deferring several of its bond-issue Judgment Days, the LSE negotiated a five-year extension, to January 1, 1925. (This, in turn, was later extended to 1933.) Despite the company's overall profitability, Moore and Coen continued to conserve its cash; no type of dividend had been paid since 1915 and none ever would again.

An outstanding passenger year was symbolized on October 13, 1919, when 27 extra LSE cars moved 1,500 Masonic Knights Templar to Norwalk from various nearby origins, including four off-line points. Ten cars came from Toledo, two from Fremont, four from Cleveland, two from Lorain, two from Sandusky, two each from Fostoria, Findlay, and Tiffin, and one from Bowling Green. Yet some shadows showed. The 1919 version of the Fremont fair — which had always produced huge loads for the interurban — was oddly disappointing. Fair attendance records were broken, but afterward LSE superintendent Milt Trueman was quoted as saying: "We did not have half the travel of former years." Many of those former riders came in automobiles.

Late in 1919 passenger operations were disrupted when employees of the the Toledo streetcar system went on a month-long strike lasting from November 8 to December 6. During that time LSE cars were forced to end their runs at the city limit, where passengers transferred to jitneys and makeshift buses. The strike was complicated by long-standing and complex political and franchise issues, and finally was personally settled by Henry Doherty, the company's New York owner and head of Cities Service. Labor and political trouble again shut down the Toledo system briefly in April 1920, and Doherty got permission to raise fares as part of the resolution.

Beyond buying new streetcars for Sandusky and acquiring freight equipment, physical improvements were limited mostly to completing the drawn-out Lorain program, rebuilding some city trackwork in Sandusky, and replacing a few fire losses such as the station in Clyde. The off-and-on Fremont–Genoa cutoff proposal switched on again briefly in 1919. This time the catalyst was a repaving project for the Maumee Pike, which would require the LSE to relocate its roadside track. The problems were resolved, however; the interurban track remained where it was, and the Genoa cutoff idea disappeared for the last time.

Another street-use problem surfaced in Fremont in 1920 when the city faced up to the necessity to replace the three-span iron truss bridge which carried State Street and the LSE line over the Sandusky River. The 1877 structure was legally condemned and plans drawn up for a new high-capacity concrete replacement. The project eventually took over five years to reach reality.

The arrival of Sandusky's Birney fleet in 1920 swept virtually all the city's older trolleys off the streets. A typical example, double-ended No. 124, is inbound on the Soldiers Home line, running alongside Columbus Avenue at the carhouse entrance just south of Perkins Avenue in 1934. (Ralph A. Perkin photo)

Another idea which took time to gestate was first broached in 1920 when the LSE began studying full conversion to commercially purchased 60-cycle electric power. Half the job already was done, since the jointly owned Ballville plant had been supplying power for the western part of the system since 1916. That left only Beach Park which, although completely rebuilt 14 years earlier, was obsolete once again. The ultimate plan was to shut down the 25-cycle plant and buy power from the Cleveland Electric Illuminating Company.

As business continued rising, the Lake Shore could congratulate itself that its safety problems finally seemed well under control. There was only one reasonably serious incident during the 1919–1920 period, and that did not even involve passengers. On March 7, 1919, steel freight motor 34 met newly built wood motor 36 head-on south of Berlin Heights, once again the result of misunderstood orders. Surprisingly the steel car was destroyed by fire but the wood motor went back to Sandusky for repairs.

Just a month earlier, the LSE was the double victim of a freak pair of accidents in Sandusky. During slippery weather on February 12 a heavily loaded truck owned by the Fremont Iron and Metal Company skidded into a single-truck city car on Camp Street, wrecking its fender. The truck then proceeded to Columbus and Washington Avenues where it hit city car 110 amidship, knocking it off the track and sending it sliding down Columbus Avenue. At the end of its trip motorman John Butts and conductor Fred Knupke found themselves and their little car between a pole and a tree on the southwest corner of Washington Row. Big Brill combine No. 63 came out and hauled the 110 back onto the track.

Outright jubilation was not one of the reserved Fred Coen's normal emotions, but the results for 1920 surely justified it. Every kind of statistic showed a spectacular upward climb. System passenger counts were up 16 percent over the previous year and 29 percent over wartime 1918; gross revenues of $3.3 million were 26 percent higher than 1919 and a full 50 percent more than 1918. Most encouraging of all, the reported profit of $376,693 exceeded that of 1919 by 31 percent and 1918 by 131 percent — and that despite the wage and cost inflation. In addition, another Ohioan, the pleasant and affable Warren G. Harding, was heading for the White House and all seemed right with the world.

Inbound for Cleveland, the 167 negotiates the reverse curves at Detroit Road in Rocky River, where the LSE employed its only crossing watchman. The date was June 27, 1936.
(W. A. McCaleb photo)

The Tide Recedes: 1921 – 1922

Even as the LSE was experiencing its best year ever, the national economy was beginning to suffer a postwar letdown. By 1921 many businesses were deep in the throes of production cuts, layoffs, and wage reductions. The Railroad Labor Board authorized a 12 percent wage cut and the U.S. Steel Corporation, Lorain's largest employer, reduced wages three times during the year. Inevitably it was a turbulent time in railroad labor relations, with another wage cut in 1922 and a shop crafts strike which ended in union defeat.

Soon enough the Lake Shore Electric found itself watching a ridership drop which eventually amounted to 12 percent. Now the statistics ran in reverse. Gross revenues for 1921 were $2.6 million, 22 percent below 1920, and the line was lucky to eke out a $51,773 profit — an 86 percent drop.

Needless to say, LSE trainmen suffered along with their steam railroad brothers. On June 15, 1921, their top wage went from 60 cents an hour back to 52 cents, a 13 percent cut. (There was no report of what happened to Fred Coen's salary.)

By that time the traffic losses were all too evident. In an interview, Fred Coen reported that in July, normally the LSE's busiest month, the line carried 259,430 fewer passengers than the year before — essentially the same level as in midwinter. And while Coen blamed the national recession for much of the problem, he also noted that the increasing use of autos was "another great factor." The Fremont fair in late September again made that point clear. Reported the *Fremont Daily News*:

> Traffic on the interurban lines was not heavy Thursday despite the crowd attending the fair. Service was doubled until noon on the Lake Shore Electric and Fostoria & Fremont, but the cars were not crowded. . . .

Coen also was becoming desperate in Sandusky. Despite his new Birney cars and the fare increase, the Hancock Street route to the Soldiers Home and the West Monroe shuttle line were hopeless losers. In May 1921 he asked the city commission for permission to abandon most of both lines. Probably not to his surprise, he was turned down athough even the city commissioners agreed that losing the West Monroe Street line would be no disaster. Regardless, it would plug on until 1928, and would even receive newer equipment in 1926.

The Lake Shore handled one especially interesting piece of "freight" business in 1921. Fifty newly built Peter Witt–type streetcars for Detroit were run under their own power from the Kuhlman Car Company plant on Cleveland's east side to Detroit via the interurban. Since they lacked headlights powerful enough for nighttime operation on the LSE's lines, they had to be sandwiched in between the regular daytime limiteds and locals.

Other shadows edged forward. The chronically anemic Sandusky, Norwalk & Mansfield, which was struggling along under its second receivership, abruptly disappeared in early 1921 and the LSE lost its second feeder line. Without electric generating facilities of its own, it had been buying its power from the Cleveland Southwestern and fell six months in arrears, at which point the Southwestern simply shut it down. On March 24 motorman James Trimmer ran the SN&M's last electric car. (Trimmer later hired out to the LSE and carried his luck with him. On May 15, 1938, he also operated the Lake Shore Electric's last run.) The battered SN&M was not quite dead, however. It was eventually sold and later emerged as the Norwalk & Shelby Railroad, but in the interim the track remained quiet for 21 months and electric cars were never to return. The new owners bought two gasoline-powered railbuses built by the Elyria Foundry & Machine Company and resumed running December 28, 1922, but ultimately were no more successful. The line expired for the last time in 1924.

The SN&M's demise could be shrugged off as a case of a congenital weakling which probably never should have existed in the first place. But larger and more ominous shadows quickly followed. In 1921 the sprawling Ohio Electric Railway system went bankrupt and on August 16, 1922, it was sold at auction to its bondholders, ending the dream of a united interurban system in southern and western Ohio. Much closer to home, the large and important Cleveland Southwestern went into receivership January 21, 1922. Although neither the former Ohio Electric lines nor the Cleveland Southwestern immediately disappeared, the message was unsettling for those who chose to read it: the interurban industry was slipping into serious trouble. But for the time being at least, the Southwestern's problems were the Lake Shore's gains; in less than two years the LSE had the Norwalk business to itself and had picked up the Southwestern's Oberlin Avenue streetcar line in Lorain.

Given the dismal events of 1921, little was spent on improvements — either then or in 1922. The only equipment additions were four more box freight trailers in 1921 and nothing the next year. In Fremont the old State Street bridge was moved north 12 feet in preparation for the new bridge work, and the LSE's track approaches were realigned. Otherwise, the only significant work was in Lorain, where the long-running rebuilding project was finally completed in 1921. The last phase consisted of double-tracking the Lorain Street Railroad's line on 28th Street from Pearl to Grove Avenue and included what was billed as "beautification" work, with the tracks in a parklike center-street private-right-of-way. It was a nice touch, but since 28th Street formed the southern border of a large, busy, noisy, and dirty steel mill, it was difficult to raise the general aesthetic level of the area.

With the Lorain track reconstruction work done, the LSE added a new local streetcar line along its interurban route on West Erie Avenue in 1922, tying it into the recently built Colorado Avenue line on the east side. After being displaced from Sandusky by the Birneys, the five ex-Atlantic City cars were brought over to Lorain to work the route and other operations in the area, and in 1922 were rebuilt for one-man operation.

Along with the Lake Shore Electric's other neighbors, the Western Ohio also was weakening and in 1921 the Union Trust Company of Cleveland attempted to put it into receivership. Nothing came of it at that point, and the company tried to rescue itself by modernizing. In 1922 it and the allied Fostoria & Fremont replaced their heavy wood cars with new Kuhlman-built lightweight equipment. The Fostoria & Fremont put its new two-car fleet in service August 29th, giving the LSE's Fremont shop workers their first experience maintaining modern equipment. It was to be their only experience, since the LSE itself stuck with its big steel Jewetts (which, after all, were almost new) and older wood cars, and never succumbed to the more economical lightweights.

At the same time the through Cleveland–Lima limited services went through some up-and-down gyrations. With the encouragement of the Indiana Service Corporation, one of the two daily Cleveland–Lima trips was extended to Fort Wayne, Indiana, on July 17. The 222-mile through run was the longest at the time, but was short-lived; precise documentation is now difficult, but it lasted no more than two years. The second of the two traditional Cleveland–Lima limited schedules disappeared September 6th when the run was cut into a pair of connecting services, with the Western Ohio running as far as Fremont to meet the LSE limited. The Western Ohio also dropped out of the Cleveland–Lima–Fort Wayne equipment pool, and an LSE car normally handled this run as long as it lasted. When it ended (in 1924 or earlier), all through Cleveland–Lima service also ceased and connecting trips were scheduled to meet at Fremont.

Jitney buses in Lorain remained a serious irritation — much more so now that the LSE had finished spending half a million dollars and five years of work rebuilding the car lines and had also

The pioneering Sandusky–Milan–Norwalk line lived apart from the main lines in its own quieter world. Demoted to such local services, a southbound ex-TF&N Barney & Smith car rolls through Milan in the early 1920s. (Ralph H. Sayles collection)

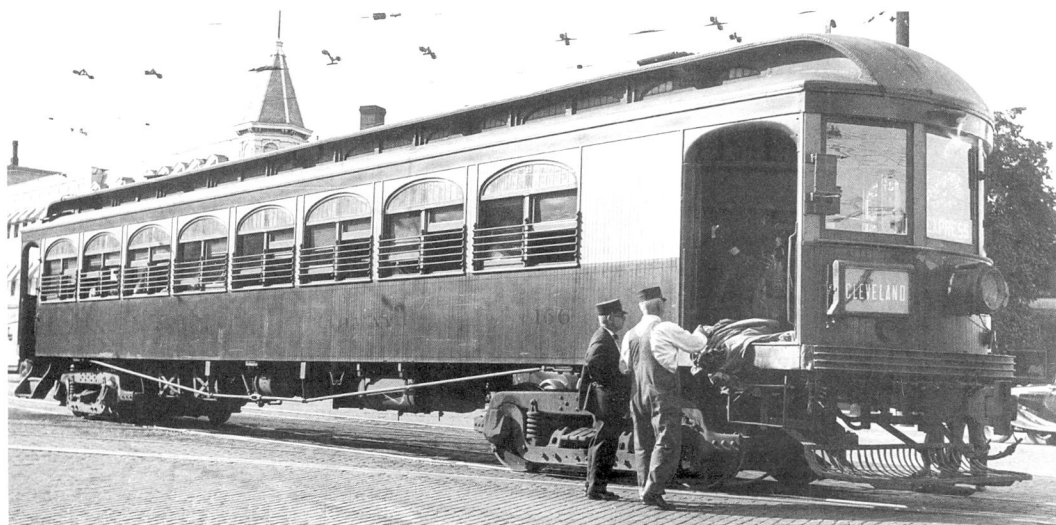

Mail for Fremont is unloaded from the 166 in 1936. (C. E. Helms photo)

bought five new cars for them. In April 1922 Coen gave an ultimatum to Lorain's city council, threatening to abandon all streetcar service unless the jitneys were regulated. He claimed that the LSE and Lorain Street Railroad lost over $44,000 on the service in 1921 and that 1922 was showing the same pattern. The city fathers listened, and the next year they passed an ordinance putting the buses out of business. Unfortunately the jitney operators got together and challenged the law in court, and the case was not finally decided in the railway's favor until 1925.

Some things remained happily unchanged. On Saturday July 29, 1922, 800 National Carbon workers and their families from Fremont climbed aboard 11 special cars to a company outing at Crystal Beach, east of Vermilion. Others came from National Carbon's Cleveland plant. But even that event had its clouds; the Fremont newspaper also noted that "in addition to the specials 20 or more automobile parties will make the trip to the beach."

Moore and Coen could at least be encouraged that 1922 turned out better than 1921 — albeit only slightly. Passenger counts were up 2 percent, although this was not reflected in gross income, which dropped a marginal 1 percent. But the net profit looked better; at $175,053 it was 238 percent greater than the lackluster 1921 performance. This was probably mostly thanks to the wage cuts and other expense reductions, since not much else really improved. The financial results did show that whatever financial strength there was lay in the long-haul interurban operations. Riding on the Lorain Street Railroad took a dismal 24 percent dive, and as already noted, that subsidiary was showing a direct loss. It was little wonder that Coen was so concerned about the economic situations in Lorain and Sandusky, since it seemed clear that the city streetcar lines were bleeding what still was thought to be a reasonably healthy interurban system.

That, however, was increasingly uncertain too. During the four years from the war's end, motor vehicle registrations in Ohio increased an average of 19 percent every year. By 1922 there were 882,840 vehicles registered in the state — almost exactly twice as many as in 1918. For the Lake Shore Electric it was not much of an introduction to the Roaring Twenties.

LSE cars started their runs at Cleveland's Public Square, the hub of the city's transit system. Toledo-bound 182 pulls out of the Square onto Superior Avenue in September 1936. (Ralph A. Perkin photo)

CHAPTER 6

A SNAPSHOT AT THE SUMMIT

The Lake Shore Electric in 1923

True to the perverse cycles of corporate fortunes, the Lake Shore Electric reached the zenith of its physical growth in 1923, three years after its traffic and income had peaked and had begun to decline. That year marked its last line acquisition when, on November 5, its Lorain Street Railroad subsidiary picked up the bankrupt Cleveland Southwestern's Oberlin Avenue streetcar line in Lorain. At that time too, the system still operated all its original lines including several weaklings it would soon shed. Including its various subsidiaries, the company's route mileage totaled almost 210 miles. Later it would add its Sandusky cutoff, but by then several branches and city lines were gone, so the system never again would be as large or as active. Thus late 1923 is an opportune point to pause in the historical narrative and look at the Lake Shore Electric system in some detail.

Despite its size, the LSE was an uncomplicated system essentially consisting of a Cleveland–Toledo main line with several secondary and feeder branches and local city lines in Lorain, Sandusky, and Norwalk.

At Cleveland, passengers boarded the big orange Lake Shore Electric cars at Public Square, the common terminal for virtually all of the city's public transportation which reached downtown. Looping around the Square's four separate quadrants not only were Cleveland Railway streetcar lines reaching all parts of the city, but four other interurban lines which exchanged passengers with the LSE to one degree or another. From the south came the deep red cars of the Northern Ohio Traction & Light Company, connecting Cleveland with Akron, Canton, Massillon, Kent, Ravenna, and New Philadelphia. The Cleveland Southwestern & Columbus Railway (more commonly called simply the "Southwestern" or "Green Line") reached Elyria, Oberlin, Medina, Wooster, and Bucyrus. To the east, the Cleveland, Painesville & Eastern followed the lake shore to Painesville with a connection to Ashtabula. Finally, the chronically ailing Cleveland & Eastern Traction Company reached eastward into hilly, rural Geauga County to serve the tiny towns of Chardon and Middlefield.

Also sharing the Square terminal was Cleveland's newest and most exciting electric line — the three-year-old Cleveland Interurban Railroad, better known as the "Shaker Rapid." The ever-expansive Van Sweringen brothers had created the CIRR as a swift means of reaching their rarified suburban Shaker Heights development. While its trains of specially modified city streetcars left the Square on city streets, they took to their own heavily built rapid transit right-of-way at East 34th Street. At the end of its South Moreland (now Van Aken) Boulevard branch at Lynnfield Road, the "Rapid" met the cars of a fifth interurban line, the remnant of the much-reorganized and now-truncated Cleveland & Chagrin Falls Railway, which continued east to Chagrin Falls.

From Cleveland the Lake Shore Electric's main line followed the Lake Erie shore west through Lorain and Vermilion. Alongside the lake at Ceylon Junction it divided into the two alternate routes which reunited at Fremont — one via Huron, Sandusky, and Castalia; the other via Norwalk, Monroeville, Bellevue, and Clyde. Westward from Fremont it passed through Woodville and Genoa before reaching Toledo. Through passenger trains ran between Cleveland and Detroit via Toledo and the Detroit United system's subsidiary, the Detroit, Monroe & Toledo Short Line Railway Company.

Other important passenger and freight connections were also made at Toledo with interurbans reaching into western and southern Ohio and northern Indiana. Extending west were the Toledo & Indiana Railroad and Toledo & Western Railroad; to the south ran the Lima–Toledo Railroad, the Toledo, Bowling Green & Southern Traction Company, and the Toledo, Fostoria & Findlay Railway. The Lima–Toledo was especially significant; as part of the recently dissolved Ohio Electric Railway system it had working connections to Dayton, Cincinnati, Columbus, and lines in Indiana. (In 1930 it became part of the Cincinnati & Lake Erie and continued as one of the LSE's strongest and longest-lived freight connections.) Also in Toledo — as well as at Holt's Corners in Genoa — the LSE had relatively minor passenger and freight interchanges with the Toledo, Port Clinton & Lakeside, soon to be part of Henry Doherty's Ohio Public Service.

Fremont was another important interline junction point. Here the LSE joined the Fostoria & Fremont Railway, the access line to the "Lima Route" through western and southern Ohio. Although the Fostoria & Fremont was controlled by the Western Ohio Railway, it was operated out of the LSE's Fremont carhouse, used mostly LSE crews, and was run by LSE dispatchers and supervisors.

At Norwalk were two emphatically lesser connections. First was the Cleveland Southwestern's Norwalk extension, which used the LSE's East Main street track to enter town. The Southwestern line was mostly a thorn in the Lake Shore Electric's side since it was a competitor between Norwalk and Cleveland, but the two lines did exchange passengers for intermediate points such as Oberlin and Elyria. Good or bad, it disappeared November 7, 1923, when the bankrupt Southwestern cut back to Oberlin. The second connection was equally doomed. By 1923 the Sandusky, Norwalk & Mansfield Electric Railway had collapsed and undergone an uncertain rebirth as the Norwalk & Shelby Railroad, operating two gasoline rail cars on a three-hour headway between the two cities of its name. In April 1924 it too died.

The LSE's four branches were a mixed assortment. Shortest was the three-mile spur from Gibsonburg Junction, west of Fremont, to Gibsonburg. Strictly a "trolley that meets all the trains" shuttle operation, it had its own assigned car, which connected with most main-line limiteds and locals. Next was the 17-mile Sandusky–Milan–Norwalk branch, one of the LSE's earliest ancestors. But by 1923 it was a secondary route which did not particularly fit into the LSE's major traffic flows. The last two branches were operated by the subsidiary Lorain Street Railroad and were a pair of opposites: the heavily patronized suburban-interurban line between Lorain and Elyria and the lonely and neglected Avon Beach & Southern, connecting the LSE main line at Beach Park with the LSRR at 31st Street in South Lorain.

At Lorain, the LSE itself owned three local city routes — East Erie Avenue, West Erie, and Colorado Avenue. Besides its Elyria route — which was also a heavy local city line serving the U. S. Steel plant — the Lorain Street Railroad had titular ownership of the just-acquired Oberlin Avenue line. As a practical matter, however, LSE and Lorain Street Railroad operations in Lorain were integrated under one management and operated from the LSRR's South Lorain carhouse. Lorain's heavy industry made it a key point on the system; based on number of passengers, the Lorain Street Railroad accounted for 35 percent of the system's total passenger traffic. (Its income contribution was proportionately much less, of course, since the riding was short-haul.)

Sandusky was much more sedate, with four modestly patronized local lines — Depot Belt, Soldiers Home Belt, East Monroe–Tiffin Avenue, and West Monroe. The first two were continuous loop, or "belt" routes and the last, West Monroe, was a strange orphan operation with little traffic or future. Norwalk's short single-car single-route city line dutifully fulfilled a franchise requirement but otherwise made little contribution to the LSE's coffers.

For operating purposes this system was divided into four divisions: The Cleveland Division, headquartered at Beach Park, controlled main line operations east of Norwalk and Sandusky. At the west end, the Toledo Division, with headquarters at Fremont, operated the main lines west of Norwalk and Sandusky, the Gibsonburg branch, and local service on the Fostoria & Fremont. From its offices in Sandusky, the Sandusky Division controlled the Norwalk and Sandusky city streetcar lines and the Sandusky–Milan–Norwalk interurban route. Finally, the Lorain Street Railroad, based at the South Lorain carhouse, operated all LSRR and LSE-owned city and suburban lines at Lorain plus the Avon Beach & Southern branch. (Before 1919 the LSE's Cleveland Division had jurisdiction over the East Erie car line.)

Despite its one time self-awarded title of "The Greatest Electric Railway in the United States," the Lake Shore Electric was physically a very typical Midwest interurban — meaning mostly that it was lightly and economically built. In many locations it took advantage of existing rights-of-way, such as in streets, alongside highways, and over public bridges. And wherever they were located, Lake Shore tracks tended to roll up and down with the topography. Fortunately that topography was gentle, mostly flat, and open. Cleveland, in fact, really marks the last vestiges of the Alleghenies and the beginning of the Midwest's Great Plains, particularly in the territory close to Lake Erie. The major hurdles were the many rivers and streams which drained into the lake, usually running at right angles to the interurban's route; otherwise the terrain was mostly unchallenging and the track, if not always level, was usually fairly straight.

Except for the busy Cleveland–Lorain section and the suburban Lorain–Elyria branch the system was almost entirely single-track; double or single, all of it was unsignaled. Typically too, LSE interurbans entered their two terminal cities on the tracks of the local streetcar companies, 2.7 miles in Toledo and a lengthy 8.1 miles in Cleveland, via Clifton Boulevard. They also trundled down the main streets of many intermediate towns and cities — namely Lorain, Elyria, Vermilion, Sandusky, Norwalk, Bellevue, Clyde, Fremont, Gibsonburg, and Genoa. (Before 1918 the alignment through Huron also was laid in

At four locations the LSE overpassed major steam railroad lines on its own bridges. This one was located east of Bellevue and crossed the paralleling Wheeling & Lake Erie main line and New York Central (ex-LS&MS) Norwalk Branch. (W. A. McCaleb collection)

More common were grade crossings of railroad lines of all descriptions, ranging from busy main lines to industrial spurs. Here a westbound Niles car clatters over the New York Central's "Big Four" branch at Clyde in the early 1930s. The railroad line extended from Sandusky to Springfield, Ohio. Note the extra pole on the car's roof, a standard LSE practice to prevent delays when poles were damaged en route. (W. A. McCaleb collection)

streets.) LSE cars also never seemed far from a steam railroad crossing of one type or another, and highway grade crossings were innumerable.

Just as the Lake Shore's right-of-way was typical of Midwestern interurbans, so were its passenger stations — or lack of them. Economy was the ruling law in sheltering riders; in contrast to the high level of equipment and service, station facilities were mostly minimal and unimposing. At major towns and way points the company usually either rented space in a commercial building or included a waiting room and ticket office in a substation or some other such structure. Storefront ticket offices served passengers at Cleveland, Sandusky, and Toledo, as well as at Norwalk, Bellevue, Gibsonburg, and at Coulter's Drug Store on Detroit Avenue in the Cleveland suburb of Lakewood.

Elsewhere, several architecturally attractive brick substation structures also housed ticket offices and small waiting rooms. These stood at Vermilion, Berlin Heights, Monroeville, Hessville, and Genoa. The last three were inherited from the Toledo, Fremont & Fostoria and dated to that line's construction in 1900; Vermilion and Berlin Heights followed their pattern and were built in 1903. (Berlin Heights had been altered after a 1919 fire.) A 1918 station-substation built of moulded concrete block served Huron, a product of the Huron cutoff project which replaced another storefront facility in the center of town on Main Street north of Homan Street.

But the LSE's most impressive "passenger station" was the large Beach Park carhouse, which also housed passenger facilities originally designed to serve the company's lakefront park just to its north. Built by the Lorain & Cleveland in 1897, its elaborate fortresslike north facade, facing the tracks and park, included decorative brickwork, a long row of arched upper windows, small end parapets, and the station name carved in stone on a large central parapet.

Riders transferring at Ceylon Junction could escape the winter Lake Erie winds inside a solid moulded concrete station built in 1911; across the track (and also fronting on the Lake Road) was a picturesque, privately owned building selling sandwiches and refreshments. Gibsonburg Junction passengers waited in a similar but smaller structure built in 1913. Wooden stations of various heritages and aesthetic virtues also accommodated passengers at Clyde, Castalia (both former dwellings), Lorain, the Soldiers Home, and Wood-

(*Above*) Several LSE substations also doubled as passenger stations, such as this attractive former TF&N structure at Monroeville. In this 1914 photo, agent Williams is throwing the manual derail protecting the Baltimore & Ohio Railroad crossing to allow an eastbound car to pass. (W. A. McCaleb collection)

(*Below*) Another station-substation combination served Berlin Heights. Originally similar to Monroeville, it was damaged by fire in 1913 and rebuilt. Niles Car 149 is westbound for Norwalk and Fremont in 1935. (Ralph H. Sayles photo)

(*Above*) The Beach Park station and carhouse was the operating center for the LSE's Cleveland Division and once also served the company-owned lakefront park. Westbound 176 handling a Lorain local stops at the 1897 structure about 1936. (Karel Liebenauer photo)

(*Below*) Looking west in August 1934, the 171 is ready to leave while line car 453 (the onetime Sandusky & Interurban's *Delta*) and crew wait in the clear. (Ralph A. Perkin photo)

ville. Otherwise, LSE local passengers braved the elements or, at best, huddled in small three-sided shelters — some of them provided by real estate promoters or property owners.

The LSE's 1923 main line schedules represented the railway at its peak form. Every hour on the hour, locals left Cleveland, alternately destined to Lorain or to Toledo via Norwalk. Limiteds left every hour on the half hour. Again, half of them terminated at Lorain; the alternate limiteds ran all the way to Detroit via Toledo. The Detroit runs consisted of at least two cars, which split at Ceylon Junction and rejoined at Fremont. Three-car limited trains were often necessary, usually on the trips leaving at 9:30 a.m., 11:30 a.m., and 1:30 p.m. In these cases, the first car ran to Detroit via Norwalk, the second car to Sandusky only, and the third to Toledo via Sandusky. Cars of the Detroit United Railway regularly appeared on the Detroit limiteds, which took six-and-a-half hours to make the full trip. By 1923 at least one of the two traditional through limiteds to Lima and Wapakoneta had been replaced by a direct transfer at Fremont, but there is evidence that the 7:30 a.m. departure from Cleveland still carried a through Fremont–Lima–Fort Wayne car running via Sandusky.

To handle these schedules and the various other short-turn and branch line runs, the Lake Shore fielded 66 interurban cars of varying types and ages. These included 19 of the original turn-of-the-century Barney & Smith–built cars inherited from the Toledo, Fremont & Norwalk, one of the original Sandusky & Interurban Jewett-built combines, nine of the original ten deluxe 1903 Brill combines (including a Kuhlman replacement), one of the 1904 Stephenson coaches, 15 of the 19 1906–07 Niles wood coaches, four of the five wood Niles combines, the two "Lima Route" Jewett wood combines, and 15 steel Jewett coaches dating to the 1915–18 period. This fleet was supplemented by 18 Detroit United cars used in the Detroit limited pool.

Local riders could usually expect one of the old, austere, and rugged Barney & Smith cars; the Brill and Niles combines also were assigned as needed, especially for runs carrying express, newspapers, and the like. Limited trains typically consisted of the wood Niles and steel Jewett multiple-unit coaches and their DUR counterparts. The two multiple-unit Niles combines were added on summer Saturdays for extra seating capacity. Car 44, a rebuilt ex-Sandusky & Interurban Jewett combine, was the faithful regular on the Gibsonburg shuttle. The Sandusky–Milan–Norwalk branch used one wood coach and one combine from the pool of local-service cars, and the 1904 Stephenson car 72 usually held down service on the Avon Beach & Southern.

The roster of city and suburban cars was almost as large as the interurban fleet. Between the Lorain Street Railroad and the LSE's own city lines, the system required a total of 50 such cars — 23 for the LSRR and 27 for the LSE. By 1923, 16 little single-truck Birneys had taken over most of the Lake Shore's Sandusky routes, although two of the original 1901 Brill single-truckers creaked along on the West Monroe line. Lorain was a melting pot of new, old, and secondhand double-truck cars owned by both the LSE and Lorain Street Railroad. The LSRR's Lorain–Elyria trunk line rostered an intriguing mix which included five former Lorain & Cleveland Brill cars from 1896, five former Cleveland Railway Brill city cars, five wood Kuhlman suburban cars from 1906, five 1918 Jewett-built steel cars, and three trailers inherited from the old Lorain Street Railway. Two of these were peculiar Stephenson-built cars dating to the mid-1890s and one was an American Car Company product. Otherwise in Lorain the LSE assigned ex–Lorain & Cleveland 1896 Brill car 50 to the East Erie line and Kuhlman-built 54(II) and 57(II) to the Colorado Avenue–West Erie route. Former Atlantic City Brill cars 118–122 filled in on both routes and the Avon Beach & Southern branch. After the Oberlin Avenue line was acquired in November, some of the five former Cleveland Railway cars were assigned to that route. Finally, at the other end of the scale, Norwalk still had its 1898 Pullman-built car 101 plodding along alone.

The Lake Shore Electric of 1923 was still overwhelmingly a passenger carrier; freight traffic was still mostly a sideline, but a growing one. Total revenues from freight, express, milk, and carload switching amounted to only $480,000 while passenger revenues (excluding the Lorain Street Railroad) were $1.5 million. Furthermore, 66 percent of that freight

A lone local passenger
boards an eastbound car at
Hayes substation, alongside
Woodville Road east of
Toledo, while work motor
402 waits in the siding.
(Ralph H. Sayles photo)

income came from express handled by the Electric Package Agency. The LSE's own less-than-carload and carload freight business was only just beginning to blossom. At the time the company had ten freight motors and 20 box trailers, plus the use of elderly rebuilt combines 41 and 43 for single-unit freight, express, and fish service. Interline freight traffic was developing, and "foreign" freight motors and trailers were regular visitors, particularly those of the Northern Ohio and the Detroit United Railway.

In all, the LSE was busy, relatively prosperous, and seemingly still strong. Competition from steam railroads was no worse than it had ever been and perhaps was less severe, since the railroads already were beginning to reduce their local and branch line services. Intercity bus lines barely existed in the LSE's territory, although jitney operators still were stealing city streetcar riders. But the shadows were now lengthening. Autos in particular were more clearly affecting the Lake Shore's income statements. As noted in the previous chapter, passenger revenues had peaked in 1920 but dropped 13 percent by 1922, which interurban officials partly ascribed to the postwar recession which began the year before. But although national prosperity returned, the interurban's passengers did not; 1923 turned out to be a bit better than 1922 for the LSE, but passenger revenues still were 11 percent below the 1920 level.

The new era was clearly visible from the interurban car windows. By 1923 most of the main highways in the Lake Shore's area had been paved and designated state highways: State Route 2 (later U.S. Route 20) was paved between Elyria and Toledo via Norwalk and Fremont. State Route 12 (later U.S. Route 6 and Ohio Route 2) was paved between Cleveland, Lorain, and Sandusky, and newly paved Route 101 linked Sandusky with Clyde. Lesser roads had been similarly improved or were then in the process. For example, paving was completed on State Route 30 between Norwalk, Milan, and Avery, although the balance between Avery and Sandusky was still unimproved. It soon would be completed and claim the LSE's earliest interurban predecessor as its victim.

In a typical LSE scene, Jewett Car 172 heads east at Stop 105, just west of Lorain. The Lake Road (U.S. Route 6) is at the left and Lake Erie is just to the right. (Ralph A. Perkin photo)

The view from an eastbound
Cleveland express as
Toledo-bound 169 passes at
Water Works siding on the
west edge of Lorain about
1937. (George Krambles
collection)

CHAPTER 7

TRANSITION

1923 – 1929

By 1923 the Lake Shore Electric was settling down from its World War I turmoil and inflation problems, although already it was facing new kinds of trauma. But those were not yet severe, and its management turned its attention to developing its newly emerging freight business and to upgrading its physical plant, most of which was some 25 years old by now.

Rebuilding and Reorienting: 1923 – 1926

The LSE's first order of business in 1923 was to purchase ten new box freight trailers. And as part of its freight expansion it built or expanded freight houses in Lorain, Vermilion, Norwalk, Clyde, Fremont, Woodville, and Castalia during the year. The following year it bought some land on the east side of Toledo from the Sun Oil Company for development as a new freight house and yard for interchanging freight with its various Toledo connections. Called Glendale, the new facility eventually enabled the LSE to handle freight interchange with its connections and its local shipments in a more spacious and uncongested off-street location. On the passenger side it also began a program of lengthening its wood Niles cars to 60 feet, but gave up after only two cars were completed.

Aware of the potential threat of motor bus competition, but nonetheless cautious and frugal, the Lake Shore's Fred Coen decided to set up a bus subsidiary — but made no immediate move to put it into business. On April 19, 1923, he created the Lake Shore Coach Company, then filed away the incorporation papers to await developments.

And indeed, by 1924 new bus operators at last appeared in the LSE's territory. At least three were in some form of business by the end of that year, most of them rather shakily. A company called the Cleveland–Elyria–Toledo Bus Company started in 1924 with seven 20-passenger buses and eight touring cars. At about the same time the Cleveland–Lorain–Sandusky Bus Company began running a menagerie of used buses and touring cars between its terminal cities, directly paralleling the LSE along the Lake Road. Finally, the Cleveland–Lorain Highway Coach Company operated a single bus over a southerly route between Cleveland and Lorain, using Detroit Road (present Ohio Route 254) and entering Lorain via South Lorain and Broadway. While this route did not challenge the LSE at intermediate points, it could serve passengers at a variety of downtown destinations in Lorain, whereas the interurban stopped at only one point.

The Cleveland–Lorain–
Sandusky Bus Company
began challenging the LSE
in 1923 and was later bought
by the railway. It had the
distinction of owning what is
believed to be the only bus
ever built by Clyde's Clydesdale Motor Truck Com-
pany, shown here when
new. When the LSE took
over the bus line in 1927, the
rugged but oddball Clydesdale was transferred to the
Lorain Street Railroad
where it worked as a line
truck until 1938. (Bruce
Dicken collection)

But Coen continued to concentrate exclusively on the railway line and spent considerable money to upgrade it, particularly bridges and street track. A major maintenance
problem was the large wooden trestle over Cahoon Creek at Bay Village on the old Lorain
& Cleveland line. In a complex engineering project which stretched over three years
between 1923 and 1925, LSE forces replaced it with a combination of steel girders on concrete piers while maintaining traffic on the constantly busy double-track line. The hurriedly
built former Sandusky & Interurban line west of Lorain also needed more attention. In 1923
the overpass over the Nickel Plate Road main line at Linwood, east of Vermilion, was realigned and replaced. This was followed the next year by new overpasses over the New York
Central main line at Slate Cut (east of Sandusky) and Ceylon on the Ceylon Junction–
Norwalk route — plus the LSE's single highway overpass at Wells Corners on the same line
and the bridge over Old Woman's Creek near Huron. (The ex-S&I line continued to give
the LSE grief, and in 1927 it found that it had to replace all of the poles on the Ceylon
Junction–Norwalk line.) In the same period, street track was replaced on a portion of East
State Street in Fremont (1923), Lodi Street in Elyria (1924), and in Lorain on West Erie and
on the newly acquired Oberlin route on 21st Street and on Washington (also 1924).

Paying for these and other needed improvements was becoming worrisome, however.
More so was the LSE's large bonded debt inherited from its predecessors and its own construction. Two large bond issues were scheduled to mature during the 1920s, the first being a mortgage of $1.6 million from 1903 which was due February 1, 1923. The company
was still profitable, but the margins were noticeably thinner and perceptive managers could

see a disturbing downward trend. During the all-time peak year of 1920, net income was $376,693. Following the recession dip of 1921, it had recovered to only $175,053 in 1922 and dropped slightly to $172,461 for 1923.

Faced with this situation, Moore, Coen, and the company's financial associates took three steps to generate capital, with varying degrees of success. First, the dangling sword of the 1903 bond issue was temporarily removed by extending the due date ten years, to February 1, 1933. At the time that seemed like it might allow a safe breathing space; obviously nobody then could know what 1933 would bring. Next, on May 14, 1923, the LSE's board approved creating a new issue of $2 million in 7 percent preferred stock in an attempt to reduce some of the debt and to finance new physical plant improvements. At the same time it authorized an additional $500,000 issue of its existing 6 percent preferred stock. The hope was that employees, customers, and on-line communities would buy to help support the line. It was a naive hope, perhaps. The LSE had not paid a dividend on any of its existing preferred stock since 1915, so it is not surprising that there was no enthusiasm for this new issue. The stock was never issued, and instead a more modest (and somewhat more secure) $800,000 bond issue was floated in 1924 to pay off some unsecured debt. This too was scheduled to mature in January 1933.

The final financial move generated immediate cash in addition to promising long-range economies. In 1923, the Lake Shore sold its lakefront Beach Park property in Avon Lake to the Cleveland Electric Illuminating Company for $300,000. CEI planned a large modern commercial power plant on the site, which, when complete, also would sell power to the LSE and replace the interurban's own Beach Park plant.

Lake Erie is not always noted for benign weather, and during its lifetime the Lake Shore battled more than its fair share of blizzards, ice storms, floods, and high winds. But June 28, 1924, brought the worst natural disaster yet — in fact one of the worst ever to be visited on the territory. Tornado-velocity winds swept across the western part of the lake, touching Sandusky, Cleveland, and Akron — but hitting Lorain dead center and devastating the city. Seventy-eight people were killed outright, many hundreds injured, and about 7,000 left homeless — one-fifth of the city's population. The Lorain police department, which at the time was reduced to a skeleton force because of municipal bankruptcy, could not maintain order, and National Guard troops were called in, supplemented by police from Cleveland and other nearby communities. Two trolleys were thrown off the tracks, including LSE city car 118, which was dumped onto its side on East Erie. Wire and transmission lines were down everywhere. Crews and equipment from the Cleveland Railway and Cleveland Southwestern were rushed to the scene to help repair the prostrate LSE and Lorain Street Railroad, but it was a week before normal services could be resumed.

The Lorain tornado seemed to usher in a string of fresh disasters. Two fatal accidents in 1924 marred the LSE's improving safety record. At Green Creek, near Toledo, conductor Clarence Keiser was killed when his work train derailed, and on October 23 a westbound car hit a school bus at Bennett Road, west of Beach Park, killing four children on the bus. The bus accident unfortunately dramatized an increasingly serious problem for the Lake Shore — the growing number of motor vehicles mixing with high-speed electric cars at the many grade crossings which, at best, were protected only by warning signs. Even worse accidents were yet to come.

Then, in March 1925, some unsettling news arrived: the Detroit United Railway had been put into receivership. Although there was little immediate effect, the future of a key LSE passenger and freight connection was suddenly in doubt.

Next came the fiery demise of the Lake Shore's Beach Park power plant, the last company-operated electric generating plant on the system. On August 23, 1925, a generator exploded and — fueled by a wood interior structure and accumulated oil and grease — the plant caught fire and burned down. The disaster not only crippled the LSE's lines east of Ceylon Junction but cut off power for many communities from Bay Village to Vermilion and Milan.

Lorain lies prostrate after the June 28, 1924, tornado. Both of these views look north on Broadway, the city's main street and the Lorain Street Railroad's main line, *(above)* from 4th Street (W. A. McCaleb collection), and *(below)* from Erie Avenue (Albert C. Doane photo). The car shown is LSE's second No. 54.

The Norwalk & Shelby Railroad succeeded the defunct Sandusky, Norwalk & Mansfield
and attempted to continue service with a pair of Elyria-built gasoline rail buses. Snow was
the least of its problems; spring had barely arrived in 1924 when the hapless line died.
(W. A. McCaleb collection)

The aftermath of the explosion and fire which wiped out the Beach Park power house on August 21, 1925, crippling the line's eastern half. The little single-truck switcher at the right, No. 405, had moved coal cars at the plant. (Ralph H. Sayles collection)

The loss came at just the wrong time. Although the Cleveland Electric Illuminating Company had bought the Beach Park site two years earlier, its new plant — which was to supply power for the LSE — was not yet complete. After a frantic scramble, the Ohio Public Service Company's Lorain plant and Sandusky Gas & Electric temporarily filled in, and a semblance of normal operations was restored within 72 hours. It was no simple job, however, since the deceased power plant had produced 25-cycle power, which was now obsolete; by then all of the commercial utilities generated at 60 cycles. As a result, substations in the territory had to be quickly re-equipped with 60-cycle converters from the Cleveland Railway and defunct Cleveland & Eastern. One positive outcome was that the Lake Shore collected some much-needed cash in the form of a $192,000 insurance settlement.

Also in 1925 the company finally took its first steps toward rationalizing its rail system. First to be shed was the Avon Beach & Southern branch between Beach Park and South Lorain. Although this line was originally built to give the LSE a competitive route between Cleveland and Elyria, it was never really exploited as such and long before had devolved into a one-car shuttle between Beach Park and South Lorain — essentially nowhere to nowhere, with nothing in between. Operation was suspended March 31, 1925, and the next day most of the property was turned over to a Cleveland Electric Illuminating Company subsidiary called the Avon Railroad, which intended to use parts of it to provide steam railroad access for CEI's new Beach Park (Avon Lake) power plant then under construction. The LSE kept a short stub on 31st Street at the South Lorain end as a branch of the Lorain–Elyria route. The Lake Shore received $250,000 for its unwanted orphan, another welcome cash infusion. Between the original Beach Park property sale to CEI, the insurance money from the power house fire, and the AB&S sale, Coen had collected a healthy $742,000.

Five months later he got rid of a lesser nuisance, the East Erie local city line in Lorain. Another one-car operation, this old and weary little Toonerville route was doomed by a street repaving project. On September 6 it became the LSE's first bus substitution. Possibly to avoid franchise problems, however, Coen still did not activate his dormant Lake Shore Coach Company and instead operated the new service with three newly purchased buses directly owned by the Lake Shore Electric.

Otherwise, the Lorain operations received a substantial boon in 1925 when the long-boiling controversy over jitney competition was resolved. Finally upholding a 1923 Lorain city ordinance, the Ohio State Supreme Court ordered the vehicles off the streets effective July 6, 1925. The displaced operators then tried to organize themselves as the Lorain Motor Coach Company, but the voters rejected the ordinance allowing its operation by a two-to-one margin. The LSE's victory paid off; patronage on the Lorain Street Railroad had dropped 23 percent between 1920 and 1925, but by 1928 it had climbed back almost to the 1920 level again.

The big steel Jewett interurbans of 1917–1918 essentially completed the Lake Shore's interurban car purchases, but the need for some more modern city cars continued. In 1924, five former Cleveland Railway steel Peter Witt–type cars were added to the Lorain Street Railroad roster, replacing two of the three 1890s-era trailers and releasing equipment for use on the Oberlin Avenue line. The next year three secondhand single-truck Birneys were bought from Baltimore to replace Norwalk's 1898 relic and the last of the 1901 Brills on Sandusky's West Monroe line.

The LSE bought its first buses in 1925 to convert its East Erie Avenue route in Lorain. Two came new from White and this one, the B-3, was a secondhand White built in 1922. (LSE photo, John A. Rehor collection)

(*Above*) Steel Jewett 173 stops at Vermilion's combination station-substation on its way to Detroit in February 1927. The station (which was eventually adapted as a bank) is at the far right. Note the train order semaphore at the curb. (Frohman Collection, Hayes Presidential Center)

(*Below*) The LSE's final expansion came in early November, 1923, when it took over the Oberlin Avenue streetcar route in Lorain from the bankrupt Cleveland Southwestern. Lorain Street Railroad 88, a much-rebuilt former Cleveland Railway open car, works the new acquisition about 1925. (Black River Historical Society collection)

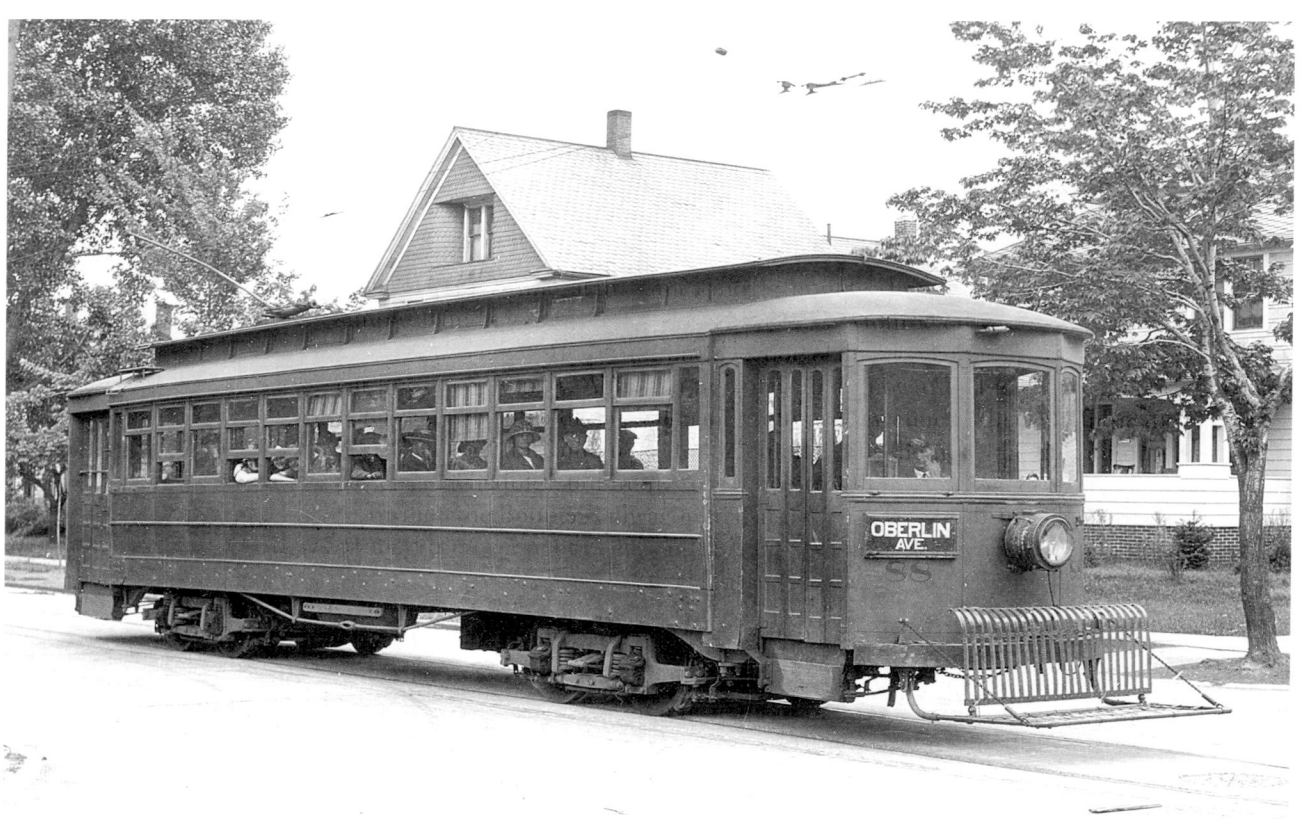

More physical improvements came in the mid-1920s, although the major ones were the result of local civic improvements rather than the railway's needs or initiatives. After several years of planning, Fremont replaced its picturesque multi-span 1877 State Street iron truss bridge over the Sandusky River with a new concrete arch structure. In the process, Coen inevitably was involved in delicate negotiations with the county commissioners over how much the LSE would contribute. Initially the company was expected to pay half the cost; eventually this was worked down to $10,000 in cash and a yearly rental of $1,000. The LSE's double-track operation was phased in during 1925 and 1926.

Similarly, in 1926 the city of Sandusky started work on a new underpass to eliminate the busy and highly dangerous three-way grade crossing of Columbus Avenue, the New York Central main line, and a Baltimore & Ohio Railroad branch. The construction work was to last two years and necessitated temporarily severing the Lake Shore's Columbus Avenue track, which carried both interurbans and city cars on the Soldiers Home Belt line. New track connections were built at the Soldiers Home to allow interurban and freight trains to use Milan Road as the eastern access to the city.

By the mid-1920s the Lake Shore's safety campaigns had helped to get its accident rate under control, and there were few subsequent serious wrecks which could be blamed on operational failures. But the Undergrade crossing west of Lorain had one last say. Early in the morning of March 6, 1926, motorman Edgar Crump lost control of his eastbound four-car freight on the "S" curve and piled up into the Nickel Plate bridge abutment. Crump and his conductor, Herbert Courtney, were crushed in the wreckage and cremated by a fire started by the freight motor's stove. Freight motor 36 and a Northern Ohio trailer also were lost to the fire.

But if the LSE had its own operations under tighter control, the grade crossing accident problem became relentlessly more lethal. The interurban followed two of Ohio's busiest highways, the Lake Road (later U. S. Route 6) along the lake shore and the later U. S. Route 20 west of Norwalk. In addition, LSE motormen skimming along at 60 mph faced at least one crossroad every mile and numerous driveways. The casualty list began to mount: On November 10, 1925, an interurban hit an auto at present Ohio Route 4 east of Bellevue; the driver was killed and 27 people injured when the interurban derailed. Two were killed at Bay Village March 23, 1926, when an LSE car hit an auto in dense fog. Then on July 20 a 16-year-old girl driver and her father were killed coming out of their driveway in Clyde. Early August saw three people killed at the Lake Road crossing east of Vermilion on August 4 and an auto and its camping trailer demolished at Monroeville August 7 — happily with no fatalities to the seven family members in the car and its trailer.

New Hands at the Helm — But Whose? (1926 – 1927)

As the year 1925 was waning, so was the Everett-Moore era on the Lake Shore Electric. The financial group which had created the company and nursed it through several crises now seemed ready to give up and cash in. Henry Everett already had been gone over eight years; in failing health, he had moved to California in early 1917 and died there that April at age 60. Barney Mahler died at 73 in March 1924. And now Edward Moore found himself following Everett's path. The LSE's co-promoter and longtime president was 61, also infirm, and was spending most of his time in California. (In fact, he had less than three years to live; he died in May 1928.)

Furthermore the syndicate itself had to decide its future in the interurban business. Gradually its holdings had dropped away through sales and bankruptcies. By the end of 1925 its interests in such major operations as the Northern Ohio Traction & Light, the Toledo system, and the Detroit United Railway were gone, and what was left had dubious futures. The syndicate's Cleveland, Painesville & Eastern was losing money, although not yet bankrupt, and the group decided to let it go before things got any worse. It was shut down May

20, 1926, leaving the Lake Shore as the last of the old Everett-Moore properties still in the fold. The LSE was still showing a profit through the end of 1925, but the earnings trend was stagnant and the passenger traffic trend clearly was slipping downward. In 1926 the company would show its first deficit.

There was one bright spot — commercial power sales. In 1925 the company grossed $584,000 from selling electric power to commercial and residential customers in its territory, about 20 percent of the system's revenues. More to the point, this income had grown by almost 420 percent in the five years since 1920. Possibly as a prelude for a sale of the LSE system, at the end of 1925 the company incorporated this most promising part of its operations as a separate subsidiary, the Lake Erie Power & Light Company. At the time, the LSE not only sold its own power to numerous communities in its territory (Lorain and Sandusky were the primary exceptions) but shared ownership of Ohio State Power's Ballville plant at Fremont with the American Gas & Electric Company. It also owned three separate minor power companies — the Bellevue Illuminating & Power Company, Bellevue Light & Power, and People's Light & Power — which it merged into Lake Erie Power & Light in May 1926.

Over a 12-month period during 1926 and 1927 a sale of the Lake Shore Electric system was indeed consummated, but the transition turned out to be turbulent and, to an outside observer, mystifying and even bizarre. In bare outline, this was the succession of events:

First, at the LSE's January 1926 board meeting, Fred Coen abruptly resigned his position as vice president and general manager, and ostensibly severed his ties with the company. It seemed a jarring surprise. No reason was given for the sudden departure, nor were there any reports of internal management disagreements. Although Edward Moore was the LSE's titular president, Coen was really its full-time chief executive and had been for many years — and was well-respected both inside and outside the company. Furthermore Coen was certainly no management job-hopper; he was devoted to the Lake Shore Electric above virtually all else in life. Why would he suddenly and inexplicably leave? That was merely the first of several successive mysteries.

Left with no full-time chief executive or general manager, the Lake Shore then made another odd move. Rather than promote anyone from within the company's ranks, the directors brought in Charles S. Thrasher, president of the Youngstown & Ohio River, to take Coen's vice presidential duties; Thrasher in turn hired another outsider, Martin F. Ackerman, as general manager. Ackerman was once a dispatcher for the LSE until he left in 1908; currently he was manager of the Cincinnati & Dayton Traction Company. Both men, it turned out, were associated with a management firm run by Warren Bicknell, the onetime LSE president and Everett-Moore associate who then ran the Cleveland Construction Company. Thus the appointments had a temporary look about them, but the new team did not act like a caretaker management. Among other things it substantially restructured schedules, effectively doubling limited services between Cleveland and Toledo to meet bus and auto competition. It also made operating management changes; in January 1927 three of the four division superintendents were replaced, two of them with former motormen and one with a claims agent.

In the meantime, Coen reportedly became a vice president of the Cleveland Electric Illuminating Company, Cleveland's principal utility. While CEI had previously purchased the LSE's Beach Park property and was then preparing to take over power generation for the interurban, there was no corporate connection between the two.

On August 10, 1926, the LSE's new utility subsidiary, Lake Erie Power & Light, sold its commercial facilities and business in the area between Rocky River and Lorain. Much of the territory went to Cleveland Electric Illuminating (which supposedly was now Coen's new home) with some sold to Ohio Public Service, a subsidiary of Henry L. Doherty's Cities Service Company which served Lorain. (At this point readers should be reminded that Cities Service was by then a vast nationwide holding company, which controlled petroleum producers and some major electric utilities, including OPS and Toledo Edison. It was what in later times would be called an energy conglomerate, and survives today in somewhat different form under the name of Citgo. As a byproduct of its electric utilities acquisitions, Cities Service also owned several city and interurban electric railways.)

Then came the biggest surprise: On March 24, 1927, it was announced that Fred Coen not only was back but had personally purchased the Lake Shore Electric from the Everett-Moore interests for $200,000 cash and the assumption of all liabilities. According to newspaper reports, he was backed by unnamed associates which included "Philadelphia interests." The same reports mentioned that Cities Service had been interested in buying the LSE's electric power operations, but Cities Service flatly disclaimed any involvement and Coen emphasized that the Lake Shore was to be run independently and "without connection with other interests."

And that certainly seemed so. The new board of directors — usually a reliable indicator of who controls a company — was clearly independent and dominated by in-house LSE managers. Of the board's eight members, a majority of five — including Coen — were LSE line officers. A sixth member, Cleveland attorney Thomas H. Hogsett, was the sole holdover from the old Everett-Moore board and for many years had served as the company's corporate counsel. Coen, of course, replaced Edward Moore as chairman and president.

Thrasher promptly disappeared from the LSE and Martin Ackerman reverted to the ranks as a conductor, also working regularly as an extra dispatcher at Beach Park. Lewis K. Burge, Coen's longtime (since 1907) general superintendent, resumed his old position as the LSE's chief operating officer and also became a director. But the schedule changes made by the Thrasher-Ackerman regime were retained, as were two of the three recently promoted superintendents. Coen did reinstate Warren Gregg, the former Beach Park superintendent, whom Thrasher had retired.

Yet there was still something strange lurking beneath the surface. Anyone looking at Coen's internal mail might well have wondered who really controlled the company — but if so, they were left to wonder. Coen regularly referred all major policy and financial matters to someone named "A. Hayes, Esq.," at 65 Pine Street in New York City, for approval or further action. But oddly, no correspondence ever showed a corporate affiliation or title for Hayes and, in fact, nobody by that name was listed at the Pine Street address in city directories or telephone books. Nonetheless the mysterious and elusive Mr. Hayes obviously was critically influential in Lake Shore Electric management.

More curiously, the responses which came back to Coen on "A. Hayes's" letterhead never seemed to be signed by Hayes himself, but rather by various other shadowy individuals — most notably Paul R. Jones, G. G. Brownell, and R. E. Burger. None of these showed any kind of identification on their letters either. Were they clerks, perhaps, for the perennially preoccupied Mr. Hayes? Not quite. All were high-level Cities Service officers — Jones was secretary of the Cities Service Company and Brownell was its treasurer; Burger was general manager of Cities Service Power & Light Company, the holding company which controlled the conglomerate's electric utility companies. And indeed, the address of the spectral Mr. Hayes — 65 Pine Street — actually was the back entrance to 60 Wall Street, the headquarters of Cities Service.

So Cities Service was the Lake Shore's real buyer all along, and — although this is speculative — it seems likely that Coen's year-long absence was really a form of "detached duty" for the Everett-Moore group to negotiate and effect the sale secretly. But the big mystery still remains: why was this elaborate charade thought to be necessary? Cities Service control seemed to be more-or-less common knowledge both outside and inside the company. And during the late 1920s there was a gradual infusion of management people from other Cities Service properties, such as E. V. Emery from its Toledo subsidiary, who became the LSE's chief engineer. But the "A. Hayes" subterfuge was continued into the early 1930s and the true control situation did not become clear until after the LSE's bankruptcy in 1933.

Cities Service's mechanism for its Lake Shore control was a holding company called the Ohio Utilities Finance Company. Like the whole purchase process, this entity was hidden at first in the shadows, but through some means it acquired a large proportion of the LSE's securities. It was capitalized at $8.6 million, which apparently covered the initial $200,000 purchase price for the stock plus $6.2 million in outstanding bonds.

The precise original structure of Ohio Utilities Finance is unknown, since it was strictly an internal Cities Service entity with no publicly traded securities. But in late 1931 or early 1932 the company was "sold" to the two Cities Service subsidiaries in the LSE's territory — Toledo Edison, which took a majority five-eighths interest, and Ohio Public Service, which had the remaining three-eighths. This laid the foundation for the eventual breakup and transfer of the Lake Shore's properties, although that was not to happen for another seven years. In the meantime Ohio Utilities Finance funded the LSE's new Sandusky cutoff line, to be described shortly, and, as evidenced by the shadowy "A. Hayes" correspondence, it dictated the interurban's basic policies and financial commitments.

Changed Priorities: 1926 – 1929

Regardless of the ultimate interests of the Lake Shore's new masters, Coen (with Cities Service blessings) was committed to keeping the railway alive and struggled to adjust it to the changing environment. By the time of his "second coming" in early 1927, two patterns were clear: the interurban passenger business was steadily declining and probably would continue to do so. But on the other hand, freight was growing — so much so that the combined revenues from freight, express, milk, and mail were almost equalling passenger revenues. Lorain was its own special case, however. Thanks to the U. S. Steel plant and the city's other industry, local streetcar patronage was heavy and healthy. In the three years since the local jitney operators were put out of business in 1925, the Lorain Street Railroad's passenger counts had grown to the point where they now well surpassed those of the LSE's declining interurban lines.

This was not to say that Coen intended to ignore the company's traditional passenger markets. As just noted, the interim Thrasher management took some radical steps to stop the decline brought on by rubber-tired competition. By 1926 several intercity bus operators were threatening the LSE's long-haul Cleveland–Toledo–Detroit business. One was Cardinal Stage Lines, a Greyhound predecessor which operated between Cleveland and Detroit as part of a longer Chicago–Philadelphia route. Up until then the Lake Shore Electric had a substantial part of this business, except for the Detroit & Cleveland Line steamships. (At that time the New York Central had no direct train service between the two

The newly formed Greyhound system was a growing thorn in the LSE's side during the late 1920s, offering direct service between Cleveland and Detroit. A fleet of its new buses lines up at the Rainbow Gardens opposite their older competitor. (Frohman Collection, Hayes Presidential Center)

In an effort to hold its inter-city passenger business, the LSE refitted its Jewett inter-urbans with comfortable bucket seats during the late 1920s. The camera looks toward the rear of car 178, with the smoking section in the foreground. (Karel Liebenauer collection)

cities; passengers transferred at Toledo.) While initially not nearly as frequent as the inter-urban limiteds, the bus service was faster. Ohio refused to allow Cardinal to do any intra-state business, a blessing which the intercity bus company probably did not appreciate at the time. Relieved of the necessity of making a lot of intermediate stops, the buses could make very good time. Buses were improving very rapidly in this period, and were becoming quite comfortable, with individual "parlor car" seats and curtained windows.

By January 1927, or perhaps even earlier, the LSE's long-established schedule pattern of operating Cleveland–Toledo limiteds every two hours was doubled to hourly service. Every second limited went on to Detroit, and close connections at Toledo were made for those which did not. Perhaps surprisingly, this added service was accomplished at mini-mum expense. Traditionally, two-car trains had handled the two-hourly schedules, each manned with full crews; single cars operated the new hourly service with the same total number of crews. Coen continued this pattern, hoping to hold the more profitable long-distance market. He also began a program of refitting the big steel Jewett interurbans with more comfortable leather bucket seats and new flooring; eventually 15 steel cars along with two wooden ones were so converted. A new image was also tried. In June 1927 the LSE introduced a new diamond logo on the side of car 156 and applied it to various other cars during the next twelve months.

But at the same time Coen had to face up to what was happening to the local business, never much of a moneymaker anyway. Commuter traffic in the suburban area between Cleveland and Lorain was strong, and a similar but lesser business was developing east from Toledo. Elsewhere, however, local riders increasingly were using their new Model Ts and Chevrolets for the short hops from farm to town, a day at the beach, a visit to relatives, or whatever. In November 1927 he eliminated all through Cleveland–Toledo locals in favor of a revised pattern of shorter runs which tried to recognize these shifts. As part of this, in 1927 two old Barney & Smith interurban cars (Nos. 18 and 23) were rebuilt for double-end operation to establish a new Toledo–Genoa local commuter service. Double-enders were necessary because there was no turning wye or loop at Genoa.

Coen also finally recognized the role of the bus in solving his marginal short-haul and city service problems. Aside from the replacement of the East Erie route in Lorain with LSE buses in 1925 — which had been forced by the repaving project — the company so far had chosen to stay out of the bus business. Although the subsidiary Lake Shore Coach Company was created in 1923, it had slumbered so far as an inactive "paper" entity. On June 3, 1927, however, it came to life when Coen bought the operating certificate of the struggling Cleveland–Lorain–Sandusky Bus Company and its motley assortment of ten buses and touring cars. Initially Lake Shore Coach concentrated its services in the Cleveland–Lorain area with one daily trip as far as Sandusky, and between 1928 and 1929 it bought a fleet of new White and Yellow Coach buses to replace the inherited relics.

With Lake Shore Coach finally in place, Coen then went after some of his weaker rail lines. The first to go was the historic but otherwise problematic Sandusky–Milan–Norwalk branch, which needed trestle and track replacement work. The bus conversion was scheduled for April 1, 1928, but a late winter storm stopped the electric cars for good on March 29. He also negotiated a new franchise with the city of Sandusky allowing him to substitute buses for streetcars where needed. The franchise became effective July 9, 1928, and Coen wasted no time. On September 13 the lightly used and almost purposeless West Monroe line — which had become a local legend for its erratic service and ancient 1901 Brill cars — was abandoned save for a short section at its west end. Another change came on October 20, when the new Columbus Avenue underpass at the New York Central Railroad crossing was finally opened for streetcars. At that time the interurban and Soldiers Home streetcar line routings returned to Columbus Avenue and the redundant Hancock Street–Milan Road route was partly converted to a bus line and partly abandoned outright.

In the meantime another financial doomsday was averted in 1927 when a maturing Lorain & Cleveland bond issue was extended — to that magic date of early 1933 again.

Freight, however, rightly got increasing management attention. By 1928 the picture was all too clear. The LSE's passenger revenues (excluding the Lorain Street Railroad) had dropped from the 1920 peak of $3,286,353 to a dismal $902,016. On the other hand, the combination of freight, express, and switching brought in $884,196 — virtually the same as the passenger business, but still growing. By then the LSE was a key carrier in a far-reaching network of interurban freight services covering western Pennsylvania, Ohio, Indiana, and Michigan. Multi-car trains operated overnight to points like Detroit, Dayton, Fort Wayne, Akron, and Youngstown, providing a kind of expedited freight service that the steam railroads were unable to match.

Thus the mid- and late 1920s saw more freight equipment added, including the rebuilding of interurban passenger cars to freight motors and the purchase of new box trailers. Continuing a program begun in 1924, the company converted a total of five of the 1900-era Barney & Smith coaches to freight motors by 1926, and in 1926 also bought 20 trailers built to Central Electric Railway Association interline standards. With business still rising and taxing its equipment, it created six more freight motors in 1929 from its 1907 Niles-built passenger coaches and added 14 second-hand freight trailers from the already-defunct Michigan Electric Railway.

And in a move to improve the effectiveness and efficiency of their interline freight operations, the LSE, together with four partner lines including the Northern Ohio and the Penn–Ohio system, incorporated the Electric Railways Freight Company on November

(Facing page) Cleveland's Eagle Avenue freight terminal was an increasingly busy spot during the 1920s, serving all six interurban companies entering the city and the electric package agency. LSE equipment is prominent in both views, which date to about 1926. (Ralph H. Sayles collection)

Small-lot freight and express
was handled in combines
such as the 166, shown
loading what may be bar-
reled, iced fish at Fremont.
The truck is owned by
Elway Transit, a subsidiary
of the jointly owned Electric
Railways Freight Company.
(Ralph H. Sayles photo)

1, 1928. A trucking subsidiary, Elway Transit, also soon appeared. These agencies took over
both the physical and administrative work involved in freight handling and solicitation for
the owners, who then split the net proceeds among themselves.

While all this helped the Lake Shore handle its swelling business — and, it hoped,
added capacity for more — Fred Coen knew that it ultimately was just a holding action.
By the late twenties trucks were proving a potentially fatal threat, moving everywhere the
railway could not and picking up and delivering loads at the customers' doors. If the LSE
and its sister interurbans had any hope of holding and expanding their freight traffic, it was
essential to develop a method of combining truck and rail movement without transferring
goods between vehicles. Already two of Samuel Insull's Chicago interurbans had adopted
a trailer-on-flatcar system, but this required high clearances and was not suitable for the
Lake Shore.

Instead Coen decided to gamble on an ingenious and innovative invention of Colonel Joseph C. Bonner, a colorful Toledo entrepreneur, politician, and banker. The Bonner Railwagon
system theoretically promised a low-cost, operationally simple method of carrying truck trailers on rail cars, with none of the disadvantages of other container or trailer-on-flatcar systems.
Bonner, who turned 73 in 1928, had originally developed it in the 1890s and had been unsuccessfully trying to interest railways in his idea for well over three decades. But even this late in
life he was refining it and pushing it with enthusiasm, and reportedly it had caught the interest of Cities Service president Henry Doherty. In 1929 the Lake Shore ordered a prototype
Bonner flatcar and single semitrailer, intending to add more semitrailers and operate a full
commercial test. Unhappily, at that point Bonner balked over the contract and the additional
equipment and testing were temporarily deferred.

Despite its generally declining fortunes, the LSE continued to show modest faith in its
future by spending some money to improve its facilities. During 1929 it picked up four
interurban passenger cars at a bargain price from the defunct Michigan Electric Railway.
While these were to replace obsolete wooden cars, the primary aim was to rebuild them

with facilities that would attract more charter movements. As it turned out, only two would ever see service. Also in that year it replaced its double track line and switches on Columbus Avenue in downtown Sandusky between Water and Scott Streets. Track on 19th Street in Lorain was also renewed, including a passing siding, and the old span wire installation between Ruggles Beach and Vermilion was replaced with new mast arms.

One other type of improvement came through tragedy. The Lake Shore's increasingly perilous relationship with highway grade crossings and motor vehicles came to a catastrophic head early in 1929. During a blinding snowstorm on January 22 a Greyhound bus en route from Pittsburgh to Detroit approached the LSE crossing on old U. S. Route 20 east of Bellevue. Unable to see at the crossing, the bus driver stopped, got out to try to look down the track, then started across; the bus was hit broadside by LSE car 164 and 19 bus passengers were killed instantly or died later. Exactly one month later an eastbound car smashed into an errant gasoline truck near Genoa. Miraculously, nobody was killed this time, but steel Jewett car 175 was cremated in what could have been a disastrous holocaust.

Traditionally, these highway grade crossings had been protected only by warning signs. But with the growing motor vehicle traffic and simultaneously multiplying crossing accidents, the interurban had found itself under ever-increasing pressure to install automatic flasher-light protection at many of them. The first — and only one so far — had been installed in 1925 at Stop 126 at Vermilion-on-the-Lake, a particularly dangerous crossing of

One of the LSE's last major improvements was renewal of the heavily used track at the foot of Columbus Avenue in Sandusky, done in 1929. The track at the left is a temporary "shoofly" or runaround. (Frohman Collection, Hayes Presidential Center)

In 1930 the company proudly (if belatedly) displayed the new equipment it was rushing to install. The flatcar actually is well-car 408, originally built for hauling substation transformers. (Ralph H. Sayles collection)

the Lake Road (Ohio Route 2). But as a result of the Bellevue catastrophe the LSE was ordered to begin installing automatic warning flashers at its major grade crossings and obliged by carrying out a large-scale program during 1929 and 1930. Beginning in June 1929 with the Bellevue crossing the Lake Shore rapidly installed such signals at many points; by the end of 1932, 41 such crossings were protected, 18 of them in the territory between Rocky River and Lorain. All used the trolley-pole-actuated Nachod system, although the original 1925 installation first employed a railroad-style d.c. track circuit.

In any event, with growing freight traffic, perhaps the Bonner intermodal system, and continued national prosperity, maybe the LSE had some hope. Then, on October 28 and 29 the stock market crashed and the world changed.

(*Facing page, top*) Little remains of the Greyhound bus which met LSE 164 at the old U.S. Route 20 (now Bauer Road) crossing east of Bellevue January 22, 1929. (W. A. McCaleb collection)

(*Facing page, bottom*) An immediate aftermath of the Greyhound disaster was an order to install automatic electric warning flashers at busy LSE grade crossings. This array of signs and flashers protected an especially dangerous blind crossing of the Lake Road (U.S. Route 6) east of Vermilion. (Karel Liebenauer collection)

Looming behind tired-looking Barney & Smith Combine 5 is the Van Sweringen brothers' 1930 Terminal Tower building, Cleveland's new symbol — and a symbol of the LSE's frustrated hopes. Beneath the soaring tower is an elaborate interurban terminal the company would never be able to use. The interurban is making its terminal loop on West 3rd Street about 1934. (Ralph A. Perkin photo)

CHAPTER 8

THE END OF THE LINE

1930 – 1938

The stock market had taken a dive, to be sure, but most people believed it was only a temporary hiccup — perhaps a little worse than in 1921, but nothing for serious concern. Even so, interurban lines like the Lake Shore had much to worry about. On January 18, 1930, Fred Coen wrote his mysterious master, "A. Hayes," and began:

> The time is not far distant when the question of the future policy to be followed in regard to the Lake Shore Electric must be determined. In other words, whether this railway can be rejuvenated and rebuilt so that it would be the same as an electrified steam railroad and made a profitable institution or whether it is to be abandoned, or partially abandoned, and recover therefrom as much as possible in the way of salvage or sale as a going concern.

He went on to propose a consulting study to determine the LSE's fate. Coen then hinted at his own feelings by recommending the consultants who had helped Samuel Insull successfully rebuild and modernize his Chicago, North Shore & Milwaukee and Chicago, South Shore & South Bend — implying that perhaps the LSE might be made into "an electrified steam railroad." Whether or not there was any such hope, the letter clearly recognized that continuing to operate the system as it then existed was undoubtedly doomed.

"Hayes's" response is unknown, but in the end no study was made and no rebuilding was considered — hardly surprising considering the circumstances in 1930 and 1931. But neither was abandonment or sale considered. The Lake Shore was left to stagger along as it was, attempting business as usual in what turned out to be a rapidly disintegrating environment.

Minor Ups and Major Downs: 1930 – 1932

The disintegration was less visible in 1930 when the LSE made the decision to buy ten new lightweight steel city-suburban cars for the Lorain Street Railroad. Actually it represented less a faith in the future than a very attractive means of cutting labor costs. Although some single-truck one-man Birneys had filtered in from Sandusky for use on lighter lines such as Oberlin Avenue, most of the Lorain streetcar lines still used cars requiring a two-person crew. In addition, many were now old and expensive to maintain and operate. Only ten of the 27 cars used in Lorain–Elyria service could be rebuilt for one-person operation;

the remaining 17 would have fallen apart. As for financing, Coen worked out a lease-purchase agreement with the cars' builder, the St. Louis Car Company, which saved the LSE
from initially laying out most of the purchase price.

Coen also seemed determined to do everything he could to hold the Cleveland–Toledo
passenger business. Although new timetables issued in early 1930 inevitably contained cuts
in service to reflect the dismal economics, the Cleveland–Toledo–Detroit schedules not
only were left largely intact but several were speeded up. Lake Shore limiteds traditionally
had made the Cleveland-Toledo run in four hours and 20 minutes; now four round trips
— labeled "Fast Limiteds" — were scheduled for a breathtaking three hours and 45 minutes. It was the fastest ever attempted — a bit too fast, in fact, since ten minutes were added
to the running time in October. But the effort was continued for two years.

On June 28, 1930, LSE passengers and crews grinding through Cleveland's downtown
streets could snatch glimpses of the notables gathering for the formal opening of the Cleveland Union Terminal, the grand new railroad passenger station at the Public Square promoted by the Van Sweringen brothers and largely built by the New York Central. It was
the consummation of the Van Sweringens' 15-year struggle to bring the railroads, interurban lines, and a new rapid transit system directly to the city's heart — and perhaps one basis
for Coen's hope that the Lake Shore could be transformed. For inside the terminal was an
entire separate section to accommodate the Lake Shore Electric and the other Cleveland
interurbans, with elaborate concourses, stairways, and underground platforms.

Furthermore, the station's builders had provided a full right-of-way for rapid transit and
interurban use over most of the terminal railroad's line, including westward on the huge
Cuyahoga River viaduct. Combined with a separate right-of-way built earlier as part of the
Nickel Plate Road's 1915–22 West Side grade separation project, the Lake Shore now had

On October 27, 1931, LSE
officials and local notables
gathered to celebrate the
opening of the Sandusky
cutoff, the company's very
last construction project.
The new line along the
city's south side allowed the
abandonment of some costly
city trackage as well as
greater freight train capacity.
(Frohman Collection,
Hayes Presidential Center)

a potential direct high-speed entrance from West 98th Street to the new underground terminal at the Square. This in turn could be extended west to Rocky River alongside the Nickel Plate line to avoid city street running entirely.

But it had come too late. Now neither the LSE nor its surviving interurban sisters had the resources to lay track and and put up wire to reach the long-promised Valhalla. Although almost all the basic work had all been done, it could not be completed. The fully graded routes would lie fallow for another quarter century before they were finally utilized for the Cleveland Transit System's east–west rapid transit line. To the end, LSE cars continued to lumber through the streets, and the terminal's interurban section remained forever deserted and dark.

The Lake Shore did embark on one last major construction project, however — although once again the primary purpose was cost saving rather than service betterment. In Sandusky, interurban cars and freight trains fought their way in and out of the city over the streets, entering from the east on Columbus Avenue and exiting west to Fremont via Water Street and Tiffin Avenue. The routing was a hindrance to the growing freight traffic, since train length was limited to a motor and two trailers; half of the freights went over the Norwalk route to avoid the streets, sharp curves, and complaints from the city of Sandusky. Even more pressing, in 1930 the city announced a three-year plan to repave several of the streets on the route including Water Street and Tiffin Avenue, requiring the LSE to spend about $96,000 to rebuild its track and contribute to the repaving.

Several times earlier the company had talked about a bypass line around the city. Now, with the ability to substitute buses for the local routes on the affected streets, it felt the time had finally come. A new right-of-way was laid out which left the Columbus Avenue track

Facing the Van Sweringens' new Terminal Tower–Union Terminal–Hotel Cleveland complex, LSE No. 178 makes ready to leave for Toledo in July 1937. (Franklyn P. Kellogg photo)

Operating on the new Sandusky cutoff, an east-bound limited waits while its conductor walks ahead to unlock the derail guarding the Baltimore & Ohio Railroad crossing. Perkins Avenue is at the rear. (John A. Rehor collection)

at Perkins Avenue, followed the side of Perkins west along the southern city limits, then swung northwest on private track to meet the Fremont line at Venice Road west of Tiffin Avenue. The cost originally was estimated at $130,000, a sum the now-destitute interurban did not have and could never raise itself. Nonetheless it calculated a 16 percent return on investment by avoiding the repaving work and saving on maintenance and operating costs — plus the important intangible benefits of speeding freight service and increasing its capacity.

Despite the deepening depression Cities Service was persuaded, and Ohio Utilities Finance put up the money in the form of $125,000 in the stock of a newly created LSE subsidiary, the Sandusky Connecting Railway. Arrangements were completed in early 1931, and the new cutoff route opened on October 28 of the same year. Primarily because of a crossing squabble with the Baltimore & Ohio Railroad the final cost turned out to be about $150,000. On the day the cutoff opened, Lake Shore Coach buses took over the Tiffin Avenue streetcar line; at the same time the northwestern section of the Depot Belt line was simply abandoned. On November 11 the East Monroe city route was converted to bus, leaving the Soldiers Home line and a section of the Depot route as the only surviving street-car lines in Sandusky. Although the interurbans now used the cutoff, they continued to enter downtown Sandusky, following Columbus Avenue to the waterfront and then doubling back out the same route to the cutoff. Thus the new line did nothing to improve passenger schedules, but in the new scheme of things that was of lesser importance.

By then the Bonner Railwagon trial also was under way. Beginning September 1, 1930, a round trip overnight Cleveland–Toledo service regularly operated with the single prototype rail car and six semitrailers. Coen quickly pronounced it a success, and on January 29, 1931, he enthusiastically proposed to "Hayes" — that is, Cities Service — that a company be created to buy a large fleet of Bonner flatcars and semitrailers for lease to the LSE and other interurbans in the area.

Again the response has disappeared but nothing was done. The single flatcar and six trailers continued running into 1932 — but that year the Ohio PUC determined that the LSE needed a motor carrier certificate to operate the service, which it lacked. After a court battle the LSE capitulated and the Railwagon operation was gone by the end of the year.

The rejection of this potentially promising system is sad, but by then there was good reason to forget about substantial new investments in equipment or anything else. The red ink which first appeared in 1926 had become relentlessly redder through the rest of the decade; the 1926 system deficit of $13,398 had grown to $409,606 by 1929 — years when most American businesses were booming. By 1931 it reached an appalling $1,087,874.

Even more worrisome for the long term, the Midwestern interurban network was now quickly collapsing, which was especially ominous for the LSE's still-promising freight business. The first direct sign of trouble came October 1, 1930, when the Toledo, Bowling Green & Southern and the Toledo, Fostoria & Findlay both abandoned service. The TF&F linked the Fostoria & Fremont at Fostoria with the Western Ohio at Findlay and thus was essential to the "Lima Route" operations between Cleveland, Lima, and Dayton.

This strategic crisis spurred the now-shaky Western Ohio to work out a complete realignment of operations west of Fremont. On October 1 of that year interests associated with the Western Ohio took over operation of the Fostoria–Findlay section of the defunct TF&F, renaming it the Findlay, Arcadia & Fostoria Railway. At the same time the Western Ohio assumed complete operation of the Fostoria & Fremont. Passenger schedules between Dayton and Fremont were integrated, with two-hourly locals running through via the Dayton & Troy–Western Ohio–FA&F–Fostoria & Fremont route. All the F&F and Western Ohio two-man lightweight equipment was converted to one-man operation and pooled with four newly built Dayton & Troy lightweights for the service. (For peak loadings the Western Ohio's original two-man Kuhlmans and one 1911 Jewett car, WO No. 199, were used until the end.)

The TBG&S and TF&F abandonments also affected the Lake Shore indirectly. The Western Ohio had depended on the Toledo, Bowling Green & Southern for its own interline freight traffic to and from Toledo. With both it and the Toledo, Fostoria & Findlay gone it was stranded at Lima. Relationships between the LSE and Western Ohio were somewhat strained since the LSE and newly-formed Cincinnati & Lake Erie had attempted to make exclusive freight agreements in the Western Ohio's territory, but the Lake Shore nonetheless came to the WO's aid. "Lima Route" freights between Dayton and Toledo were routed via Fostoria and Fremont, then used LSE trackage rights between Fremont and Toledo. This arrangement lasted until the end of the Western Ohio, which came soon enough.

Next came a serious direct hit. On July 1, 1931, the Northern Ohio system ceased carrying freight, closing off connections to such industrial markets as Akron, Canton, Massillon, and Youngstown. With it too went the rationale for the jointly owned Electric Railways Freight Company, and the almost-new agency was dissolved. The following year the Northern Ohio abandoned its entire system.

Freight motor No. 43(II) with the LSE's last bright hope, the Bonner Railwagons. The single flatcar holds three 18-foot semitrailers. Note that their highway wheels rest below the flatcar's frame, giving the equipment a low profile impossible with conventional trailer-on-flatcar systems. The Bonner system was successfully used for two years but was finally killed by legal, not technical, problems. (George Krambles collection)

The financial condition of the vital Eastern Michigan–Toledo railroad connection is plainly evident in this view of tattered EM-T Cars 7086 and 7092 at Detroit. Helping to keep the line going is a steel LSE Jewett at the far left. (Ralph A. Perkin photo)

At the same time, the critical link to Detroit was undergoing a chaotic decline. In the aftermath of the Detroit United Railway's 1925 bankruptcy, the Detroit–Toledo line had emerged in September 1928 as the Eastern Michigan–Toledo Railroad, but was in trouble from the beginning. Beset by financial problems and lack of equipment, it attempted to abandon its line in April 1931 but was stopped by legal action from the Lake Shore Electric and Cincinnati & Lake Erie. It then promptly cancelled its interline passenger agreements with the LSE and C&LE and the through Cleveland–Detroit limited runs temporarily ceased and were cut back to Toledo. Then on June 18 the Eastern Michigan–Toledo went into receivership. The Lake Shore and C&LE paid for an appraisal of the property with the idea of buying it, primarily to preserve the freight entry to Detroit. Through passenger service resumed on July 20, partly because the EM-T was so short of cars that it had to use LSE equipment even for its own Detroit–Toledo services, but it was only a temporary breather.

And as the Detroit connection was entering its death throes, the Fremont–Fostoria–Lima route vanished. Back in the heady days of 1929 a Philadelphia-based utilities holding company called Empire Public Service had bought the Western Ohio, but by November 1931 Empire was in receivership and forced the Western Ohio to follow. Caught in the collapse, the affiliated Fostoria & Fremont went into receivership November 13, in this instance instigated by the LSE over unpaid power bills. On January 16, 1932, both the Western Ohio and Fostoria & Fremont gave up and ceased operations.

The anticipated bad news from Michigan came later that year. After more legal wrangling, the Eastern Michigan–Toledo finally received permission to abandon on September 21, 1932, and ran its last car October 4. By then, the Lake Shore was left as the last of the six interurban companies once radiating from Cleveland.

Service — which had been progressively reduced during 1930 and 1931 — was drastically cut again with the September 6, 1932, timetable. Cleveland–Toledo expresses now departed every three hours, rather than two-hourly; the vaunted "fast limiteds" disappeared entirely, as did many local runs. By then the Cleveland–Toledo "expresses" essentially were handling most remaining local services west of Lorain.

Physically, however, the Lake Shore system remained intact with only one minor exception: on June 11, 1932, the outer end of the Colorado Avenue city line in Lorain was abandoned without replacement, since the Cromwell Steel plant at its terminal no longer existed and planned new homes in the area never appeared.

The deepening gloom was punctuated by one human bright spot: on August 24, 1932, motorman William Lang was nearing Lorain when he was horrified to see a 22-month-old girl on the track ahead of him. Lang instantly threw his brakes into emergency, scrambled out of his cab onto the car's front fender, twisted down and snatched her up. His heroism won him a Carnegie medal and a special Interstate Commerce Commission award personally given him by President Franklin D. Roosevelt. The girl, Leila Jean Smith, grew up and remained a friend the rest of his life.

Motorman William Lang poses in Cleveland with Lila Jane Smith and her father after his heroic rescue. Somehow, Lang was able to scramble out of his cab and onto the car's front fender to scoop the girl off the track. Note the Bonner Railwagon trailer at the far left. (Richard Krisak collection)

Bankruptcy

Beginning July 1, 1932, the Lake Shore Electric started defaulting on the various bond issues covering itself and several of its subsidiaries and underliers, as their interest came due. Furthermore, it also had to face what promised to be a major financial crisis early the following year. During the 1920s the maturity dates of various bond issues for the LSE and some of its underliers had been extended as they fell due, in effect postponing the day of reckoning. As a result, outstanding bonds totaling over $5.7 million were all now scheduled to mature in the period between January 1 and February 1, 1933. Clearly there was no prospect of refinancing or extending them further, much less paying them off.

The inevitable finally came on October 5, 1932, when the Ohio Utilities Finance Company moved to put the Lake Shore Electric into bankruptcy. Ohio Utilities Finance, of course, was a stand-in for Cities Service; this holding company — by then jointly owned by Toledo Edison and Ohio Public Service — essentially controlled the railway and was its major creditor. Technically, the action was taken by Chase National Bank of New York as trustee for Ohio Utilities Finance in Federal District Court for the northern district of Ohio. Named in the suit were the Lake Shore Electric, the Lorain Street Railroad, the Sandusky, Fremont & Southern, and the Union Trust Company of Cleveland, the trustee of most of the LSE's various mortgages. Three LSE subsidiaries generated sufficient cash flows for themselves and thus escaped inclusion in the bankruptcy proceedings — the Lake Shore Coach Company, Lake Erie Power & Light, and the Sandusky Connecting Railway. (The Connecting Railway built and owned the recently completed Sandusky cutoff. Lest anyone wonder how it remained solvent, it had been financed through a stock issue taken by Ohio Utilities Finance, and had no significant debt as such. It covered its expenses from rental payments from the LSE.) Elway Transit, the onetime Electric Railways Freight Company trucking subsidiary, also was excluded — as was the Electric Package Agency, which by then essentially was strictly an LSE entity, but also still surprisingly solvent.

Almost three months passed before the court formally declared the company bankrupt on January 30, 1933. From then on the interurban became the ward of Federal Judge Paul Jones, who named LSE president Fred Coen as receiver. The appointment signaled a "friendly" bankruptcy, which essentially maintained the LSE's existing management at all levels.

Coen faced a bleak outlook. Revenues for the year 1933 were only one-third of the 1929 level — and 1929 itself had been a discouraging year; they were less than one-quarter of the peak year of 1920. Indeed, the company had already recognized that its rail operations probably were ultimately hopeless — particularly its passenger business.

Even so, Coen was determined not to liquidate immediately and to try to ride out the immediate effects of the Depression, which by then had become the worst that the country had experienced. Not the least of his motives was a strong desire to protect the employees at a time when outside job opportunities were minimal and pension rights nonexistent. Already the LSE had the germ of a bus operation and, with luck, could eventually expand it to replace its rail lines — although some major legal and financial hurdles had to be overcome. Thus the cars ran for over five years more as Coen struggled through the transition — while at the same time maintaining rights to its physical properties, which were valuable for its public utility creditors.

Inevitably there was a human cost. During the 1930–1932 period there were substantial layoffs and job consolidations as train services and maintenance were trimmed — but so far the basic wage and salary rates of the survivors were untouched. In May 1933, however, these were slashed an average of 23 percent across the board. Some classes of workers fared even worse; interurban motormen, for example, were cut 31 percent, from 58 cents an hour to 40 cents. Track laborers received only 29 cents an hour.

The Last Struggles: 1934 – 1936

Committed to rail operations — for the time being, at least — Coen moved to improve the schedules somewhat. The Lake Shore's June 18, 1934, timetable brought back the two-hourly Cleveland–Toledo expresses — which, although now also covering various local stops, still covered the full distance in the traditional four hours and ten minutes. But making the time safely became an increasing challenge to crews as track and wire maintenance was pared to the absolute essentials.

Niles Interurban 143 looked clean and well-kept as it passed Linda Street in Rocky River on its way to Cleveland, but the right-of-way was another story. (Louis Szakas photo)

It also became necessary to purchase several short but key pieces of trackage which the LSE used, but which were actually owned by the now-defunct Cleveland Southwestern and the Fostoria & Fremont. On May 19, 1934, the LSE took title to the Cleveland Southwestern's tracks on Broadway in Lorain between 21st and 28th Streets and a segment on 21st between Reid and Broadway. The Broadway section was especially vital since it had formed part of the Lorain–Elyria route since 1919; the 21st Street piece was used by Oberlin Belt cars. At Fremont, Coen bought the downtown wye track from the Fostoria & Fremont's receiver on March 28.

Despite his efforts to preserve jobs by keeping the company operating, Coen soon faced labor problems. The 1933 wage cuts were borne for a while, but in August 1934 the employees threatened to strike. Coen responded with a letter sent personally to every LSE worker, stressing the dire financial situation and the general disintegration of the Midwest interurban system. Should a serious service interruption occur, he warned, the property would have to be immediately abandoned. He offered to speak with anybody at any time, unions or individuals, and finished with this heartfelt plea:

> Most of you know that I have been connected with this property during practically its entire period of operation. It has been my hope that these railroads could be kept going through this depression and that four hundred and fifty employees could be kept on the payroll, thereby providing the necessities of life for the employees and their families, totaling directly about 3000 people and indirectly many more.

It was touch and go, but no strike occurred. Coincidentally, Congress passed the first version of the Railroad Retirement Act in late 1934 and after some changes it finally became effective March 1, 1936. Thanks to Coen's extended balancing act, many LSE workers were covered under the new government-backed pension system. (Technically the LSE was an "interurban" and not a "railroad," but somehow Coen was able to qualify it under the law. Cincinnati & Lake Erie employees also were covered by the Railroad Retirement Act.)

Most critical to the LSE's future as a rail carrier was its freight business, which had grown substantially during the 1920s and was contributing an increasingly large share of the company's revenues. By the time the Lake Shore entered bankruptcy in 1933 many major interline freight movements were lost, including all routes south and east of Cleveland, everything routed through Fremont and Lima, and everything in Michigan. But oddly enough, freight revenues continued to grow.

Two promising connections remained at Toledo which still gave access to many key markets in the Midwest. Most important was the Cincinnati & Lake Erie, which could handle traffic to Columbus, Dayton, and Cincinnati; in addition the C&LE reached Indianapolis and other points on the extensive Indiana Railroad system via the Dayton & Western Railway at Dayton. The Toledo & Indiana line between Toledo and Bryan, Ohio, also had developed into a busy connection after the demise of the Fort Wayne–Lima route. In 1932 the LSE and T&I had teamed up to provide a fast less-than-carload service between Cleveland and Fort Wayne, Indiana, using a truck connection between the T&I's Bryan terminal and Fort Wayne. From Fort Wayne, the Indiana Railroad took the freight to and from Indianapolis and Louisville.

Freight was still a major contributor to LSE revenues in 1936 when Cincinnati & Lake Erie motor 634 brought three box trailers eastbound across Detroit Road in Rocky River that June. (W. A. McCaleb photo)

But sadly the freight business was proving fully as vulnerable as the passenger side — perhaps more so, since it depended heavily on its western network connections over which it had no control. The first blow came May 2, 1934, when the LSE lost its direct track connection with the Toledo & Indiana. Toledo's local streetcar company, Community Traction, had converted its Dorr Street car line to trolley bus, removing the T&I's entry into downtown Toledo and forcing it to cut back all operations to its Vulcan station in West Toledo.

More freight trauma followed. In Cleveland the downtown freight terminal at East 9th Street and Eagle Avenue had thus far survived with the LSE now its sole tenant. Located in the heart of the retail district and in the city's geographic center, it was at a strategically strong spot to draw traffic. But on April 4, 1935, the LSE's access route over Cleveland's rickety Central Viaduct was abruptly cut off by the bridge's condemnation. Frantically the LSE and Cleveland Railway cobbled together a roundabout and awkward alternate route via the Clark Avenue viaduct, which necessitated using the equally shaky Kingsbury Run viaduct on East 34th Street. That lasted only until April 26, when LSE freight trains were ordered off of the 34th Street structure.

The next stopgap site was the Cleveland Railway's East 34th Street storage yard just south of the forbidden bridge near Trumbull Avenue, which had been built in 1923 for Shaker Heights cars but closed in 1930. Barney & Smith combine No. 16 was moved to the site as an office. But this was also unsatisfactory, and in the end the Cleveland Railway built the Lake Shore a new freight house at its Rocky River yard in Lakewood, over seven miles from the city's center. The new facility opened August 1, 1935; afterward the LSE had to truck its freight to and from this extreme west-side location.

In Sandusky, a street repaving project doomed the Hayes–Depot city line, the surviving remnant of the old Depot Belt route. The change to bus was made July 1, 1935, at absolute minimum cost. The two Birney cars operating the line were replaced by a single bus brought over from the Lake Shore's Cleveland–Lorain bus route, a weary 1924 White which had been in storage since 1932. Repainted for its new service, the reincarnated veteran, No. 157, chugged on until 1938. The conversion left the Columbus Avenue–Soldiers Home route as the sole Sandusky city line.

Things brightened slightly in 1936. Riding improved by 14 percent over 1935 and almost 50 percent better than dismal 1933. In fact the Lake Shore actually showed a slim operating profit of $24,000 — but of course this did not include the accumulated bond interest which had been unpaid since 1932. By 1936 this amounted to almost $800,000. Much of the improvement came from the Great Lakes Exposition in Cleveland, although increased steel mill employment helped the Lorain Street Railroad. But needless to say, equipment and roadway maintenance continued to be Spartan; the unpainted cars looked increasingly shabby and rode roughly on the deteriorating track.

An indication of the nature of the Lake Shore's passenger business in its last days was provided by Felix Reifschneider, a traction enthusiast and professional street railway manager who traveled extensively on the interurbans during the 1930s. Describing a November 1937 trip on the LSE from Toledo to Cleveland, he noted: "There might have been 20 or 25 passengers on board leaving the terminal, but by the time we were a mile or two beyond the Toledo city limits, there were exactly three passengers on board and no one was picked up until we reached Fremont and a few more at Sandusky. I was the only through passenger from Toledo to Cleveland." For all practical purposes, the line's traffic now consisted mostly of short-haul commuter and suburban business in the area between Cleveland and Lorain — from communities the Lake Shore had been instrumental in developing. The Lorain city lines, fed by the city's slowly recovering industry, contributed an especially large share of the company's traffic. Finally, a modest commuter business had developed east of Toledo. But in between there was little left. During the final years Coen consistently tried to persuade the Cleveland Railway to take over the line as far as Lorain, but to no avail.

It is about 1:25 p.m. on Superior Street in Toledo on July 20, 1936, and there is still some life left at the Union Interurban (and bus) Depot. Cincinnati & Lake Erie 117, one of the famous high-speed lightweight "Red Devils" loads for a limited trip to Springfield, Ohio, while LSE 183 hulks behind waiting its turn to depart for Cleveland. (W. A. McCaleb photo)

The End of Hope: 1937 – 1938

The dreary downward slide resumed in 1937, spurred by a disheartening national economic recession. It proved to be terminal. On May 9 the Dayton & Western Railway was abandoned, removing the only freight link with the Indiana Railroad system and leaving the LSE and Cincinnati & Lake Erie to lean solely on each other for any freight traffic. They had little time to lean. Apparently heedless of how precarious their jobs now were, the LSE's Cleveland freight handlers picked this particular time to protest their low wages. On May 15 they went on strike. This time Coen did not plead; instead he swiftly announced that all freight service on the Lake Shore was finished. No more revenue freight trains ever rolled. The effect on the Cincinnati & Lake Erie was catastrophic; shorn of its vital freight interchange at Toledo, it abandoned its entire 138-mile Springfield–Toledo division on November 19 of that unhappy year.

The end was now nearing for the Lake Shore Electric itself. By mid-1937 it was finally decided to begin liquidating the various LSE properties and terminating the bankruptcy. Again, however, it was an "in-house" liquidation in that the properties initially went directly into the hands of the Ohio Utilities Finance Company — which effectively meant Toledo Edison and Ohio Public Service. The basic plan was to turn over the LSE's commercial electric power business to the two utilities along with the rail rights-of-way for transmission line use. The rail lines were considered hopeless as such — but efforts were to be made to continue operating the transportation system with motor buses under the LSE's old management.

Thanks to minimal maintenance, the LSE's main line began disappearing in a carpet of grass and weeds. Here car 151 skims alongside the McPherson Highway (U.S. Route 20) at Clyde in August 1937. (James P. Shuman photo)

Thus the stage was set for the last act — Lake Shore's final twelve months of active life. That final act, however, was fated to follow a complex and sometimes confusing script, with some unanticipated twists, suspenseful pauses, and fast on-stage improvising. To accomplish the aims of the LSE's owners, two separate major tasks had to be carried on simultaneously: First, the legal and corporate mechanisms had to be put in place to transfer the Lake Shore's properties and dissolve the company; at the same time the legal rights had to be established to operate buses in the LSE's territory. The corporate job was fairly straightforward and simple since it was mostly a matter of moving assets between the pockets of the owners. But the bus situation was another matter.

Electric railway fans flocked to the dying Lake Shore Electric during its last two years. In one typical outing, members of the recently formed Electric Railroaders Association posed with their chartered car 170 at Beach Park on August 1, 1937.
(W. A. McCaleb photo)

Another such group rode 1903 Brill Combine 69 into Gibsonburg on a gloomy April 3, 1938. Sister Car 65, the regular Gibsonburg shuttle, waits behind. (Karel Liebenauer photo)

To take the corporate shuffles first, the initial step was a formal sale of the bankrupt companies. First to go was the Lorain Street Railroad. On June 23 Judge Jones ordered the company's sale; on August 2 it was sold at Lorain County courthouse in Elyria to Ohio Utilities Finance. E. V. Emery, the LSE's chief engineer, became its titular operator. Sale of the Lake Shore Electric and its SF&S subsidiary was set for December 2, but was postponed a month. When it finally took place on January 4, 1938, the buyer for both properties was once again Ohio Utilities Finance. In the interim the LSE had petitioned the Public Utilities Commission of Ohio (PUCO) to abandon its rail lines, and the commission gave its blessings August 25, 1937. But the actual abandonment had to await resolution of the bus operating rights problem — which was proving messy, as will be described in a moment.

Interestingly, as the LSE entered its terminal year, another institution had just been born and was rapidly growing — the organized railroad enthusiast movement. During the railway's last two years, photographers and "last chance" riders flocked to it from everywhere in the country, often chartering excursions.

In addition, several even went beyond recording the death throes and made a serious, if ill-fated effort to save the line. In February 1938 five Cleveland-area enthusiasts put together a proposal for LSE employees to buy most of the interurban lines for $350,000. Their slimmed-down system consisted of a Cleveland–Norwalk–Toledo main line with a stub-end branch from Ceylon Junction to Sandusky, thus omitting the Lorain Street Railroad and the Sandusky, Fremont & Southern. An operating plan was developed which included buying lightweight passenger cars for an improved Cleveland–Lorain service, while keeping the old steel Jewetts for Cleveland–Sandusky and Cleveland–Norwalk–Toledo services. Several enthusiastic meetings of employees were held at Beach Park, Sandusky, and Fremont, but the financial realities quickly doomed the idea. Among other things, a $176,000 loss was projected for the first year and major expenditures were needed for track upgrading and several other capital projects. (As will be explained later, by then the line was severed at Bellevue by a new underpass project; this would need to be restored too.) Within a month the plan was dropped.

Unfazed by this diversion, the LSE's owners began the process of putting their railway out of business. First the corporate structure was reshuffled. In early 1938 Ohio Utilities Finance — which by then was wholly owned by Toledo Edison — was liquidated and the LSE's physical properties passed directly to Toledo Edison. The Lake Shore Electric as a corporation passed out of existence in March, although its cars were still running. Obviously uninterested in running the doomed railway itself, Toledo Edison leased operation of the line to Lake Shore Coach Company as an interim expediency. Ownership of Lake Shore Coach itself went to the Cities Service holding company which controlled Toledo Edison. Toledo Edison also inherited Elway Transit, the trucking subsidiary which had been passed down from the old Electric Railways Freight Company. Through all this, Fred Coen and the LSE's other officers and employees remained working at their customary jobs, although now concentrating on converting the railway to a full bus operation.

To do so was not a simple matter of stopping the trains one day and starting buses the next. Up to that point the LSE's legal right to operate buses was limited to certain specific routes and communities, not its entire system. So, while the corporate liquidation was proceeding, Coen also had to establish clear — and hopefully exclusive — state regulatory permits and local franchises where he lacked them. As of early 1937 the LSE's bus subsidiary, the Lake Shore Coach Company, had "interurban" operating rights only between Cleveland, Lorain, and Sandusky — an inheritance from the old Cleveland–Lorain–Sandusky Bus Company it bought in 1927. (Its earlier Sandusky–Norwalk permit was sold to another operator in 1931.) It also had a city franchise in Sandusky, but not Lorain. In Lorain, the LSE itself operated buses on the old East Erie route, a minor line with a dubious future; otherwise all of the routes were still rail and operating under street railway franchises.

The first necessity was to create the corporate vehicles to cover the areas where the LSE or Lake Shore Coach did not have existing bus rights — namely the remaining Lorain local routes and the interurban lines west of Sandusky and west from Ceylon Junction via Norwalk and Bellevue. On August 2, 1937, Lake Shore Coach set up a new subsidiary called Lorain Transit Company, Inc., to operate all replacement bus services in the Lorain–Elyria area — which included both the Lorain Street Railroad and the LSE-owned city car routes. And on August 25 it established still another company, Lake Shore Coach Lines, Inc., which was to operate the former LSE interurban routes west of Sandusky and Ceylon Junction. (The distinction between the Lake Shore Coach Company and Lake Shore Coach *Lines* was confusing enough in itself. But it was a distinction without a difference; the two entities were necessary for financial and legal reasons, but were intended to operate as one.) Specifically, Lake Shore Coach *Lines* would cover the route from Ceylon Junction to Toledo via Norwalk and Fremont; a second LSCL route would connect Sandusky with Clyde. Combined with Lake Shore Coach Company's earlier Cleveland–Sandusky rights, this would effectively provide a slightly modified version of the traditional LSE Cleveland–Toledo alternate routes via Sandusky and via Norwalk. The Gibsonburg branch was purposely forgotten.

Lake Shore Coach also received PUCO permission to buy and finance 17 new buses for its various routes and subsidiaries — eight interurban-type for Lake Shore Coach Lines, five interurban-type for Lake Shore Coach Company itself, and four city buses to supplement those already used on the Sandusky local lines. Lorain Transit purposely delayed any new bus commitments for reasons that will be seen.

But establishing the rights was not so simple. Other bus operators were anxious to enter the LSE's territory and, in fact, already had a foothold. Back in March 1937 the Ohio Public Utilities Commission had allowed Central Greyhound Lines and Buckeye Stages to handle local passengers in the Norwalk–Toledo territory. (At the time, Central Greyhound was allied with the New York Central Railroad, and it in turn owned 20 percent of Buckeye Stages.) Lake Shore Coach protested and on August 29 the Commission reversed itself, permitting the LSE's future successor to operate the bus replacement. Greyhound and Buckeye Stages then took the case to the Ohio Supreme Court, which scheduled hearings beginning February 16, 1938. That put the rail-to-bus transition in limbo until the case could be heard and decided.

In the midst of this a combined legal, financial, and operating problem came up right in the center of the disputed Norwalk–Toledo territory. Bellevue, located between Norwalk and Fremont, had begun building a highway subway in the center of town to eliminate the busy and dangerous Main Street grade crossings of the Nickel Plate Road and Pennsylvania Railroad. The LSE, which used the street, was required to stop operating at the site for 50 days and also pay $10,000 to have new track installed and paved in the underpass. Since abandonment of the rail line was now a foregone conclusion, there clearly was no reason to pay the $10,000 to re-establish the line once the project was finished. In fact, the 50-day service suspension normally would have precipitated immediate bus replacement for the entire interurban route through the area. But the timing put Coen and Judge Jones in a quandary. LSE's bus operating rights were uncertain, and until the Ohio Supreme Court case was settled, it had to maintain the rail operation — and, presumably, pay the $10,000 to maintain its rights.

As a result a makeshift operation had to be put together to maintain the semblance of through rail service between Norwalk and Fremont. On November 15, 1937, the rail line at Bellevue was cut and split into two segments operated by shuttle cars. Two double-end cars were assigned to work between Ceylon Junction, Norwalk, and the east end of the Bellevue underpass at East Main and McKim Streets; one single-end car covered the balance of the route from the Bellevue wye on West Main Street to Fremont. By December 1st, however, traffic congestion and a bad accident at the East Main–McKim terminal caused the east-end shuttle cars to terminate their runs at the Bellevue city limits where

the track entered East Main Street. Taxis were used to ferry passengers between the various temporary Bellevue terminals. The 50-day operating moratorium ended January 4, 1938, but the LSE obviously did not pay the $10,000 to restore its track and the patchwork shuttle-transfer arrangement continued. Ironically, the Norwalk–Bellevue end of the shuttle operation was worked by the same Barney & Smith cars which had first worked the route for the Toledo, Fremont & Norwalk. In this case, history made a complete cycle.

At about the same time, Norwalk city officials considered preserving their one-trolley city "system," using power from the municipal light plant. They did not think long after looking over the track condition on West Main Street.

As noted earlier, in late 1937 the PUCO gave Lake Shore Coach Lines permission to buy eight new buses for the anticipated interurban replacements. Gambling that it eventually would win its case, LSCL ordered the new vehicles, and by January 1938 three had arrived on the property — Yellow Coach Model 739s carrying 23 passengers. Coen decided to take a chance and put these in service between Ceylon Junction, Norwalk, and Fremont as quickly as possible, and on Sunday, January 23, they began running over the route on the interurban car schedules. But as a hedge against the uncertainties of the pending rights case, he also continued to run the rail cars on identical schedules — giving elaborately duplicated services for few passengers. Not surprisingly this lasted only two weeks; effective February 7 Judge Jones ordered the rail service reduced to a single token franchise run — a morning round-trip service between Ceylon Junction, Norwalk, and Fremont. Because of the line break at Bellevue — which now was clearly permanent — two shuttle cars handled the schedule with (if needed) the taxi connection at Bellevue. For all practical purposes, the LSCL buses then took over all service on the route, legally or not.

Coen's problems on his Southern Division were not ended, however. On February 18, 1938, a severe ice storm hit the area, downing wires and poles and knocking out rail service on the Ceylon Junction–Fremont franchise shuttles and Norwalk's little city line. This seemed like the ideal time to give up rail operations over this section completely, but with the bus rights case still undecided Coen continued to be cautious. He ordered the damage repaired and resumed running the franchise shuttle cars and the Main Street service on March 3.

Work on Bellevue's new Main Street underpass is well under way in this scene shot August 28, 1937, but the LSE still could operate over the railroad crossings on a temporary track. Afterward the link was cut, severing the Norwalk–Fremont line forever. (Ralph H. Sayles photo)

(Above) With the line cut at Bellevue, the LSE was forced to operate shuttles over the two severed segments. On the east end, double-ended Barney & Smith cars ran from Ceylon Junction through Norwalk to this spot on the town's far east side, where passengers were taxied to complete their trips or connect with cars on the western end. This 1938 view looks east on U.S. Route 20, which curves to the right beyond the waiting taxi. (Ralph H. Sayles photo)

(Below) Lake Shore Coach Lines' 120 was one of three Yellow Coach (GM) Model 739s which supplemented and then replaced the interurban shuttle cars between Ceylon Junction and Fremont in 1938. The 23-passenger bus has stopped at Clyde. (Paul Jenck collection)

(*Above*) In a scene all too symbolic of the LSE's future, one of the Bellevue shuttle cars waits forlornly at Ceylon Junction during the winter of 1937–38. The car, Barney & Smith–built No. 23, had worked the company's entire lifetime, and more. (Karel Liebenauer photo)

(*Below*) While bus 120 is parked at the curb at Clyde, interurban 157 rolls past en route to Bellevue. (Ralph H. Sayles photo)

Norwalk's last "train" readies to depart town on May 13, 1938. Veteran ex-TF&N 18, one of the Ceylon Junction–Bellevue shuttle cars, has been coupled to the resident Norwalk City streetcar 115(II) with a drawbar to haul it back to Sandusky shop. Standing by his little Birney car is perennial motorman Fred Gassman, who had regularly worked the route since 1906. (Firelands Museum collection)

In April the Ohio State Supreme Court finally ruled for the Lake Shore and allowed the PUCO plan to go into effect, denying certification to Greyhound and Buckeye Stages. On May 13, 1938, the faithful little Birney car 115 ran down Norwalk's Main Street for the last time; the following day the franchise shuttles between Ceylon Junction and Fremont ended. Barney & Smith car 18, which handled the eastern end of the run, hauled the Norwalk Birney back to the Sandusky shops on its final trip.

In the meantime, the planned bus replacement program in Lorain had become equally confused. As noted earlier, the LSE had created its Lorain Transit subsidiary to take over all existing local LSE and Lorain Street Railroad rail and bus routes within the city, including the Lorain–Elyria line. Here, however, the company had to deal with two different jurisdictions for its rights — the city of Lorain for a franchise for all routes within the city, and the PUCO for any portions outside the city. The state utilities commission was the easier of the two, giving Lorain Transit permission for an intercity route replacing the Lorain–Elyria car line. Since the rail route operated largely on private right-of-way (later paved over as Ohio Route 57), the replacement buses were to use Pearl Avenue. Lake Shore Coach Company also already had a PUCO certificate to operate between Lorain and Elyria over a more westerly route via Penfield Junction, which it had purchased earlier from the Cleveland Southwestern.

But the city of Lorain gave Coen an unpleasant surprise. Instead of routinely transferring the rail franchises to the LSE's new local bus subsidiary, the city fathers put them up for bidding from anyone who might want to run the services. Lorain Transit thus had to submit a proposal along with three other hopeful operators. Even more surprisingly, one of Coen's three competitors was a company called Employees Transit Lines, Inc. — purportedly a cooperative venture of 33 of his own employees of the Lorain Street Railroad and the Lake Shore Electric's Lorain lines. The city council then moved to approve the employees' proposal in what looked to the other bidders like unseemly haste. Some questions were raised about who was really behind the enterprise and how fully it represented the employees. Its primary financial backer was John W. Schmauch, a Lorain automobile dealer, who later became president; its first president also happened to serve as city treasurer. In any event, in early March 1938 — and at the behest of Lorain mayor George Bretz — the city council quickly awarded the franchises to Employees Transit and that was that. To be included were the Colorado–West Erie and Oberlin Belt streetcar lines, the city portion of the Lorain–Elyria route as far as 36th and Grove, and the East Erie bus line. The LSE's Lorain Transit was left with only the "interurban" section of the Lorain–Elyria line.

In the interim a street paving project made it necessary to convert the Lorain Street Railroad's short branch on 31st Street between Grove and Norfolk — the southern stub of the onetime Avon Beach & Southern. The changeover was made September 5, 1937, using a single bus on a 30-minute headway. Since the LSRR did not own any buses, it rented one from Lake Shore Coach Company or the LSE.

When it became apparent that Lorain Transit would not have the local bus franchise, officials of Employees Transit, Lake Shore Coach Company, and the Lorain Street Railroad sat down to work out an orderly transfer of operations. Employees Transit ordered 18 new Ford buses, but these would not be available until sometime in the spring of 1938. To show its willingness to start the conversion program, the new company borrowed a Ford demonstrator bus, which on March 11, 1938, replaced the Lorain Street Railroad's borrowed shuttle bus on the already-converted 31st Street line.

Ready or not, Employees Transit took over its second line three weeks later. Ohio bus registration renewals were due April 1, and on March 31 the Lorain Street Railroad announced that it would not re-register the three LSE buses used on the East Erie Avenue route. Employees Transit scurried around and leased one bus from the Elyria Coach Company in time to take over the route April 1. It then made almost daily announcements about the pending arrival of its new fleet of 18 Fords, but nothing actually happened until May 1 when it was finally able to convert all of the remaining Lorain routes and return its borrowed equipment.

That should have ended all local rail service in Lorain, but it did not quite. Lorain Transit, which was to operate the Lorain–Elyria intercity route, now also found itself with no equipment. As a result the Elyria cars staggered on for another week until Lorain Transit replaced them on May 8 with six antique 1928 and 1930 White buses leased from Toledo's Community Traction Company. By May 15, three of these were reassigned to cover some abandoned interurban services and were replaced by Lake Shore Coach equipment.

With its Lorain tangle resolved and all its local Lorain lines finally gone, the Lake Shore Electric readied itself for the last and largest event — the end of all remaining interurban operations plus the single surviving Sandusky city line, the Soldiers Home route. By that time, of course, the interurban bus operating rights case had been settled and ten 37-passenger Yellow Coach Model 742 buses were delivered to convert the Cleveland–Lorain–Sandusky–Toledo services. The previous three smaller Yellow 739s were to continue on the already-converted Ceylon Junction–Norwalk–Clyde line. Four new 21-passenger Yellow Model 733s were available for the Soldiers Home route in Sandusky. The last full day for all LSE rail services was set for Saturday, May 14, 1938.

And so it happened — mostly. Steel Jewett interurban No. 174, running as the 7:30 p.m. Toledo express, pulled away from Cleveland's Public Square on the evening of May 14 for the final revenue trip over the Lake Shore's full length; after arriving there at 11:40, it was returned to the Fremont carhouse. The final interurban run of any kind, however, was car 167 with the lowly midnight Cleveland–Lorain local, which actually struggled out of the Public Square at 12:41 a.m. on May 15. At the controls was James Trimmer, closing down his second interurban line.

That left the little Birney cars on Sandusky's Soldiers Home line, which were also supposed to cease running on May 14 but did not. Unlike Lorain, the LSE's franchise situation in Sandusky was clear and the legalities seemed simple. Its first move was to transfer the three bus lines it already directly operated — Hayes Avenue, East End, and West End

(*Above*) To replace the LSE's main-line interurban services, Lake Shore Coach bought ten Yellow Coach 37-passenger Model 742s, lined up here in Sandusky after delivery. (LSE photo, John A. Rehor collection)

(*Below*) The end. Ready for the last LSE interurban run, car 167 waits briefly at the Public Square station after midnight May 15, 1938, before heading into the longest night. (Bruce Triplett photo)

At the end of its run, Conductor E. R. Jamieson and Motorman James Trimmer dutifully but sadly pose for the requisite ceremonial handshake. (John A. Rehor collection)

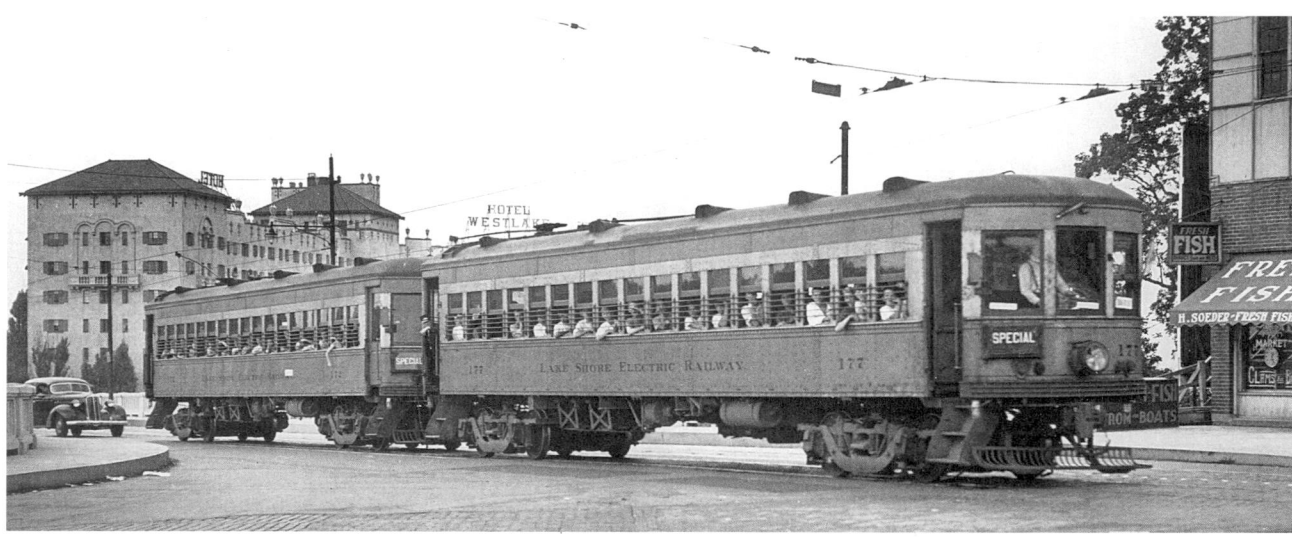

(Above) Charters and excursions continued to the end. In the summer of 1937 a two-car Lorain Boys' Club special comes off the Rocky River Bridge into Lakewood. (William R. Heller photo)

(Below) What is identified as the LSE's last freight train, a cleanout extra, leaves the Rocky River freight station in Lakewood on its way west. (William R. Heller photo)

— to the Lake Shore Coach Company. Since Lake Shore Coach had the franchise to run buses locally within Sandusky, it seemed that nothing more was needed to complete the process by motorizing the Soldiers Home line with the four newly ordered city buses. But in its rush, the company apparently forgot that the route's outer end, from Perkins Avenue to the Soldiers Home, was outside Sandusky's city limits and thus under Ohio PUC jurisdiction. No one had applied to the utilities commission.

After hurrying to do so, the company was allowed to make the bus conversion on May 25. But even then the Lake Shore Electric was not completely dead. On Memorial Day, May 30, three interurban cars and two Birneys emerged again to run special trips between downtown Sandusky and Oakland Cemetery. Afterward Birney No. 116 made one final trip to the Soldiers Home and, at last, it was all over for the LSE.

Or rather, revenue rail operations were over. But the Lake Shore Electric story was not.

CHAPTER 9

EPILOGUE

The Afterlife

One certainty during the LSE's last several years was that finality was a flexible concept. Nothing seemed to end cleanly or exactly as planned.

All Lake Shore Electric revenue services ceased May 15, 1938 — or May 25, or May 30, depending on one's preference. But even afterward, genuine LSE trains, with LSE crews, ran for another two years. Unlike many defunct interurban lines, the LSE was not turned over to commercial scrappers. Fred Coen remained very much on the scene, now managing the Lake Shore Coach Company and still responsible for the deceased but still-intact railway. Apparently under no pressure from Toledo Edison to vacate the rights-of-way, Coen decided that his own employees would dismantle the line themselves — thus keeping many of them employed for some time longer. For accounting purposes, all remaining rail employees were transferred to the Toledo Edison payroll on July 1, 1938, but during 1938, 1939, and early 1940 they regularly operated salvage trains with LSE work motors and line cars under Coen's management.

First to go were the two outer ends of the system. During the remainder of 1938 the Cleveland–Lorain and Toledo–Norwalk sections were dismantled, along with the Lorain Street Railroad and the Ceylon Junction–Norwalk branch. Freight motor No. 33 worked west from Rocky River, and leased Cleveland Railway crane car No. 0741 removed several of the bridges in this section. Line car 453 handled wire removal. Motor 31 and line car 455 worked their ways eastward from Toledo to Norwalk and Ceylon Junction.

Track and wire removal continued during 1939 and by the end of the year virtually all of the remainder of the LSE was gone. This included the main line from Lorain west to the Wagner quarry siding, south of Soldiers Home outside Sandusky, and from Sandusky shops to Fremont. Before the Sandusky–Fremont section was removed, however, it had a last fling of interurban operation — of a sort. In an effort to provide space for salvaging operations at the Sandusky shops and yard, the 1917 steel Jewett cars — considered the company's most salable equipment — were moved to Fremont and later moved back to Sandusky. During the dismantling operations west of Lorain an embarrassing incident occurred when crews accidentally dropped the LSE bridge into the Vermilion River, blocking pleasure boats and canoes and irritating Vermilion city officials.

Also in 1939, Coen cleaned up the corporate structure of his bus operations. On May 31, the Lake Shore Coach Lines and Lorain Transit Company were merged back into the parent Lake Shore Coach Company, putting all the onetime LSE routes in the Cleveland–Toledo territory under a single company.

LSE crews were kept employed as long as possible after abandonment. East of Bellevue Work Motor 401 and a maintenance gang winch up the rails for scrap. (Ralph H. Sayles photo)

(Above) By the time freight motor 33 paused by the boarded-up Beach Park station and carhouse in 1938, it had lived longer than the Lake Shore Electric itself. Built in 1900, the former TF&N motor was helping dismantle the Cleveland–Lorain section. One of the two main line tracks already has been lifted. (Karel Liebenauer photo)

(Below) The onetime Sandusky & Interurban shop complex at Sandusky had survived as a bus garage when this photo was made in October 1955. It has since been demolished. (John A. Rehor photo)

By 1940 one small vestige of the LSE still remained, an operating track between the Sandusky shops and the Wagner quarry siding south of the Soldiers Home on the former line to Cleveland, about two miles in total. This line connected at the quarry with a B&O Railroad spur and was thus used to ship out materials. Several cars were also moved to the quarry for stripping. Work motors 400, 407, and 410, line car 455, freight trailer 807, and six work flatcars remained on the active roster at this time. By late spring this operation ended, and the LSE was finally history.

Concurrently with scrapping operations, the company slowly disposed of its equipment. Again, the process was leisurely and was relatively unusual in that most cars were not cut up for scrap. The company, of course, hoped to sell at least its newer equipment for operation elsewhere. But the few potential buyers which remained were primarily interested in one-man lightweight equipment. Sadly, only three steel Jewetts found an operating home, on the Des Moines & Central Iowa; otherwise there were no takers for the interurban cars. Fifteen of the Lorain Street Railroad's newer cars found new homes, but that was the extent of any sales to operating companies. Of these, the ten 1930 steel suburban cars ended up back in the hands of their builder, the St. Louis Car Company, after payments on their trust agreement ceased. St. Louis promptly rebuilt and resold them to the Birmingham (Alabama) Electric Company, which gave them another eleven years of active life. Five former Cleveland Peter Witts went to the Indianapolis Railways and operated until 1947. Work motor 401 went to work at the Ohio Power Company's Ballville generating plant at Fremont, and Ohio Public Service bought sprinkler trailer 446 for its Toledo–Port Clinton interurban operation.

Aside from these few cars sold for further operation, most of the LSE's roster was spread across northern Ohio in the form of residences, summer cottages, diners, storage sheds, and the like. While the precise number probably will never be known, at least 77 interurban cars, freight motors, and Birneys — plus 46 freight trailers and three sweepers — were stripped of trucks and

Perry (Iowa) has replaced Toledo in the destination sign box of former LSE 180, now Des Moines & Central Iowa 1714, shown at its new terminal in July 1940. Among other changes, the DM&CI has added a baggage-express compartment, truss rods, and a locomotive bell. (George Krambles collection)

electrical gear and their bodies sold to private individuals and companies for continued use. As a result, more of the LSE's equipment survived — and survived longer — than any other interurban, albeit in humbled form. Many carbodies still existed in the late 1990s, six decades after the line's demise and far longer than they ever ran in service.

The year 1940 marked more than just the physical end of the Lake Shore. Soon after the last scrapping operations ended, Fred Coen finally retired at the age of 68. Coen had been more than merely the company's manager; Fred Coen and the Lake Shore Electric were one, beginning with that chance assignment in 1893 when, as a 21-year-old small-town banker, he was sent to oversee the predecessor Sandusky, Milan & Norwalk. By 1940 Coen had headed the company through its flush years and its decline; he had saved it as a transportation company, if not a railway, and had completed the job of dismantling his lifetime work. He lived less than two years after leaving, dying in Lakewood, Ohio, on January 24, 1942.

But the LSE itself, now in the form of Lake Shore Coach Company, continued to soldier on. Soon, though, it was pulled away from its roots. On September 9, 1943, most of the system was sold to Harry W. Arnold, president of Ohio Rapid Transit, Inc. Ohio Rapid Transit was a holding company controlling several city and intercity bus operations in an extensive territory primarily in central and southern Ohio; it was linked to the Lake Shore through a route from Columbus and Newark to Sandusky. Afterward Arnold adopted "Lake Shore System" as the common marketing name for his growing collection of Ohio companies, although Lake Shore Coach and the other individual Arnold companies retained their legal names and properties. Lake Shore's Sandusky city routes were split off and incorporated as a separate Arnold subsidiary, Sandusky Rapid Transit Company — although Lake Shore Coach retained the Soldiers Home route, which extended outside the city limits. Arnold also adopted the Lake Shore's orange livery for his system, continuing the tradition begun with the interurban cars over 40 years before.

But less than six years later Arnold concluded that the Lake Shore Coach routes did not really fit his system, and decided to concentrate on strengthening himself in his original

The Lorain Street Railroad's five 1917 Jewett–built 95-series suburban cars went to the former LSE beachfront property at Sages Grove, east of Huron, where they and several LSE and Toledo cars served as summer cottages for Toledo Edison employees. (J. W. Vigrass photo, January 1955)

territory. At the same time, Greyhound still wanted its long-sought local-service rights between Cleveland and Toledo.

Thus another of the Lake Shore's many endings came on June 20, 1949, when Arnold traded off all his onetime LSE routes to Valley Greyhound Lines, a small and relatively new Greyhound subsidiary operating from Columbus into southern and southeastern Ohio. Valley Greyhound took over all the former Lake Shore Coach routes except the local Soldiers Home line in Sandusky, which once again had become the odd line out; it was turned over to Sandusky Rapid Transit. The Greyhound company also inherited the Lake Shore's 41-bus fleet and its garage in Lorain. Valley Greyhound was then almost immediately absorbed by Central Greyhound, the operator of the interstate routes in the LSE's old territory. In exchange, Lake Shore Coach Company absorbed several Greyhound routes radiating from Columbus to points such as Portsmouth, Pomeroy, Chillicothe, and Athens.

Sandusky Rapid Transit remained under Arnold's wing, continuing the last "Lake Shore Lines" presence in the LSE's old territory for another decade. It was finally sold to local interests August 2, 1958. But before it was, another kind of era ended when the company's superintendent, Frank C. Gilcher, retired. Gilcher symbolized Sandusky's entire local transportation history in human form. He was the son of Charles Gilcher, one of two brothers who started the city's first public transit service in 1882, a horse-drawn omnibus system which they called the Herdic Lines. Within six years the Gilchers' Herdic Lines was out of business, a casualty of the Sandusky Street Railway's horsecars. But young Frank let bygones be bygones and at age 18 he embraced the new technology; in 1896 he hired out as a conductor on the People's Electric Railway — which then happened to be run by his uncle, William Gilcher. By 1906 he was an LSE trainmaster at Norwalk and a year later became superintendent of the interurban's Sandusky Division, which included the Sandusky and Norwalk city lines and the Milan branch. Gilcher remained running the local streetcar and bus operations in Sandusky through the eras of the Lake Shore Electric, Lake Shore Coach Company, and Sandusky Rapid Transit until he retired at 73 in July 1951.

Elsewhere, "Lake Shore Lines" remained on Arnold's intercity buses, but now they no longer came near the lake shore except on charters. Only the name and their orange paint was left as a reminder of what had been. Like the Cheshire Cat, everything had slowly disappeared except the smile. Even that dissolved in 1974 when Lake Shore Coach Company went out of business after a long strike.

Travel in Lake Shore Electric Territory in the 1990s

When the Lake Shore Electric began life in 1901 virtually its only competition came from a multitude of steam railroad lines. Ultimately, some of these did not fare much better than the interurban against motor vehicles and their own economics. The onetime Lake Shore & Michigan Southern's Norwalk branch, which largely paralleled the LSE between Norwalk and Toledo, is gone, although the paralleling Wheeling & Lake Erie line remained intact. Sandusky's five rail lines shrank to two — the former LS&MS main line and the Pennsylvania Railroad's coal-carrying Sandusky branch, both of which were part of Norfolk Southern in 1999. Gone are the Lake Erie & Western line to Fremont and Fostoria, the New York Central's Big Four branch from Sandusky (Ohio's first railroad), and the Baltimore & Ohio's Sandusky branch. The former Nickel Plate Road main line remained active as another part of Norfolk Southern.

Thanks to the almost complete triumph of the automobile, public passenger transportation of all types has withered to only a few nominal services in much of the old Lake Shore Electric territory. Many former LSE communities have no service whatever. In 1997 Greyhound — financially unsteady itself — ran three daily round trips between Cleveland and Toledo, using Interstates 80 and 90 where possible. These highways were located to bypass every major community between the two cities, so there was no direct service into such points as Lorain or Sandusky. Instead, Greyhound buses stopped on the north side of Elyria at Ohio Route 57, which occupies the old main line of the Lorain Street Railroad. They also stopped at a point halfway between Sandusky and Norwalk, at U.S. Route 250 — which the original Sandusky, Milan & Norwalk followed. For reasons unknown they also made one flag stop each day in both directions at Huron, a town that even the LSE bypassed in 1918.

Portions of the heavily built-up area between Cleveland and Lorain were served in 1998 by two different public transit agencies. The Greater Cleveland Regional Transit Authority operated buses between Cleveland and Beach Park, although only a few rush-hour trips ran west of Bay Village. Between Avon Beach (from Lear Road west) and Lorain, the Lorain County Transit operated seven weekday trips on its East Route — which followed the route of the old LSE East Erie local line. On the west side of Lorain, Lorain County Transit's West Loop route covered the LSE's West Erie local line with nine weekday round trips. The route continued west along the Lake Road to the site of the LSE's Kolbe siding, and also covered most of the old LSE Oberlin Avenue line.

Lorain County Transit also still operated the Lorain–Elyria line, including the 31st Street branch — the onetime remnant of the Avon Beach & Southern. Ten weekday round trips, six Saturday trips, and three Sunday trips were scheduled over what was the Lorain Street Railroad's main stem.

Otherwise, the LSE's communities — including Vermilion, Norwalk, Bellevue, Fremont, and Genoa — were left to survive without any form of public transportation.

Sandusky was only slightly luckier. It had neither local nor intercity bus service, but rail passenger trains on the former Lake Shore & Michigan Southern main line continued operating almost one hundred years after the Lake Shore Electric first challenged them. As of 1999, Amtrak offered three trains each way between Cleveland, Toledo, and Chicago, two of which stopped at Sandusky's restored 1892 stone station — the same station where cars of the primeval Sandusky Street Railway once waited to take passengers downtown. Reaching this station was the reason that the Lake Shore Electric's earliest ancestor was created, so in a sense the story ends where it began. But while the building and a few trains still survive, almost everything else has long since slipped away.

Most LSE cars went to more mundane uses. The former 171 served steaks, sandwiches, and soft drinks in Monroeville in 1955. A large number of LSE carbodies still survived in the late 1990s. The 171, in fact, now reposes at the Seashore Museum in Maine awaiting restoration. (John A. Rehor photo)

PART II

THE ORIGINS

Helping to build the pioneering Sandusky, Milan & Norwalk interurban line in 1893 was this little onetime elevated loco-motive from New York's Manhattan Railway. The SM&N's route followed alongside public roads, but three trestles such as this were necessary to ease grades through various stream valleys. (Frohman Collection, Hayes Presidential Center)

CHAPTER 10

THE PREDECESSORS

1883 – 1906

The Lake Shore Electric's family tree dated back to the electric railways' equivalent of Pilgrim Father days and included some especially distinguished pioneers. Inevitably too, it was a complex assemblage of different personalities and lineages. At least ten different company names showed up at one time or another, but by the time the LSE was created in 1901 these had boiled down to four — the Lorain & Cleveland, the Toledo, Fremont & Norwalk, and two Sandusky-based companies, the Sandusky & Interurban and the Sandusky, Norwalk & Southern. A fifth, the Lorain Street Railway, joined the family in 1906.

Three of these had comparatively simple, straightforward histories, but the city of Sandusky seemed to spawn financial and corporate instability for its two railways — perhaps the result of too much competition in a stagnant and marginal market. Whatever the reasons, the Sandusky predecessors were both the oldest and the most complex.

Sandusky & Inter-Urban Electric Railway
Sandusky Street Railway

Sandusky's modest street railway system had its origin in the Sandusky Street Railway, a locally promoted horsecar line which was built primarily to connect its steamship piers and downtown area with the then-remote Lake Shore & Michigan Southern Railway station. The LS&MS main line was the city's primary rail route, and originally had entered town from the east along the waterfront. In 1872, however, it was relocated a mile south of the city's center, and reaching it became a hardship. The first solution was a horse-drawn omnibus line organized by Sandusky's Gilcher brothers in 1882. But even by then competition was brewing; another group of local businessmen headed by Clark Rude had incorporated the Sandusky Street Railway on August 3, 1881.

Nothing happened immediately. Rude and his backers had no intention of building the line themselves, but hoped to interest others in the project while rewarding themselves for their foresight through the sale of franchises and other rights. On May 8, 1883, they sold out to a group of Berea, Ohio, businessmen headed by Alson H. Pomeroy, who built it quickly and began operating that August. The route began on Columbus Avenue south of Water Street at the West House, Sandusky's principal hotel, and ran south to the depot via Columbus Avenue, Hayes Avenue, and North Depot Street.

The genesis of the Lake Shore Electric was this little horsecar line built by the Sandusky Street Railway in 1883. This contemporary view looks south on Columbus Avenue from the waterfront and Water Street, the car line's terminal. In the distance another car approaches. (Bishop photo, W. A. McCaleb collection)

Pomeroy and his associates then became interested in building a similar line in their home town of Berea and, needing capital for that, sold the Sandusky operation back to the local merchants in January 1885. (Pomeroy later founded the Pomeroy-Mandelbaum financial syndicate which built the Cleveland Southwestern and various other Midwestern interurban lines.) Jay O. Moss, a Sandusky banker, became president and Clark Rude was retained to operate it. Rude then proceeded to extend the route west on North Depot Street to Camp Street and back north into town via Camp, Washington Street, and Washington Row, forming a loop or "belt" route. The new line was built in two months and opened in July 1885. A year later a spur was built south on Columbus Avenue to the Erie County fairgrounds at Scott Street for seasonal service. The company owned seven cars and 28 horses, which operated out of a carbarn on the southeast corner of Hayes Avenue and North Depot Street.

By 1890 more competition appeared in the form of a newly incorporated (but as yet unbuilt) electric street railway, to be called the People's Electric Street Railway. Spurred by this threat, the horsecar company electrified its route in 1890 and extended it south on Columbus Avenue to the Ohio Soldiers and Sailors Home, a total distance of 3.5 miles from the downtown terminal on Columbus Avenue. It also built a crosstown feeder route from Columbus to Monroe and King Streets in the west end of town, using West Park and Monroe. Its new electric cars were lettered "Sandusky Electric Railway" although it is uncertain whether the corporate name was formally changed from Sandusky Street Railway. The People's Electric Street Railway finally appeared in 1892. When it did, Sanduskians distinguished the two companies by the color of their cars — the Sandusky Street Railway was universally known as the "Brown Line" and People's as the "White Line." In 1893 the Brown Line was listed as owning 12 single-truck motor cars and two trailers.

In 1897 the city put the Brown Line in receivership over an unpaid paving assessment, a portent of the poor relationship that developed between Sandusky and its street railways, which was inherited by the Lake Shore Electric and continued for the years to come. Clark Rude, then the company's superintendent, was appointed receiver.

(*Above*) Sandusky Street Railway open car 5 is working the Columbus Avenue–LS&MS depot line in the mid-1890s. (Firelands Museum collection)

(*Below*) In the mid-1890s early Sandusky streetcar competitors keep their distance from one another at the West House at the foot of Columbus Avenue. At the left on Columbus Avenue is Sandusky Street Railway No. 9; at right is People's Electric Street Railway No. 16, one of the company's unusual "convertible" double-deckers. (Frohman Collection, Hayes Presidential Center)

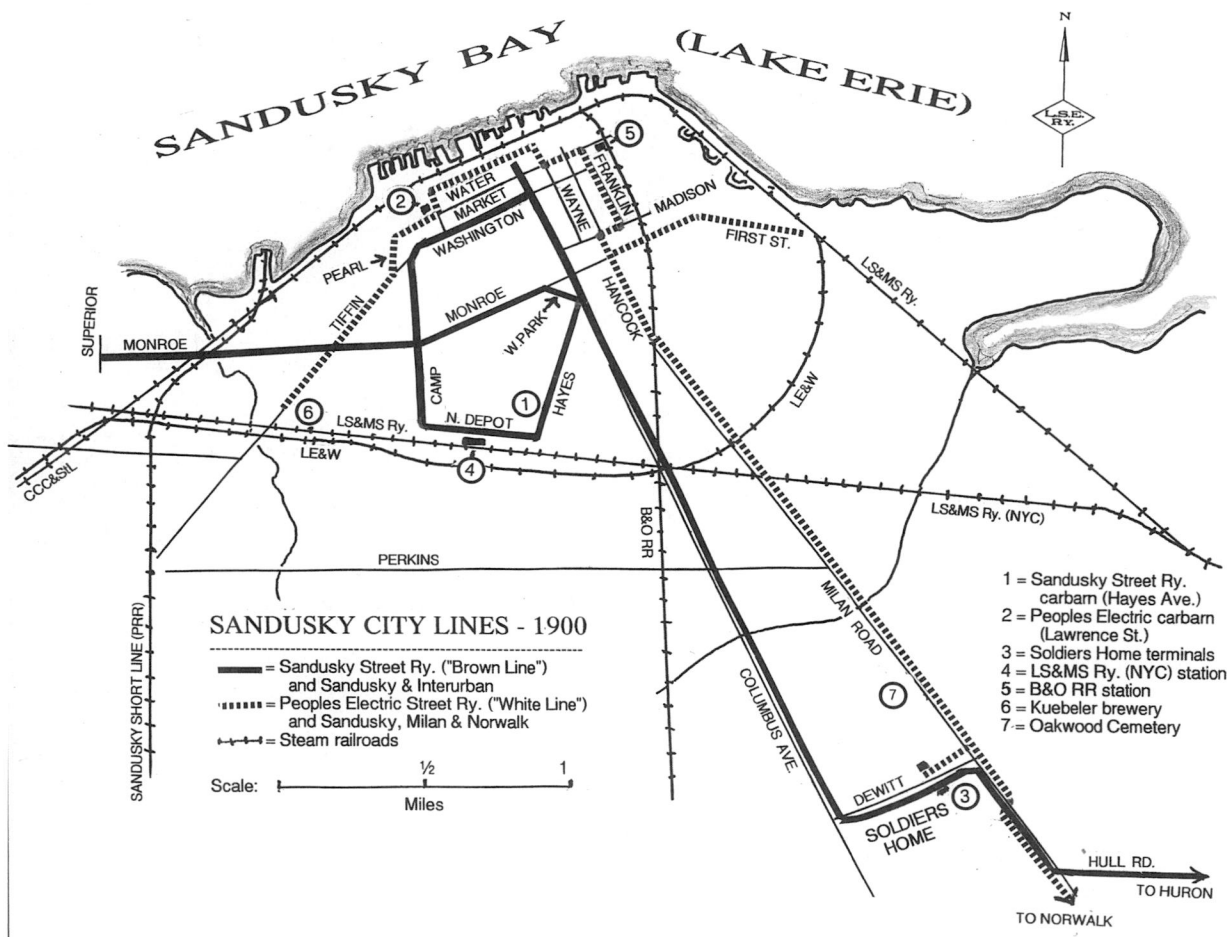

Sandusky city streetcar lines, 1900.

On July 9, 1898, Rude sold the property for $60,000 to Thomas Wood, an engineer and an early promoter of gas fuel and electric illumination in Sandusky. In the late 1880s Wood had been superintendent of the Sandusky Electric Light, Fuel & Gas Company; more recently he was general manager of the competing People's Electric Railway and the Sandusky, Milan & Norwalk interurban line. A Judge Bentry arranged the financing, but it would appear that Everett and Moore were lurking in the background. Wood formed a new company formally called the Sandusky & Inter-Urban Electric Railway — more commonly spelled simply "Interurban" by both outsiders and the company itself. By July 1899 the new S&I had absorbed the Sandusky Street Railway and planned to obtain a new Sandusky city franchise. More ambitiously it intended to build a 32-mile interurban line east along the Lake Erie shore from Sandusky to Lorain. At Lorain it would connect with Everett-Moore's Lorain & Cleveland to form a route between Sandusky and Cleveland. (The company was, by the way, one of the earliest electric lines to use the word "interurban" in its title.)

As an afterthought the S&I also planned a branch from Ceylon Junction (located between Huron and Vermilion) to Norwalk. This branch would permit a through route between Cleveland and Norwalk via Lorain and Vermilion, and was a strategic move in the rapidly developing interurban power politics of the area. Its purpose was to head off a line being built by the Pomeroy-Mandelbaum syndicate's Cleveland, Elyria & Western, which was to reach Norwalk via Elyria and Oberlin. At Norwalk it would connect with another nascent line, the Toledo, Fremont & Norwalk, which would carry the route on to Toledo. In short, the S&I was to be a link in what would be a through Cleveland–Toledo line — controlled by Everett-Moore rather than Pomeroy-Mandelbaum.

The new Sandusky & Interurban built east from Sandusky, using the Sandusky Street Railway's route out of town to the Soldiers Home and continuing toward Huron via Milan Road and Hull Road. The first segment opened as far as Huron on November 4, 1899, temporarily using single-truck Sandusky Street Railway cars. Five new interurban cars were ordered from the Jewett Car Company and arrived in 1900. Two of them were promptly sent on to the new Toledo & Western Railroad; the remaining three were "numbered" *Alpha*, *Beta*, and *Gamma*. June 1, 1900, marked the first trip with the new equipment. An express motor, *Delta*, came the next year.

But the S&I never made it east of Huron in its lifetime. Problems in using the public road bridges at Huron and Vermilion first stymied the project; a franchise fight in Berlin Heights on the Norwalk branch caused further delays. (As it turned out, the Huron bridge was to remain a barrier until early 1903.) In the meantime the company built a new car shop and powerhouse on Columbus Avenue just south of the Sandusky city line, completing it in December 1899.

It was in this state that the Sandusky & Interurban was fully taken over by the Everett-Moore syndicate and, on September 21, 1901, became part of the Lake Shore Electric. It came with a mixed legacy. Its primary value, of course, was its charter and franchises for what would become the LSE's main line from Lorain to Norwalk and Sandusky — but that was more paper than physical fact in the fall of 1901. Otherwise, its Sandusky shop was substantial and became the LSE's primary shop facility, but its almost-new power plant was already obsolete and was barely adequate to operate the existing Sandusky–Huron line and the Sandusky city routes — which by then had been combined with those of the former People's Railway. The city streetcar lines in themselves turned out to be mostly a liability, and neither the city cars nor the S&I's three interurbans would be of much use to their new owner.

The LSE took over construction of the incomplete Lorain and Norwalk lines under the S&I charter and franchises, hurriedly completing them in 1902 and 1903.

In 1899 the Sandusky & Interurban built this substantial stone carhouse and powerhouse complex just south of the city at Columbus and Perkins Avenues. Later the Lake Shore Electric expanded it to be its primary heavy repair and construction shop. In this 1902 photo, an s&I *Alpha*-class interurban is at the far left, a new LSE Brill city car is in the center, and the former Sandusky, Milan & Norwalk's Norwalk city car 17 — temporarily renumbered 4 — is at the right. (Karel Liebenauer collection)

Sandusky, Norwalk & Southern
Sandusky, Milan & Norwalk
People's Electric Street Railway

Competition for the Sandusky Street Railway appeared in the early 1890s in the form of the People's Electric Street Railway — the White Line. Behind it was another group of

(*Above and below*) The rival Sandusky Street Railway and People's Railway met on separate paralleling tracks at the Soldiers Home, where each built an elaborate terminal station. Seen here is the People's Railway station, which was also used by the affiliated Sandusky, Milan & Norwalk. (Frohman Collection, Hayes Presidential Center)

Sandusky businessmen including William H. Gilcher (one of the original omnibus company owners), Thomas Wood, G. H. DeWitt, and C. L. DeWitt. Organized in 1890 and completed in 1892, the White Line's route roughly paralleled the Brown Line from downtown Sandusky to the Soldiers Home. And like the Brown Line it also built a crosstown route, which in this case served both sides of town via the waterfront.

The Soldiers Home line began on the waterfront on Water Street at Columbus Avenue and followed a complex, winding route paralleling Columbus Avenue to its east, eventually ending up on Hancock Street and its continuation, Milan Road, to the Soldiers Home at DeWitt Avenue. The east–west crosstown route began on the east side on First Street a few blocks east of the end of Monroe. From there it traveled west on First and on Monroe to Hancock, where it joined the Soldiers Home route into downtown at Water Street and Columbus Avenue. It then continued west and southwest, eventually following Tiffin Avenue to a terminal at the Kuebeler Brewery near Sandusky Street. Along the way it served stations of the Sandusky & Columbus Short Line (later part of the Pennsylvania Railroad) and the Cleveland, Cincinnati, Chicago & St. Louis (a New York Central subsidiary, known by all as the "Big Four") on Water Street, plus the Baltimore & Ohio depot east of Franklin Street.

As its corporate title proudly stated, the People's Electric Street Railway was electrified from the beginning. It built a carbarn and powerhouse at Market and Lawrence streets and initially owned four single-truck closed cars and four opens. Two unusual Brill-built single-truck double-deckers were added by 1896 to cope with summertime crowds — some of the very few double-deck streetcars ever used in the United States.

The early 1890s building, located on De Witt Avenue, still stood in 1997. (Bishop photo, W. A. McCaleb collection)

Operating on the Soldiers Home Line, a People's Railway open car stops on Hancock Street at Monroe. (Frohman Collection, Hayes Presidential Center)

(Above) Ex–Sandusky Street Ry. No. 18 and its dapper young motorman are at the Kuebeler Brewery at the end of the Tiffin Avenue line. (Karel Liebenauer collection)

(Below) For handling peak summertime loads, People's Railway bought two single-truckers, Nos. 14 and 16, which could be converted to double-deckers by installing benches on the roof and portable stairways. These oddities were among the very few single-truck double-deckers in the United States. (W. A. McCaleb collection)

As part of its original fleet the SM&N also bought two "open" cars, actually simply windowless open-platform coaches. Soon after, it rebuilt one of them — No. 7 — as this motorized combine, definitely one of a kind. (John A. Rehor collection)

As People's was completing its line to the Soldiers Home, another company was created to continue the route southeast to Milan and Norwalk, a total of 18 miles from Sandusky. Originally called the Sandusky, Milan & Huron Railway, it was organized on July 21, 1892, and became one of the two earliest interurbans in the United States. (The other, the Oregon City line of Portland's East Side Railway, opened February 16, 1893, beating the Norwalk line by seven months.) Judging by its somewhat confusing corporate name (which omitted Norwalk as a terminal) the company also planned a branch to Huron, but as already noted, nothing was done about this for another seven years. In any event the Sandusky–Milan–Norwalk route was a much-needed line and offered good potential because there was no direct steam railroad link between the three communities.

The new SM&H was closely allied with the People's Electric Street Railway, although the commonality of ownership and management were not complete. In 1893, however, Tom Wood served as general manager of both companies and A. W. Prout of Sandusky was their joint treasurer. The new interurban line planned to use the White Line tracks into Sandusky from the Soldiers Home terminal. Although its headquarters were located at the People's Railway carhouse on Lawrence Street in Sandusky, the SM&H built its own carbarn and power house in the Huron River valley at Milan. For equipment it ordered three interurban motor cars and two open-air trailers from Jewett, plus a single-truck city car to fulfill its franchise obligation to provide local streetcar service in Norwalk. Like the People's Railway fleet, SM&H cars were painted white.

The line was built alongside various public highways the entire distance from the Soldiers Home to Norwalk, with a dinky 0-4-2 tank locomotive — a veteran of the New York Elevated Railroad and Manhattan Railway — hauling construction trains. Some of the topography was rough; the major topographic challenge was the deep Huron River valley at Milan, where the highway plunged down a steep grade, crossed the river on a truss bridge, and swung up the other side.

Operations began piecemeal as sections were completed. The first service ran July 18, 1893, between the Soldiers Home and the north side of the Huron River valley hill, using People's Railway streetcars. Construction from there into Milan and on south to Norwalk turned out to be a problem when the Erie County commissioners refused permission for the construction train to use the Huron River highway bridge. According to legend, Tom Wood waited until the dead of night and had his crew lay rails over the bridge before anyone got an injunction, allowing construction to proceed and making himself a local hero

MAIN STREET
S.M.& N.E.RY
DEPOTS

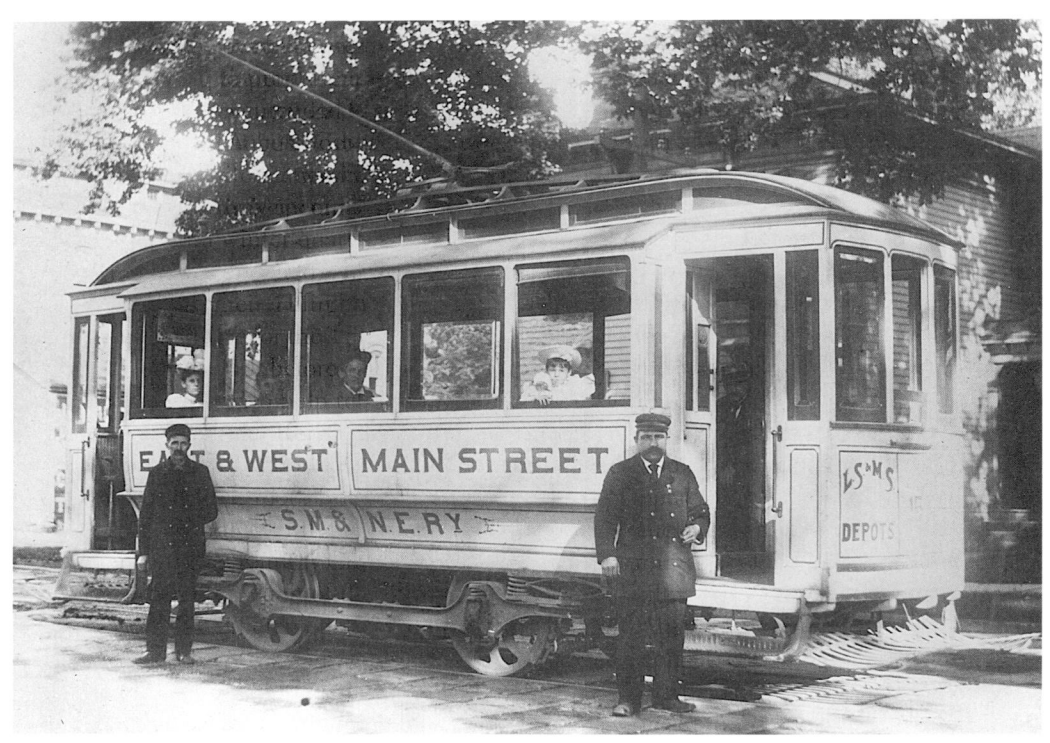

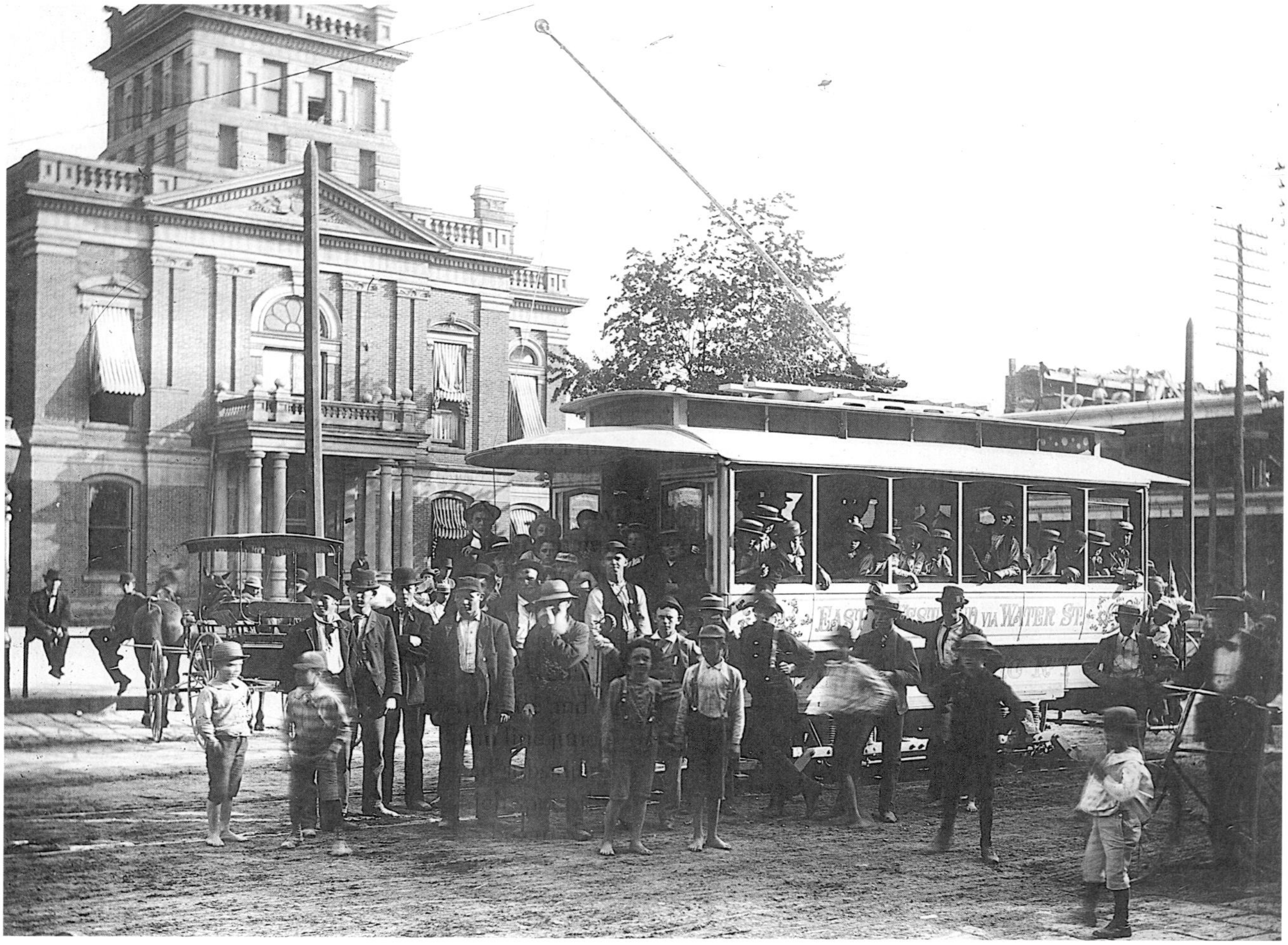
VIA WATER ST

of sorts. The railway did strengthen the bridge for regular operation. By August 15 it was as far as Allings Corners, just outside Norwalk. Entering Norwalk, two similar problems awaited — one at the grade crossing with the Lake Shore & Michigan Southern Railway and one at the East Main Street bridge over the Wheeling & Lake Erie railroad tracks, where the W&LE had obtained an injunction. By the same legend, Wood used his midnight Milan bridge technique again. Finally on September 5 through Sandusky–Norwalk service began along with the short Norwalk city streetcar service on East and West Main Street.

In the meantime, however, the 1893 national financial panic dried up capital and forced the company into a brief bankruptcy on August 21. Its heaviest creditor was the Erie County Banking Company of Vermilion and the bank's president, Captain J. C. Gilchrist, was made receiver. On October 8 — a red letter day for the future — Gilchrist brought in the bank's office assistant, a 21-year-old Fred Coen, as his representative. Enough cash was raised to end the receivership October 10 and the company emerged as the Sandusky, Milan & Norwalk Railway — but Coen remained as watchdog with the title of cashier and then secretary.

With no existing steam railroad service between its terminals, the SM&N not only carried passengers but mail, express, and freight. Eight trips a day were run each way with an initial running time of an hour and 50 minutes. It was reported that on heavy traffic days the little ex-elevated locomotive was put to work hauling trailers.

At Avery, about midway on its route, the SM&N crossed the Nickel Plate Road. While most steam railroads of the time refused to have anything to do with the new electric lines, the Nickel Plate was an exception. A secondary line in a competitive territory, it needed all the business it could get and made joint ticketing arrangements with the SM&N so that the interurban acted as its feeder at Avery for Sandusky and Norwalk traffic.

The steep hills on either side of the Huron River valley just north of Milan were the bane of SM&N operations. The worst was on the Milan side, where the grade averaged over 7 percent; reportedly, part of it was a harrowing 12 percent. In addition it included a reverse curve and a grade crossing of the Wheeling & Lake Erie's Huron branch at the bottom. Reported the *Street Railway Journal* in December 1895: "All cars come to a full stop on the top of the grade and descend with a man at each brake, the brakes being independent. The cars stop halfway down the grade and proceed only to a semaphore signal [at the W&LE crossing] and also stop again before crossing the railroad tracks." The cautious procedure worked, and with all of the Lake Shore Electric's accidents elsewhere, nothing serious ever happened on the old SM&N line. Getting cars up the hill was still another story.

The People's Railway and the Sandusky, Milan & Norwalk continued in their individual but intertwined ways for several more years, but in July 1899 both companies were sold to S. R. Bullock. Bullock was backed by the C. D. Barney investment banking firm of Philadelphia, which proceeded to take over his interests in late 1900. On November 16, 1900, Barney incorporated the Sandusky, Norwalk & Southern Railway to consolidate the two lines, which was fully accomplished by the year's end. It would appear that once again the Everett-Moore syndicate was really behind the maneuverings, which then put both the Sandusky & Interurban and the new Sandusky, Norwalk & Southern under common interests.

(Facing page, top) Little single-truck SM&N 15 was bought for its franchise-required streetcar service on Main Street in Norwalk. It was the first of only three cars which regularly operated this route over its entire 45-year history. (John A. Rehor collection)

(Facing page, bottom) The SM&N's first official run into Norwalk was made by People's Railway No. 2, a single-truck Sandusky city car, on August 15, 1893. (C. S. Bateham photo, Firelands Museum collection)

For its regular services, the SM&N relied on two interurban coaches and a combine built by
Jewett in 1893. *(Above)* The combine, No. 9, is shown on Main Street in Norwalk in 1893
(C. S. Bateham photo, John A. Rehor collection), and *(below)* coach 11 stops at the Milan
Square at about the same time (Milan Museum collection). The SM&N apparently had an
identity problem then. In each photo, the car's front is lettered "SM&H" (the "H" for
"Huron," the original company name), while the letterboards on the side read "Sandusky,
Milan & Norwalk."

Following Old State Road between Milan and Norwalk, the Sandusky, Milan & Norwalk had to deal with steep grades in and out of Rattlesnake Creek valley. *(Above)* Its spindly trestle is shown here (Frohman Collection, Hayes Presidential Center) during construction in 1893, and *(below)* soon afterwards (H. C. Morrison photo), uncertainly supporting SM&N car 9.

By this time too, the Toledo, Fremont & Norwalk was building east from Toledo to Norwalk, where it would connect with the SN&S and the incomplete Sandusky & Interurban branch from Ceylon Junction. On November 24, 1900, the SN&S made an agreement with the TF&N allowing it to use its track on West Main Street in Norwalk to enter the city.

During the first half of 1901 the Sandusky, Norwalk & Southern and Sandusky & Interurban began physically and corporately moving together. On March 13 the two companies agreed to route all interurban passenger runs into Sandusky on the S&I's Columbus Avenue line and the freight and express cars over the SN&S's Hancock Avenue–Milan Road route. Two weeks later, on March 27, the SN&S moved into the S&I's new car shop and yard in Sandusky, leaving the old People's Railway facility downtown on Lawrence Street for storage and freight use. By July 10 both operations were managed as one although not legally merged.

When the Lake Shore Electric succeeded the SN&S on September 25, 1901, it received for its efforts a poorly built interurban line, another marginal city system, and car equipment that represented the earliest street and interurban railway technology, which already was obsolete.

The Lorain & Cleveland Railway

Another pioneer in the industry, the Lorain & Cleveland was the third project in the rapid-fire series of Everett-Moore interurban promotions in Cleveland. (It followed the Akron, Bedford & Cleveland of 1894–95 and the Cleveland, Painesville & Eastern of 1895–96.) West of Cleveland was another excellent potential passenger market. As noted in Chapter 2, the Lake Erie port of Lorain, 27 miles west, began an industrial boom in 1895 with the completion of Tom L. Johnson's steel mill. And while the intermediate territory consisted mostly of fruit farms, the adjacent lake beaches offered convenient summer relief for Cleveland's swelling population of industrial workers.

In company with Barney Mahler, the two promoters chartered the Lorain & Cleveland Railway on November 11, 1895, and the young Fred Coen was brought over from the Sandusky, Milan & Norwalk as assistant secretary.

Their concept for the L&C was different from their first two projects, however — different, in fact, from any interurbans of the time. They would locate, build, and equip the Lorain & Cleveland for what was then considered very high-speed operation — meaning sustained 50-plus mph running. To do so, they located their line almost entirely on private right-of-way, roughly following the Lake Road along the shore, but slightly inland and generally straighter. Cars were to be powered by four motors, rather than the two more common on city and suburban lines.

Unfortunately, getting the line out of Cleveland was something else. It was necessary to use the entire length of the Cleveland Electric Railway's Detroit Avenue streetcar line, 7.5 miles from Cleveland's Public Square to the Rocky River at the west end of Lakewood. At that point came another problem — crossing the deep gorge of the Rocky River itself to the tiny village of Rocky River where its own right-of-way began. This was accomplished by obtaining rights to use the county-owned high-level highway bridge, an iron truss structure built in 1890.

From Rocky River the L&C's single-track route curved west and north to pass under the Nickel Plate Road's main line, then turned west and struck out in almost a straight line for Lorain. It built its carbarn and power plant at Beach Park, or Avon Beach, seven miles east of Lorain. Like the Sandusky, Milan & Norwalk and the Sandusky & Interurban, the L&C arrived just too early to take advantage of the new high-voltage alternating current transmission technology, and its power plant produced direct current. The power plant site consisted of 65 acres of beachfront property, most of which the company developed as a swimming, picnicking, and amusement park.

(Above) Lorain & Cleveland No. 15, an 1896 Brill coach, is on Ontario Street at Huron Road in Cleveland about 1900. (Karel Liebenauer collection)

(Below) The Lorain & Cleveland could make fast time on its straight, single-track route through the flat, open countryside along the lake. The LSE double-tracked this section in 1906; today the area is densely suburbanized. (John A. Rehor collection)

Beach Park, in Avon Lake, was the site of the L&C's carhouse and power house, as well as a company-owned lakefront park. The 1897 carhouse therefore also doubled as a passenger station. In this 1902 view looking east, former East Lorain Street Railway Car No. 1 is peeking out of the door. (Gilbert Hodges photo, Bob Lorenz collection)

Entering Lorain the L&C again reverted to the streets, turning north onto Arizona Avenue to East Erie Avenue, and then using the line of the East Lorain Street Railway into town on East Erie. The physical antithesis of the Lorain & Cleveland, the East Lorain Street Railway nonetheless had the only practical right-of-way into Lorain, since its route on East Erie Avenue used the highway swing bridge over the Black River. The L&C bought the little streetcar company in late 1896, locking up its Lorain entry, but giving itself and the later LSE an unwanted local city route to support for the next four decades.

The Lorain & Cleveland ordered eight passenger cars from Brill similar to 20 others bought at the same time for the Everett-Moore–controlled Akron, Bedford & Cleveland and Cleveland, Painesville & Eastern. While looking much like double-truck city street-cars, they were equipped with four 50-hp motors and, once on their own track, could move along at a very respectable 55 mph.

Scheduled Cleveland–Lorain service began October 6, 1897, and cars ran every half hour. The line's speed impressed even the trade magazine *Electrical Engineer*, which enthused in 1898:

> The schedule speed . . . on some of the long straight sections is fifty-five miles per hour; on speed tests the cars have run as high as sixty . . . One who has never had experience in riding on an electric car at this speed can form no idea of how rapid a pace this is — the sensation is so different from that experienced on steam cars. It is usually highly enjoyable, for no one seems to have any sense of danger, or at least, not so much as many people experience on steam cars running at this speed.

The L&C was successful from the start, taking most of the Nickel Plate Road's Cleveland–Lorain business, among other things. (Most likely it was business the railroad was happy to see disappear.) Soon after its opening the line ordered two additional passenger cars from Brill, plus two combines for carrying express. (In 1898 the L&C became one of the joint owners of the Electric Package Company, which shipped express over its line.) Equipment appears to have been traded with the Cleveland, Painesville & Eastern, but 12 cars were always assigned to the L&C and were eventually passed on to the Lake Shore Electric.

Barney Mahler served as the Lorain & Cleveland's president during its independent life, and was a major stockholder. While the line was built and financed by Everett, Moore, and Mahler, their syndicate did not actually own the company until July 27, 1898. The new Lake Shore Electric absorbed the L&C September 23, 1901, inheriting a well-built high-speed line with already-obsolete cars and power system.

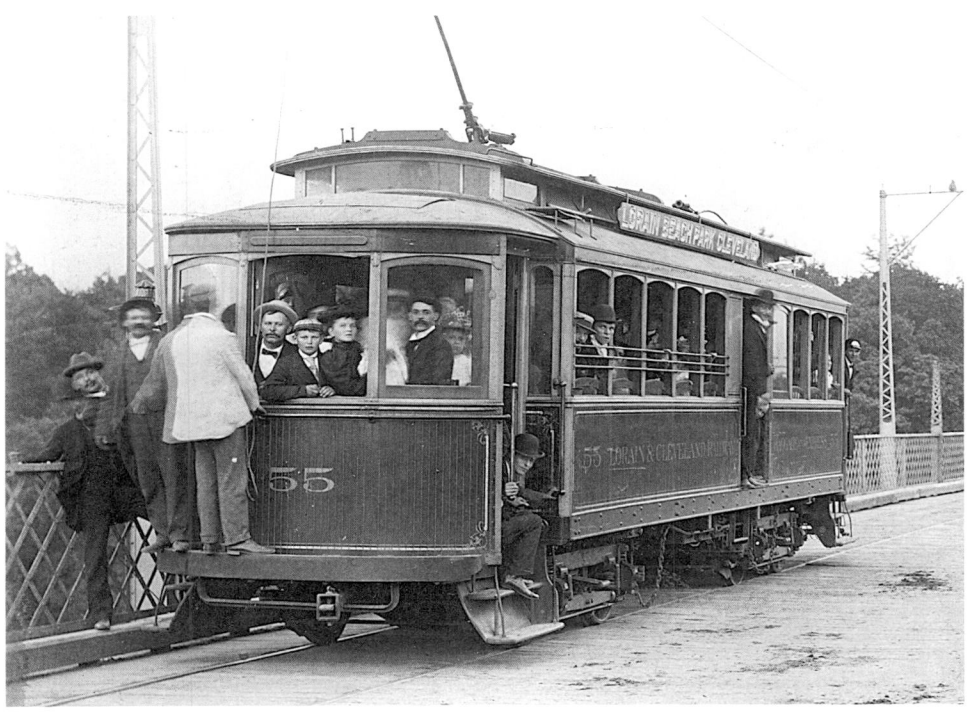

(Above) L&C combine 55 came from Brill in 1898 when the line began handling express business. Here it heads east toward Cleveland on the 1890 Rocky River highway viaduct. (George Krambles collection)

(Below) Lorain & Cleveland Brill car 64 is at Stop 12 in the area of present Bay Village in 1902. (Gilbert Hodges photo, John A. Rehor collection)

East Lorain Street Railway

Eventually becoming the western end of the Lorain & Cleveland, the little East Lorain Street Railway predated its later owner by slightly more than a year. It was chartered June 5, 1895, by local Lorain interests to build a streetcar route along East Erie Avenue from downtown Lorain to Root Road, about 2.6 miles to the east at the border of Sheffield township. Its first and only closed car showed up on February 3, 1896, a small 16-foot (carbody length) car purchased secondhand from a Chicago company. It was housed in a barn owned by Walter Root located at the end of the line at the southeast corner of Root Road and East Erie — where a mule was also kept for insurance.

On February 6, three days after the car arrived, operation began — but stopped on February 20 because of the winter weather. By March 21 service resumed with three round trips a day, and by May the car ran every 30 minutes. At some point the single closed car was joined by an eight-bench open car; these two then constituted the line's entire roster. J. W. McReynolds was the manager and senior motorman and a Mr. O'Neill was the other motorman. In the first few months of operation both of them managed to take the closed car into the barn without opening the barn door.

It was in keeping with the line's casual character. During its first year the little car carried not only a sparse load of passengers but flour, lumber, and provisions — clearly the purest and most primitive of Toonerville Trolleys. While the line's traffic became more conventional later, its character never changed. In season, however, it carried crowds to Randall's Grove, a lakeside park and half-mile track for horse and bicycle racing near Root Road, built by George Randall in 1890.

Reportedly the company originally planned to continue east to Cleveland, following the extension of East Erie, which became the Lake Road and formed the main highway along the lake shore (and which later became Ohio Route 2 and U.S. Route 6). But its independent life was short; by January 24, 1896, the Lorain & Cleveland had received a 90-day purchase option and in late 1896 bought the line for $16,000. Operations were then moved to the L&C's Beach Park carhouse.

Toledo, Fremont & Norwalk Railroad

Of all the Lake Shore Electric's predecessors, the Toledo, Fremont & Norwalk was the newest, longest, and most technologically advanced. That it followed the Lorain & Cleveland by only four years is a dramatic commentary on the speed of technical development in the new industry. On the other hand it represented a back-step from the Lorain & Cleveland's concept of a high-speed line completely located on private right-of-way.

This 61-mile route between Toledo and Norwalk was organized on September 14, 1899, by Detroit interests, led by interurban promoters Samuel F. Angus, James D. Hawks, and Henry A. Haigh, with financial backing from Michigan lumber barons A. W. and W. C. Comstock. Angus and Hawks were fresh from building the Detroit, Ypsilanti & Ann Arbor (the "Ypsi-Ann" as it was called from its earlier days), and now looked eastward from Toledo with a line which was intended to form the western half of a Toledo–Cleveland interurban route. The eastern link was uncertain, but was assumed to be the Cleveland, Elyria & Western, which by then extended from Cleveland to Oberlin. It was thought that either the TF&N would build east as far as Oberlin or the CE&W would continue west to meet the TF&N at Norwalk. In the interim, Norwalk became the primary goal. (The CE&W later became part of the Pomeroy-Mandelbaum syndicate's Cleveland Southwestern.)

Whatever the long-range hopes, the TF&N's own territory seemed to have plenty of potential. The largest city, Fremont, was the county seat of Sandusky County with diversified industry — most notably the Thomson-Houston (later National Carbon) carbon brush mill, cutlery and furniture plants, a beet sugar mill, kraut canneries, and early auto

The TF&N was mostly a roadside interurban and, as this photo shows, a better choice than the road. The location is Woodville Road at Groll Street, just outside Toledo, about 1900. (Karel Liebenauer collection)

parts plants. Clyde, the model for Sherwood Anderson's *Winesburg, Ohio*, was a lesser manufacturing center and, among other things, built the early Elmore automobile. (Later it was the home of the Clydesdale Motor Truck Company, which produced trucks and at least one bus to compete with the Lake Shore Electric.) Bellevue was a major railroad center, a division point on the Nickel Plate Road and junction with three other lines.

There were steam railroads aplenty in the territory including two lines which directly paralleled the TF&N's planned route — the Wheeling & Lake Erie's main line between Toledo and Wheeling, and the Lake Shore & Michigan Southern's Norwalk branch, which before 1872 had been the LS&MS's Toledo–Cleveland main line. But neither of these was a heavy passenger carrier, and none of the railroads in the area actively opposed the new interurban.

The countryside was mostly flat, agricultural land and the line was largely located in or alongside public roads and turnpikes, making construction work comparatively quick and easy. Going east from Toledo, the Toledo, Fremont & Norwalk passed through Genoa, then swung southeast on a 4.7-mile stretch of private right-of-way to Woodville. Picking up the old Maumee & Western Reserve Turnpike (now U.S. Route 20), it continued on through Fremont, Clyde, and Bellevue. En route it met its major physical challenge, the Sandusky River in Fremont, which it crossed on the State Street highway bridge. From Bellevue a

At about the same time, TF&N car 2 is shown between Genoa and Woodville. (Karel Liebenauer collection)

combination of roadside and private right-of-way took the line to Norwalk by way of Monroeville. At both terminals the TF&N negotiated trackage rights to enter town — at Toledo over the Toledo Traction Company's East Broadway line and the Sandusky, Milan & Norwalk's West Main Street track at Norwalk. Fremont, the line's halfway point, housed its operating headquarters, car shop, and power plant.

Spliced into its mostly roadside route were street operation franchises in Genoa, Fremont, and Bellevue. A similar franchise was planned in Woodville but was changed to private right-of-way to avoid two crossings of the Pennsylvania Railroad, a notably cantankerous, if not impossible, company to deal with. Most steam railroads were crossed at grade, but an underpass-subway was necessary at Millbury for the busy Lake Shore & Michigan Southern main line, as well as an overpass east of Bellevue where the route crossed both the W&LE and the LS&MS Norwalk branch.

Physically and technologically, the TF&N was very typical of the state-of-the-art, turn-of-the-century interurban — which by then was a considerable advance from lines like the Lorain & Cleveland and the Sandusky, Milan & Norwalk. Instead of the older direct current generation, its Fremont power plant produced 15,000-volt 25-cycle alternating current for distribution to six substations where it was converted to 600 volts d.c. for traction power.

In addition its equipment was larger, heavier, and more specifically designed for long-distance service. The company ordered 22 large interurban coaches and three similar express-freight box motors from the Barney & Smith Car Company in Dayton, Ohio, who had built the first cars for Angus's Ypsi-Ann. The coaches were slightly over 50 feet long and carried 56 passengers, compared to the Lorain & Cleveland's 42-foot-long Brills which seated 42. The number of cars ordered was clearly more than were needed for the projected hourly service between Toledo and Norwalk, and presumably were bought in anticipation of eventual interline service to Cleveland.

In other ways, however, the Toledo, Fremont & Norwalk betrayed its original mission as a low-cost local-service carrier with its roadside and in-street locations, wooden bridges, and austere, underpowered two-motored cars.

During the line's construction in 1900, the Toledo, Fremont & Norwalk's work motor *Mary Jane* and crew roll across the new Huron River Bridge at Monroeville. (Frohman Collection, Hayes Presidential Center)

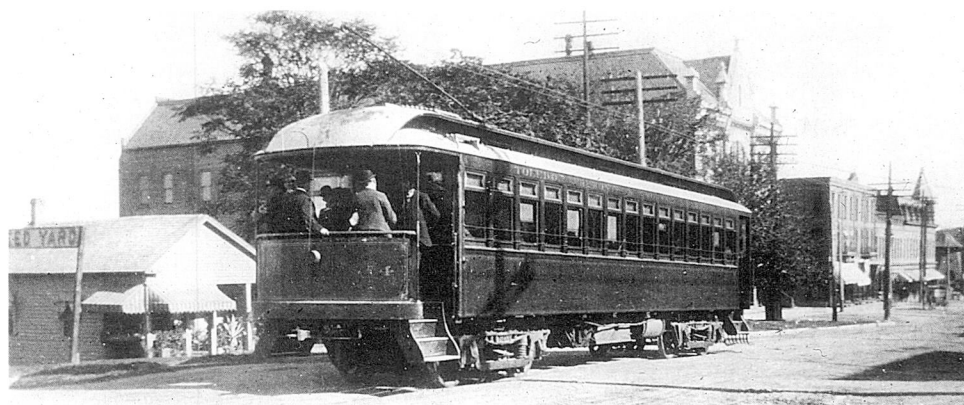

TF&N No. 4 rolls east on State Street in Fremont. The photo is believed to show the first trip between Toledo and Fremont in early September of 1900. (Ralph H. Sayles collection)

Construction began immediately — in fact, the first contract was let two weeks before the company's formal incorporation — and by modern standards went unbelievably quickly. There were the usual thorny local street franchise problems, but the constant presence of the promoters engendered warm and effective relationships with local politicians, businesses, and the press. Fremont was especially enthusiastic about the line — Bellevue less so. In fact, for the Lake Shore Electric, Bellevue would become one of those spots which seemed always to produce more problems than revenues.

By April 2, 1900, the TF&N had hired its new general manager, Furman J. Stout, a 42-year-old former general superintendent of the Wheeling & Lake Erie. Stout put his past experience to use on the TF&N by instituting standard steam railroad rules and operating methods— the first on any interurban line. Thanks in large part to him, the TF&N was very well planned and organized, and once operating it turned in a remarkable on-time performance.

Within a year of the company's organization, cars were running over half of the line. By September 8, 1900, hourly service was being operated between Toledo and Fremont; by September 15 it had been extended to Clyde. On October 2 a shuttle car ran between Clyde and Bellevue every two hours. Service as far east as Monroeville started January 9, 1901, and through operations between Toledo and Norwalk were finally inaugurated on May 1. From company organization to full service had taken fewer than 18 months.

Amid construction debris, new TF&N Barney & Smith–built car 13 visits Bellevue on October 2, 1900, the first day of service to this point. In the center of the car's rear platform is W. C. Comstock, one of the company's financial backers; on the right is TF&N General Manager Furman J. Stout, later LSE's general manager. Interestingly, this same car ran regular trips on the LSE the day before its abandonment. (Ron Jedlicka collection)

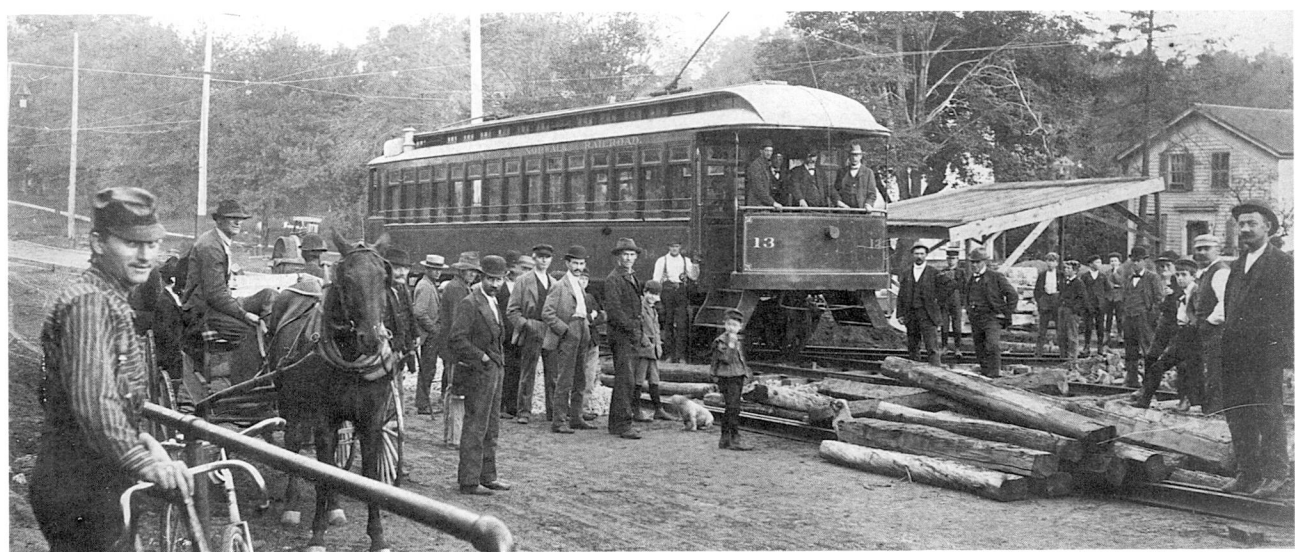

But even before the line had fully opened, its owners were negotiating to sell it — possibly because they knew that the two powerful Cleveland interurban syndicates were both trying to form a Cleveland–Toledo line and the timing was right for a good price. The Everett-Moore group won and bought the TF&N on August 7, 1901; by September 30 it was part of the Lake Shore Electric.

Perhaps the time was right for the TF&N's principal owners in another way. By 1908 all of them had died. Angus himself died February 6, 1908, at the age of 52 and the last of the group, A. W. Comstock, followed him in April.

Lorain Street Railway

There actually were two Lorains in history — Lorain Before Johnson and Lorain After Johnson. It was in the Before Johnson era that then-sleepy little Lorain got its first public transit, a tiny, financially faltering horsecar line befitting the nondescript backwater village on Lake Erie.

The community's population was only about 1,600 people when eight Lorain businessmen formed the Lorain Street Railway in 1881. Their primary purpose was to provide public transportation from the center of town to the Hayden Brass Works, which had just been established in the area around present Broadway and 19th Street. With about 400 employees, Hayden became the town's leading industry. Led by F. P. Vernam (who became the company's general manager and superintendent) the group obtained a franchise to operate a horsecar line south on Broadway (then called Penfield Avenue) from Erie Avenue to 19th Street.

By 1885 the horsecars were rolling, and in 1887 the line was extended slightly southward to 21st Street near St. Joseph's Hospital. At its fullest extent the railway was 1.5 miles long and owned nine horses, two closed cars, and two open cars.

But the brass works closed during the financial panic of 1893 and the always-unprofitable horsecar company lapsed into receivership that year, with F. C. Norcross as receiver. Happily, however, Tom L. Johnson made the decision to locate in Lorain in March 1894 and bought the railway.

Johnson located his new mill and worker housing south of Lorain itself on 4,000 undeveloped acres fronting on the Black River surrounding the old hamlet of Globeville. Of that area, 2300 acres south of the present 28th Street (then Tenth Avenue) were set aside for a town, to become South Lorain, and 70 acres went for a park.

The original Lorain Street Railway's carbarn and stable was at the end of its line near 19th and Broadway, which at this point was then called Penfield Avenue. Horsecars 6 and 36 pose in the late 1880s. (Photo from Albert C. Doane)

By June 1894 work had begun on a new powerhouse for the electrified street railway, which was to be extended south and east from its old 21st Street terminal to 28th Street to serve the mill and new community. In order to tap another source of labor, Johnson continued the line south to Elyria, about five miles from South Lorain. The original route turned east from Broadway onto 21st Street and followed 21st Street and North Fulton to 28th Street; it then ran east on 28th along the south side of the mill and north side of the residential development. At Grove Avenue it turned south and headed for Elyria, mostly on private right-of-way. The northerly terminal in the center of Lorain at Broadway and Erie consisted of a loop track right in the middle of the intersection — a layout which would produce chaos in later years. The carhouse and power house were built on 28th Street at Seneca in South Lorain. (See map, p. 197.)

The old horsecars made their last trip on July 14, 1894, and on August 16 Johnson's new electrified line began running between Broadway and Erie Avenue and the South Lorain carhouse. Elyria service started September 15. When fully completed the line was 11.5 miles long.

The Lorain Street Railway's early roster consisted of 17 single-truck motor cars and two trailers, all reportedly built by Stephenson. But eventually it owned at least 11 double-truck cars — five of them Stephenson products and six from the American Car Company.

In 1894 Tom Johnson's new version of the Lorain Street Railway built its carhouse at what is now 28th and Seneca Streets in South Lorain, then virtually a wilderness. The bucolic environment changed quickly as the steel mill rose behind the carhouse and the area was developed for worker housing. The carhouse itself was soon expanded; it survives in the late 1990s. (Photo from Albert C. Doane)

Tom Johnson began his Lorain–Elyria Service in 1894 with single-truckers such as this Stephenson-built product. The ornate lettering includes a painting of clasped hands representing the uniting of the two cities. (John A. Rehor collection)

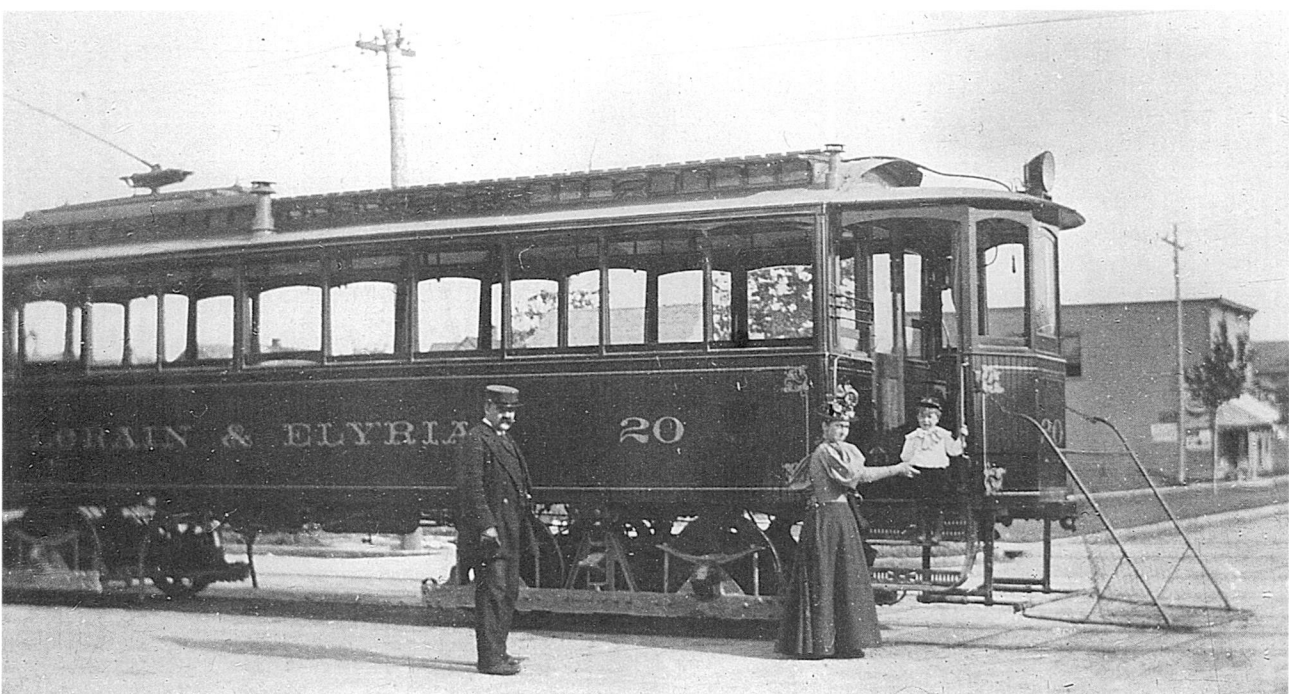

Fearsome-looking Lorain
Street Railway No. 20 was
one of five Stephenson-built
suburban cars of uncertain
lineage, but possibly rebuilt
from single-truckers. In the
early years of the LSE era
they were used as trailers on
rush-hour trips. Thanks to
its high clearances, one —
No. 79 — served as part of
the LSE's "high water train"
during the 1912–16 period.
(Karel Liebenauer collec-
tion)

The mill first opened in February 1895 and expanded quickly. In 1898 its name was changed from the Johnson Steel Company to Lorain Steel, and in 1899 a blast furnace and ore docks were added. Cleveland Shipbuilding Company was established in 1897 on the east bank of the Black River and launched its first ship, *Superior City*, in April 1898. The following year the Thew Automatic Shovel Company established a plant on 28th Street to produce steam shovels.

In 1901 Johnson sold the mill to the newly formed U.S. Steel Corporation, which substantially expanded the complex between 1903 and 1906 with a tube works. By 1906 it employed 9,500 men. Another 1,550 worked at the shipyard, by then called the American Shipbuilding Company. In brief, Lorain had become a major industrial city and the Lorain Street Railway was its circulation system.

But by then Johnson had moved on. In May 1901 he was elected mayor of Cleveland and became one of its most legendary political figures. He kept his interest in the Lorain Street Railway until March 1905, however, when he sold it to some principals in the Everett-Moore group for $400,000. The new owners immediately built an extension from 31st and Grove Avenue in South Lorain to the Lake Shore Electric's Cleveland–Lorain line at Beach Park. Separately incorporated as the Avon Beach & Southern, the line was primarily intended to give the LSE a Cleveland–Elyria route but was built as a Lorain Street Railway subsidiary.

The Lorain Street Railway's corporate end came August 3, 1906, when the Lake Shore Electric formally took control of the company and re-incorporated the property as the Lorain Street Railroad. But unlike the LSE's four original predecessors, it was never merged into its parent. While it shared a common management with the LSE and, to some extent, pooled equipment and operating crews, the Lorain Street Railroad remained a separate corporation for the rest of its operational life.

Fremont Street Railway

Fremont's short-lived and always-ragged little streetcar line was never part of the Lake Shore Electric. But although it was never intended that way, it became a sort of a relative by marriage and a key part of the LSE story. For that reason — and also because the line's life is unlikely to be recorded anywhere else — it is included here as an "honorary predecessor."

The relationship was created when the newly formed Fostoria & Fremont Railway decided to use the car line as its entry to Fremont and its connection to the Lake Shore Electric. When it did so, it acquired what was surely one of Ohio's smallest, most obscure, and ill-documented electric railways. Dates and even corporate names are uncertain to one degree or another.

Its precise starting date is unknown, for example, but on December 5, 1888, the city passed an ordinance granting the Fremont Street Railway its franchise. Presumably the animal-powered line began operating in the next year, with a short route on Front Street from Birchard to Croghan and on Croghan to the Lake Shore & Michigan Southern Railway station. A December 1893 ordinance allowed the company to electrify, and it acquired two cars — one single-truck open, numbered 51, and one closed car, number unknown.

If the company's history is misty, one thing is clear: erratic operation and shifting own-erships were the prevailing forces in its life. On November 18, 1895, it was sold at a receiver's sale to Dr. Frank Creager, an early promoter of electric lighting in the city who owned the Creager Electric Light and Power Company. Some time afterward it was extended south along Front Street and Tiffin Street to Park Avenue.

Creager soon gave up on it. A March 27, 1901, report in the *Sandusky Weekly Register* stated that "The Fremont Street Railway, for some time defunct, has been sold to the pro-jectors of the Lakeside, Napoleon & Western Railway, to connect Lakeside with Port Clinton, Fremont, Gibsonburg, Bowling Green, and Napoleon." The *Fremont Daily News* then noted on April 12 that "cars on the Fremont Street Railway began making regular trips today; two cars are in service."

One of the Fremont Street Railway's two original electric cars, open single-trucker 51, curves out of Croghan Street onto Front Street. (Hayes Presidential Center Collection)

The new owners were the brothers E. M. and Richard Kerlin of Toledo, who actually were trying to promote a route from Lakeside and Port Clinton to Tiffin via Fremont. Evidently they intended to use the streetcar line as their passage through Fremont en route to Tiffin. By August 1901 its route was extended south along Tiffin Road to the Ballville bridge over the Sandusky River. But regular operation remained questionable. Said the *Fremont Daily News* on March 10, 1902: "Trips to Ballville to be Resumed Soon: Street car comes from winter quarters next week. . . . [The] Kerlins to push things . . ." At this time the line was operated by H. P. Reiter under contract to the Kerlins, who were getting nowhere with their Tiffin line. At some point about half a mile of track was laid south of the Ballville bridge for the Tiffin extension — but there was no track on the bridge itself, which had to be rebuilt before cars could operate over it. The rails were never used, and were removed in 1907 to help rebuild the operating line.

Service under Kerlin ownership apparently continued to be erratic through 1906, with varying talk of complete abandonment or an extension. A double-truck open car was acquired in June 1906. But in May 1907 ownership apparently changed again, with E. M. Kerlin turning over the Fremont Street Railway's franchises to a new company called the Fremont City Railway Company. In August 1907 its route was changed to start at Front and State Streets. Much of the line reportedly was rebuilt with new rail and an extension to Oakwood Cemetery, beyond Ballville, was started. At the same time the original line on Croghan Street was given up. Half-hourly service seems to have been offered using one car at a time.

The equipment was not too dependable, so in the summer of 1908 a work car was fitted up with seats and canopies, and in January 1911 it was reported that the open car was used in place of the ailing closed car and was promptly dubbed "the pneumonia special."

The newly formed Fostoria & Fremont signed an option to purchase the line October 25, 1909, although the Fremont streetcars were left to operate as they had before until the F&F was completed. At the time of sale the line was 2.4 miles long, 1.2 miles of which were in brick pavement, with 70-pound rails; its roster consisted of two 12-bench open cars and a work car.

Once the Fostoria & Fremont began local service in June 1911 it did its best to dump the chronically money-losing local streetcars. Operations were relegated to off-again, on-again summer service to Oakwood Cemetery, the last reported year being 1914.

As the eastern end of the Fostoria & Fremont, the line itself continued and, in fact, its western section in the area of Ballville and Oakwood Cemetery managed to outlive both the F&F and Lake Shore Electric by a substantial margin. When a steam plant was added to the original hydroelectric facilities at the Ballville power plant about 1916, the F&F brought coal into it from its interchange with the Lake Erie & Western about two miles to the northwest. After the F&F's demise in 1932, the Ohio Power Company, owner of the Ballville plant, bought these two miles to operate itself; at the same time it acquired F&F freight motor No. 150 to switch the railroad cars. (Lake Shore Electric "monitor" motor 401 was added in 1939.) This operation lasted until 1953.

PART III

THE OPERATIONS

As Cleveland's other interurban lines withered away, track space at the joint Eagle Avenue freight terminal was used to store LSE cars laying over between runs. Here cars 168, 149, and another steel Jewett take in some mid-day sun in the mid-1930s. (Louis Szakacs photo)

CHAPTER 11

PASSENGER SERVICES

The historical text of this book broadly described the Lake Shore Electric's interurban services. But for those more specifically interested in the subject, this chapter takes a more detailed look at these schedule and general service patterns. Even so, it should be remembered that the LSE's passenger schedules were often adjusted for traffic peaks, valleys, and shifts in riding patterns — sometimes on an ad hoc basis. This was especially so in the summer, when hordes would head for Cedar Point and the numerous parks and resort communities lining Lake Erie's shore.

Predecessors' Services

The primeval Sandusky, Milan & Norwalk's earliest known timetable is dated December 1, 1893, and shows not only the line's service but the specific car numbers for each run. Cars 9 and 11 alternated, with runs every two hours between Sandusky and Norwalk; the 18-mile trip took an extremely leisurely one hour and 50 minutes, a terminal-to-terminal average of ten mph. (For some SM&N riders the specific car numbers were relevant, since combine No. 9 carried baggage; coach No. 11 did not.) Virtually every run connected with one or more steam railroad local trains, which also were shown on the timetable. SM&N cars regularly exchanged passengers with trains of the Lake Shore & Michigan Southern and the Wheeling & Lake Erie at Norwalk, the W&LE's Huron branch at Milan, the Nickel Plate at Avery, and no less than five railroads at Sandusky — the LS&MS, Big Four, Lake Erie & Western, Baltimore & Ohio, and Sandusky & Columbus Short Line (later Pennsylvania Railroad).

Two-hour headways were also the norm when the Sandusky & Interurban inaugurated service between the West House terminal in Sandusky and Huron on November 4, 1899. Initially the S&I used single-truck Sandusky Street Railway city cars, but by May 3, 1900, the three *Alpha*-class Jewett interurbans had taken over the run.

The early Lorain & Cleveland was a different kind of animal, with far faster and denser service than the two Sandusky lines. During the winter months the L&C operated hourly between Cleveland and Lorain, with half-hourly service during the summer. L&C cars were slowed by 7.5 miles of city street running in Cleveland over Superior and Detroit avenues, but once on their own almost-straight, private right-of-way between Rocky River and Lorain they were expected to average 30 mph, including all stops. According to the May 1899 *Street Railway Journal* this required running speeds of 45–50 mph.

The Lake Shore's fourth predecessor, the Toledo, Fremont & Norwalk, offered hourly cars between Toledo and Norwalk. Its large, lumbering two-motored Barney & Smith–built interurbans were scheduled to cover the 61 miles in two and a half hours, an average of slightly more than 24 mph. Designed for low-cost local operations rather than high speeds, they were further slowed by city street running in Toledo and several intermediate towns.

LSE Main Line Local Services

Throughout the Lake Shore Electric's life, its interurban services between Cleveland and Toledo really consisted of two separate types of operations — its locals and its limited-stop schedules. These served different markets and over the years followed different paths of development and service patterns. The plodding all-stop local schedules were geared to small communities, the numerous little beach resorts, farmers, and suburban dwellers — markets which the automobile took as its first victims. Thus, although the LSE began life with frequent local cars, by the end these services had contracted to concentrate on the Cleveland and Toledo suburbs.

While the 60-mph limiteds eventually gave the company its distinction, prestige, and profitability, it necessarily had to begin operations with strictly local cars. Two turbulent years passed after its 1901 formation before the LSE could even begin to offer the fast services its promoters planned. In fact, it was not even until early 1902 that it could offer the semblance of a through local service between Cleveland and Toledo via Norwalk, and it was a rough semblance. Portions of the route between Lorain and Norwalk were still essentially unfinished, and initially, "through" Cleveland–Toledo cars ran every two hours and took seven hours with two transfers — an average of 17 mph for those who stuck it through. But on the older sections between Norwalk and Toledo and Cleveland and Lorain, cars were hourly and ran faster.

Things improved substantially on September 8, 1902, when hourly through local service began and the running time was cut to six hours, although through passengers reportedly transferred at both Norwalk and Fremont. A Fremont newspaper reported that the Norwalk change was eliminated July 12, 1903. But throughout the LSE's history, both its public and operating timetables are unclear as to whether the advertised "through" local cars between Cleveland and Toledo actually ran through, or whether passengers transferred to a connecting car at some point. Once the limiteds began running in 1903, it is doubtful that many people rode a local for the entire distance. In any event, hourly Cleveland–Toledo locals became the LSE's early basic service pattern. As long as the through locals ran, they took about six hours, a terminal-to-terminal average speed of about 20 mph.

During this early period Lake Shore management's first priority was to put the Cleveland–Norwalk–Toledo service in shape. The Huron bridge problem still prevented direct services between Sandusky and points east of Huron. What was advertised as a "through" service between Sandusky and Ceylon Junction began November 15, 1902, but passengers still had to get off and get themselves across the Huron River bridge to a waiting car on the other side. Direct service to Sandusky finally started early in 1903. When the Sandusky–Fremont line opened in 1907, routing of the hourly through locals usually alternated between Norwalk and Sandusky.

By September 1908, with limited service now well-established, daytime local service west of Lorain was cut to every two hours. Hourly Cleveland–Lorain locals continued and, as in earlier years, apparently were augmented during the summer months. For example, a June 1910 local timetable showed half-hourly local cars over this busy segment of the system. Two Cleveland–Beach Park commuter trips were added about 1915. Otherwise, this two-hour through local service pattern (with hourly Cleveland–Lorain service) continued until July 1922, when service west of Lorain essentially was cut to a three-hour headway. But as part of overall main-line service improvements in January 1927, Cleveland–Toledo local service (via Norwalk) reverted to every two hours.

Fremont was always a busy loading and transfer point for the LSE. This westbound express is taking passengers about 1937. The Wheeling & Lake Erie main line crosses State Street in the foreground, and the LSE's turning wye at Front Street is at the left. (Ralph H. Sayles photo)

That proved short-lived. A major restructuring took place with the November 18, 1927, timetable and all through Cleveland–Toledo locals abruptly disappeared, never to return. They were replaced by a patchwork of short-turn local services and the reclassification of some Cleveland–Toledo limiteds as "expresses" to handle certain local traffic without compromising their running times. Hourly locals continued between Cleveland and Lorain; east from Toledo several locals operated in a somewhat irregular pattern. Some ran between Toledo and Fremont or Norwalk, and some operated only as far as Genoa, 14 miles to the east. Several additional rush-hour and evening locals ran between Fremont and Norwalk or Fremont and Bellevue.

The Depression officially arrived on October 28 and 29, 1929, and by either January or early February 1930 the Lake Shore made its first big service cuts. The traditional hourly local service between Cleveland and Lorain was reduced to a car every 90 minutes, supplemented by more rush hour cars between Cleveland and Beach Park, and even a morning short-turn trip to the Cleveland Railway's Rocky River carhouse in Lakewood, where the Detroit Avenue and Clifton Boulevard city lines terminated. This was a school service and operated until the LSE's end, although it was not shown on timetables during later years.

More cuts came September 6, 1932. Local Cleveland–Lorain cars ran only daytimes, 90 minutes apart, along with three Beach Park commuter trips, one of which in the morning turned at the Cleveland Railway's Rocky River carhouse. On the Toledo end only one lonely double-ended rush hour car left Toledo for Genoa at 4 p.m. Also, one local rush hour round trip remained between Fremont and Sandusky, plus a similar rush hour round trip between Sandusky and Cleveland. By June 1934 the various "expresses" were splitting up virtually all local duties between Lorain and Toledo. Most remaining local business, however, was now concentrated in the Cleveland–Lorain suburban territory and, to a lesser extent, Toledo's eastern suburbs.

Main Line Limited Services

The long-awaited limited-stop services finally began in mid-October of 1903 when the newly delivered high-speed Brill interurban combines began pacing off the distance in four hours and 45 minutes. As a beginning, three such limiteds were added each way to the basic hourly local services, leaving the terminals in early morning, early afternoon, and late afternoon. In November 1904 two similar fast trips each way were added between Cleveland and Sandusky.

Ceylon Junction, 3½ miles east of Huron, was the LSE's other key transfer point for the Sandusky and Norwalk routes. In this April 1937 scene the camera looks east from the Sandusky line as Toledo-bound 168 meets Niles car 150 on the Norwalk line. The station is behind the 150 while a popular private sandwich shop is to the left of the 168. To the left of that is the Lake Road, now bypassed and abandoned because of lake erosion. (Ralph A. Perkin photo)

The limited-stop concept quickly became the cornerstone of the LSE's future operations. On the Cleveland–Norwalk–Toledo route there were over 310 designated local stops, an average of almost three a mile. While most were seldom-used "flag" stops, local cars were obligated to pick up or drop off passengers at any of them if someone wanted. The new limiteds stopped only at major intermediate towns. While these varied slightly over the years, there were only about 14 or 15 on the same route. Going west from Cleveland they were: Rocky River, Beach Park, Lorain, Vermilion, Ceylon Junction, Berlin Heights, Norwalk, Monroeville, Bellevue, Clyde, Fremont, Gibsonburg Junction (often a conditional stop), Woodville, and Genoa. Beginning in 1907 with the opening of the Sandusky–Fremont line, limiteds also operated via Sandusky, stopping at Huron, Sandusky, Castalia, Whitmore, and Vickery.

The new Sandusky–Fremont line was completed July 21, 1907, giving an alternate route between Cleveland and Toledo and allowing through services via Sandusky — previously a dead-end terminal. The Lake Shore's January 5, 1908, timetable showed the limiteds scheduled two hours apart and alternating routings between Sandusky and Norwalk. With some occasional variations, this basic two-hour headway remained the pattern for the LSE's entire life. Cleveland–Toledo running time was cut to four hours and 25 minutes.

The year 1911 was a landmark in the LSE's history and, in fact, in the history of the Midwest interurban industry. Almost simultaneously, through long-distance interline operations were inaugurated between Cleveland and Detroit — 177 miles — and Cleveland and Lima, Ohio, 157 miles. First to begin was the Detroit service on June 22, 1911. In essence, the LSE's two-hourly Cleveland–Toledo limited service was extended to Detroit, with a total running time of six hours. On the 57-mile Toledo–Detroit leg, limiteds stopped only at Monroe, Michigan. Of the six daily round trips, three were routed via Sandusky and three via Norwalk.

Lima runs followed the Detroit service slightly more than a month later. The initial trial trip left Lima at 8:15 a.m. July 31, 1911, and, after a minor mishap in Cleveland with a snagged trolley wire, reached the Public Square at 2:50 p.m., one hour and 20 minutes late. Although the new Fostoria & Fremont required a lot of work before high-speed operation could be risked over its track, the through Lima Limiteds were put into scheduled operation August 3, only three days after the trial run. Two round trips were made daily with running times of five hours and 25 minutes westbound and five hours 35 minutes eastbound.

Two of the four pooled LSE and Western Ohio Jewett combines could handle the Lima–Cleveland schedules. Lima patrons could leave at 6:15 a.m., arrive in Cleveland just before lunch at 11:50, have some time to shop or transact business, and leave at 5:30 p.m. Clevelanders going to Lima, however, had to figure on staying there overnight, because if they arrived on schedule at 1:05 p.m., they would have only an hour and ten minutes before the afternoon eastbound departed. The Lima limited schedules remained largely unchanged over the lifetime of the service. The cars always ran via Sandusky, partly to give western Ohio communities direct access to Cedar Point.

Actually, the Lima service went even farther than normally advertised, since trains usually operated to the Western Ohio's shop at Wapakoneta, Ohio, 16 miles southwest of Lima. In the earlier years the Western Ohio also occasionally tied the Cleveland runs and equipment into some of its other services. For example, for a time after the runs were established, the evening train out of Cleveland ran all the way to St. Mary's, Ohio, a total distance of 182 miles. After laying over at St. Mary's, the car headed east at 5:15 a.m. and arrived in Cleveland as LSE train No. 104 at 11:50 a.m. Another short-lived extension was indicated in the Western Ohio's March 1918 schedule, which showed the trains originating and terminating at Piqua, 47 miles south of Lima and 204 miles from Cleveland.

In addition to the two Lima limiteds each way, the F&F's own local cars shuttled between Fostoria and Fremont every two hours, making Fremont a busy transfer point for people going to and from various LSE points. Beginning in 1911 and probably extending into 1922, these two-hourly Fostoria–Fremont locals ran all the way through to Sandusky during the summer season for the Lake Erie resort riders.

Closely concurrent with the Detroit and Lima interline schedules came regular operation of multiple-unit trains. From then until 1927, limiteds usually ran with two and sometimes three cars — particularly during the summer resort season. The LSE ran its first four-car train in 1914, but trains of this length were rare. Both the Detroit and Lima services were run with pooled multiple-unit equipment — LSE and Detroit United Railway cars in the case of Detroit, and, for the Lima route, the four new Jewett combines owned by

An eastbound Detroit–Cleveland limited is reassembled at Ceylon Junction as a Detroit United Railway car — which has come via Norwalk — is backed to couple onto an LSE Jewett from the Sandusky route. (Karel Liebenauer collection)

the Lake Shore and the Western Ohio. For the first ten months of the Cleveland–Detroit service, LSE Niles coaches handled all the through schedules since the DUR had no equipment suitable for interline operations. But beginning in April 1912 four new DUR Niles coaches went into the pool service; numbered 7073–7076, they were multiple-unit cars fully compatible with the LSE's equipment. By 1916 this group had grown to 26 cars (Nos. 7073–76, 7084–96, 7308–12, 7520–21, and 7745–46) and in 1917 eight similar Jewetts (7522–29) were added to the pool.

Typically, multi-car trains were broken up and reassembled en route on a tightly coordinated schedule which allowed little room for delays or failures. Westbound, a two-car limited would be uncoupled at Ceylon Junction, with one car each running over the Sandusky and Norwalk routes; the cars met again at Fremont and were then re-coupled as a train to complete the run to Toledo. Going east the procedure was reversed. To avoid coupling on the curve at Ceylon Junction, the eastbound car from Norwalk would come through the turnout and then back down to the Sandusky car. For the same reason, westbound trains out of Cleveland had the Sandusky car on the head end. This usually required a switching move at Cleveland to get the cars in the proper order. After off-loading at West 3rd and Superior, the inbound trains pulled down to the turnout from West 3rd to St. Clair. After uncoupling, the lead car pulled into the clear in the turnout, after which the trailing car pulled ahead into the layover track on West 3rd north of St. Clair. The former lead car then backed into West 3rd and pulled ahead behind the erstwhile trailing car.

A three-car limited heads west on Clifton Boulevard in Cleveland about 1915. On this multiple-destination train the lead car, an LSE Niles, is marked "Toledo via Sandusky." The second car will go to Lima, also via Sandusky and Fremont. The third, destined for Detroit, will run via Norwalk and meet the first car again at Fremont. (Robert Runyan collection)

According to several eyewitness accounts, two-car trains carried a motorman and conductor on each car over the entire route, even though the extra motorman was needed only for the Ceylon Junction–Fremont split. For the LSE's type of operation and schedule pattern, this unusual practice apparently was more efficient than assigning a motorman strictly to shuttle between Ceylon Junction and Fremont. Nonetheless it negated any significant cost savings from train operation, although there were operational and safety advantages.

The expanded limited schedules and interline runs established in 1911 quickly became the backbone of the LSE's operations and its key to prosperity into the early 1920s. The limiteds generally were well-patronized and produced consistently high earnings by any type of measurement.

The Lake Shore's revenue leader during this period was its train 212, the 3:30 p.m. eastbound limited out of Toledo which arrived in Cleveland at 7:50 p.m. — in time to connect with the night boat to Buffalo. It also probably represented the epitome of the LSE's complex but closely coordinated interline and alternate routing operations. This single train consisted of cars originating at both Detroit and Lima, which in turn were split and reassembled over the LSE's alternate Fremont–Ceylon Junction routes.

Train 212 was a two-car train from Detroit to Ceylon Junction via Sandusky, and a three-car train from Ceylon Junction to Cleveland. Out of Detroit it consisted of an LSE car and a 58-foot Detroit United Railway Niles or Jewett car. The DUR car was cut off at Fremont and proceeded east to Ceylon Junction via Norwalk; it was replaced at Fremont by the afternoon limited car out of Lima, which then ran in multiple with the LSE car from Detroit to Ceylon Junction by way of Sandusky. At Ceylon Junction the two-car Sandusky

train was rejoined by the DUR car
which had gone through Norwalk,
and became a three-car train from
there to Cleveland. To facilitate the
recoupling at Ceylon Junction, the
Michigan car usually was placed as
the lead car at that point, an unpopu-
lar arrangement with LSE crews who
disdainfully called the DUR equipment "tubs." (Routing the longer
"tubs" through Norwalk apparently
was done to avoid the sharp curves in
Sandusky's streets.) On westbound
trains from Cleveland, the "tubs"
were the rearmost car.

Thus train 212 and similar LSE
limiteds were unique among interurban lines anywhere — a single
train not only provided service over two different LSE routes at the same time, but also
operated two separate interline services.

Two-car trains were typical on the LSE until 1927 but rare after that except for special movements. Here express train 207, with the 174 and 167, is westbound alongside Perkins Avenue on the Sandusky cutoff in March 1935. (Lee N. Birch photo, George Krambles collection)

The train's earnings were as impressive as its physical operation. During August 1918,
for example, train 212 averaged $308 in revenue per trip, or $1.044 per revenue car mile,
seven days a week. This was somewhere close to three times the industry average at the time
— a sensational performance. The train's revenue per car-hour was $30.40, at a time when
crew members were paid about 40 cents an hour. Its occupancy rate was about 90 percent.

While the early morning and late evening runs inevitably carried light loads, other
daytime limiteds were also healthy earners. The 9:30 a.m. westbound from Cleveland even
outperformed train 212 in August 1918. Operated with a third car as far as Sandusky, it averaged $1.05 per car mile. The 1:30 and 3:30 p.m. westbounds and 11:30 a.m. and 1:30 p.m.
eastbounds did nearly as well, each averaging about $1.02 per car mile.

In 1922 the Lima service belatedly and briefly blossomed into a breathtaking 222-mile through
run between Cleveland and Fort Wayne, Indiana — the longest such scheduled operation in
the country at the time. (The Cincinnati & Lake Erie later bested it with a 282-mile Cincinnati–Detroit service inaugurated in December 1930.) On July 17 of that year, one of the two
through Cleveland–Lima schedules was extended to Fort Wayne via the Fort Wayne, Van Wert
& Lima, at that time controlled by the Indiana Service Corporation. Under one kind of arrangement or another, the Cleveland–Fort Wayne cars traveled over the tracks of no less than seven
different companies — the Cleveland Railway; Lake Shore Electric; Fostoria & Fremont; Toledo, Fostoria & Findlay; Western Ohio; the Fort Wayne, Van Wert & Lima; and finally entering Fort Wayne on the Indiana Service Corp.

Running times for the joint service totaled eight hours westbound and seven hours and
35 minutes eastbound. Clevelanders riding to Fort Wayne left the Public Square at 7:30 a.m.
and arrived at 2:30 p.m. Central Time. A direct connection with the ISC's "Wabash Valley Flyer" took any interested passengers to Indianapolis, putting them into the great Indianapolis Traction Terminal at 7:55 p.m. From Fort Wayne the Cleveland car left in late
morning at 11:15, arriving (as before) at 7:50 p.m. in time to make the Buffalo night boat.
This train, too, connected with the "Wabash Valley Flyer," which left Indianapolis at 7 a.m.
— an 11-hour-and-50-minute trip to Cleveland with one transfer.

Lower fares notwithstanding, one must wonder how many people preferred this gruel-
ing interurban route over the sootier but much faster steam railroads — at least between
the principal terminals. The Nickel Plate Road was 35 miles shorter between Cleveland
and Fort Wayne; westbound it beat the interurban's time by 2½ hours and eastbound by
three hours. The slowest Cleveland–Indianapolis train on the New York Central's Big Four
Route took about 8½ hours.

In any event the Fort Wayne run was doomed to an early death, as was all through Lima service. In the fall of 1922 the financially troubled Western Ohio pulled out of the through Cleveland–Lima equipment pool and sold one of the two cars it had bought for the service. As a result one of the two LSE interline services ceased on September 6, 1922, replaced by connecting limiteds at Fremont. A Western Ohio schedule dated May 7, 1923, shows one Wapakoneta–Lima–Cleveland "through" schedule, but with a change of cars at Fremont; the Fort Wayne–Lima–Cleveland run, however, was still advertised as a genuine through service, using LSE equipment. This may have lasted as such into 1924; after this, both of the old Cleveland–Lima limited runs were broken at Fremont, where passengers transferred.

The Detroit service also underwent some lesser trauma, which turned out to be short-lived anyway. Back in 1922 the Detroit United Railway had lost its Detroit city streetcar lines in a forced sale to the city. In an effort to reduce running time and now-costly street operations into downtown Detroit, it embarked on an ambitious plan to transfer passengers to parlor buses at outlying city terminals. As part of this it built an elaborate transfer station for its Toledo line on Fort Avenue at Oakwood, six miles south of the city's center. Beginning April 14, 1925, most Detroit–Toledo runs began or ended at Oakwood, presumably including the Cleveland limiteds. It was an operational success — transferring passengers saved as much as 15 minutes — but a commercial failure. The experiment ended October 21, 1926, and all cars reverted to the long street running into the city.

Intercity bus competition in the Cleveland–Toledo–Detroit market appeared in 1926, at the time the LSE was in the midst of its ownership change and the temporary management headed by Charles Thrasher. In January 1927 the company dramatically revised its limited schedules, now offering hourly limiteds between Cleveland and Toledo in place of the traditional train every two hours; every second train went through to Detroit. Routing alternated between Sandusky and Norwalk. The limiteds which originated or terminated at Toledo made tight five-minute connections with DUR limiteds so that, in effect, an hourly Cleveland–Detroit limited service could be advertised.

With Cleveland–Toledo service doubled, single cars took the place of the former two-car trains. The limited trips via Norwalk always had connecting cars at Ceylon Junction for Sandusky, with some even operating through to Fremont. From then until the end of service in 1938, single cars handled the Lake Shore's basic services; multiple-car trains were run only for certain peak traffic periods and for charter trips.

Newspapers are transferred at Fremont between car 151, running on the Norwalk route, and a Sandusky–Cleveland car behind. The two cars will meet again at Ceylon Junction. The 1937 photo was shot by J. F. Cook. (George Krambles collection)

A westbound express enters Toledo in April 1938. (Franklyn P. Kellogg photo)

A semantic change came with the November 18, 1927, timetable. The Cleveland–Detroit runs continued to be classified as "limiteds" and ran via Sandusky; the alternate-hour Toledo limiteds now were "expresses" running via Norwalk with a Huron–Sandusky–Fremont shuttle connection at Ceylon Junction. (Some shuttle runs operated through Sandusky to Fremont; some went only as far as Sandusky.) The "expresses" picked up some of the duties left by the discontinuance of through Cleveland–Toledo locals, but their running times remained the same.

How did the LSE compare with its railroad competition during this era — particularly in the premier Cleveland–Toledo service corridor? Based on terminal-to-terminal running time, the interurban inevitably was slower by a substantial margin. Taking 1928 as a more-or-less typical year, New York Central expresses covered the distance in anywhere from two hours and 20 minutes to two hours and 47 minutes, stopping only at Elyria, Sandusky, and sometimes Port Clinton or LaCarne. Its slowest local took three hours and 47 minutes. The Lake Shore Electric's limiteds normally took four hours and 20 minutes, and the best that the interurban ever regularly accomplished (which was in the 1930–31 period) was three hours and 55 minutes.

Service frequency, schedule times, and general convenience were another matter. In 1928, of course, the LSE had a clear advantage in service frequency with its hourly limiteds versus only six or seven NYC expresses during the normal travel hours. (Some other Central expresses were scheduled for the New York–Chicago overnight trade, and passed through this territory in the middle of the night.) Even its previous two-hour headway pattern gave it some advantage. In 1916, for example, the Central scheduled four or five daytime expresses versus seven or eight LSE limiteds (frequency varied by direction). Furthermore the interurban offered a consistent, regular headway over the span of the day; the steam railroad's schedules tended to be bunched in the morning, noontime, and late afternoon and evening. Station locations also favored the interurban; the electric cars arrived and departed from the centers of both Cleveland and Toledo, while the Central's lakefront station in Cleveland and its Toledo station were on the fringe. (The Central's situation in Cleveland was vastly improved when Cleveland Union Terminal opened in 1930 on the Public Square.)

At this time there was no through steam railroad service between Cleveland and Detroit; New York Central passengers had to change trains at Toledo. Even so, they beat the interurban's time by a good margin. Four daytime NYC schedules each way ranged from four hours and three minutes to five hours 20 minutes total — versus the LSE–DUR route's 6½ hours.

The electric did better against its steam railroad competitors at most intermediate points, such as Lorain, Huron, Norwalk, Bellevue, Clyde, and Fremont. For such towns, the competitive running times were roughly equal, although still slightly to the railroads' advantage — but the railroads offered only infrequent local service. (Sandusky, however, was a regular stop for most of the New York Central's Cleveland–Toledo expresses.) For example, in 1928 the LSE took two hours and ten minutes between Cleveland and Norwalk; New York Central Norwalk branch locals covered the distance in anywhere from an hour and 38 minutes to two hours and 15 minutes. The story was much the same along the balance of the Central's Norwalk branch, which connected both Cleveland and Toledo with Norwalk, Monroeville, Bellevue, Clyde, Fremont, and Genoa. But the Norwalk branch only offered three westbound trains a day and two eastbounds over the entire line, plus a single commuter round trip between Cleveland and Norwalk.

Bellevue was one of the more competitive intermediate points, served by four steam railroads — although all of them were secondary or branch lines. For Cleveland–Bellevue business, however, the Nickel Plate's four trains each way were not only an hour faster than the interurban's limiteds, but Bellevue was heavily a Nickel Plate "railroad town," a division point with yards and shops. The Lake Shore's consolation, perhaps, was that many NKP passengers thus were employee pass-riders.

The first Depression-era timetable, February 1930, cut local services significantly. But at the same time the long-distance schedules were upgraded in what proved to be a dramatic last attempt to win back the fast-diminishing business. "Express" trains left Cleveland for Toledo and Detroit every two hours between 5:30 a.m. and 7:30 p.m., usually running via Norwalk. These were supplemented by four Cleveland–Toledo limited trains spaced two hours apart. Running time of the expresses was four hours and 20 minutes, the same as the traditional limiteds of years before. The new limiteds — called "Fast Limiteds" in the timetables — were fast indeed; they made the trip in a spectacular three hours and 45 minutes, the fastest ever scheduled. One trip showed a connection to Lima, leaving both terminals in the afternoon.

It was not to last. On October 11, 1930, Cleveland–Toledo service went back to a basic two-hour headway, but three of the "fast limiteds" remained. The earlier three-hour-and-45-minute schedule apparently proved a bit too tight, and ten minutes were added to the running time. As before, the "fast limiteds" ran only to Toledo and the "expresses" continued to Detroit. By this time too, almost all through Cleveland–Toledo cars ran via Sandusky, with a connecting car running between Ceylon Junction and Fremont via Norwalk.

Southern route cars pass at Main and Hester Streets in Norwalk in August 1937. The 158 is bound for Ceylon Junction, the 155 for Fremont. (James P. Shuman photo)

Patterns were shifted on February 22, 1931, when the "fast limiteds" (although now merely labeled as "limiteds") were moved to the Detroit schedules, providing a record six-hour running time between the two terminals. But the Detroit service was now approaching its end. On April 28, 1931, the financially destitute Eastern Michigan–Toledo Railroad, the successor to the bankrupt Detroit United's DM&TSL line, tried to cancel its interline services with both the LSE and the Cincinnati & Lake Erie. Through Cleveland–Detroit services were suspended until July 20, when they resumed, including the three "fast limiteds" and two expresses each way. By then the Eastern Michigan–Toledo was so short of its own operable equipment that it had to depend on LSE and C&LE cars.

The September 6, 1932, timetable marked the nadir of LSE service. Six express trips each way operated on a three-hour headway between Cleveland and Toledo and all continued to Detroit — although some had lengthy layovers in Toledo. The "fast limited" schedules disappeared entirely, putting all Cleveland–Toledo running times back to four hours and 20 minutes.

One month later an era ended. On the evening of October 4, 1932, the Eastern Michigan–Toledo Railroad abandoned all service, taking with it the LSE's Detroit link; thereafter Toledo was the farthest western terminal.

A new and, surprisingly, slightly improved schedule took effect June 18, 1934; it was destined to be the LSE's last, serving essentially unchanged for the company's final four years. Regular daytime service consisted of Cleveland–Toledo express trains every two hours; all ran via Sandusky with a connecting car between Ceylon Junction and Fremont via Norwalk. These bi-hourly "expresses" handled all service west of Lorain including most local stops, yet they covered the Cleveland–Toledo distance in only four hours and ten minutes — a sad symptom of the sparse traffic.

By this time extra trips were rarely run, although LSE general superintendent L. K. Burge testified at a public hearing in 1937 that an express trip was run every Saturday from Cleveland to Fremont via Norwalk, probably at 1:30 p.m. Also, three Sunday evening expresses were always doubleheaded from somewhere to Cleveland. In addition a Genoa extra car doubleheaded most Toledo trips during the Saturday daytime hours.

In the leafy Cleveland suburb of Lakewood, westbound 174 takes on passengers at Coulter's drug store at Sloane and Detroit Avenues in the mid-1930s. (Louis Szakacs photo)

Sandusky–Milan–Norwalk Branch

This backwater of the Lake Shore system seemed to arouse little management attention, and its schedules were left largely untouched for most of its life. As noted earlier, the Sandusky, Milan & Norwalk's original service in 1893 consisted of two cars operating on a two-hour headway, with each trip taking an hour and 50 minutes. By 1903 the LSE had improved the frequency and speed somewhat — cars now operated every 90 minutes between 5:30 a.m. and 10:00 p.m. and took only an hour to negotiate the 18 miles. Two cars still held down all service. Except for slight variations in leaving times to connect better with main line interurban cars at Norwalk, this basic schedule remained in effect at least through the summer of 1921.

Wood interurban-type cars were normally used; one was stored overnight at Sandusky car-house and the other at the small Milan carhouse. The latter car made an early morning run

(Above) Entering Milan from Sandusky, LSE cars had to climb a steep hill out of the Huron River valley. This early view looks south toward the town as a former Sandusky, Milan & Norwalk combine heads north toward the highway bridge over the river. (W. A. McCaleb collection)

(Below) The summer-only through operations between Mansfield and Sandusky were rarely recorded, but this photo survived. An LSE Barney & Smith car loads a crowd for Cedar Point at Plymouth, Ohio, on the Sandusky, Norwalk & Mansfield about 1908. (W. A. McCaleb collection)

from Milan to Norwalk to begin its day and returned to its stable as a late evening Norwalk–Milan trip.

The branch's routine was enlivened in the 1908–1911 period by brief and only spottily documented through summer-only services between Mansfield, Ohio, and Sandusky, primarily run for the Cedar Point day-trip trade. These interline operations involved the LSE between Sandusky and Norwalk, the Sandusky, Norwalk & Mansfield Railway from Norwalk to Plymouth, the Plymouth and Shelby Traction Company between those towns, and finally the Mansfield Railway, Light & Power Company between Shelby and Mansfield. Apparently LSE cars handled all of these runs, operated by SN&M crews.

At least one charter trip was run over part of the route as early as August 1907, when an LSE car ran from Plymouth, Ohio, to Sandusky and back for a Cedar Point excursion. Regular service began the next year. A July 18, 1908, Sandusky, Norwalk & Mansfield timetable showed one scheduled through round trip a day, a limited which left Mansfield at 7:30 a.m. and arrived at Sandusky at 9:50, undoubtedly depositing most of its load for the Cedar Point steamer. The excursionists steamed back to Sandusky from Cedar Point in time to leave on the limited at 6:45 p.m., arriving wearily back home in Mansfield at 9:05. This schedule reportedly was run through August. In June 1909 local newspapers reported that an hourly through service was being planned for that summer, and some through runs were reported in the summer of 1910, but no timetables exist from either period to document what actually ran.

Finally, a June 1, 1911, Sandusky newspaper account noted that the LSE and Sandusky, Norwalk & Mansfield were planning two daily round-trip limited trains for that summer beginning June 15. Again no timetables survive to confirm that this service operated as planned, but by implication at least one regular trip must have been scheduled; the *Sandusky Register* of July 8, 1911, carried the news that "the SN&M Cedar Point limited car from Mansfield was delayed 15 minutes on Benedict Ave. in Norwalk due to a wagon loaded with hay being upset in the street." Whatever ran that year was the last regular interline service over this route.

The chronically wobbly SN&M itself expired in 1921 and its short-lived successor, the Norwalk & Shelby, gave up in April 1924. Perhaps reflecting the loss of this connection, the LSE's September 3, 1924, timetable shows that its Sandusky–Milan–Norwalk line was down to one car running at various intervals between two hours and four hours, with most daytime runs scheduled three hours apart. The car was stored overnight at the Norwalk freight house and serviced at Sandusky. This minimal schedule lasted through the end of service — which was scheduled for March 31, 1928, but came March 29 after an ice storm disabled the line.

This was the first branch to be taken over by the LSE's Lake Shore Coach Company subsidiary, which scheduled one bus on a two-hour headway from April 6, 1928, until the route was sold October 24, 1931. This lone bus was housed and serviced at the Sandusky carhouse.

The Gibsonburg Branch

Little Gibsonburg, located on the 3.4-mile dead-end spur from Gibsonburg Junction, never warranted through service to other LSE terminals except for excursions and operational moves. The branch thus spent its entire life as a classic one-car shuttle operation scheduled to meet main line runs at the junction. Its normal running time was ten minutes. Service on this interurban Toonerville Trolley was handled by a single obsolete wooden combine of one type or another which spent years — if not decades — on the branch. The first regular car was the 42, a rebuilt 1893 Sandusky, Milan & Norwalk veteran; its service (and life) was cut short when it was wrecked at the junction in August 1906. The Jewett-built No. 44, originally the Sandusky & Interurban's *Beta*, then took up residence and faithfully shuttled to Gibsonburg for the next 21 years. It was finally replaced in 1927 by No. 65, one of the onetime deluxe 1903 Brills, which completed the branch's roster; it served until the end in 1938. The resident car was stored overnight at either Gibsonburg or the junction, and was serviced at the Fremont carhouse. The single-end cars turned on wyes located at both Gibsonburg and the junction.

The branch opened December 21, 1901. A December 15, 1903, timetable shows 13 daytime round trips operating from 6 a.m. to 7 p.m. with additional evening service on Saturdays and Sundays — a pattern which lasted until June of 1918. After this date the spread of service remained the same but the number of trips was gradually reduced to eight by 1921, with three weekend evening trips. In the interim, some sort of record was set on August 2, 1907, when it was reported that 2,000 people rode the branch. The occasion which brought so many people to (or from) Gibsonburg, unfortunately, was not reported — nor was there any explanation of how, or whether, the single interurban combine handled all this business.

Interestingly, in 1927 or earlier, the branch car crew was reduced to only one man, and remained so until the end.

Riders on the tranquil Gibsonburg Branch could always expect car 65, a 1903 Brill combine long since downgraded from limited service. Shown here in 1936, it had already served the branch for nine years and would continue to the end. (Ralph A. Perkin photo)

By November 27, 1929, however, service had been dramatically improved again, with 14 daytime round trips. Evening service was run only on Sunday nights; this was handled by the last regular Toledo–Fremont local run of the night, which simply made a side trip to Gibsonburg on its way to Fremont. If one of the 60-foot-long steel Jewett interurbans (or the lengthened Niles cars 143 or 149) was used on this trip, the car had to back up from Gibsonburg to the junction because long cars could not use the junction wye. The last evening trip ended around August 10, 1930.

The 1930s saw some downs and an up: 13 daily round trips (as of August 11, 1930), 12 trips (July 20, 1931), then only nine trips (September 6, 1932). But 13 round trips returned with the June 18, 1934, schedule and remained running until the last day of service May 14, 1938.

Avon Beach & Southern Branch

This seven-mile single-track line connected the Lorain Street Railroad's Lorain–Elyria line with the LSE main line at Beach Park and was originally built to provide a cutoff route between Elyria and Cleveland via the LSRR and LSE to compete with the Cleveland Southwestern's Elyria–Cleveland main line. Its route left the LSRR's Elyria line at 31st Street and Grove Avenue in South Lorain, crossed the Black River gorge on an impressive combination trestle and truss bridge, then continued east and north on a private right-of-way to the main line junction near the Beach Park carhouse. Although technically a Lorain Street Railroad subsidiary, it was usually operated with LSE equipment from the Beach Park pool which spent the night at South Lorain carhouse.

The AB&S began operations December 21, 1905, and for slightly less than a year it attempted to fulfill its intended mission. Hourly trips ran between Cleveland and Elyria from 6:30 a.m. to 9:30 p.m., and the cars took an hour and a half between terminals — roughly comparable to the Southwestern's local service at the time.

But whatever the initial hopes, the AB&S must have quickly proved a disappointment. By the September 16, 1906, timetable only a single car based at Beach Park was shuttling back and forth on a two-hour headway between 31st and Grove in South Lorain and Beach Park. Passengers hardy enough to attempt the Elyria–Cleveland trip over this route transferred twice — a highly unlikely occurrence considering the Cleveland Southwestern's direct service. A one-transfer service appeared on the January 5, 1908, timetable, with a single car making ten round trips between Elyria and Beach Park on the two-hour headway. Total running time was 40 minutes.

But by September 1908 service had once again reverted to a two-hourly one-car shuttle between South Lorain carhouse and Beach Park, offering a total of seven round trips out of Beach Park between 7:10 a.m. and 7:10 p.m. The trip took 25 minutes. As before, an LSE interurban car handled the runs, but after 1923 this was replaced by one of the LSE's former Atlantic City Brill city streetcars in the 118-series, rebuilt for one-man operation.

Some minor modifications were made to this September 1908 schedule in 1916 and 1919, but essentially this was to be the AB&S's life story — a story of hopes thwarted. But for its first 12 years the line at least served a secondary use: until 1918, it formed the only direct track connection between the LSE and Lorain Street Railroad, and any equipment transfers had to move over the route.

The last scheduled AB&S car ran March 31, 1925. At South Lorain a stub end was retained as far as 31st and Norfolk Avenue for use by certain Lorain city runs and survived as such until September 4, 1937. The balance of the line, from 31st and Norfolk northward to Beach Park, was sold to a Cleveland Electric Illuminating Company subsidiary called the Avon Railroad. CEI originally intended to use most of the AB&S right-of-way as a means of connecting its Avon Beach power plant with the various steam railroads entering Lorain, but in the end it used only part of the northerly section between the Nickel Plate Road interchange and the Avon Beach plant. As of the late 1990s this track was still carrying coal into the plant. Ironically, this line — the least successful in the LSE system — was the last active segment of the onetime interurban.

Photos of the Avon Beach & Southern Branch are at the hen's-teeth level of scarcity, and those which seem to exist are poor. Here LSE's Stephenson-built car 70 (itself a rarity) waits at the Elyria terminal loop on Lodi Street before making the inaugural through trip to Cleveland on December 20, 1905. Dimly visible in the background is the Lake Shore & Michigan Southern's main line grade crossing, later eliminated by a grade elevation. (Karel Liebenauer collection)

The LSE's heaviest city line — and, in fact, the heaviest segment of the entire Lake Shore Electric System — was the Lorain Street Railroad's Lorain–Elyria route. It also received the last new cars ever bought by the railway, ten modern one-man suburban cars turned out by the St. Louis Car Company in 1930. One of them, the 205, has just arrived at the Elyria terminal about 1936. (W. A. McCaleb photo)

CHAPTER 12

CITY OPERATIONS

Although noted primarily as an interurban system, the Lake Shore Electric operated extensive local city routes in Lorain and Sandusky plus a single franchise-required service in Norwalk. Their traffic and economic characteristics varied enormously, from heavily burdened, industrially oriented lines to casual and folksy little Toonervilles with no visible means of support.

Sandusky's city streetcar lines were a perennially vexing financial burden, but because its interurban services depended on city franchises the company could not walk away from them. Its problems stemmed partly from early competitive overbuilding and partly from the nature and development of the city. When its horsecars began running in 1883, Sandusky's population was more than 16,000 and it was Ohio's eighth largest city. But afterward the city attracted little new industry and experienced little growth. There was only an 8 percent population gain between 1890 and 1910, the period when most of the streetcar lines were built. By 1920 Sandusky ranked only 24th among Ohio cities. The lines built into the outlying areas never attracted new residential subdivisions as they surely would have if Sandusky had enjoyed the remarkable expansion of some other Lake Erie shoreline cities. As a result, much of the territory served by the city cars was always relatively unproductive.

The industrial city of Lorain was much the opposite. As noted in Chapter 2, Lorain was transformed in the mid-1890s by Tom L. Johnson's new steel mill, which was absorbed by the U.S. Steel Corporation in 1901 and subsequently expanded. The American Shipbuilding yard and Thew shovel plant added to the industrial complexion; in the 15 years between 1890 and 1905 population soared a breathtaking 425 percent to 25,000 people. Never much more than a gritty city, Lorain lacked Sandusky's Victorian charm but it supplied heavy loads and a more understanding political environment for the railway. Here too, though, the LSE had some losers in the form of franchise-mandated operations.

Unfortunately, timetables for many LSE city lines are lacking before the early 1930s (if they even existed), so it is difficult to document how services changed over the years. In most cases, however, it may be assumed that the lines ran on reasonably consistent 15- or 30-minute headways during most daytime hours.

The Lorain–Elyria Line (Lorain Street Railroad)

Ironically, the busiest line on the entire Lake Shore Electric system was this ten-mile Lorain Street Railroad route between Lorain and Elyria, a combination of a heavy city line and a suburban operation with some interurban overtones.

The Lorain Street Railroad's Lorain–Elyria Line had all the ingredients of a heavily trafficked car line — downtown Lorain, its steel mill and shovel works, working-class suburbs, and a short intercity route to Elyria. LSRR No. 201, one of the 1930 St. Louis cars, is northbound on Broadway at Erie Avenue about 1937. (John A. Rehor collection)

Most of the route dated to 1894, built on the base of an 1888 horsecar line on Broadway from Erie Avenue to 21st Street. Tom Johnson created it primarily to carry workers from Lorain and Elyria to his South Lorain steel plant, so its route was oriented to the area along 28th Street, the border between the mill and the South Lorain workers' community. But since it ran much of the length of Broadway, Lorain's main street, and connected Lorain with the equally thriving city of Elyria, it also carried a healthy general traffic. Suburban and city-type cars were always used, although LSE interurbans occasionally appeared on special movements.

During much of the LSE era the Elyria line was almost entirely double track, much of it on center-boulevard or private right-of-way. The original route began at a loop right in the middle of the intersection of Broadway and Erie Avenue in Lorain's center. On August 21, 1919, this was relocated to an off-street loop on Broadway north of Erie. The line followed Broadway south to 21st Street, turned east on 21st across the Baltimore & Ohio Railroad tracks to North Fulton Road, then southeast on North Fulton to 28th Street, crossing three other sets of industrial tracks on the way. It then continued east on 28th along the southern border of the steel mill, passing the LSRR's carhouse, shop, and powerhouse at Seneca Street. Part of this section of the line was relocated in 1918 to bypass the operational tangle along 21st Street and North Fulton. Afterward Elyria cars were routed south on Broadway to 28th Street, using Cleveland Southwestern tracks between 21st and 28th Streets; at 28th Street they turned east to meet the original alignment, crossing beneath the B&O in a newly built underpass.

At 28th Street and Grove Avenue the line turned south, passed the Avon Beach & Southern junction at 31st Street, and entered a private right-of-way which took it to the north side of Elyria. (After the line's abandonment this was paved over as Ohio Route 57.) Cars entered Elyria on Lodi Street (later called Lake Avenue), turning at a wye and small station immediately north of the New York Central Railroad main line tracks at North Street. This wye replaced the Lorain Street Railway's original center-of-the-street loop when the railroad tracks were elevated in the 1910–15 period.

Lorain–Elyria service seems to have had a consistent history of a 20-minute headway, operating from 4:30 a.m. to 12:30 a.m. daily until the Depression. Terminal-to-terminal running time was about 40 minutes, with five cars assigned for normal base service. In addition, a short-turn city service was operated over the line as far as the 31st and Grove wye-junction; three cars ran on a 20-minute headway over this segment, giving riders a car every ten minutes north of 31st Street. Extra cars and (in earlier days) trailers were added for rush hours as required by shift changes at the mill.

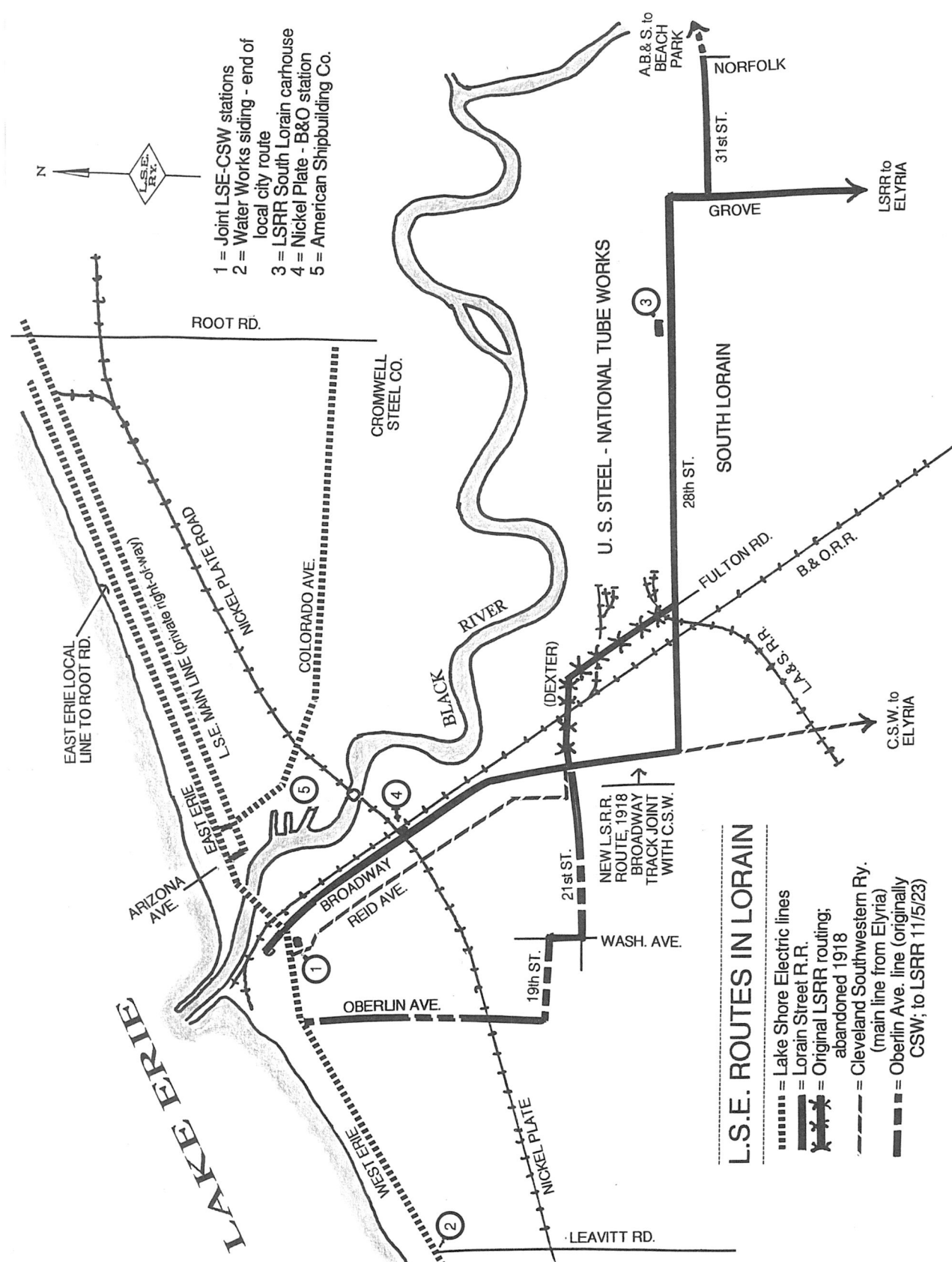

N

L.S.E. RY.

1 = Joint LSE-CSW stations
2 = Water Works siding - end of local city route
3 = LSRR South Lorain carhouse
4 = Nickel Plate - B&O station
5 = American Shipbuilding Co.

ROOT RD.

A.B.& S. to BEACH PARK

NORFOLK

31st ST.

GROVE

LSRR to ELYRIA

CROMWELL STEEL CO.

③

SOUTH LORAIN

U. S. STEEL - NATIONAL TUBE WORKS

28th ST.

EAST ERIE LOCAL LINE TO ROOT RD.

L.S.E. MAIN LINE (private right-of-way)

NICKEL PLATE ROAD

COLORADO AVE.

BLACK RIVER

FULTON RD.

B. & O.R.R.

L.A.& S. R.R.

C.S.W. to ELYRIA

EAST ERIE

ARIZONA AVE

⑤

(DEXTER)

④

BROADWAY

REID AVE.

NEW L.S.R.R. ROUTE, 1918 BROADWAY TRACK JOINT WITH C.S.W.

21st ST.

WASH. AVE.

19th ST.

①

OBERLIN AVE.

LAKE ERIE

WEST ERIE

NICKEL PLATE

②

LEAVITT RD.

L.S.E. ROUTES IN LORAIN

.... = Lake Shore Electric lines

━━━ = Lorain Street R.R.

✕✕✕ = Original LSRR routing; abandoned 1918

– – – = Cleveland Southwestern Ry. (main line from Elyria)

▬ ▬ ▬ = Oberlin Ave. line (originally CSW; to LSRR 11/5/23)

LSE lines in Lorain.

(Above) Heading for downtown Lorain from Elyria, St. Louis–built 206 rolls along the center boulevard reservation on 28th Street in South Lorain in July 1937. (W. A. McCaleb photo)

(Below) The southern half of the Lorain–Elyria Line was mostly on a straight, fast, private right-of-way. This typical scene near Elyria dates to 1937. After abandonment, this section was paved over as part of Ohio Route 57. (Ralph A. Perkin photo)

The cars used for base service to Elyria were always the newest, largest, and fastest on the Lorain Street Railroad's roster at any given time — first the wood 90–94 series Kuhlmans of 1906, then the steel 1917–18 Jewetts numbered 95–99, and finally the 200-series St. Louis cars bought in 1930. Rush hours brought out the older double-truck cars, plus the former Cleveland wood cars (LSRR 73 and 86–89) and ex-Cleveland Peter Witts (LSRR 80–84 [II]). Through the World War I period trailers 75–79 and motor cars 80–85 also were used.

At some point, some of the 31st Street city runs were extended over the Avon Beach & Southern branch several blocks to a wye at Norfolk Avenue, but surviving timetables do not document when this began or how often such trips ran. By the mid-1930s, however, all 31st Street trips were running to 31st and Norfolk. This stub operated until September 4, 1937, ending before other Lorain Street Railroad routes.

Beginning January 15, 1931, the schedules shrank somewhat, although the route remained well-served. The twenty-minute Lorain–Elyria headway (with ten minute service as far as 31st) operated only in the morning rush hours; the rest of the day both the Elyria and 31st Street cars ran only every half hour, giving 15-minute service on the inner part of the line. Again, extra cars ran for steel mill shift changes and, later, for high school students. This was the basic pattern on May 7, 1938, when all Lorain Street Railroad service ceased.

Lorain Street Railroad 83(II) is at the end of the South Lorain spur on 31st Street at Norfolk in 1930. Originally this spur formed the south end of the doomed Avon Beach & Southern branch, most of which was abandoned in 1925. The car is a 1918 Cincinnati Car Co. product with a checkered history. Originally built for Rochester, N.Y., it was diverted to the Cleveland Railway to relieve World War I pressures, and in turn was sold to the LSRR in 1924. (Ralph H. Sayles collection)

Lorain–East Erie Avenue (Lake Shore Electric)

The opposite of the busy Elyria line, this obscure and lonely single-track, single-car route originally extended 2.5 miles eastward along Erie Avenue from Broadway in Lorain to Root Road. A Lake Shore Electric operation, it was inherited from the Lorain & Cleveland and dated back to the East Lorain Street Railway of 1895. A single small secondhand single-truck car inaugurated service on February 6, 1896, and was later supplemented by an open car. The line was always a sub-marginal Toonerville, but was kept because its franchise provided the LSE's main-line entrance to downtown Lorain.

For over 20 years the regular car on the deservedly neglected East Erie Avenue route in Lorain was LSE 50, an 1898 veteran from the Lorain & Cleveland. (Karel Liebenauer collection)

The single car provided a 30-minute headway between 6 a.m. and 6 p.m. (Saturdays until 9 p.m.); passengers boarding the first inbound and last outbound trips, however, boarded on the LSE line a short distance south of East Erie, since the car was kept at the LSE's Beach Park carhouse. After 1902 LSE car 50, an 1897 Brill veteran from the L&C, was double-ended and assigned as the regular car. If it was unavailable for any reason, the line simply did not operate; passengers used the nearby interurbans.

Thanks to its deteriorating track, the route was an early casualty; Lake Shore Electric buses replaced the streetcars on September 6, 1925. A bus timetable of March 6, 1931, shows a 20-minute headway from 5:00 a.m. to 11:25 p.m., using two buses which were housed and serviced at the South Lorain carhouse. By 1935 only a single bus held down a half-hourly headway. Its last day of operation was March 31, 1938.

Lorain–West Erie Avenue (Lake Shore Electric)

West Erie Avenue carried the LSE's interurban main line westward from Lorain's center to its western city limits, but the company's franchise on the street also required local city service. Little is known about the early days of this service, but since interurban operations began over the street on August 25, 1902, it may be assumed that the regular interurban locals handled the business at 30-minute or hourly headways. Beginning in 1923 the LSE's Colorado Avenue line (see below) was tied into a new West Erie local line using two 118-series ex–Atlantic City cars which had been converted to one-man operation. In addition the route was sometimes served by Cleveland–Lorain interurban locals, which terminated at the Water Works wye at the west end of town. For example, employee timetables for the period between September 21, 1915, and September 3, 1924, and during 1927, show the hourly Cleveland–Lorain local runs operating through Lorain to this terminal.

A timetable dated March 16, 1931, shows the through-routed West Erie–Colorado Avenue cars running on a 30-minute headway between 4:55 a.m. and 11:00 p.m. Two cars still handled the schedule. When the Colorado Avenue end was cut back to the Nickel Plate railroad crossing June 11, 1932, only one car was needed.

During this period it is believed that the LSE used its double-truck ex–Atlantic City Brill cars on the route until displaced Birneys from Sandusky arrived in November 1931. Afterward a lone double-end Birney shuttled back and forth over the two lines until service ended April 30, 1938.

Lorain–Colorado Avenue (Lake Shore Electric)

On August 21, 1919, the Lake Shore Electric opened a new single-track branch off its East Erie Avenue line on the east side of the Black River to serve the American Shipbuilding

(Above) Beyond the Lorain–Elyria route, the single-truck Birney eventually became the LSE's predominant city streetcar. In 1920 the company modernized virtually all its Sandusky lines with the little bobbers, and by 1931 they also had taken over all Lorain operations but the Elyria Line. A typical example, No. 125, is on West Erie Avenue at Broadway in Lorain in 1936. (W. L. Hay photo)

(Left) The hub of the Lorain Streetcar system was Erie Avenue and Broadway. Two LSE Birneys are evident in this 1937 view looking west on Erie at the intersection. One probably is working the Oberlin Belt Line and will turn south (left in this view) on Broadway, while the other will continue east on Erie and Colorado Avenue (center tracks). This track also carried LSE interurbans. (Ray Ewers collection)

complex and the Cromwell Steel Company plant, a new facility built during World War I. It left downtown Lorain on East Erie Avenue, turned southeast at Colorado Avenue, then followed Colorado (mostly on the side of the road) to a wye at the Cromwell plant west of Root Road. In earlier years it was tied into the Lorain Street Railroad's Lorain–South Lorain services, but in 1923 was through-routed with the new West Erie line to the Water Works wye on the west side of town.

And like the West Erie route it ran in obscurity most of its life. The March 16, 1931, timetable shows it through-routed with West Erie. When the line opened in 1919 it probably was served by Lorain Street Railroad cars and LSE Nos. 54 and 57, a pair of odd 1902 Kuhlman-built light interurbans originally built for the Cleveland, Elyria & Western but never delivered. These were succeeded in 1923 by two elderly ex–Atlantic City Brill cars, which handled service for the two routes, running every half hour from 5:00 a.m. to 11:25 p.m. About 15 minutes were needed from the center of Lorain to Root Road.

By the onset of the Depression the Cromwell plant had closed and anticipated new housing in the area never developed. As a result, on June 11, 1932, the car line was cut back to the north side of the Nickel Plate Road grade crossing on Colorado Avenue. From then until the end on April 30, 1938, a single Birney operated the 30-minute headway over the two lines.

Lorain–Oberlin Belt Line (Lorain Street Railroad)

The Cleveland Southwestern also served Lorain with both its competitive Elyria line and a single local city route. The Elyria line entered town on Broadway, then turned west on 21st to Reid Avenue and north on Reid to the joint LSE-CSW station on West Erie west of Broadway.

Its city route, known as Oberlin Avenue, covered the west side of Lorain, starting at 21st and Reid Avenue and Broadway, then running west on West 21st Street, north on Washington, west again on 19th Street, then north on Oberlin Avenue to West Erie. On November 5, 1923, the LSE's Lorain Street Railroad took over this line, initially operating the same route. But on March 24, 1925, it was integrated with LSRR and LSE trackage, and afterward was operated as a continuous loop route serving both the central and western sections of the city. (The CSW retained the Reid Avenue track for its Elyria interurbans.) Cars ran in both directions around the belt. Going clockwise, they began in the city's center at Broadway and Erie, then went south on Broadway on the Lorain Street Railroad's line. At 21st Street they swung west onto the original CSW route, going west on 21st, north on Washington Avenue, west on 19th, north again on Oberlin Avenue. At Oberlin and West Erie they turned east onto the LSE main line and followed it back to Broadway to complete the loop. The portions of the route which used the LSE and LSRR lines on West Erie and Broadway were double-track; the balance was single with a passing siding on 19th Street.

Since the original CSW line was stub-ended at both ends, the LSRR used a double-ended LSE 118-series car from the line's acquisition in 1923 to its conversion in 1925. From then until 1928 various single-end city cars were used. Afterward it was normally run with single-end LSE Birneys displaced from Sandusky, supplemented by LSRR double-truckers as needed.

As of March 1931 the Oberlin Belt offered 15-minute headways running in both directions on the loop during daytime hours and half-hourly after 7:20 p.m. Cars made each circuit in half an hour. Four cars serviced the route during daytime hours and two at night. After 1935 service was cut to 30 minutes during most hours with 15-minute rush hour headways in one of the directions, requiring two cars for the base and three in rush hour. Mill and school tripper cars also ran between Oberlin Avenue and South Lorain. The line finally died on April 30, 1938.

LSE Birneys 138 and 132 pass on 19th Street in Lorain while making their respective circuits on the Oberlin Belt route. (Tom Heinrich collection)

Sandusky–Depot Belt Line

The Depot Belt was the Sandusky Street Railway's first horsecar route and the LSE's earliest predecessor, dating in part to 1883 and originally conceived to reach the then-remote Lake Shore & Michigan Southern Railway station. Its earliest segment ran south on Columbus Avenue from Water Street, turning southwest on Hayes Avenue to North Depot Street and the railroad station. In 1885 the line was turned into a loop by extending it west on North Depot Street to Camp Steet, north on Camp to Washington, east on Washington to Jackson, north on Jackson to Washington Row, then east on Washington Row to Columbus Avenue. After the LSE took over all the Sandusky city lines in 1901 it abandoned the Washington–Jackson–Washington Row portion, and the northwestern part of the Depot Belt was rerouted via Camp, Washington, Lawrence Street, and Water Street to Columbus Avenue. The large loop was operated in both directions.

The line's February 10, 1930, timetable shows a ten-minute headway for both directions between 5:30 a.m. and 11 p.m., with a running time of 20 minutes. Four cars were needed — which before 1920 consisted of Brill single-truck cars. Afterward single-end Birneys handled all runs.

The continuous belt routing was broken October 28, 1931, when the northwestern portion of the loop north of Camp and Jefferson Streets was abandoned. The remainder of the line continued running every 15 minutes using two double-end Birneys. That, in turn, ceased July 1, 1935, when they were replaced by a single bus running every 20 minutes. The bus was leased from Lake Shore Coach Company but technically operated by the railway.

Sandusky–Soldiers Home Belt Line

Like the Depot Belt line, this route operated as a continuous loop in both directions. It was put together by the LSE in 1901 from portions of the 1883 (and later) Sandusky Street Railway route on Columbus Avenue and the former People's Electric Railway's Hancock

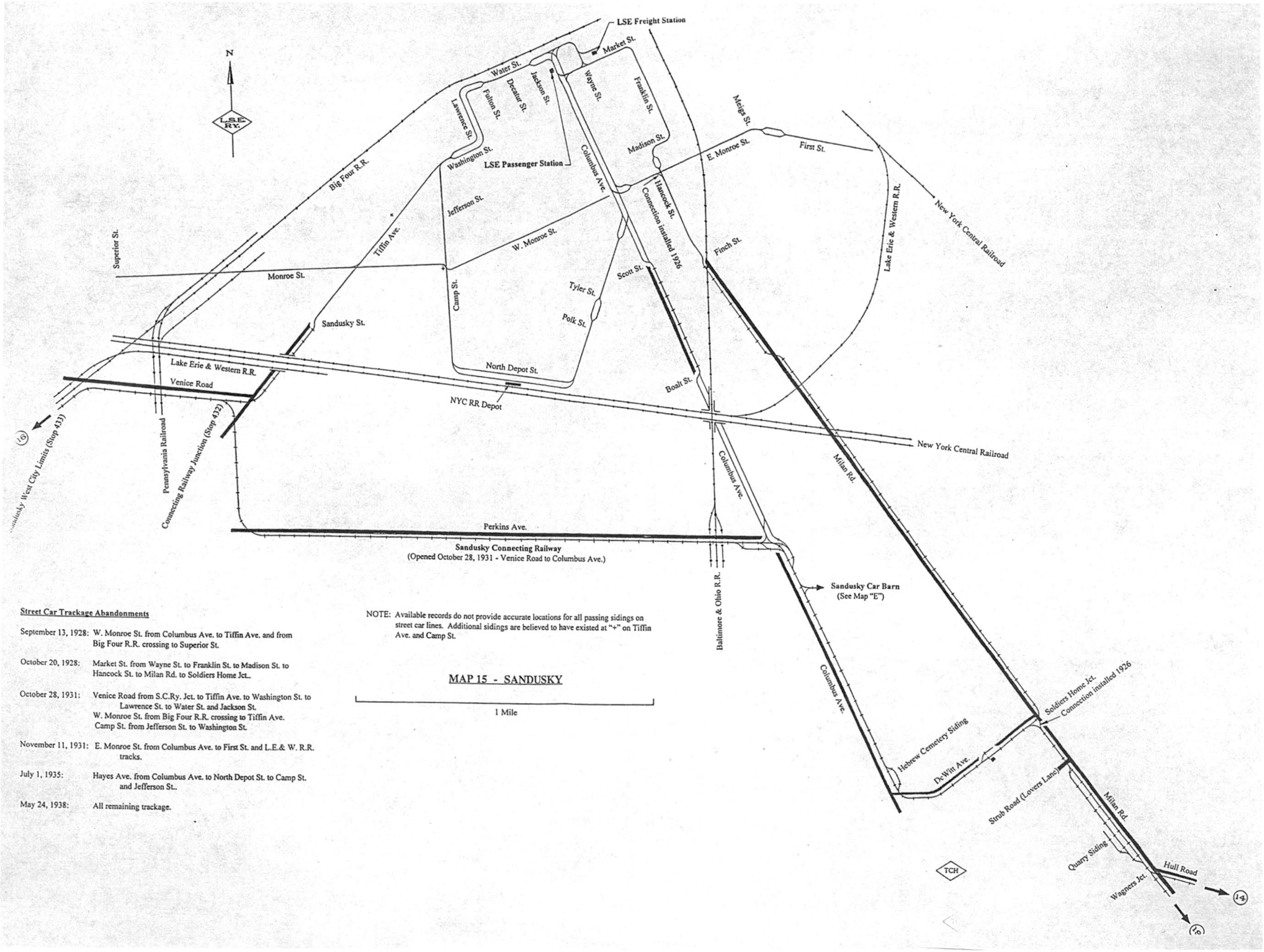
MAP 15 - SANDUSKY
N
L.S.E. RY.
LSE Freight Station
Market St.
Water St.
Jackson St.
Decatur St.
Fulton St.
Lawrence St.
Wayne St.
Franklin St.
Madison St.
Washington St.
LSE Passenger Station
Columbus Ave.
Hancock St.
Connection installed 1926
Meigs St.
E. Monroe St.
First St.
Big Four R.R.
Jefferson St.
W. Monroe St.
Tiffin Ave.
Superior St.
Monroe St.
Camp St.
Tyler St.
Polk St.
Scott St.
Finch St.
Lake Erie & Western R.R.
New York Central Railroad
Sandusky St.
North Depot St.
NYC RR Depot
Boalt St.
Venice Road
Pennsylvania Railroad
Connecting Railway Junction (Stop 432)
Sandusky West City Limits (Stop 433)
16
Milan Rd.
Perkins Ave.
Sandusky Connecting Railway
(Opened October 28, 1931 - Venice Road to Columbus Ave.)
Baltimore & Ohio R.R.
Sandusky Car Barn
(See Map "E")
Street Car Trackage Abandonments
September 13, 1928: W. Monroe St. from Columbus Ave. to Tiffin Ave. and from Big Four R.R. crossing to Superior St.
October 20, 1928: Market St. from Wayne St. to Franklin St. to Madison St. to Hancock St. to Milan Rd. to Soldiers Home Jct..
October 28, 1931: Venice Road from S.C.Ry. Jct. to Tiffin Ave. to Washington St. to Lawrence St. to Water St. and Jackson St.
W. Monroe St. from Big Four R.R. crossing to Tiffin Ave.
Camp St. from Jefferson St. to Washington St.
November 11, 1931: E. Monroe St. from Columbus Ave. to First St. and L.E.& W. R.R. tracks.
July 1, 1935: Hayes Ave. from Columbus Ave. to North Depot St. to Camp St. and Jefferson St..
May 24, 1938: All remaining trackage.
NOTE: Available records do not provide accurate locations for all passing sidings on street car lines. Additional sidings are believed to have existed at "+" on Tiffin Ave. and Camp St.
1 Mile
Soldiers Home Jct.
Connection installed 1926
Hebrew Cemetery Siding
DeWitt Ave.
Strub Road (Lovers Lane)
Quarry Siding
Wagners Jct.
Hull Road
TCH
14
16

Lake Shore Electric Sandusky city lines after 1907. (Tom Heinrich)

Street–Milan Road line, which had been built in the early 1890s. The terminal point was the Ohio Soldiers and Sailors Home, a sprawling collection of buildings opened in 1889 on a 300-acre tract between Columbus Avenue and Milan Road about a mile south of the city limits.

Going clockwise, the Soldiers Home Belt started on Columbus Avenue at Market Street, ran east on Market to Franklin, south on Franklin to its intersection with Madison Street and Huron Avenue, jogged a block west on Madison to Hancock, then turned south on Hancock Street (which became Milan Road) for 1.6 miles to the Soldiers Home. Cars then turned west into DeWitt Avenue, where the picturesque waiting station stood on the north side of the Soldiers Home property.

After pausing at the station, they continued west on DeWitt to Columbus Avenue, then turned north alongside Columbus to return to downtown Sandusky. Before 1926 Columbus Avenue cars had to negotiate an especially nasty grade crossing of both the New York Central main line and Baltimore & Ohio at the same point. The car tracks were in city streets in downtown Sandusky, but alongside Milan Road south of the B&O crossing, and alongside Columbus Avenue south of Scott Street.

Up through the mid-1920s it is believed that the belt route ran a 20-minute headway in both directions; the entire loop consumed about 40 minutes and probably required four cars — which consisted of old single-truckers until 1913, then open and closed secondhand double-truck cars from Atlantic City. These in turn were replaced by single-end Birneys beginning July 5, 1920.

The Soldiers Home line was always a financially marginal operation, and as early as 1921 the LSE proposed to abandon the Hancock Street side of the belt. This section had been built by People's Railway to compete directly with the Sandusky Street Railway's Columbus Avenue route and as such it was always redundant; much of the route was only two blocks from the paralleling Columbus Avenue portion. But strong public opposition forced its continuance at that time.

The new single-end Birneys were destined for a short life on the line. The belt routing was broken in 1926 when construction began on the Columbus Avenue underpass at the New York Central–B&O railroad crossing. Through service on Columbus Avenue through the completed underpass resumed October 20, 1928. But simultaneously the LSE accomplished its aim of eliminating rail operations on the Hancock Street–Milan Road side of the belt. On the same date it replaced this route with the Lake Shore Coach Company's East End bus line and, to some extent, by the Lake Shore's Sandusky–Norwalk intercity bus line which had begun earlier that year. A pair of double-end Birneys then operated the remaining 20-minute service out Columbus Avenue to the Soldiers Home.

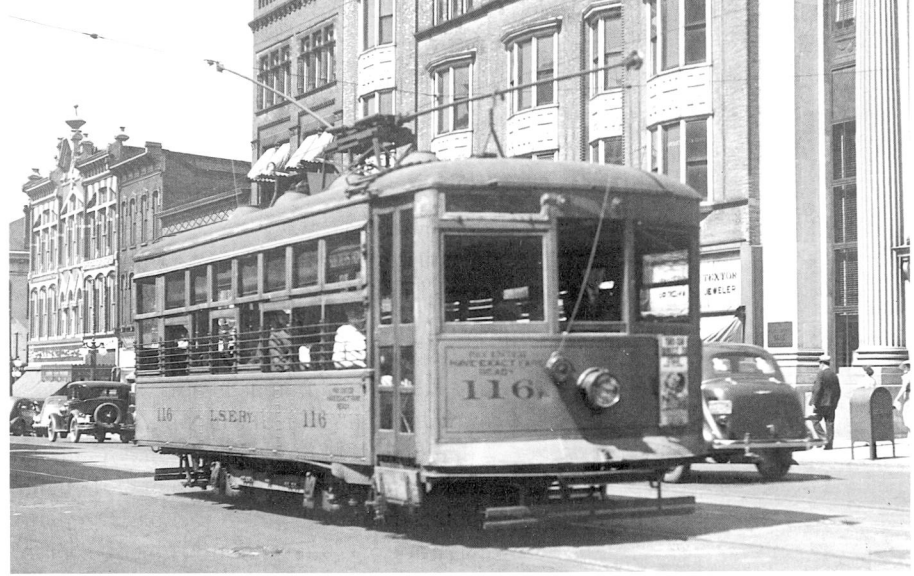

Outbound for the Soldiers Home, ex–Baltimore Birney 116 (II) heads south on Columbus Avenue south of Market Street in downtown Sandusky in August 1937. (William R. Heller photo)

Despite the LSE's unhappiness with the little Soldiers Home line, its surviving remnant outlived everything else on the system, including the grand interurban limiteds. Its last regular day came May 24, 1938, when a lone Lake Shore Coach bus replaced the two Birneys. Even then it was not completely dead; on Memorial Day, May 30, specials were run all day to Oakland Cemetery, using two city cars and three interurbans.

Sandusky's Tiffin Avenue Line ended at the hulking Kuebeler Brewery on the city's southwest side. Clearly, Kuebeler had a healthy market among Sandusky's heavily German population of the time. The Kuebelers also helped finance the Cedar Point resort, and their beer was sold exclusively there until Prohibition. (Henry Timman photo)

Sandusky–East Monroe–Tiffin Avenue

The east–west East Monroe–Tiffin Avenue route was put together from lines originally built by the People's Electric Railway. From east to west, it began on Sandusky's east side at First and Lane Streets, near the waterfront and adjacent to a New York Central branch, once its main line into the city from the east. Cars followed First Street to the Meigs Street/ East Monroe intersection, East Monroe to Columbus Avenue, Columbus Avenue north to Water Street, west on West Water Street, south on Lawrence Street (passing the original People's Electric Railway carbarn and power house), west on Washington Street to the "Five Points" intersection with Tiffin Avenue, and finally out Tiffin Avenue to the Kuebeler brewery just beyond Broadway. After 1907 LSE interurbans to Fremont continued on out Tiffin Avenue past Venice Road. The city cars could make downtown turnbacks by looping around Columbus Avenue, East Water Street, Wayne Street, and Market.

Base service in early 1930 was every 15 minutes, using three cars. Starting September 14, 1928, every other Tiffin Avenue car branched onto West Monroe Street as far as the Big Four railroad crossing, replacing part of the West Monroe line (below). Double-end Birneys held down all service beginning July 1, 1920, succeeding the 1901 Brill single-truck cars.

The Tiffin Avenue end of the line was replaced by the Lake Shore Coach West End bus on October 28, 1931; an expanded East End bus line replaced the East Monroe section on November 11 of that year.

Sandusky–West Monroe Street

This odd line was a relic from the Sandusky Street Railway, a clearly unloved orphan which never seemed to fit into the LSE's Sandusky route system. For a brief period around

1901 it was part of a through crosstown line on West and East Monroe, connecting the Enterprise Glass factory at Superior and West Monroe with First Street at the New York Central (LS&MS) crossing. But for most of its life under the LSE it operated as a shuttle line serving Sandusky's west side, and never ran all the way downtown. (In fact, there was no track connection for it to do so.) When it ran — which sometimes was infrequently — it began on West Monroe Street at Columbus Avenue and followed Monroe west, crossing other car lines at Camp Street and Tiffin Avenue, crossing the Big Four and Pennsylvania Railroad tracks west of King Street, and finally ending at the western city limits at Superior Street. At this end was Winnebago Park, a small park on Sandusky Bay which still exists as Lion's Park. One or, at most, two double-end cars carried the patient passengers. Before late 1925 that meant one of the weary 1901 Brill single-truckers; afterward a former Baltimore Birney took over.

None of the LSE's four Sandusky city lines were strong financial performers, but West Monroe was the champion loser. During the 1915–16 period it carried an average of only 2.3 passengers paying a total of ten cents on each 1.6-mile trip. Typically, the crew members must have outnumbered the passengers.

Most of the line — the section between Columbus Avenue and Tiffin Avenue, and the western end from the Big Four railroad crossing to Superior Street — was abandoned September 13, 1928; the remaining western stub from Tiffin Avenue to the Big Four crossing was served by alternate Tiffin Avenue cars until that line ended on October 27, 1931.

Filling in for the regular No. 101, LSE's 1901 Brill city car 111(II) picks up a passenger on a slushy winter day in Norwalk. (Firelands Museum collection)

Norwalk

As a condition of the original Sandusky, Milan & Huron Railway's franchise on Main Street in Norwalk, the company (which became the Sandusky, Milan & Norwalk) was obligated to run a local city car on Main Street between the east side of town at Old State Road and the western city limit. The service began in 1893, and when the Toledo, Fremont & Norwalk arrived in Norwalk on May 1, 1901, it used the western end of the line as its entry to town.

A lone single-truck double-end car gave hourly service each day, but perhaps not always on Sundays — various sources differ. It was stored overnight at the freight house on Whittlesey Avenue and, in earlier days, probably was shopped at the Milan carhouse. After that was closed it was sent to Sandusky for work. The vehicle was virtually a permanent Norwalk resident. For 27 years the regular was LSE 101, an 1898 Pullman product which the SM&N had bought for the service; this aging veteran was replaced in December 1925 by No. 115, a former Baltimore Birney which carried on for almost 13 years afterward.

(*Above*) Norwalk's single-car Main Street line was regularly worked by only three cars over its 45-year lifetime. This was the second, built by Pullman in 1898 as Sandusky, Milan & Norwalk No. 17 and later renumbered LSE 101. It served until 1925. (Pullman photo, George Krambles collection)

(*Below*) Succeeding No. 101 in 1925 was ex–Baltimore Birney 115(II). But whatever the car, it seemed to be the personal property of Fred Gassman, its conductor and then motorman since 1906. Here Gassman poses with his charge at the line's east end at Allings Corners in early 1938. He was, of course, there for the last run. (W. L. Hay photo)

CHAPTER 13

FREIGHT SERVICES

Passengers were the Lake Shore Electric's primary business, or so it originally thought. But after a belated start, the company established a substantial and far-flung freight operation which eventually overtook passengers in importance. Indeed, by the early 1930s freight appeared to be the key to whatever future the railway had. Describing it is more difficult, however. Unlike its passenger operations with their myriad timetable publications, the LSE's freight services are only spottily documented; it was a complex business, some parts of which followed no fixed patterns.

First, some definitions are needed. Actually, "freight" on the LSE (and most other rail carriers) consisted of at least four disparate types of traffic lumped under one loose definition: (1) "express" or "package freight," (2) less-than-carload freight, universally abbreviated as "LCL" by the rail lines, (3) forwarder or consolidator shipments, and (4) straight carload movements of several different types. To one degree or another each of these varieties involved different handling methods, rate scales, equipment, traffic patterns and economic characteristics. Often, too, their patterns of growth and decline varied from one another.

The Lake Shore Electric's earliest type of freight was what was variously called "express" or "package freight" — individual shipments of relatively small size, light weight, and high value. "Package freight" was merely an easy shorthand term for a mishmash of different types of small shipments. Besides packages there were trunks, crates, barrels, drums, and the like; some shipments, such as tools or small farm implements were simply tagged and sent loose. (There was at least one instance of a 3,100-pound tractor being sent express from Cleveland to Fremont.) Before 1913 the U.S. Post Office did not handle anything weighing over four pounds, so many items which later would be sent parcel post were shipped as express. Small-lot perishables such as fruits, vegetables, and Lake Erie fish were also shipped express, as were live baby chicks. (Milk, however, was a separate specialized type of business, not classed as express.) Traditionally, express was considered a premium service, and usually included door-to-door pickup and delivery. Shippers or receivers generally had to pay charges on the spot, either in advance or on delivery.

Typically, neither the steam railroads nor the interurbans attempted to operate the express business themselves. Separate companies or agencies — often railroad-owned — handled such essentials as customer solicitation and contact, pickup and delivery, loading and unloading the rail cars, storage, and collection of charges. These in turn contracted with the railways for transportation service. The contracts were usually exclusive — that is, any given railway contracted with a single express agency. Such was the case with the LSE, which primarily carried express for the Electric Package Company, which it partly owned.

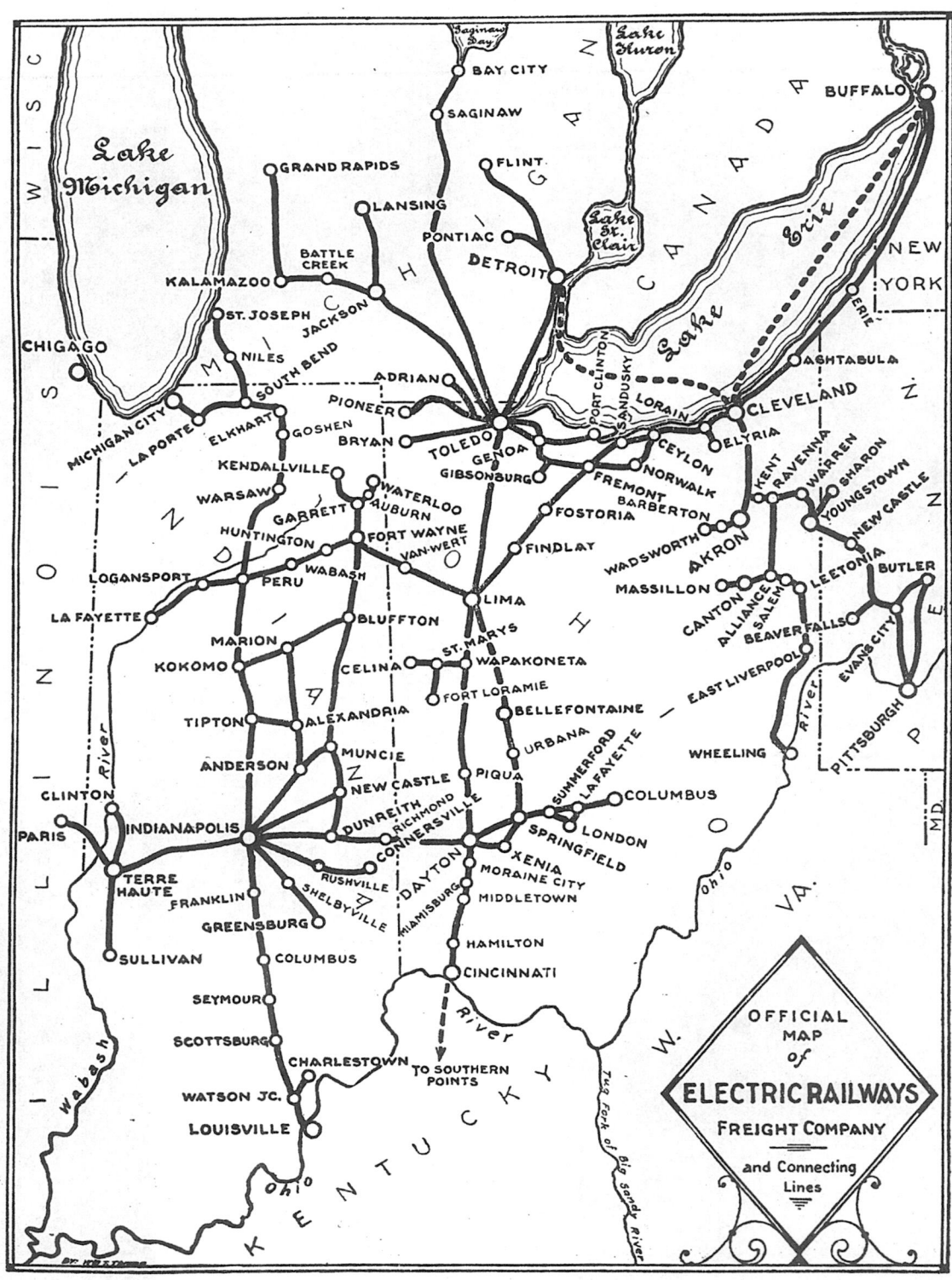

When the LSE's partly owned Electric Railways Freight Company issued this official map in April 1931, the agency could still advertise an extensive interurban service network in the Midwest. By then a few points were reached by connecting trucks, but various interurban lines served most. By the end of the following year many key lines were gone and the agency itself had been dissolved. (John A. Rehor collection)

Heavier and bulkier items were classed purely as "freight" and were shipped in two forms — carload and less-than-carload (LCL). There was some overlap of commodities and shipment size between express shipments and LCL freight, but the rate scales and services were different. LCL rate scales usually were somewhat lower than express, and the railways operated the services themselves. LCL shipments usually were brought to a railway freight house by the customer; the railway then consolidated them with other shipments in a freight motor or box trailer, and carried them to another freight house where the receiver came to pick them up.

Typical of many (but certainly not all) Midwestern interurbans, the LSE initially avoided this kind of business. While Electric Package Company express traffic could be handled principally as a by-product of passenger operations, with little extra work on the railway's part, LCL freight required dedicated facilities, forces, services, and expertise. But the market had potential. The steam railroads generally were ill-suited to handle relatively short-haul LCL shipments expeditiously; the more flexible interurbans often could offer overnight or next-day service while their railroad competitors might take several days or even weeks. The business came at a stiff price, however; LCL required manual handling at the various freight houses and was highly labor-intensive. And in many cases, the goods had to be re-handled at intermediate freight houses as they moved between different routes or carriers. As a result, rates were high, and as highways and motor truck technology improved, LCL proved most lucrative to the truckers. They could quote the same rates — or sometimes even higher rates — but offered a service that was cheaper for them to operate and superior for the customer.

In some cases, less-than-carload shipments were consolidated into full carloads and shipped terminal-to-terminal on the interurban by an independent freight forwarding company. These operators solicited the customers, picked up their shipments, consolidated them into full carloads at the freight terminal, delivered them at the other end, and collected the freight charges. Basically they made their money by charging the customer the published less-than-carload rate and paying the railway a specially negotiated lower full carload rate. In effect, the railway was simply a middleman in the movement, but it welcomed this type of traffic since it was relieved of the expenses and numerous problems of soliciting and handling the "retail" end of the small-shipment business. The freight shippers also were happy to use these forwarding companies since they gave better service for the money. Eventually the LSE handled large amounts of this kind of traffic. Its only drawback was that it was limited to markets where the forwarder could count on regular high-volume loads. For the LSE this meant such city pairs as Cleveland–Detroit or Cleveland–Cincinnati.

The next freight category was merchandise traffic in full carload lots. Cars were loaded and unloaded by the customers, either at a private siding or at a public railway siding (or "team track") where the customer's wagon or truck could back up to the car. The railway needed only to place the empty car for loading, take it to the destination, and place it for unloading. As a result, carload rates were lower than less-than-carload, sometimes substantially so. But it was profitable business — and again, interurbans such as the LSE usually could beat the steam railroads' transit time within their service territory. The principal problem was that few manufacturing plants had interurban sidings, and this was particularly true in the Lake Shore's on-line territory. Some of the LSE's interline connections were better situated, however. The Northern Ohio, for example, served Hoover at North Canton and some steel products producers at Massillon; the Penn-Ohio reached Sharon Steel Company, and the Toledo & Western had access to the Overland division of the Willys-Overland automobile company at Toledo.

Whatever the type of freight, the Lake Shore generally handled it either in its own equipment or the cars of its connecting interurban lines. Interchange with steam railroads and the use of standard railroad freight cars in revenue interline movements was minimal and, in fact, most major railroads refused to make interline rates with the LSE. After all, virtually every reasonably populated point reached by the Lake Shore was also served by some steam road which already had freight facilities and sidings for local industries; these railroads were hardly anxious either to share this business with the interurban or establish interline routes which would shorthaul themselves. To work with the steam railroads, an interurban had to generate traffic which the railroad wanted to handle — which usually meant developing its own on-line industries. Several of the LSE's neighbors did so to one degree or another — notably the Northern Ohio, the Toledo & Indiana, the Toledo & Western, and the Toledo, Port Clinton & Lakeside — but for whatever reasons, the Lake Shore did not.

The LSE did switch steam railroad cars, mostly shipments of its own supplies and materials. The largest volume was coal for its generating plant at Beach Park, which was received via the Nickel Plate Road at an interchange at Root Road east of Lorain. After the Beach Park plant's demise in 1925, the Cleveland Electric Illuminating Company built a new commercial generating plant on the site, and although a direct connection with the Nickel Plate was established over part of the old Avon Beach & Southern line, the LSE continued to bring in at least some CEI coal. Similarly, at Fremont the LSE received coal cars for its power plant from an adjacent Wheeling & Lake Erie interchange. Also, LSE work motors hauled coal from the W&LE interchange to Clauss Cutlery and the Herbrand Company via the LSE track on State Street under commercial switching arrangements.

One unusual type of "freight" on the LSE consisted of moving streetcars and interurbans owned by other companies under their own power, en route for rebuilding, sale, or display at trade exhibitions. The G. C. Kuhlman Car Company, a Brill subsidiary, was located on the east side of Cleveland and often its new cars were operated westward on the LSE for delivery to customers; other cars moved back and forth for rebuilding. In 1911, for example, 20 Detroit United open city cars were shipped over the LSE from Toledo to Rocky River en route to the Kuhlman plant for rebuilding into closed cars. Two months later they returned over the same route. In late 1921, 50 new Peter Witt–type cars were run from Cleveland for delivery to Detroit. In at least one case the LSE actually hauled steam railroad passenger cars; in June 1913 it moved Wheeling & Lake Erie passenger combines 097 and 099 from the Nickel Plate interchange at Root Road to the Rod and Gun Club at Beach Park.

Early Freight Operations

Most LSE predecessors limited themselves to the express business, and even then they were usually in no hurry to exploit it. The earliest component, the Sandusky, Milan & Norwalk, bought a single passenger-baggage combine for its 1893 opening and provided baggage and express service with it roughly every four hours. Later it supplemented this by rebuilding a passenger excursion trailer into a motorized full baggage car. The American Express Company, one of the old-line railroad express agencies, handled the SM&N's express business. The Sandusky & Interurban waited over a year after its opening before acquiring a new baggage motor in 1901 — the *Delta*.

Like the S&I, the Lorain & Cleveland was slow to get into the business. Although opened in 1897, it had no express-hauling ability until it bought two Brill combines between 1898 and 1899. And like the Sandusky, Milan & Norwalk, it initially contracted with the American Express Company to handle the traffic.

But in 1898 the Lorain & Cleveland joined with most of Cleveland's other interurban companies to form their own express agency, the Electric Package Company. Other owners were the predecessors of the Northern Ohio Traction & Light, the Cleveland Southwestern, and the Cleveland, Painesville & Eastern. (The Cleveland Railway, over which all these lines operated to reach downtown, also later became an owner.) Of the Cleveland interurbans, only the Cleveland & Eastern and Cleveland & Chagrin Falls did not participate; these two associated lines served a thinly populated rural territory with no direct steam railroad competition, and were a world unto themselves.

Otherwise the agency covered much of northern Ohio, taking control of all express handling over its owner lines in its own name, including door-to-door pickup and delivery (which in many cases it contracted out to local drayage companies). It also had joint arrangements with several steam railroad express companies covering points beyond its own territory. Like similar railroad express agencies, its business was limited strictly to express, or small shipments; it did not handle LCL or carload freight. Depending on location, the handling work was done by its own full-time employees, by railway employees who received an extra "commission," or by outside contractors. The unincorporated agency collected all express revenues, paid its employees and contractors, and divided the residual earnings among the owners. It did quite well by interurban industry standards and served the LSE until the end of freight operations in 1937.

Lorain & Cleveland President Barney Mahler served as the Electric Package Company's first president. On December 1, 1898, the agency opened its own Cleveland freight depot at 92 North Ontario Street, just north of the Society for Savings building at the Public Square. Subsequently its market territory expanded considerably as the LSE system was completed and other lines were extended and consolidated. By 1910 it covered 614 miles of interurban routes and had 200 employees — clearly a larger and more effective organization than any of its individual owners could afford.

Of the LSE's predecessors, only the Toledo, Fremont & Norwalk seriously attempted a true freight business, doubtless because its general manager, Furman J. Stout, had come from a steam railroad background. The TF&N issued steam railroad–type freight tariffs and bought three heavy-duty box freight motors from Barney & Smith, similar to its large passenger cars except for their arched roofs. But although Stout became the Lake Shore Electric's general superintendent when the company was put together, the TF&N's freight policies did not prevail.

After its formation the LSE adopted the "express-only" policy of most of its predecessors; it extended Electric Package Company express service systemwide, and discontinued the old TF&N freight tariffs. Its reasons are now speculative, but most likely it was a case of concentrating on what the company felt it could do best considering its markets, physical

The Toledo, Fremont & Norwalk was the only one of the LSE's predecessors to attempt full-scale freight handling. No. 31, one of its three Barney & Smith freight motors, loads at Toledo in 1901. (John A. Rehor collection)

plant, and facilities. Interurban freight trains were often unwelcome in city streets anyway. The city of Cleveland, in fact, banned freight (as distinguished from express) on its streets, limiting the LSE even if it had wanted to develop the business. (This restriction was lifted in 1913, although it was reported that no freight was handled immediately afterward.)

For equipment, the LSE carried its express shipments in combines on regular passenger runs and in a small fleet of inherited box motors. Initially only the three former TF&N box motors and several semi-obsolete combines were available for the service, but in 1903 the ten Brill-built high-speed interurban combines arrived to expand express capacity systemwide. Five new Niles combines were added in 1906 and two older combines — an ex–Lorain & Cleveland car and the rebuilt former S&I *Alpha* — were converted to box motors. Thus by 1907 the LSE had 15 interurban combines and five full baggage-express motors for its growing express operations.

In the meantime an elaborate, high-capacity off-street express and freight terminal had been created in Cleveland to serve all interurban lines entering the city and the express agency. The Electric Depot Company was formed in 1903, jointly owned by the Cleveland Electric Railway (later simply Cleveland Railway), the Northern Ohio, the Lake Shore Electric, Cleveland & Southwestern, and Cleveland, Painesville & Eastern. (As it had done with the Electric Package Company, the Eastern Ohio Traction — a short-lived consolidation of the onetime Cleveland & Eastern and Cleveland & Chagrin Falls — held itself apart. While the EOT owned no stock in the depot company, it and its successors used the terminal as tenants.) The new terminal, which opened October 24, 1903, occupied part of the block between Eagle Avenue and Bolivar Road west of East 9th Street; it was thus almost in the center of the city's central retail district — better situated, in fact, than any comparable steam railroad facility. The initial building was a large combination freight house and office stretching almost the width of the block, used primarily by the Electric Package Company.

Over the years the Eagle Avenue freight terminal was expanded several times. A major addition came in late 1911 when a new fireproof warehouse was built parallel to and immediately east of the original shed. The 25 × 267-foot brick and concrete building faced Bolivar Road and extended back to Eagle Avenue; it included an underground storage area

LSE motor 27, a rebuilt Barney & Smith passenger coach, is moving out of the terminal on Eagle Avenue in 1931. (Ralph A. Perkin photo)

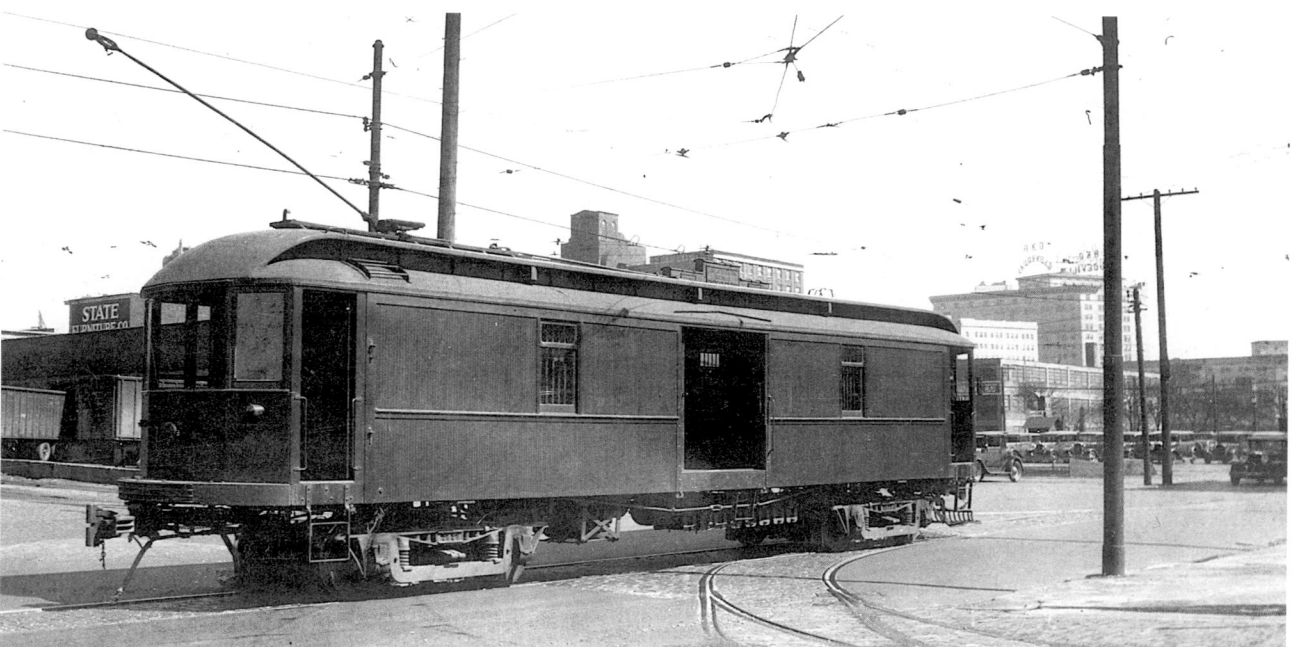

Cleveland's union freight terminal occupied most of the block bounded by Eagle Avenue, East 9th Street, and Bolivar Road. *(Above)* This late 1920s view looks north toward Bolivar road. The LSE's outbound freight house is the flat-roofed building in the center. *(Below)* A street-level view of the LSE freight house. (Both, John A. Rehor collection)

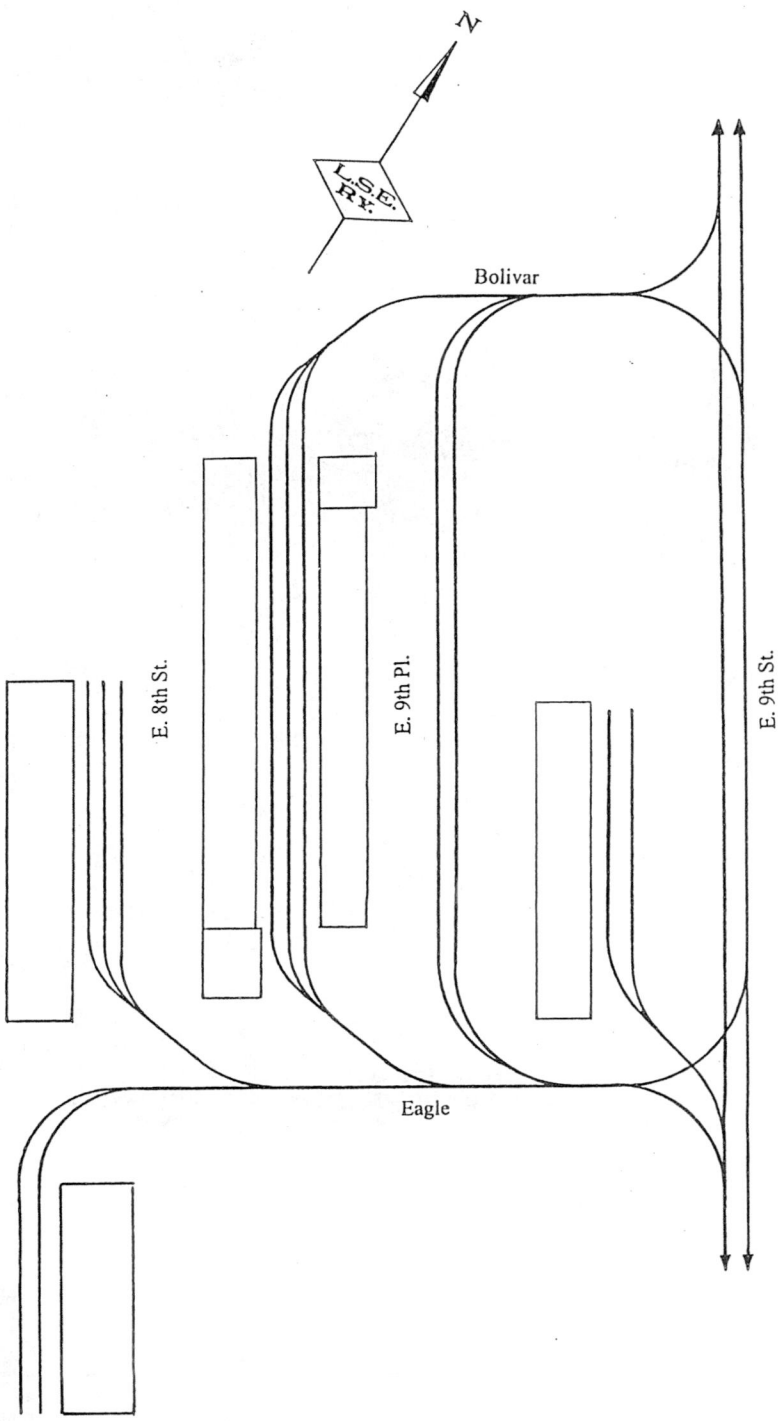

N

L.S.E. RY.

Bolivar

E. 8th St.

E. 9th Pl.

E. 9th St.

Eagle

(Left) Tracks and buildings were progressively added to the original 1903 Eagle Avenue facilities over the years. This map shows the layout at its peak in the late 1920s. Occupancy of the various freight houses also changed; space was leased to the Electric Package Agency and individual interurban lines as volume dictated. (Tom Heinrich)

for pickup and delivery vehicles, and a two-story office section. When opened, the building was used partly by the Electric Package Agency (renamed from the Electric Package Company in 1910), partly for the Cleveland & Eastern's and Cleveland, Youngstown & Eastern's LCL freight business, and partly for milk traffic. Later, when the LSE entered the LCL freight business, it became the Lake Shore's outbound freight house.

In Toledo, the LSE used a "union" downtown freight station on Huron Street which varied in size, complexion, and tenants over the years. At its height the complex consisted of a 1902 brick building at 518 Huron, a 1903 brick building at 520 Huron, and a 1919 steel warehouse at 524 (later 528) Huron built by the LSE for Electric Package Agency business. At one time the terminal was used by all interurbans entering the city except the Ohio Electric, but various dropouts later occurred. The first two buildings were razed about 1930, leaving the metal building which was then shared by the LSE, Western Ohio, and Ohio Public Service.

As an indication of the LSE's express services in the early 1900s, a 1906 Electric Package Company schedule shows four westbound trips out of Cleveland. From Cleveland to Toledo, an ex-TF&N 31-series freight motor departed at 9 a.m., and the 1 p.m. limited passenger car carried express in a 60-series Brill combine. Two Cleveland–Norwalk runs both rated ex-TF&N motors — one leaving at 4 p.m. and the second in the evening at 8 p.m. In addition, car 41 — the rebuilt ex–Lorain & Cleveland motor — ran west from Fremont to Toledo. On Sundays a 31-series motor carried newspapers from Cleveland to Norwalk. There were equivalent eastbound trips.

Beginning about 1908 the Lake Shore became interested in hauling low-value bulk materials between on-line points, primarily as a minimum-cost byproduct of its own maintenance and construction operations. By this time highway paving projects were beginning in earnest. Despite the ominous future implications, the LSE was nicely situated at least to make some immediate money from the activity. Large on-line stone quarries were located at Wagner's (south of Sandusky), Castalia, Bellevue, and Gibsonburg, and the LSE

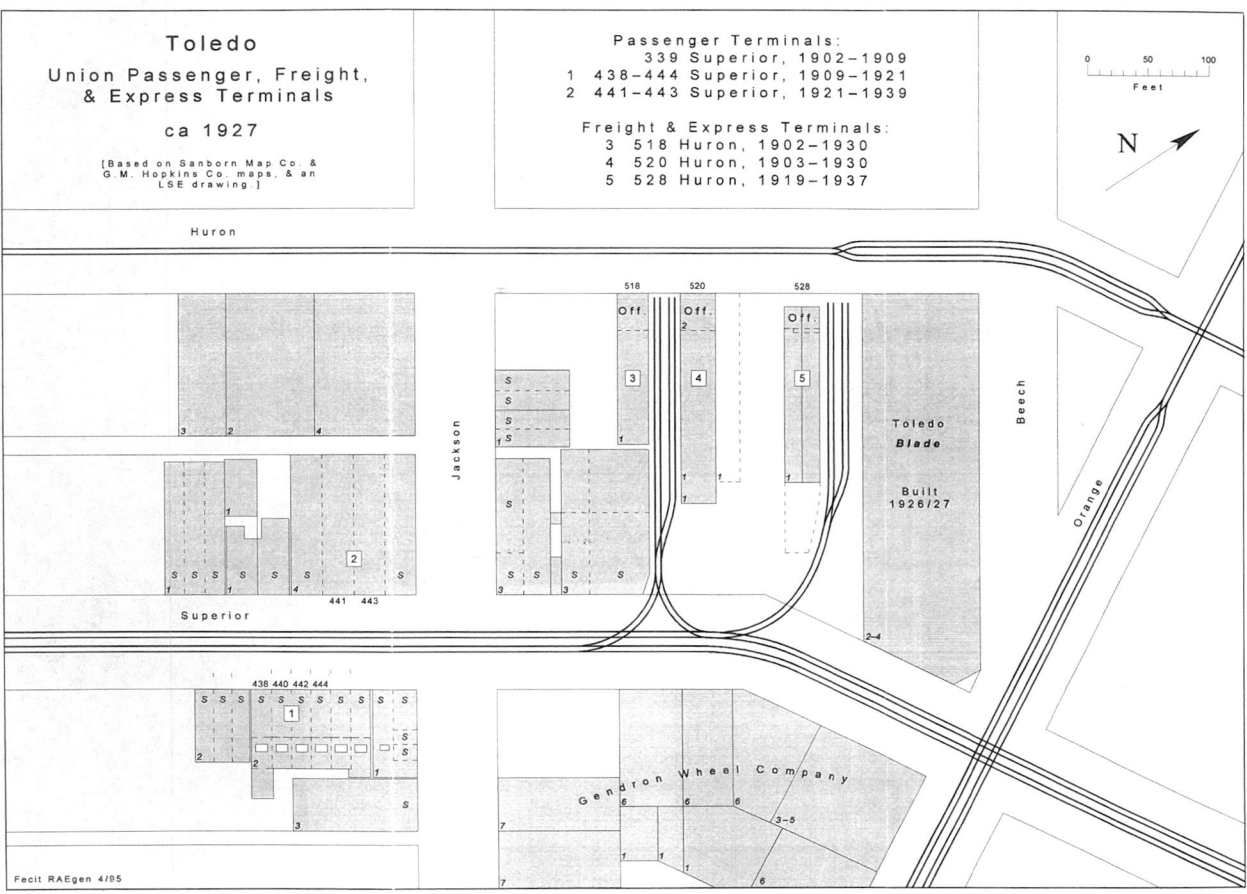

Toledo
Union Passenger, Freight,
& Express Terminals

ca 1927

[Based on Sanborn Map Co. &
G.M. Hopkins Co. maps, & an
LSE drawing.]

Passenger Terminals:
   339 Superior, 1902–1909
1 438–444 Superior, 1909–1921
2 441–443 Superior, 1921–1939

Freight & Express Terminals:
3 518 Huron, 1902–1930
4 520 Huron, 1903–1930
5 528 Huron, 1919–1937

Like Cleveland, the joint downtown freight terminal in Toledo changed form and tenants over the years. (Richard A. Egen)

mined its own sand from its lakefront properties at Beach Park and Sage's Grove for sale along with power plant cinders. On the receiving end, its tracks either were laid in the highways, next to them, or very close by, so the materials were delivered directly to the job sites. The business was handled by regular work crews and the motors, flatcars, gondolas, and ballast cars in its maintenance fleet. A 1908 issue of *Electric Traction Weekly* stated that "Practically the only freight business carried by [the LSE] is handling of crushed stone for highway work." Such movements peaked about 1914, although the LSE continued issuing new tariffs at least into the early 1920s.

A more prestigious movement occurred in 1916 when the Lake Shore acted as an intermediate carrier on a large shipment of racehorses from Lima, Ohio, to Rockport, on the southwest side of Cleveland. Two trains — one of three cars and one of four — originated on the Western Ohio at Lima and were routed WO to Findlay, then Toledo, Fostoria & Findlay to Fostoria, the Fostoria & Fremont to Fremont, LSE to Norwalk, and Cleveland Southwestern to Rockport. Unhappily, nothing is known about the motive power or cars, although at the time the LSE owned no suitable freight equipment itself.

Heavy Freight Develops in the 1920s

The turning point for Lake Shore Electric freight traffic came in World War I, although the change was somewhat slow to take hold. The immediate impetus came from the federal government, which was desperately looking for ways of relieving the overburdened and

Early in its career the LSE began handling bulk materials between various on-line points for road and other construction projects. *(Above)* Denman's sand pit was hard by Lake Erie at Sage's Grove, east of Huron. *(Right)* A major loading point was the Wagner stone quarry at Castalia, reached by a mile-long spur. (Both, W. A. McCaleb collection)

congested steam railroads. It recognized that the LSE and its neighbors were theoretically better able to handle shorter hauls, smaller shipments, and expedited services. The problem was that in 1917 it was still mostly theory. Few interurbans had the equipment, facilities, operational systems, or expertise for anything beyond their traditional express business.

Of the Cleveland-based lines, the Cleveland Southwestern was the first to inaugurate true freight service, a year earlier. Even at this early date the automobile was beginning to chew into its business, spurring it to find new markets. In October 1916 the far-flung Southwestern began daily LCL freight schedules between Cleveland and Wooster, Ashland, Mansfield, and Bucyrus, using five new or rebuilt freight motors and several trailers. Interestingly, it charged substantially higher rates than its steam railroad competitors, but because there were no direct railroad lines from Cleveland to much of its territory it could offer far faster and more dependable service. CSW freights operated from a new building at the Eagle Avenue terminal complex in Cleveland.

The neighboring Northern Ohio Traction & Light and the Toledo, Bowling Green & Southern were also quicker to respond than the Lake Shore, buying new freight motors and trailers in 1917. The LSE's only purchases in this period were a pair of new steel freight motors — No. 34 in 1916 and similar 35 in 1917 — equipped with four motors which turned out an impressive total of 560 hp. These were more than adequate for hauling trains of freight trailers but none were immediately ordered or acquired. It appears that these two motors actually were primarily intended simply as replacements for obsolescent express motors 41 and 43 rather than any planned traffic expansion.

Although the Lake Shore still owned no freight trailers, some new freight business began moving nevertheless. In 1917 it began hauling Overland autos from Toledo to Cleveland, probably using specialized Toledo, Bowling Green & Southern box trailers. (The Willys-Overland plant was located on the Toledo & Western on the west side of that city, but the new autos also were loaded at the TBG&S freight station.) Also in this year a newspaper article noted that an LSE passenger limited car pulling a freight car loaded with furniture derailed east of Slate Cut, proving that at times the company did haul freight behind passenger cars. What the car was and who was shipping furniture are mysteries, however.

It was not until 1918 that the LSE finally realized the potential for an expanded freight business and embarked on a freight motor–building program. Over the next two years the Sandusky shops fabricated six box motors (Nos. 36–40 and second 34), mostly from new components. Also between 1918 and 1919 the company built its first box trailers, five specialized cars designed — ironically enough — for hauling new automobiles. Most likely these went into Overland Motors service from Toledo.

The start of full freight train operations caused some routing problems in Cleveland, since it was necessary to avoid running trains through Public Square on their way to and from the Eagle Avenue freight terminal. A somewhat meandering bypass freight route was worked out which, instead of the Superior Viaduct, approached the freight station from the south via the Central Viaduct — an impressive 3931-foot-long combination iron truss and swing bridge over the Cuyahoga valley built in 1888. Patched together from pieces of various Cleveland Railway streetcar routes, the freight line left the Eagle Avenue terminal westbound via Central Avenue (now Carnegie) and joined the passenger route at Detroit Avenue and West 28th Street (later West 29th–Dexter). With one minor variation in 1931, this routing remained essentially the same until the Central Viaduct was condemned for streetcars in 1935.

Regularly scheduled interline freight runs began in 1919 with an expedited through service between the Northern Ohio and the Detroit United, using the Lake Shore as the intermediate line. The westbound run left Canton, Ohio, at 6 p.m. and arrived at Detroit at 7 a.m. Initially the operation was run with newly delivered Northern Ohio freight motors 1058–1061 and box trailers 1100–1103. A Youngstown–Detroit train soon followed, using Penn-Ohio, Northern Ohio, LSE, and Detroit United equipment. Over the next few

The LSE and its various interline partners hauled much of their merchandise freight in standardized box trailers such as the 810 and its sister. These two came secondhand from the Michigan Electric Railway in 1929. (George Krambles collection)

years several other scheduled through interline runs were created. In 1923, for example, new overnight trains were added between Youngstown and Detroit, Massillon and Detroit, and Alliance and Detroit. These used the Detroit–Superior High Level Bridge in Cleveland for the first time. In order to avoid running through Public Square, the westbound trains were routed north on East 9th Street, west on St. Clair, and south on West 3rd Street to Superior, where they joined the passenger route.

Another early and important overnight service was inaugurated over the "Lima Route" between Cleveland and Dayton, via the Fostoria & Fremont, TF&F, Western Ohio, and Dayton & Troy. In 1921 the newly independent (from Ohio Electric) Fort Wayne, Van Wert & Lima Traction Company established a through connecting schedule between Fort Wayne, Indiana, and Cleveland, advertising second morning delivery. The Fort Wayne line operated its trains to Lima, where they connected with "Lima Route" motors running to Cleveland and Toledo. Fort Wayne freight thus ran over two alternate LSE routes — one via Fremont and the "Lima Route," the other via Toledo.

In addition to these through operations, which usually involved pooling freight motors and box trailers, the Lake Shore and the rest of the Midwestern interurban network gradually developed rate and service agreements among themselves to handle LCL and carload shipments between a vast variety of places. For the most part they adopted steam railroad freight classification systems, rate scales, and interline accounting practices; rates were published both by individual interurbans, such as the LSE, and by agencies acting for a group, or all of the lines.

Their principal joint agency was the Central Electric Railway Association, first established in January 1907 strictly as a trade association for the various Midwestern lines. Soon afterward it began setting mechanical standards for such things as couplers, brakes, and wheels for interchange cars. (All LSE freight equipment was designed to be compatible for interchange.) In 1908 the CERA had set up an interline rate publishing agency, the Central Electric Traffic Association, but for many years this group was concerned almost entirely with passenger and baggage matters. Finally in 1924 it began producing a series of joint freight tariffs for the territory. A standard per diem rate of a dollar a day was also set for use of any "foreign" freight trailer on line.

Probably more important, in the same period the LSE itself made various interline rate agreements with an increasing number of individual Midwestern interurbans. By late 1927 it could quote rates and offer services from points on its lines to no less than 464 destinations on 40 different interurban companies, plus the Cleveland & Buffalo Transit Company's steamship line. LSE freight customers could ship to places as far east as Buffalo, N.Y., and Sharon, Pennsylvania; as far south as Louisville, Kentucky; and west to Michigan City, Indiana, and Paris, Illinois. The LSE could reach some of these points with direct scheduled through operations and others by interchanging trailers or by transferring LCL at intermediate freight stations. Needless to say, it is highly unlikely that freight was shipped to every one of these 464 stations, but the arrangements were in place.

As it moved more heavily into the LCL and carload merchandise business, the Lake Shore augmented its growing fleet of freight motors with 15 box freight trailers between 1920 and 1921, and ten more in 1923. Between 1924 and 1926, 20 more box trailers arrived and five freight motors were created by rebuilding Barney & Smith interurban coaches — the first physical sign of the shift in the nature of the LSE's business.

The shift showed up more emphatically on the Lake Shore's ledgers. Over the ten years between 1916 and 1926, its freight revenues had more than quadrupled. They continued rising through the rest of the decade as passenger income correspondingly declined, and by the 1928–29 period they were only marginally less than LSE interurban passenger revenues.

Rebuilt Barney & Smith motor 30 waits with box trailer 700 on State Street in Fremont in the late 1920s. (J. W. Vigrass collection)

The Lake Shore also built or expanded its freight stations throughout the 1920s. In 1923 alone, it built new facilities at Lorain (at 113 West Erie, shared with the Cleveland Southwestern), Vermilion, Woodville, and Castalia; the existing freight houses at Norwalk and Fremont were expanded. In one form or another, virtually every community of any size on the LSE had a freight house, including Elyria on the Lorain Street Railroad. While the larger cities — such as Sandusky, Norwalk, Fremont, and Elyria — could dispatch and receive full freight motor or trailerloads, most of the on-line communities were served by the interurban's equivalent of a railroad "peddler" service. A motor, sometimes with trailer, would stop at each point, loading and unloading shipments from the car.

In 1926 the LSE and Northern Ohio jointly leased track space in the Cleveland Railway's East 34th Street carbarn and yard near Trumbull Avenue to facilitate the interchange of equipment and crews between the companies. The following year the LSE established an outbound freight house on the north side of the Cleveland Railway's carhouse at West 117th Street and Madison to service the heavy concentration of industry on Cleveland's west side.

Improvements came at Toledo about 1927 with a new freight station at Glendale, on Woodville Road at Towers Road on the city's east side. As an off-street facility away from downtown congestion, it was a better location to interchange trailers and LCL shipments with connecting lines such as the Detroit United, Toledo & Indiana, and Lima–Toledo Railroad (soon to become part of the Cincinnati & Lake Erie). The downtown Toledo freight station on Huron Street was retained for local freight handling, and one portion of this complex remained active until the end of LSE freight services in 1937. LSE crews regularly operated transfer runs between Glendale and the Detroit United's Novi yard just north of Toledo's city limits.

The growing importance and complexity of the freight business also brought some commercial complications. Passenger and freight marketing are two entirely different kinds of animals, one reason why the LSE originally avoided the freight business. Attracting passengers, the LSE's traditional stock in trade, was done through advertising and other mass-marketing techniques, and by soliciting large organizations for outings. It was rela-

Outside downtown Cleveland and Toledo, the LSE's freight facilities were nothing more than utilitarian wooden warehouses, as these two examples show. *(Top)* Glendale station was built on Toledo's outskirts in 1927. *(Bottom)* Beginning in 1929, Elyria was served by this station at Bath Street. (Both, LSE photos, John A. Rehor collection)

tively simple and few people were needed to do it. But freight selling required direct personal contact with a large number of geographically scattered customers who had widely differing types of shipments and needs. Rate structures, routings, and billing procedures were more complex and variable, requiring more people and greater specialized expertise.

To do these jobs more effectively and efficiently, the Lake Shore and four neighboring lines — the Northern Ohio, the Penn-Ohio system, the Toledo & Indiana, and the Ohio Public Service Company's Port Clinton division — decided to create a single joint freight handling agency which could act for all the lines together. On November 1, 1928, they organized the Electric Railways Freight Company, with the LSE, NOT&L, and P-O as joint majority stockholders and the T&I and OPS as minority owners. Not to be confused with the Electric Package Agency — which continued to specialize strictly in express shipments — the new freight company was closely patterned on the express agency. Among other things it handled customer solicitation, waybilling, billing and revenue collection, interline agreements and revenue divisions, and (where necessary) door-to-door pickup and delivery in its own name. Revenues and expenses were split among the owners on the basis of their traffic. The company was headquartered in the Cleveland freight terminal at 704 Eagle Avenue with David R. Thomas as president; LSE employees directly involved in freight solicitation and handling were transferred to its payroll.

There was perhaps another motive for creating the freight company: by late 1928 truck competition, with its door-to-door service, was becoming a serious threat; at the same time, some components of the Midwest interurban network were seriously weakening and even beginning to drop away. Lines like the LSE needed the ability to offer truck pickup and delivery services, and also needed to work out substituted connecting truck services when a rail connection died. An immediate problem was the 1928–29 demise of Michigan Electric Railway and Michigan Railroad connections to such points as Battle Creek, Lansing, Kalamazoo, Grand Rapids, and the Saginaw–Bay City area. For those reasons, the new freight agency in turn created Elway Transit (presumably for "ELectric railWAY") as a trucking subsidiary.

Operations in the 1928 – 1929 Peak

Despite increasing truck competition and the loss of the central Michigan connections, LSE freight revenues hit an all-time high of almost $894,000 in 1929 — 48 percent of the entire gross revenue of LSE's interurban operations (that is, excluding the Lorain Street Railroad and non-rail subsidiaries). The "byproduct" was within a hair of becoming the main product.

By this time, several freight forwarding companies were consolidating LCL shipments and shipping them in full carload lots between major cities on the LSE and its connections; in some cases, the interurban operated specific dedicated train schedules for these shippers. The largest single carload flow was westbound from Cleveland to the Detroit area. During October 1929, for example, the Q-D Forwarding Company moved 48 cars to Detroit; at the same time Elway Transit shipped 23 carloads to Oakwood terminal on Detroit's southern outskirts. (According to a 1931 Electric Railways Freight Company shipping guide, Elway was handling freight to and from the various central Michigan cities "lost" when the Michigan interurbans abandoned.) Elway also moved eight cars from Sandusky to Oakwood. The Michigan runs were informally called "Q-D's" and the "Oakwood Nighthawk." Cincinnati was the second largest carload destination. During the same month, Universal Carloading Company shipped 45 cars from Cleveland to Cincinnati, plus two to Dayton. Eastbound the picture was much the same, although the Cincinnati–Dayton area seemed to predominate: Universal moved 46 carloads from Cincinnati to Cleveland and 33 from Dayton. Q-D Forwarding contributed 20 cars from Detroit but, mysteriously, no eastbound shipments from Oakwood or any Elway shipments show up. The largest traffic from an industrial customer consisted of 13 cars of refrigerators from Frigidaire in Moraine, Ohio (near Dayton), to Cleveland.

In addition to these regular volume movements, there were numerous scattered carload shipments, mostly of a limited or one-shot nature. Elway shipped two cars from Akron to Oakwood for distribution in Michigan. Single carload shipments during this same October included conduit carried from Barberton, Ohio (on the Northern Ohio), to Fort Wayne, Indiana, steel from Youngstown to Lansing, Michigan (delivered by truck), steel from Massillon, Ohio, to Flint, Michigan, paper from Marion, bottles from Toledo to Alliance, Ohio, brake shoes from Toledo to Cuyahoga Falls, Ohio, paper from several points in Ohio and Indiana to Cleveland, and sauerkraut in tins from Huron, Ohio, to Massillon.

The Lake Shore and its various interline partners regularly pooled equipment to carry these and the heavy volumes of LCL freight. On what might be a typical day — March 20, 1928 — four "foreign" freight motors operated on LSE lines: Dayton & Troy 225, Western Ohio 160, Detroit United 1948, and Northern Ohio 1060. In addition, there were box trailers of the Dayton & Troy, the Terre Haute, Indianapolis & Eastern, the Cincinnati, Hamilton & Dayton (later Cincinnati & Lake Erie), the Toledo, Fostoria & Findlay, the Western Ohio, the Dayton & Western, the Union Traction of Indiana, and the Chicago, Lake Shore & South Bend on line. (The last is somewhat mysterious since the CLS&SB's 1925 successor, the Chicago, South Shore & South Bend, was not part of the Central Electric Traffic Association.) During the same day, the LSE operated nine of its own freight motors and 15 of its trailers.

In some cases the interline services came close to steam railroad

Lima–Toledo Railroad box motor 766, one of many "foreign" visitors to the LSE, is at the Eagle Avenue freight terminal about 1932. By this time the L–T was part of the Cincinnati & Lake Erie, the LSE's principal connection to western and southern Ohio. (Richard Krisak collection)

LSE steel motor 39(II) is eastbound with two box trailers on Clifton Boulevard at West 117th Street in Cleveland about 1936. (W. A. McCaleb photo)

operations in complexity. One interesting example was the overnight Cleveland–Fort Wayne run, routed via Toledo and established about 1929. The train left Cleveland with trailers loaded with freight for Cincinnati, Columbus, and Dayton in addition to Fort Wayne. The Lima–Toledo Railroad picked up the train at Toledo, adding cars from Detroit and Toledo itself. At Lima the cars for central and southern Ohio were dropped for forwarding on another train, and cars from those points to Fort Wayne and beyond were added. Thus a single train service, with its closely coordinated connections, could provide overnight service to Fort Wayne from Cleveland, Detroit, Toledo, Columbus, Dayton, and Cincinnati — as well as overnight service between Cleveland and the major cities in central and southern Ohio. No doubt it was necessary to operate more than one section on busy days. The Lake Shore regularly assigned its most powerful freight motors to the heavy run — the No. 35 (which was the line's fastest) and the home-built 34 and 37–40 group.

In addition to the all-rail runs, shipments were routed from Cleveland to Fort Wayne, Indiana, as well as Jackson, Michigan, via the Toledo & Indiana to its western terminal at Bryan, Ohio, where they were transferred to truck for Fort Wayne and Jackson.

Although express was typically carried in combines on passenger runs, several dedicated express runs were scheduled with freight motors. Charles Hanville, a onetime LSE motorman, recalled working one regular express trip which would leave Fremont in late afternoon, pick up barreled fish from Huron and other communities along the lake, and arrive in Cleveland about 11 p.m. It then took newspapers back to Fremont.

Generally, LSE freights in and out of Cleveland were limited to a motor and two box trailers in the daytime and four at night. In cases where through trains carried more trailers, the extra cars were shuttled between the Eagle Avenue station and Beach Park or Wagar Road siding in Rocky River, where they were switched in and out of the trains. (Usually a wood freight motor was kept at the Eagle Avenue freight station for these moves and for freight house switching.) West of Beach Park, up to five cars have been observed in some

Lake Erie fish were shipped express in ice-filled barrels and were clearly heavy business for the interurban. A load awaits the arrival of an LSE combine at Huron's old Main Street station in the spring of 1916. LSE Agent George H. Windau is on the baggage cart while Wells Fargo Route Agent W. J. MacGreevy stands below amid puddles from the melting ice. (John A. Rehor collection)

trains, but this was probably close to the
LSE's practical limit. While its steel
freight motors were theoretically capable
of hauling up to 15 cars on level track,
there were few places where anything
close to this could be done. Among other
things the trains had to contend with steep
grades on various railroad overpasses and
underpasses as well as street running in
numerous spots. Before the Sandusky cutoff was opened in 1931, freights were limited to a motor and two trailers through
that city's narrow streets and sharp curves.
Freight train speeds were not overly fast—
usually about 35 mph.

With (it was thought) a steadily expanding freight business, the Lake Shore
made a further investment in equipment — what turned out to be its last, except for the
experimental Bonner Railwagons. In 1929 it rebuilt six wooden Niles passenger coaches
to freight motors (Nos. 41–46) and picked up 14 box trailers from the defunct Michigan
Electric Railway. With these additions its active freight roster totaled 21 heavy-duty freight
motors and 65 trailers.

Cincinnati & Lake Erie
motor 632 takes three trailers west at Beach Park about
1936. (Franklyn P. Kellogg
photo)

But by this time the Lake Shore's Fred Coen and David Thomas of the Electric Railways Freight Company clearly recognized the rubber-tired threat to their existence. They
realized that they must have some means of combining the railway's terminal-to-terminal
line haul with door-to-door truck service — without the laborious, costly, and damage-
prone manual transfer of goods through a freight house. In 1926 Samuel Insull's Chicago,
North Shore & Milwaukee inaugurated what became a successful trailer-on-flatcar operation, one of the first of its kind; the next year his Chicago, South Shore & South Bend
followed with a similar service. The two were the forerunners of the "piggyback" system
belatedly adopted by the railroads a quarter of a century later, and except for the size of the
vehicles and the tiedown techniques, the technology was identical. The method had some
drawbacks, however, not the least of which were clearance problems with overhead wires,
underpasses, and the like, which precluded use on the LSE and its connections. In addition, it was somewhat limited in flexibility since the rail–truck transfer terminals required
extra space, a loading/unloading ramp, and manpower to load the trailers onto the cars, tie
them down, and unload them.

Possibly influenced by Cities Service president Henry Doherty, Coen asked Thomas to
investigate the Bonner Railwagon system in mid-1928. This combination of semitrailer and
flatcar designs promised simple, automated loading and unloading, minimal terminal space
and installations, and a low profile for clearances. Coen then decided to go ahead with a
commercial test of the system. In July 1929 Kuhlman constructed a prototype flatcar and
Kuhlman's parent, the J. G. Brill Company, built a single semitrailer, both of them specially designed under the Bonner patents. But afterward negotiations with Colonel Bonner
came to a standstill and remained there at least through mid-1930, so nothing ran and —
for the moment — no more semitrailers were ordered.

The 1930s

While the Bonner project sat in limbo, the shape and nature of the LSE's interline
freight system began a radical and mostly negative change. The first event was reasonably
bright, however. New Year's Day of 1930 introduced an important new freight partner for

the LSE — the Cincinnati & Lake Erie Railroad. The C&LE had been put together by the creative and aggressive Dr. Thomas W. Conway from three former pieces of the old Ohio Electric system — the Lima–Toledo Railroad, the Indiana, Columbus & Eastern, and the Cincinnati, Hamilton & Dayton. The new company formed a single line between Toledo, Dayton, and Cincinnati, with a branch to Columbus. The LSE had, of course, interchanged substantial amounts of freight with the C&LE's predecessors and operated several through services. But with an integrated system and Conway's imagination and dedication to keeping business (as exemplified in his famous high-speed "Red Devil" lightweight passenger cars), the C&LE was a potentially powerful partner in an environment which was increasingly depressing.

Their first joint move was a misstep. The LSE and C&LE made an effort to create exclusive rates and routings between themselves, which would cut out interline agreements with each other's competitors — the "Lima Route" in the C&LE's case and the Cleveland Southwestern for the Lake Shore Electric. As part of this, the Lake Shore canceled its through rates and routes with the "Lima Route" lines in 1930. The intent was to push all Cleveland–Dayton–Cincinnati–Fort Wayne business through the C&LE at Toledo, rather than via Fremont and the Fostoria & Fremont–Western Ohio connection. In turn, the C&LE canceled its joint routes with the Cleveland Southwestern which competed with LSE routes. (The Southwestern operated its own through Cleveland–Dayton service.) The Lima Route lines immediately hauled the Lake Shore before the Ohio Public Utilities Commission and had the old tariffs and routings reinstated.

Ironically, at about the same time that this scuffle was going on, the Lake Shore consented to help the Western Ohio in another area. With the abandonment of the Toledo, Bowling Green & Southern and parts of the Toledo, Fostoria & Findlay in September 1930, the Western Ohio lost its own links to Toledo — through which it directly competed with the C&LE. The LSE agreed to handle the WO's Dayton–Lima–Toledo business through Fremont, thence the Lake Shore to Toledo. This continued until the Western Ohio finally expired in January 1932.

As of April 1930 the Bonner Railwagon situation was still unresolved. David Thomas of the freight company reported to Coen that "Mr. Bonner yet refuses to agree to the terms of any contract that is submitted to him." With time moving on and truck competition worsening, Thomas recommended that the LSE instead adopt a demountable container system for its Cleveland–Toledo business. As was originally intended with the Railwagon equipment, containers would be transferred between truck and rail car at Rocky River (Stop 6, Wagar Road) and at Glendale on the Toledo end. Admitting that a container system required more transfer expense and terminal space, Thomas nonetheless suggested buying six containers and rebuilding the already-delivered Bonner flatcar to begin an overnight service between the LSE's two terminals.

But for better or worse, some kind of agreement with Bonner was soon reached, and in August 1930 five additional Bonner-design semitrailers were built by Fruehauf. After brief road testing, commercial service between Cleveland and Toledo began September 1. Three semitrailers were based at each terminal, picking up and delivering freight during the daytime. The three Toledo trailers were loaded onto the flatcar in late afternoon, leaving Toledo for Cleveland at 6:30 p.m. When the car arrived at the Cleveland end, it was unloaded and the three waiting Cleveland trailers loaded for the return to Toledo, arriving about 6:30 a.m. At both terminals, the trailers were thus ready for customer deliveries and pickups by early morning. The actual rail–truck transfer terminals were located at Beach Park for Cleveland traffic and Glendale yard at Toledo. By using these locations on its own property, the LSE avoided track-use charges by the local streetcar companies in each city and also achieved a faster turnaround for the car.

After four months the trial was declared a success, and Coen immediately planned a broad expansion of the program covering not only the LSE but its major direct connections. On January 31, 1931, he formally proposed creating a separate equipment company which would acquire a total of 61 Railwagon semitrailers (55 for city delivery use and six for over-the-highway movements) and 19 flatcars. In turn, the equipment company would lease the equipment on a per diem basis to the LSE, the C&LE, the Northern Ohio, Penn-Ohio, and Eastern Michigan–Toledo.

At the same time the Electric Railways Freight Company aggressively promoted the Bonner system in its literature to shippers and connecting lines. But the Railwagon expansion project disappeared without a trace, and the issue quickly became academic anyway. On June 30, 1931, the Northern Ohio ceased its entire freight operation, which of course also took the Penn-Ohio out of the picture. And in April of that year the dying Eastern Michigan–Toledo attempted (unsuccessfully for the moment) to cancel its interline routes with the LSE and C&LE. The only other potential Railwagon user, the C&LE, developed its own demountable container system in 1930 and began operations in early 1931. The C&LE's system required overhead cranes at the transfer terminals, limiting its use to C&LE lines alone. The LSE continued to run its single Bonner flatcar and six semitrailers into 1932, but the operation ceased by the end of that year. Apparently there were complaints to the Ohio PUC about the LSE's lack of a trucking operating authority; the PUC decided that the interurban was required to have a motor carrier certificate. The LSE lost the case on appeal in late 1932 and apparently gave up. At least three Bonner semitrailers (then owned by Elway Transit) were used until the end of 1934 for local pickups and deliveries.

Indeed, the years 1931 and 1932 were disastrous to the Lake Shore's interline traffic. The loss of the Northern Ohio at the end of June 1931 wiped out the entire territory south and southeast of Cleveland, including the Ohio industrial centers of Akron, Canton, Massillon, Niles, Youngstown, and Sharon, Pennsylvania. In the same year, connections to Flint and Pontiac, Michigan, were lost. Without the Northern Ohio and Penn-Ohio, the Electric Railways Freight Company had no reason for existence, and it was dissolved in August 1931. Elway Transit was transferred to Lake Shore ownership, and former LSE freight employees returned to their old employer. On January 15, 1932, the Western Ohio and the Fostoria & Fremont gave up, finally resolving the LSE–C&LE routing problems but also removing such western Ohio traffic points as Fostoria, Findlay, Troy, Piqua, Wapakoneta, and Celina.

Next came the abandonment of the Fort Wayne–Lima line on June 30, 1932 — thus ending the direct rail service to Fort Wayne, with its westward connections to South Bend. The LSE and Toledo & Indiana attempted to keep the business through a rail–truck–rail operation, using the LSE between Cleveland and Toledo, the T&I from Toledo to Bryan, Ohio, a truck operator from Bryan to Fort Wayne, and the Indiana Service Corporation's rail line west of Fort Wayne. Despite the costly and time-consuming rail–truck transfers, a fair business was kept; in August 1932 the T&I reported 60 loaded trailers for the month — an average of two a day, predominantly westbound. The service lasted until April 1934, when the LSE–T&I connection in Toledo was severed by the abandonment of the Dorr Street streetcar line, the T&I's entry to the city.

Finally — and most damaging — the Eastern Michigan–Toledo at last succeeded in shutting itself down on October 4, 1932, ending all direct rail service into Michigan.

Despite the disintegration of the interline freight network, the LSE and C&LE retained a strong interchange business with one another, with direct Cleveland–Dayton runs (with through trailers to Cincinnati and Columbus) which began in October 1929. C&LE motors and trailers, plus some Indiana Railroad trailers, continued to be common sights in Cleveland, but now they were the only "foreign" cars to be seen. The C&LE normally assigned its best freight motors — its 630–634 series — as its contribution to the pool, and occasionally less powerful motors in the C&LE's 635–649 group also would show up. Another relatively bright spot was the opening of the Sandusky bypass October 28, 1931, taking freight trains off the difficult and roundabout city street tracks and allowing longer train operation.

Not having enough problems, in 1932 the LSE was cited before the Ohio Public Utilities Commission as the result of an effort by its competitive steam railroads to require a railroad-size full crew on its freights. Like many interurbans, the Lake Shore normally ran its trains with two men, a motorman and conductor; the railroads — now also hard-hit by the Depression — had to pay five crew members. Fortunately the interurban won the case.

Happily for posterity, detailed Electric Railways Freight Company daily reports of activity at Cleveland survive from January 1932, giving a graphic picture of the Lake Shore's freight operations and equipment use as they were just before the collapse of so many of its interline partners. At that time, scheduled through runs were made between Cleveland–Toledo–Fort Wayne, Cleveland–Dayton via Fremont and the "Lima Route," Cleveland–Dayton via Toledo and the C&LE, Cleveland–Detroit, Cleveland–Oakwood, and Cleveland–Toledo via Norwalk. But, much like steam railroad practice, not every service was run every day, nor were eastbound and westbound trips balanced each day. Specific runs were tailored to the shipping practices of the freight customers, which ran heavy on certain days and light on others. Fridays, Saturdays, and Sundays usually were heaviest days as shippers dispatched their orders for the week for delivery to their buyers early the following week. Midweek days generally were lighter, often with less than half as many trains dispatched. When they operated, the Cleveland–Fort Wayne and Cleveland–Dayton trains left between six and seven in the evening, variously carrying trailers for Lima, Dayton, Columbus–Springfield, and Cincinnati. The Detroit run generally followed between 6:30 and 7:30.

Two samples of heavy days in this period show how the patterns varied. The first, Tuesday, January 12, happened to be three days before the demise of "Lima Route" operations on January 15. On that day, seven freight runs were recorded in and out of Cleveland and nearby stations, five of which were westbound — including one destined for Dayton via the Lima Route. This day there was virtually no action in the morning. The first run to operate was LSE motor 27 on a Norwalk–Lorain–Elyria freight trip, which passed through Lorain at 1:20 p.m. It returned to Lorain and left that evening at 6:45 for Norwalk and Fremont, this time towing an LSE trailer ultimately destined for the C&LE. At about the same time came a rapid succession of westbound trains from Cleveland, which went like this:

> 6:25 p.m. — The Cleveland–Toledo–Fort Wayne run leaves, powered by C&LE motor 636 hauling a C&LE trailer for Cincinnati and an LSE trailer for Toledo & Indiana Railroad points.
>
> 6:40 p.m. — Dayton & Troy motor 245 takes out the Cleveland–Fremont–Dayton Lima Route train with two LSE trailers, one for Dayton and one for Lima.
>
> 7:00 p.m. — LSE motor 44 leaves for Toledo via Norwalk, hauling a C&LE trailer which carried dropoff and pickup freight for intermediate points.
>
> 7:10 p.m. — The Cleveland–Toledo–Dayton (via C&LE) train departs, headed by Lima–Toledo (C&LE) motor 779 loaded with Dayton freight, followed by two trailers — Indiana, Columbus & Eastern (C&LE) No. 848 with Springfield and Columbus shipments, and LSE 480 for Dayton.
>
> 9:30 p.m. — Finally ending the day at Cleveland, LSE motor 26 arrives with express from Sandusky.

On the other hand, Sunday, January 17, at Cleveland showed an equal number of trains but different patterns — this time mostly eastbound morning arrivals, and also including Detroit traffic and the Bonner Railwagons. (By then, of course, the Lima Route was gone.) This day began in the wee hours, when LSE motor 28 left Cleveland at 12:10 a.m. for Norwalk and Toledo loaded with express. Then came these arrivals and departures at Cleveland:

> 2:15 a.m. — LSE motor 32 arrives from Norwalk and Toledo, with a C&LE box trailer.
>
> 6:20 a.m. — Motor 45 and two empty LSE trailers arrive as the Detroit train (a third empty trailer was dropped at Beach Park).

8:00 a.m. — LSE motor 40 brings in the Dayton–Toledo–Cleveland (via C&LE) train, with one C&LE trailer and two Dayton & Western trailers.

8:20 a.m. — The Fort Wayne run arrives, with LSE 35. This motor had taken three empty LSE trailers as far as Beach Park.

7:00 p.m. — The Cleveland–Toledo–Oakwood train leaves with motor 37; en route it picks up the loaded Bonner Railwagon car for the Glendale station at Toledo.

9:05 p.m. — As before, the express run from Sandusky to Cleveland arrives to close out the day; it consists of motor 28 (which had left Cleveland at 12:10 a.m. the night before with express for Norwalk), loaded with express, plus a trailer of LCL freight.

During 14 more-or-less typical days of this January in 1932, LSE freight motors handled most of the runs, but C&LE 636 appeared twice on the Cleveland–Fort Wayne train and Dayton & Troy 245 brought in the one Lima Route Dayton–Cleveland run mentioned above. Trailers from the C&LE (some still lettered for predecessor lines Lima–Toledo, and Indiana, Columbus & Eastern) were numerous, and there were also occasional visits from cars of the Dayton & Western, Indiana Railroad, and Northern Indiana. The Bonner Railwagon flatcar No. 500 made almost daily trips between Beach Park and Glendale during the period.

The grim litany of lost connections continued in April 1934 when, as noted earlier, the Toledo & Indiana was forced to cut back its line to the western outskirts of Toledo. This left the Cincinnati & Lake Erie as the LSE's only interline partner. The C&LE in turn managed to maintain a route to Indianapolis via the Dayton & Western, which connected with the Indiana Railroad system at Richmond, Indiana.

A fresh disaster came in 1935 when Cleveland's now-ancient Central Viaduct was declared unsafe for streetcars and interurbans. (It was finally dynamited in 1939.) This left the LSE without direct access to its downtown freight terminal; operating freight trains over the Detroit–Superior High Level Bridge and through Public Square was out of the question. A frantic search produced what seemed to be the only practical alternative, a highly circuitous and awkward new route around the far south side of the city via the Clark Avenue viaduct over the Cuyahoga valley. Among other things, this route also involved a switchback movement at West 14th Street and Clark Avenue and the use of the old and spindly East 34th Street viaduct over Kingsbury Run.

But then, three weeks later, came a worse disaster: interurbans were banned from the Kingsbury Run viaduct, cutting off what was now their only access to the downtown freight terminal. As an expediency the Lake Shore used space in the now-unused Cleveland Railway East 34th Street carhouse, where it and the Northern Ohio had formerly interchanged crews and equipment. Finally on August 1, 1935, the Cleveland Railway completed a new freight station for the LSE at its Rocky River carhouse and yard in Lakewood, adjacent to the Rocky River bridge. Now permanently walled off from the center of the city, the company continued to maintain the Eagle Avenue–Bolivar Road freight terminal, with Elway trucks transferring the freight between the downtown terminal and this final bastion in the outskirts. (The Eagle Avenue freight terminal survived the LSE's demise by many years, but the site was finally swallowed up by Jacobs Field.)

Layout of the LSE's final Cleveland freight terminal at the Cleveland Railway's Rocky River yard in Lakewood. (Tom Heinrich)

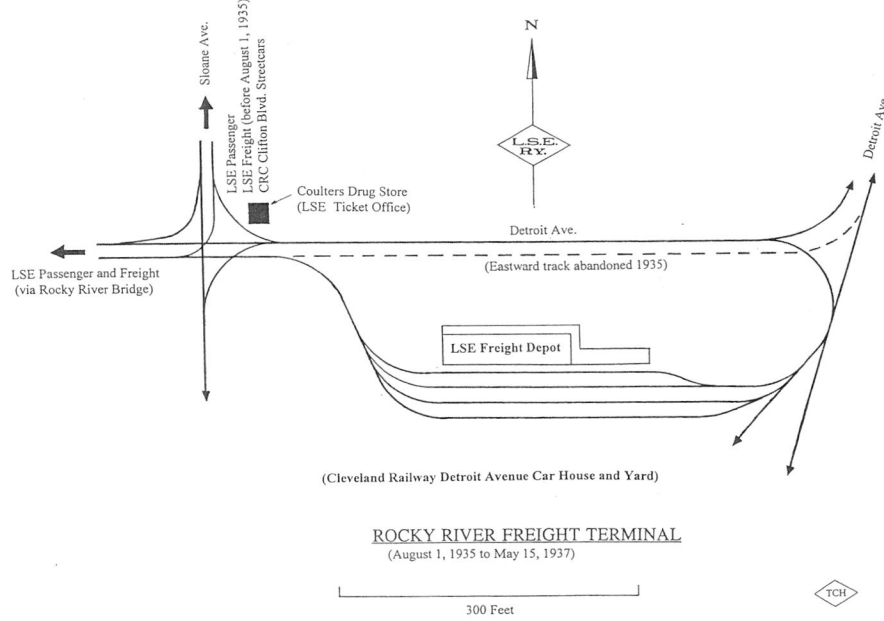

ROCKY RIVER FREIGHT TERMINAL
(August 1, 1935 to May 15, 1937)

300 Feet

Four freight motors lined up at the new Rocky River terminal give at least an illusion of prosperity in this 1936 scene. From left to right they are: LSE 38 and 37, C&LE 631, and LSE 35. (W. A. McCaleb collection)

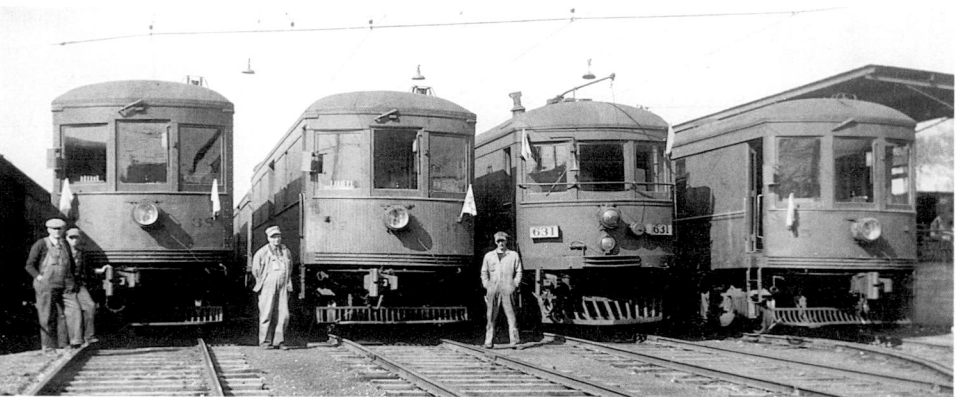

Despite the continuing agonies, the Lake Shore's freight business continued to be relatively strong through 1936 and into early 1937. But the inevitable interline disintegration continued. On May 8, 1937, the strategic Dayton & Western ceased operation, severing the last direct rail link between the surviving Ohio interurbans and what remained of the Indiana network.

Almost coincidentally, the Lake Shore's freight handlers picked this time to strike. Indeed, their substandard wages were a legitimate complaint, but the action was instant suicide. By then Coen was preparing to ease out of all railway operations, so when the strike came on May 15 he simply announced the end of freight services. Perhaps by then he had become disillusioned by the real economics of the LSE's freight business anyway. Despite the relatively healthy volume, the highly labor-intensive traffic was costly to handle, even at very low wage rates — a problem which was now aggravated by the additional trucking and rehandling necessary at Cleveland.

Quickly the Lake Shore returned all interline cars to the C&LE, including one Indiana Railroad trailer which had been caught by the shutdown of the Dayton & Western connection a week earlier. At about the same time, shabby-looking LSE motor No. 30 hauled two even more weatherbeaten box trailers loaded with company materials west out of Rocky River to end all freight operations. The Lake Shore's freight equipment was stored at the Beach Park, Sandusky, and Fremont yards and in some unused sidings and spurs, but all of it remained intact and serviceable until passenger service ended a year later.

Like its original interurban cars, the TF&N's three freight motors were long-lived on the Lake Shore Electric. No. 33, shown at Beach Park in 1932, was double-ended in 1927 and remained on the roster until 1939. (E. V. Emery–LSE photo, John Keller collection)

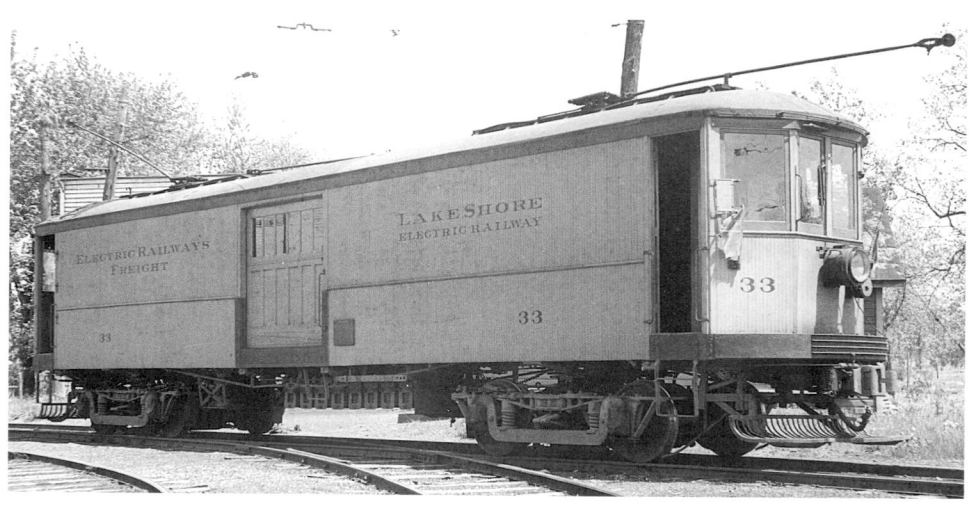

Interlude C: Cleveland to Toledo on the LSE

A Brief Geographic Tour of the Line

(*Above*) Combine 5, rebuilt from an ex-TF&N Barney & Smith coach, makes its Cleveland Terminal loop on West 3rd Street about 1932. (Ralph A. Perkin photo)

(*Below*) LSE's own right-of-way began alongside the landmark Hotel Westlake in Rocky River, seen in the background. The view looks east toward the Rocky River bridge as the 170 on a Lorain local run pauses at Stop 1 in 1936. (Louis Szakacs photo)

Westbound 180 approaches the little shelter station at Woodland Road in Bay Village on the double-track Cleveland–Lorain section in June 1934. (Ralph A. Perkin photo)

The 173 heads eastbound along the double-track Cleveland–Lorain section at Bay Village about 1936. (Karel Liebenauer photo)

(*Facing page, top*) Niles 159's shining paint belies the line's imminent demise in this 1937 photo as it moves west at the Beach Park Carhouse. (Karel Liebenauer photo)

(*Facing page, bottom*) The **Ise** entered Lorain from the east over the Erie Avenue Bridge spanning the Black River and the Baltimore & Ohio Railroad tracks. The camera looks east in November 1934 as 182 heads for Toledo. (Ralph A. Perkin photo)

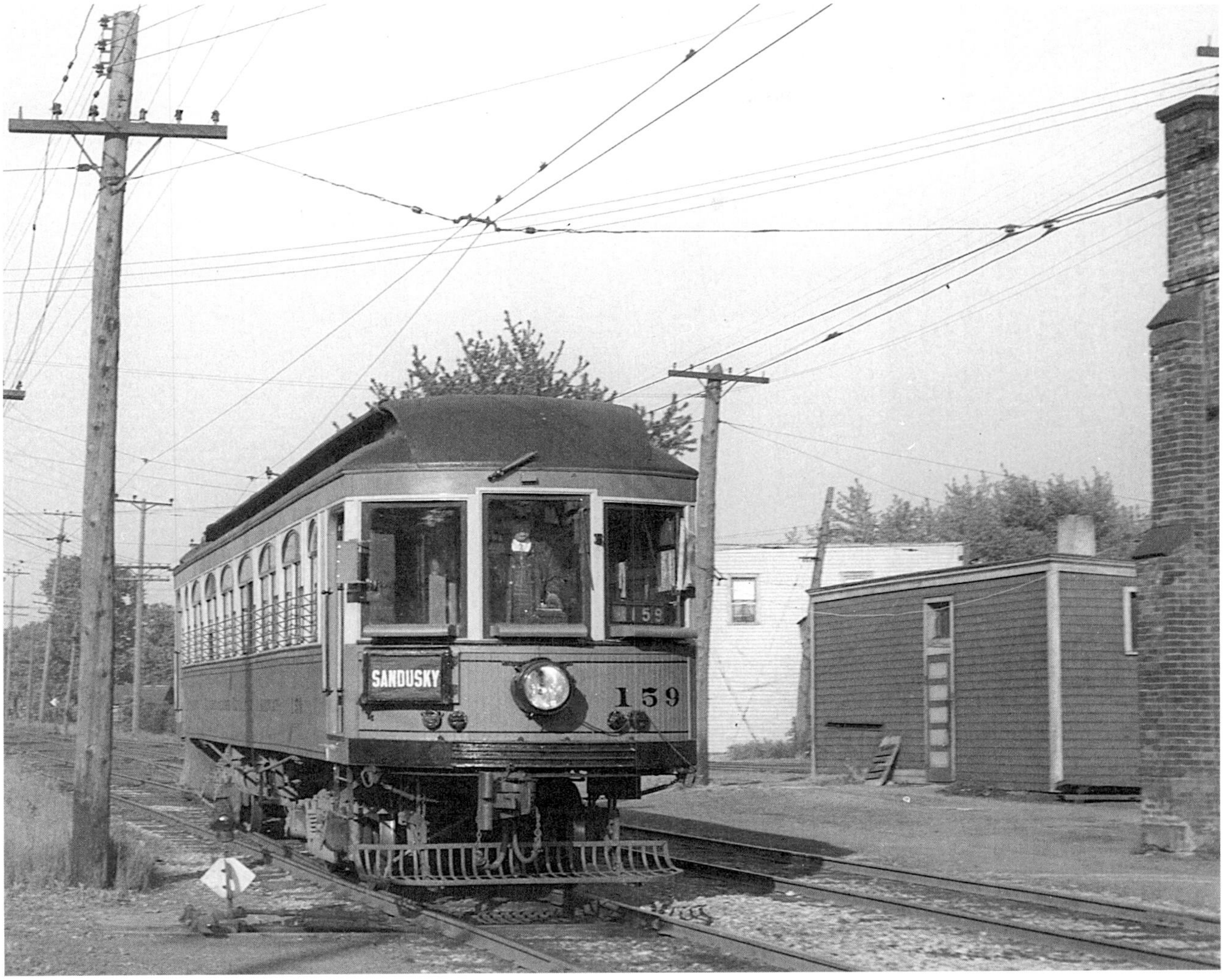
SANDUSKY
159

EXPRESS
STOP HERE

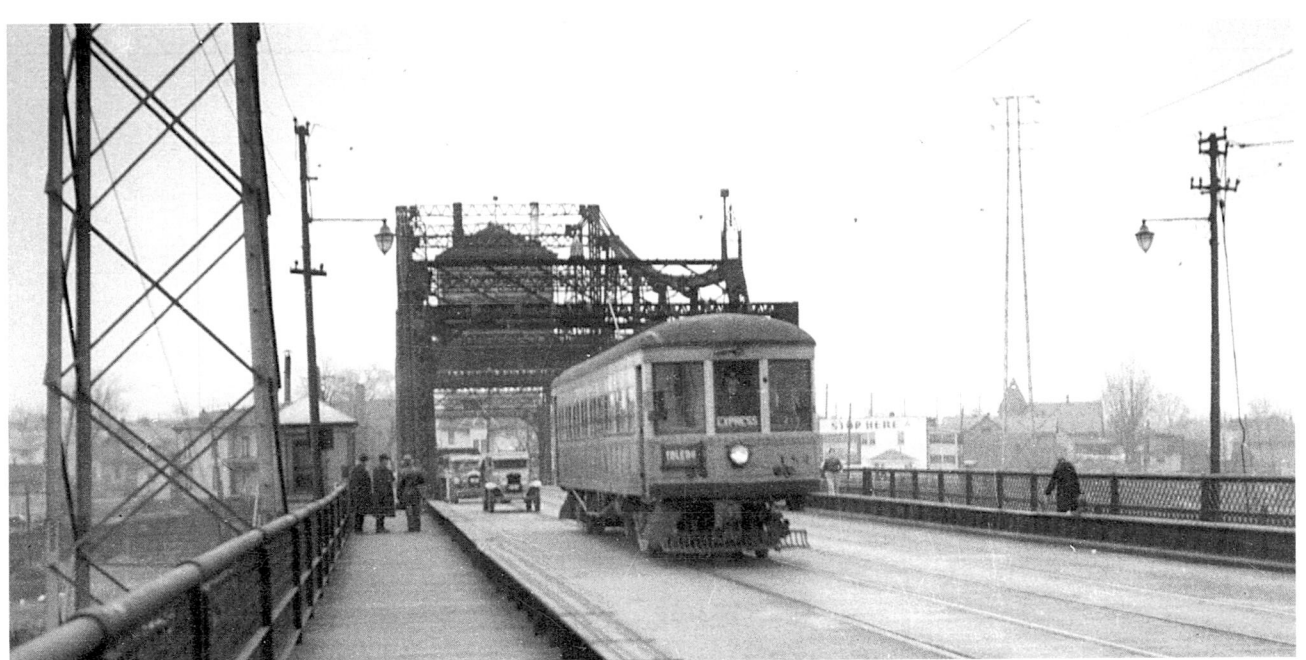

(*Above*) The LSE's chronic operating bane was the point it called Undergrade, where the interurban and the Lake Road passed under the Nickel Plate Road's main line west of Lorain. The nasty combination of sharp "S" curve, grades, and unyielding obstructions claimed four wrecked cars, five lives, and at least 16 serious injuries over the years. This 1926 view looks east. (LSE photo, John A. Rehor collection)

(*Below*) Eastbound 173 running a Toledo–Cleveland express trip meets 166, one of the 1911 Lima limited cars with a fan excursion at Lake Siding west of Vermilion on April 8, 1938. (Franklyn P. Kellogg photo)

(*Above*) On a clearly miserable November 21, 1937, westbound 183 has deposited several shivering transfer passengers for the Norwalk route car at Ceylon Junction. (Ralph A. Perkin photo)

(*Below*) On a balmier day some time in 1936, Niles 143 from Fremont and Norwalk is approaching the wye at Ceylon Junction. (Ralph A. Perkin photo)

(*Above*) Car 172 is running alongside Columbus Avenue on the outskirts of Sandusky in September 1935. City streetcars on the Soldiers Home route also shared this track.
(Karel Liebenauer photo)

(*Right*) The 1931 Sandusky cutoff crossed the Baltimore & Ohio Railroad's Willard–Sandusky Branch at Perkins Avenue. As with most of the LSE's railroad grade crossings, it was protected only by manual derails operated by the interurban crews. The conductor of eastbound 179 has opened the derail to allow the car to cross.
(James P. Shuman photo)

(*Above*) George Krambles leaned out of the rear of his Cleveland-bound car to catch a shot of westbound 182 on State Street in Fremont in September 1937. The LSE's turning wye — once also used by the Fostoria & Fremont–Lima Route connection — is on Front Street in the left foreground. (George Krambles photo)

(*Below*) Eastbound 178 pauses at Woodville's little frame station, partly visible at the car's rear. At this point the LSE once connected with the ill-starred and short-lived Lake Erie, Bowling Green & Napoleon. (Ralph H. Sayles photo)

Interurban coach 183, a former Michigan Electric Railway rebuild, shows off the typical Lake Shore Electric "face," which includes the line's unusual scoop fender design, knuckle-type coupler with a wide vertical face to compensate for sharp grade changes, and, of course, receptacles for multiple-unit cables. But unlike much multiple-unit equipment elsewhere, no LSE cars had train doors. (Ralph A. Perkin photo)

CHAPTER 14

THE EQUIPMENT

"Mishmash" is the only appropriate word to describe the Lake Shore Electric's original roster. When the company was formed on September 25, 1901, it inherited a mixed collection of rolling stock from its four predecessor companies — none of it really suitable for the type of operations its creators envisioned. In total there were 41 interurban passenger cars ("interurban" sometimes being rather loosely defined), 22 city streetcars, five box freight motors, four powered work cars, 33 work trailers, and three steam locomotives no less. Some of these cars dated to the pioneering days of interurban and street railway operations in the early 1890s and, although young in years, already were obsolescent if not completely obsolete. Only the former Toledo, Fremont & Norwalk's 22 Barney & Smith cars of 1900–1901 were usable for long-distance interurban operations, but these were rather austere and, worse, were underpowered and thus slow. Nonetheless the new company had to rely on them until it could buy equipment specifically designed for its planned high-speed, deluxe services.

Somewhat oddly, however, the LSE's first new car order was for ten Brill single-truck city cars which the cash-short company needed quickly to satisfy the requirements of a new 25-year franchise in Sandusky. They were ordered in October 1901 and delivered the following February.

But shortly after the 1902 bankruptcy quagmire the company went to Brill again for ten deluxe interurban combines which began arriving in July 1903. Three years later it received the first of a large group of classic wooden Niles interurban coaches and combines which set the company's future operating standards — most notably, speed capability of 60 mph and multiple-unit operation. These later led to 15 big steel Jewett multiple-unit interurban coaches which became the backbone of LSE operations and, to many people, the company's symbol.

Acquisition of Tom L. Johnson's Lorain Street Railway in 1906 brought in another motley assortment of city and suburban equipment, most of which was directly placed on the roster of the Lorain Street Railroad, the new LSE subsidiary created to operate the property. Throughout the remainder of the LSE's life, the Lorain company maintained its own separate roster, lettering, and color scheme, although there were occasional transfers between companies. Since the Lorain equipment was designed for local streetcar and suburban service, it normally did not wander onto LSE interurban lines. Certain smaller LSE interurban cars regularly operated on the LSRR, however, and to an extent the two companies pooled equipment on their various Lorain local lines after 1919.

Like many Midwestern traction operations, both the LSE and LSRR and their predecessors primarily used single-end equipment; double-enders were necessary only for certain city lines and short-turnback services. Virtually all freight motors also were single-end.

Unlike some similar operations, however, the LSE did not use trailers in any type of passenger service except to a modest extent on the Lorain Street Railroad. Instead the company was a pioneer in multiple-unit (m.u.) interurban operations, beginning with an early (but unused) system on its 1903 Brill combines and then standardizing on such equipment beginning with its 1906–1907 Niles cars. Restrictions on the old Rocky River viaduct initially prevented m.u. train operations into Cleveland, but after completion of the new bridge in 1911, two- and three-car trains were routinely run through the late 1920s. The 1927 schedule restructuring eliminated all regular multi-car operations, but they continued for charters and other special occasions until the end of service.

With only minor exceptions, the Lake Shore bought its interurban cars new. It was less discriminating when acquiring city and suburban cars, where low purchase cost was often a critical factor. In the earlier years its streetcar routes were operated with a mixture of new, secondhand, and inherited cars, but these were mostly replaced by 16 new single-truck Birneys in 1920 (augmented in 1925 by three more from Baltimore) and ten modern steel double-truck one-man LSRR city cars delivered in 1930.

An LSE oddity was its "flood train," used to shuttle passengers through sections of line which flooding had made impassable for ordinary equipment. This consisted of a specially designed single-truck box motor hauling a high-mounted trailer coach, a onetime Lorain Street Railway double-truck 1890s-era suburban car. The train was used extensively during the infamous March 1913 flood in Fremont, but apparently had become unnecessary after 1916.

At the time the LSE was formed, the Everett-Moore management intended to adopt a common four-digit equipment numbering system for all its properties, which was fully applied on the Detroit United Railway. As part of this scheme, the LSE's first newly ordered cars — the ten single-truck Brill city cars of 1901–1902 — were numbered 5000–5009. Former TF&N car 13 also was temporarily renumbered 8000 in 1902. But that was the end of it for the LSE; afterward the company followed its own simple system, starting with "one" and working upward, generally in chronological order as cars were received.

Interurban Passenger Cars

The TF&N Barney & Smith Cars
(TF&N 1–22 / LSE 1–24 and 8000)

Of the LSE's mixed bag of hand-me-downs from its four predecessors, the newest, best, and most suitable for long-distance service were 22 interurban passenger motors built by Dayton's Barney & Smith Car Company in 1900–1901 for the Toledo, Fremont & Norwalk Railroad. These austere-looking but large, sturdy, and highly durable wooden cars immediately became the backbone of the new LSE's operations, and in one form or another most were on the property until the end. In fact, TF&N Car 13 opened the Fremont–Bellevue line on October 2, 1900, and as LSE 23 was still available for Bellevue–Ceylon Junction service on May 14, 1938. Originally TF&N Nos. 1–22, they carried their numbers through to the LSE roster with only one major and one minor exception. TF&N car 13 briefly became LSE 8000 in 1902, but in 1903 was renumbered 23, leaving the number 13 forever vacant to reassure the superstitious. And as will be noted in a moment, No. 18 became No. 24 for about three years.

The TF&N had opened with hourly service between Toledo and Norwalk, and its schedule could be handled by six cars; hence the company had far more cars than it needed. The highly optimistic 22-car order apparently anticipated the TF&N's planned through interline service between Toledo and Cleveland. Evidence from a 1902 inventory indicates that the TF&N never fitted out cars 16–20 or 22 for service.

As originally built, these single-end TF&N "Barneys" had open rear platforms, no toilets, K-13 controls, and two 75 hp motors which were carried on the rear truck. As a result they were underpowered for their size and weight and undoubtedly had difficulty in maintaining the LSE's initial 30 mph average scheduled running speed. Once under the new LSE's wing, at least three cars were soon fitted out with various control and motor combinations for testing to determine the LSE's future standard equipment.

The most widely publicized test car was "Yellow Flyer" No. 18, which received GE equipment including four No. 66 motors of 125 hp each. (It was supposed to be a model for the new New York City subway cars.) Westinghouse equipment was installed in two other cars. No. 13, renumbered 8000, was re-fitted with an L-4 control and four Westinghouse No. 76 motors of 75 hp each; it was repainted in the maroon scheme with gold leaf trim used by Everett-Moore's Detroit United system. In a variation of this, No. 9 carried three No. 76 motors and was painted in the so-called "Big Four" orange scheme. The 8000's performance was deemed substantially equal to No. 18's, and the company settled on this motor and control combination. But the unsuccessful three-motor No. 9 did make one lasting contribution: its orange paint scheme thereafter became the LSE's standard.

Gradually re-equipped with the L-4 control and four Westinghouse No. 76 motors (and with toilets added), the "Barneys" were the backbone of LSE operations until 1907, when supplanted by the new Brill and Niles cars. They then held down local and suburban runs until the steel cars appeared in 1917–18, and remained in general utility work afterward.

The "Yellow Flyer" No. 18 soon underwent a strange renumbering, becoming No. 24 between 1903 and 1906 and then reverting to its old number again. The reason: The Cuyahoga County (Cleveland) commissioners ruled that No. 18 could not enter the city because they did not want such a "heavy" car crossing their not-too-substantial Rocky River bridge and Superior viaduct and swing bridge. LSE president Barney Mahler solved the problem by simply renumbering the car to 24 and continuing to run it over the bridges with, apparently, nobody the wiser.

Inaugurating what was to become an LSE tradition of demolishing new cars, No. 4 — an early LSE high-speed rebuild — was wrecked and burned in a head-on collision with No. 57 on December 13, 1902. Nos. 9 and 11 were also accident and fire victims. The 9 was demolished in a fiery collision at Beach Park during a blinding blizzard December 18, 1917; car 11 was lost more prosaically in the Fremont carbarn fire of October 15, 1906. Ten other members of the fleet were rebuilt in various forms at various times: Between 1924 and 1926, five cars became freight motors 26–30. Cars 5 and 16 became combine motors in 1927, and

Barney & Smith 23 went through three numbers and two rebuildings in its life. Originally Toledo, Fremont & Norwalk 13, it became the LSE's experimental No. 8000 and then 23. In 1923 it was rebuilt as a double-ender for Toledo–Genoa service. In this mid-1930s view at Fremont it displays the diamond logo briefly adopted in the 1926–27 period and applied to several cars at that time. (Anthony Krisak photo)

the 18, 20, and 23 were converted to double-end operation — the 18 and 23 in 1927 and the 20 in 1937. The remaining nine of the original 22-car fleet, all of them single-end coaches, were put in storage in 1932 but survived until 1938.

Other Inherited Interurban Cars (LSE 40–59)

The LSE's three other predecessors also provided interurban cars, albeit in lesser numbers and of considerably lesser value. From the Sandusky & Interurban the LSE inherited three double-ended passenger motors (one combine and two smoker-passenger coaches), all produced by Jewett in 1900. Although almost new when the LSE was organized, they were already obsolescent by the company's standards. Undoubtedly their greatest distinction was that the S&I had given them rather whimsical classical Greek names rather than numbers — *Alpha*, *Beta*, and *Gamma* — although on the S&I's books they were prosaically numbered 25–27. (In 1901 Jewett delivered two similar cars to the S&I, Nos. 29–30, but these soon showed up on the Everett-Moore–affiliated Toledo & Western Railway as T&W 29–30.) In the course of time the LSE rebuilt *Alpha* and *Beta* as combines numbered LSE 43 and 44 respectively. *Gamma*, however, expired after being hit by a Lake Shore & Michigan Southern train at the Columbus Avenue crossing in Sandusky February 18, 1903, and was written off without having been renumbered. The 43 and 44 lasted until 1927 and 1928 — the 43 as an express motor and the 44 as the regular Gibsonburg branch shuttle car, a service it performed for 21 years.

The Lorain & Cleveland Railway contributed ten full passenger motor cars (L&C 10–19 series and 64) and two combines (L&C 55–56), all built by Brill between 1896 and 1899. These single-end deck-roof cars had open rear ends, Brill 27E trucks, four 50 hp GE 57A motors, and B-9 controllers for magnetic brakes. Some of the full passenger motors were part of a large joint order for several Everett-Moore interurban lines, which included ten closely identical cars each for the Akron, Bedford & Cleveland (AB&C 32–50, even numbers only, with railroad-style roofs) and ten deck-roof versions for the Cleveland, Painesville & Eastern (CP&E 10–19). The L&C Nos. 55, 56, and 64 actually fitted into the CP&E's numbering scheme, indicating probable early equipment trading, either before or after delivery. Although relatively fast for their time (reportedly capable of 55 mph), the L&C cars were little more than city streetcars in interurban service. Even John G. Brill himself thought that they rode badly, and according to Barney Mahler's 1909 recollections they had to have over a ton of weight added before they could ride reasonably well at 40 mph.

The former L&C 10–19 and 64 became LSE 50–59 while combines 55–56 were renumbered LSE 40–41. But not surprisingly, the LSE had little use for most of them. Four were gone by 1905, mostly wreck victims; most of the remaining coaches soon became Lorain Street Railroad property and were in such bad shape by 1929 that the LSRR was forced to replace them with new cars. Car 59 became a line car, later LSE 451, and was retired in 1931; the longest-lived, combine 41, was rebuilt as a freight motor, becoming LSE 49 in 1929 and surviving until the end in 1938.

Last, and least, was a group of four primitive early interurban cars originally built in 1893 by Jewett for the Sandusky, Milan & Norwalk and inherited through its successor, the Sandusky, Norwalk & Southern. Two — the former SM&N 11 and 13 (later 12) — were double-ended full coaches equipped with McGuire 20 trucks and two Westinghouse 3 motors. The other two, SM&N 7 and 9, were double-end combines with different histories. No. 9 was originally built as a combine similar to the two coaches; No. 7, however, started life in 1893 as one of two "open" trailers — actually center-aisle closed coaches but with no windows and open platforms — and at some point had been rebuilt as a fully closed fearsome-looking combine motor. (Its sister, No. 5, was rebuilt as a baggage motor.) By 1902 all four of these were obsolete and in wretched shape, but the LSE was forced to continue using them on the Sandusky–Milan–Norwalk line because of a shortage of other suitable cars. It attempted to rebuild combine No. 9 into an improved combine for the Gibsonburg branch, numbered LSE 42. But on August 18, 1906, the 42 ran into its onetime sister car, Sandusky, Norwalk & Southern 11, which was being used as a portable passenger station at Gibsonburg Junction, and both became history. The remaining two cars, SN&S 7 and 12, were last used in December 1902 and soon scrapped.

The 1902 Kuhlman Cars
(LSE 54[II] and 57[II])

The LSE insisted on its own high standards and designs for its interurban car fleet and generally spurned secondhand equipment. In fact, there were only two such cases, each one a special situation. The first came soon after the company's creation, before it even was able to buy new interurbans of its own.

Following the mutual destruction of Barney & Smith car 4 and Brill combine 57 in the December 13, 1902, collision, the company hustled out for quick replacements. That year, Kuhlman had built six light interurban cars for the Cleveland, Elyria & Western (later part of the Cleveland Southwestern) which the CE&W rejected. In 1903 the LSE picked up two of the six, numbering them 4 and 57 to match their destroyed predecessors — although the second No. 4 was renumbered as second No. 54 in 1905. When the new No. 4 arrived in 1903 it was given its defunct predecessor's trucks, but in 1905 it received the original No. 54's trucks.

These two identical cars eventually rode on Brill 27E trucks but had different motors — the 54(II) had GE 57-A motors like the Lorain & Cleveland's Brill cars while 57(II) carried Westinghouse 101-D motors, rarely used by the LSE. While technically interurban cars, the two oddballs spent most of their lives in plodding local services — first on the Sandusky–Milan–Norwalk run, then shuttling between Lorain and Elyria on the Lorain Street Railroad. They last saw revenue service in early 1930 but were not scrapped until 1938.

Three other of the six Kuhlman orphans, incidentally, gravitated to what became the Rockford & Interurban Railway in Illinois and Wisconsin. The final car disappeared from the records.

An emergency purchase in 1903, LSE's second 57 was built by Kuhlman in 1902 for the Cleveland, Elyria & Western. It and Sister 54(II) worked local runs until about 1930. (W. A. McCaleb photo)

The 1903 Brill Cars
(LSE 60–69)

After emerging from its 1902 bankruptcy, the LSE hastened out to order ten new interurban passenger-baggage combines from Brill in 1903 — cars custom-designed to inaugurate the planned Cleveland–Toledo limited services. They were truly deluxe, with unusual five-part front and rear windows which included a wrap-around glass section at each corner. Inside were leather-covered seats and an enclosed curved glass smoking section incorporating semi-circular leather-covered couches. The motorman had his own separately enclosed cab at the car's right front end.

No. 69, one of the elegant 1903 Brill limited combines, shows off its distinctive curved-glass front end at Fremont in 1937. (W. L. Hay photo)

The 49'7"-long single-end cars rode on the latest Brill 27A2 trucks and were powered by four Westinghouse No. 76 motors of 75 hp each. They were delivered with Van Dorn couplers and carried large oil-fired headlights; eventually these were replaced with heavy-duty Tomlinson MCB couplers and the standard LSE electric headlights with clear lens.

The Brills also came with an early form of multiple-unit equipment, with train line wires carried between the cars via under-floor receptacles. The m.u. system did not include high-voltage power lines, however, so that each car of a train drew power from its own trolley pole. What may have been the first known instance of m.u. train operation on an overhead trolley system occurred August 5, 1903, when master mechanic Fred Heckler, at the controls of car 62, ran cars 62 and 65 together from Sandusky to Fremont via Ceylon Junction. The cars had just been set up at Sandusky and were being ferried to Fremont to be placed in service. But while this was a first for a trolley-powered interurban and the control system was used successfully elsewhere, it came to naught on the LSE. For various reasons the Brills never regularly ran in trains. The next order of multiple-unit interurbans — the 1906–1907 Niles cars — were built with a more advanced but incompatible system.

Numbered 60–69, the new cars began arriving on July 16, 1903, and after testing they entered revenue service in late August operating the newly introduced limiteds. Most of them subsequently had long but sometimes rough careers on the LSE, with the seven survivors still on the property in 1938 and four active in passenger or work service until the last day of operation. Car 66 probably broke the record for short-time service on the LSE, or any interurban line for that matter. It entered service August 29, 1903, and was promptly destroyed in a derailment at Undergrade, west of Lorain, on September 20 — an active life of 23 days. The company quickly ordered a replacement from Kuhlman, by then a Brill subsidiary, using the trucks and electrical equipment from the deceased 66 and carrying its same number. Second 66 entered service March 9, 1904, but the number seemed cursed. On June 2 of the same year it was involved in the horrific Wells Corners collision, which killed six passengers riding in its elegant smoking section. The unhappy car finally burned on the Gibsonburg branch June 4, 1928, and its number was ignominiously retired. Two others of the group also were lost: the Fremont carbarn fire of October 16, 1906, consumed car 67, and the 60 was destroyed by a New York Central train at the Milan Road crossing in Sandusky October 21, 1925.

After the arrival of the Niles cars in 1906–07 the Brills were relegated to local and branch runs which required combines. Among other things they were used on the pioneering interline runs between Sandusky and Mansfield, which sporadically operated during the summers between 1908 and 1911. Several were rebuilt in various forms afterward. In the course of wreck repairs Nos. 61, 64, and 68 lost their unique curved front corner windows, replaced by standard LSE three-window front ends; the 65 had its curved smoking section rebuilt to a conventional center-aisle layout in 1927 when it was assigned as the regular car on the Gibsonburg branch. There it plodded back and forth until the last day of LSE operation. Car 69 became the spare Gibsonburg car, and in November of 1937 was converted to double-end operation when given the added duty of handling the Saturday-only East Toledo–Genoa shuttle run. The 62 and 63 were extensively rebuilt as line cars 455 and 456 in 1931. As No. 455, the onetime 62 remained operating until early 1940 helping to remove its long-time home rails.

The 1904 Stephenson Cars
(LSE 70–72)

The LSE's second new interurban car order came in 1904, and was another sidestep from the path to high-speed intercity equipment — a small, short-lived, and rather mysterious group of three Stephenson-built straight coaches. (Like Kuhlman, Stephenson was then a Brill subsidiary.) These were part of a joint order of eight cars shared with Everett-Moore's Northern Ohio Traction and Light Company. (The NOT&L cars were used for its Akron–Cleveland services.) Records show that the LSE's portion of the order originally was to be only two cars, but possibly the loss of the *Gamma* in the Sandusky grade crossing wreck February 18, 1903 prompted the addition of one car. Numbered 70–72, they were delivered August 11, 1904. Nos. 70 and 71 were mounted on Peckham 40A trucks with four GE 57A motors; the 72 received the Brill 27E trucks and GE 57A motors from LSE 50, which in turn was given *Gamma*'s trucks and equipment.

The three Stephensons were put in local services — 70 and 71 operating on main line locals out of Beach Park carhouse and 72 on the Sandusky–Milan–Norwalk run. All three eventually gravitated to rotating use on the Avon Beach & Southern branch and Cleveland–Lorain locals. It is possible that they were transferred to the Lorain Street Railroad roster early in their careers. In any event those careers were short. Nos. 70 and 71 perished simultaneously on April 15, 1918, in the Beach Park carbarn fire. (It would appear that fire insurance settlements were slow in those days; the LSE retired the two in January 1930 after finally receiving $400 each for them.) The 72 operated inconspicuously in Lorain and on the AB&S until at least 1923 and was retired in 1928.

The 1906–1907 Niles Cars
(LSE 141–164)

In June 1906 the LSE received the first of a fleet of classic interurban cars from the Niles Car Company. Notwithstanding the elegance of the earlier Brills, many Lake Shore Electric enthusiasts feel that these were the best proportioned and most aesthetically pleasing cars the company ever owned. Their size, performance, and operating characteristics were to set the company's future equipment standards. Five (Nos. 160–164) were combines; the balance (141–159) were straight coaches. They had the classic Niles curved top windows, and within were fixed high-back seats upholstered with black leather and an expensive

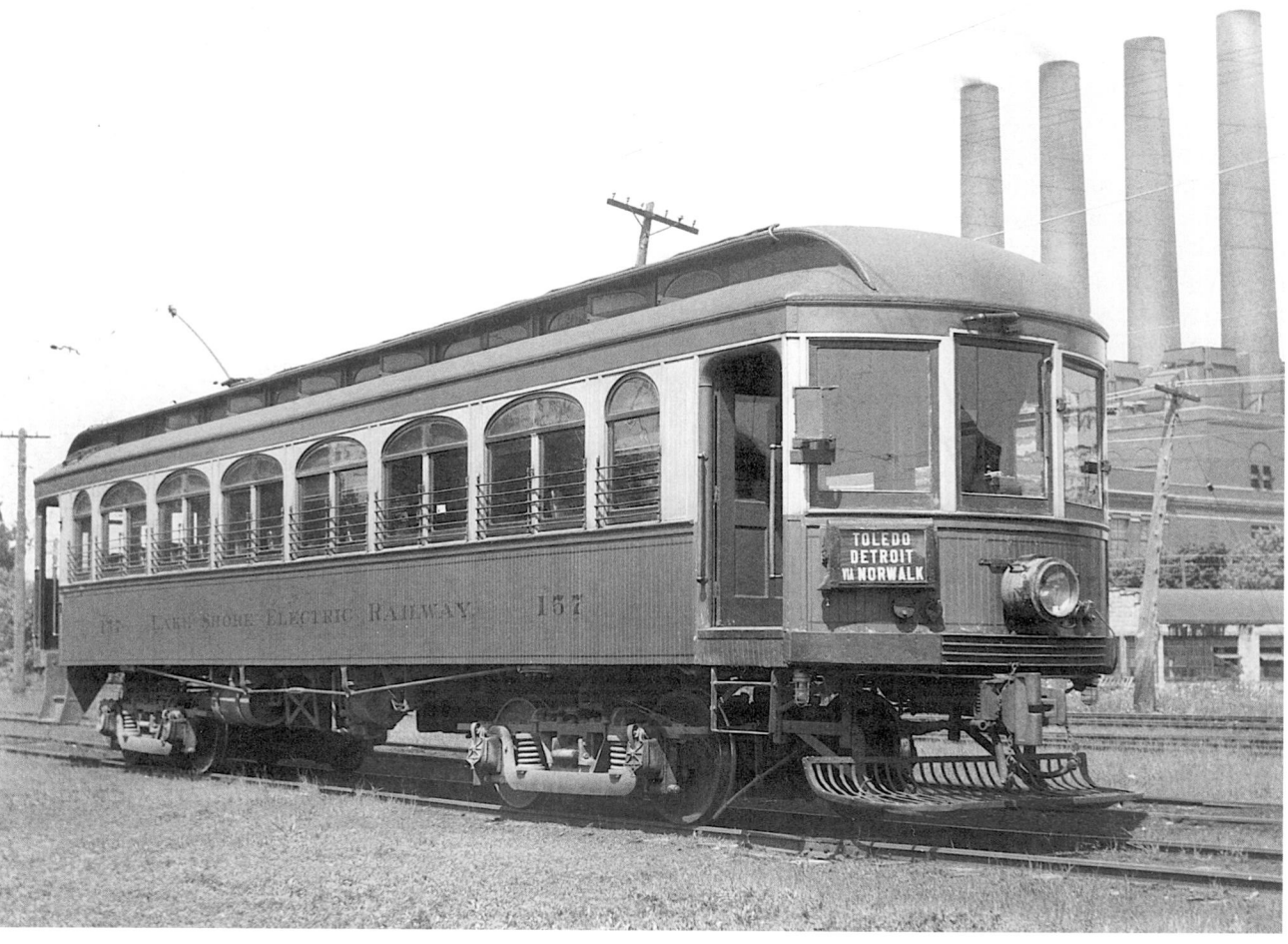

An LSE classic: 1906 Niles
coach 157 is at Beach Park
in 1937. (W. L. Hay photo)

cherry wood finish inlaid with white holly borders. The single-end Niles cars weighed about
75,000 pounds and cost (in 1906–1907 dollars) about $10,000 apiece.

They also were delivered with GE Type M automatic-accelerating multiple-unit control, with Westinghouse Type C-36 master controller and the Westinghouse Traction Brake
Company's Type AMM automatic air brake. The m.u. system was unusual for interurbans
at that time; many contemporary traction managers considered motor-trailer operation to
be a less costly and more effective way of handling peak loads. But the fine hand of LSE
general manager Furman Stout can be seen behind its decision to go m.u. (Sadly, Stout
barely outlived the delivery of his new cars.) Unlike the 1903 Brills, this m.u. system included a high voltage line between the cars, so that only one pole was necessary to draw
power for a two-car train. This feature, which all subsequent LSE m.u. cars carried, was
necessary for reasonably trouble-free high-speed operation under the LSE's simple overhead wire suspension system. A single pole also was needed to properly operate automatic
electric switches on the city streetcar lines which the trains used.

Coaches 150–159 were ordered in December 1905, and the first five delivered at Cleveland
May 28, 1906; the second half of the order came to the LSE at Bellevue via the Nickel Plate
in mid-June. Both groups were set up at Fremont, and on June 15 cars 154 and 155 were tested
in multiple-unit operation between Fremont and Norwalk, reaching a top speed of 71 mph.
(That figure probably was achieved going downhill, since their normal top operating speed was
closer to 60 mph.) The company publicized the event as the first time a train of cars was operated on a surface railway using an overhead trolley system, and for some years the Westinghouse
Traction Brake Company used a photo of the pioneer train in its advertising.

While nine of the Niles cars entered limited train service July 27, 1906, the inevitable LSE new car catastrophe followed promptly. On August 4 westbound 152 collided head-on with eastbound Barney & Smith No. 12 just west of Vermilion, killing four people. Both cars were taken to the Fremont shops for repairs but on October 15th the shop itself caught fire, catching the 152 still inside and permanently ending its life.

With the pending opening of the Sandusky–Fremont line in 1907, the ever-thrifty LSE ordered an additional 15 bodies from Niles but only 12 sets of trucks and other equipment. While essentially the same as the ten original 1906 Niles coaches, the 15 newcomers had heavier underframes. This group consisted of ten full coaches (planned as Nos. 140–149) and five combines (160–164). In the end, however, it was decided to give No. 140 the trucks, equipment, and number from the recently deceased 152, so the series actually began with No. 141. Also, combines 162 and 163 used trucks and equipment from destroyed Barney & Smith cars 4 and 11, and were not multiple-unit cars. Ten cars of this latest group — coaches 141–148 and combines 160–161 — were included in the mortgage of the Sandusky, Fremont & Southern, the technical owner of the new Sandusky–Fremont line, and were thus listed as SF&S property on the Lake Shore Electric's roster.

The new Niles coaches 141–159 went into limited train service, where they remained until 1932 when demoted to local assignments between Cleveland and Lorain and the Ceylon Junction–Norwalk–Fremont run. Combines 160–164 were used on systemwide local runs where baggage and express capacity was needed. While the coaches 141–159 often ran in trains, the three m.u.-equipped combines (160, 161, and 164) were only included in train consists for extra Sandusky service during summer weekends.

The 160 illustrates the combine version of the Niles fleet, built in 1907 and technically owned by the Sandusky, Fremont & Southern. In this 1938 view it also displays the ditch lights installed in the LSE's last year as well as an unusual Vermilion destination sign. (W. L. Hay photo)

The regal Niles fleet was hardly immune to the LSE's lifelong penchant for equipment mayhem. Aside from the original 152 already mentioned, six others were lost to wrecks, fires, or both. As they were, trucks and other equipment often were recycled for their replacement cars or for other uses. Next to go was the 153, which burned at Alexis, Ohio, on January 22, 1914, on the Detroit United Railway. It was replaced in 1915 by new steel Jewett car 167, using the 153's trucks but carrying new motors. SF&S Nos. 142 and 144 collided with one another east of Flora siding near Clyde April 28, 1915, and donated their trucks and usable equipment to steel Jewett replacements 168–169 built that year. As noted earlier, the 154 collided with Barney & Smith No. 9 at Beach Park in December 1917, and it too was fatally injured; its trucks and motors went to combine 163 to replace its odd Barney & Smith trucks, themselves recycled. On April 10, 1918, SF&S 161 caught fire and burned simply while sitting on the lead track at Fremont's Fifth Street carbarn after a run; its equipment went to home-built freight motor SF&S 36 later that year. Finally, on November 15, 1930, No. 163 was wrecked and burned at Hayes siding east of Toledo in a head-on collision with Northern Ohio freight motor 1059.

Several of the Niles cars were rebuilt in one form or another during the 1920s. In 1923 coach 149 had its original 50-foot 9-inch length extended to 60 feet; the following year the 143 was similarly lengthened. By 1929 the company had too many passenger cars and not enough freight motors, so five Niles coaches went through the shop to emerge as freight motors 41–45. In addition the LSE decided to rebuild coach 152(II) to serve double duty as a spare freight motor during the winter and a passenger-carrying car during the peak summer months. It apparently lasted only one summer in its dual role and in December 1929 was rebuilt as full freight motor 46.

Twelve Niles cars continued in passenger-carrying service until the end in 1938, although the combines were seldom used after the end of freight service May 15, 1937. After 1927 the fleet was rarely run in multiple-unit trains, although a well-photographed boys' club charter trip in August of 1937 shows the 143 and 149 running as a two-car train between Lorain and the Cleveland Railway's Rocky River carhouse in Lakewood.

The 1911 Jewett "Lima Route" Cars
(LSE 165–166)

To handle its planned new Cleveland–Lima interline service via the Fostoria & Fremont and the Western Ohio, the LSE participated with the Western Ohio and the Dayton & Troy in a joint 1911 order to Jewett for six wood combines. The LSE's portion consisted of two cars, LSE 165–166, which rode on Standard C-80P trucks, with four 100 hp GE 205E motors (a departure from the LSE's usual Westinghouse equipment) and GE multiple-unit controls and equipment. Two identical cars were built as Western Ohio 198–199, and the four

The 1911 Jewett-built Lima Route combines, when new and in 1938. (Right) The 165 carries its original lettering and Lima Route logo on its side. Note the two spare poles on the roof, a regular LSE practice for emergencies out on the line. (George Krambles collection)

(Below) The 166 is at Sandusky in April 1938. (Bruce Triplett photo)

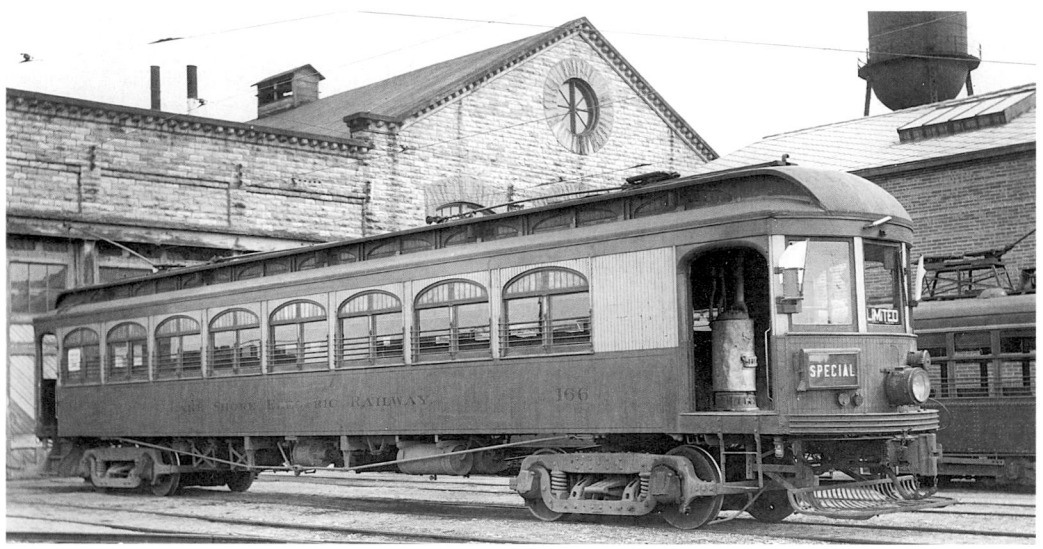

were pooled in the Lima service beginning in early August 1911. The Dayton & Troy's two-car portion, numbered D&T 300 and 310, were built for its Dayton–Toledo interline service with the Western Ohio and the Toledo, Bowling Green & Southern; their bodies were identical but they had different trucks and electrical equipment.

In appearance and operation the new Cleveland–Lima Jewetts were fully compatible with the LSE's Niles fleet, with only minor visible differences. Sixty-two passengers could be seated either on leather-covered smoker seats or green figured plush in the main passenger compartment. Although single-end cars, they also carried a front-end trolley pole and retriever. All four cars were painted the LSE's standard orange with brown trim, but they carried the lettering "Cleveland - Limited - Lima" on their letterboards in Western Ohio style along with that road's "Lima Route" emblem on their sides.

In 1922 the Western Ohio converted its lines to lightweight equipment, and the LSE–WO Lima through pool operation ended in September of that year. The Western Ohio sold its combine 198 to the Interstate Public Service Company of Indiana (it became IPSC 149) but retained the 199 to operate the connecting limited car between Lima and Fremont until those runs ended on September 30, 1930.

After leaving the Lima run, the two LSE combines were used in regular Cleveland–Toledo limited and express service. They were given new leather bucket seats in 1930, so well did the company think of them. The 165's useful life ended November 2, 1935, when it hit an auto east of Toledo and derailed, although it remained stored until retired in 1938; its sister 166 ran in both local and express service until the LSE's end.

The 1915 Steel Jewett Cars
(LSE 167, SF&S 168–169)

The Lake Shore finally entered the steel car age in 1915, albeit for less than progressive reasons. On December 18th of that year three steel Jewett-built coaches arrived to replace recently destroyed wooden Niles cars 153 (in early 1914) and SF&S 142 and 144 (in 1915). To match the ownership of their departed predecessors, the Jewetts went on the books as LSE 167 and SF&S 168–169. Although steel-bodied, these arch-roof multiple-unit coaches carried the side truss rods normally needed for wood underframe equipment.

The new Jewetts went into main-line limited train service, with the 167 also used on the Lima run. But with the usual LSE luck, SF&S 169 was caught in the Beach Park carbarn fire of April 15, 1918, and was severely burned. It was returned to Jewett for rebuilding and returned home April 2, 1919. The 167 had the dismal duty of closing down the LSE with

One of the LSE's first steel interurbans, the 169 came from Jewett in 1915 but used trucks and motors from wrecked wooden Niles coach 144. It waits for a night run at Cleveland's Public Square in 1937. (John A. Rehor collection)

the final run out of Cleveland at 12:41 a.m. on Sunday morning May 15, 1938. The three cars were then stored and retired in early 1939.

The 1917–1918 Jewett Steel Cars
(LSE 170–181)

The Lake Shore's last interurban car order and certainly its most familiar fleet was a fine group of 12 steel coaches delivered by Jewett during the trying World War I days. The company's board of directors originally authorized the purchase of 20 steel interurban cars on October 30, 1916 — 16 motor cars and four trailers. (The planned trailers are surprising since the LSE never operated trailers in interurban service. Possibly it represented pressure from its Detroit United connection, which soon ordered trailers for its own operations.) But only 12 motor cars actually were ordered, and their gestation turned out to be long and difficult. On December 2nd Jewett was sent an order for the 12 bodies, and on December 13th the Baldwin Locomotive Works received a separate order for their trucks.

The all-steel bodies measured 60 feet 2 inches and contained wide bucket seats for 64 passengers, split between a forward leather-upholstered smoking section and striped plush covering in the main passenger compartment. The new cars were powered by four 140 hp motors, the LSE's most powerful yet. Traction historian William D. Middleton noted that their weight of just over 42 tons, relatively light for their size, gave them a 152-pounds-per-horsepower ratio that was one of the most favorable of any contemporary interurban car design. "It was not until the development of the several lightweight, high-speed car designs of the early 1930s that this ratio was materially improved," he wrote.

But thanks largely to wartime shortages, construction was painfully slow. Three cars (Nos. 170–172) arrived in November of 1917, and three more (173–175) in February 1918. Hardly had they arrived when the LSE curse overtook two of them — on April 15, 1918, Nos. 173 and 174 were burned in the Beach Park carhouse fire. These went back to Jewett for rebuilding (along with the 169) and made their second appearance April 2, 1919, returning from Jewett as a three-car train. In the meantime, three more cars (176–178) filtered in during late April and early May 1918. The last three, Nos. 179–181, finally appeared that July, over a year and a half after the order was placed.

Once received, they became the steel backbone of LSE's main-line services between Cleveland, Toledo, and Detroit, often running in two- and three-car trains until 1927 and sporadically in trains for charters thereafter. The last known two-car train operation, in fact, came shortly before abandonment when the Masons chartered a train consisting of cars 170 and 182 on May 3, 1938. Only one of this group of cars was lost, somewhat of a record for

Examples of the familiar 1917–18 steel Jewetts, the 172 and 173 pose at Fremont about 1927. (J. W. Vigrass collection)

LSE equipment: on February 21, 1929, No. 175 hit a gasoline truck at Millbury, between Toledo and Genoa, and was burned beyond economical repair. Its body was cut down to become work flat car 409 in May 1930.

Through the 1930s the surviving 11 steel Jewetts continued in daily service between Cleveland and Toledo via Sandusky and on Cleveland–Lorain locals, and after the end they were stored in the hope of eventual sale. That hope was modestly fulfilled when the Des Moines & Central Iowa bought Nos. 170, 179, and 180 in March 1939, rebuilding them into combines DM&CI 1710, 1712, and 1714 — with truss rods added. In that form they operated until September 28, 1949, the last LSE interurban cars active anywhere. But the remaining eight were unwanted for any other traction operations, and their bodies were sold for housing between April and July 1939.

The 1930–1932 Michigan Electric Cars
(LSE 182–183)

The LSE's only other group of secondhand interurban cars also was its last purchase of any kind of interurban equipment — and in hindsight turned out to be a misjudgment. By 1929 the interurban industry was faltering and some excellent equipment was coming onto the used car market, but at the same time the LSE still held out some optimism for the future. So in July of that year it picked up four deluxe 1917 St. Louis–built steel passenger interurbans from the Michigan Electric Railway, intending to fully rebuild them for use in both regular and charter service. Charters were a particular marketing target, and the company planned to install a small lounge section in each for parties, equipped with a sofa and a pair of upholstered chairs. The cars selected were Michigan Electric Railway Nos. 849, 851, 853, and 855, which were to be numbered LSE 182–185.

Unhappily their arrival on the Lake Shore closely coincided with the October stock market crash, and after the early 1930 LSE service cutbacks the purchase did not look so wise. But in a strange and surprising move, two of the four were sent through the LSE shops anyway, receiving extensive and expensive rebuildings. Former Michigan Electric 851 showed up in September 1930 as LSE 182, completely rebuilt to resemble the LSE's steel Jewetts. Included were substantial exterior and interior carbody alterations, including the installation of the planned lounge compartment, new multiple-unit equipment, and almost entirely rebuilt trucks. (It did retain its truss rods, however, making it look more like the LSE's 167–169 group than the 170-series.) The car proved successful, and in July of 1932 LSE fans were happily surprised to see Michigan Electric 853 appear as LSE 183, similarly rebuilt but without the lounge. That ended the rebuilding program, however, and the 849 and 855 accumulated rust in the Sandusky yard until 1938 when their bodies were sold. But the two rebuilds remained running until the end of service, and their bodies were sold in 1939.

City Cars

The Inherited City Cars

The early history of the LSE's and Lorain Street Railway's city streetcars is much murkier than the system's interurban equipment. One certainty is that the LSE inherited a total

The 182 and 183 were substantially rebuilt from Michigan Electric Railway combines 851 and 853 respectively. *(Top)* The 183 is at Eagle Avenue in Cleveland about 1937 (Karel Liebenauer photo). *(Bottom)* The 182 displays its backside on Erie Avenue in Lorain in October 1937. (George Krambles collection)

of 22 open and closed city cars at its formation in 1901, most of which were operating in Sandusky and many of which were in such terrible shape that the new company immediately had to order ten replacements. Of the 22, 15 were single-truck closed cars varying in carbody length (exclusive of platforms) from 16 to 21 feet, and the remaining seven were eight- to ten-bench opens.

From the Sandusky & Interurban came four early 16-foot closed cars (which became LSE 109–112), three 18-foot closed cars (LSE 113–115), and three nine-bench opens (LSE 204 and 205, with one unrenumbered) — all of them hand-me-downs from the Sandusky Street Railway and originally numbered in the 1–24 block. The four 16-foot closed cars had ancient Brill No. 13 trucks and two Walker No. 4 motors each, and must have been candidates for early scrapping. The 18-foot closed cars and the opens had more modern Brill 21E trucks and two Westinghouse 3 motors. The opens shared equipment with closed cars and snow sweepers.

Sandusky's other streetcar system, the onetime People's Electric Railway, passed down a total of nine cars through LSE predecessor Sandusky, Norwalk & Southern. Six were 16-foot single-truck closed cars (Nos. 2, 4, 6, 8, 14, and 16), which became LSE 103–108; two eight-bench opens (Nos. 10 and 18) became LSE 201 and 202, and one ten-bench open (No. 20) was numbered LSE 203. The closed cars 14 and 16 were among the earliest double-deck single-truck cars, with portable end stairwells and roof seating for seasonal loads.

Another SN&S underlier, the Sandusky, Milan & Norwalk, contributed its lone Norwalk city car, an 1898 Pullman-built single-truck convertible. Originally numbered 17, it continued its short shuttlings in Norwalk as LSE 101 until it was replaced in December of 1925. Although not listed in the LSE's 1902 inventory, it is believed that the SM&N's original 1893 Norwalk city car, No. 15, became LSE 102 and was used as a line car until 1914.

Of the 13 original closed cars, eight (LSE 103–105 and 108–112) were scrapped as soon as the ten new Brill city cars came in February 1902. The other five (LSE 106, 107, and 113–115) continued running in Sandusky until 1914. (In 1905 the 106 and 107 became 116–117.) Five of the six single-truck open cars (LSE 201–205) remained in summer service through 1911; the sixth was retired in 1902 without renumbering.

The final two city hand-me-downs came from the Lorain & Cleveland, which in turn inherited them from the East Lorain Street Railway's East Erie Avenue streetcar line in Lorain. One, the former L&C No. 1, was a 16-foot closed single-trucker which the East Lorain company had obtained from the Northern Electric Railway Company of Chicago. It became LSE 120 and was used as a line car at least until 1914. The second car, an eight-bench open of unknown origin, became LSE 200 and remained in Lorain city service through 1907.

In 1906 the Lake Shore Electric acquired Tom L. Johnson's Lorain Street Railway, which added an even more shadowy collection of cars. Even the precise number is unknown, although 15 have been accounted for. All went directly onto the roster of the LSE's new Lorain Street Railroad. Those which can be identified include five Stephenson-built railroad-roof double-truck trailers which became LSRR 75–79. These originally were early motor cars on the Lorain–Elyria line, possibly numbered Lorain Street Railway 12–20 (even numbers only), and may have been rebuilt from earlier single-truck cars. They were distinguished by DuPont trucks and large wheels, which gave them a peculiar high-mounted look. Six other double-truck 1895 American Car Company cars became LSRR 80–85. In addition, it is documented that the LSRR operated four other inherited Lorain cars until 1916, but not even their LSRR numbers are known.

In any event, all of the early Lorain cars were gone by 1924 with three exceptions: trailer 79 was transferred to LSE ownership in 1912 for use on the "flood train," where its high-mounted body was a prime virtue. It returned to the LSRR in 1916 and was scrapped in 1925. LSRR 85 was rebuilt as work car LSRR 406 in 1919 and survived in that form into 1938. Finally, LSRR 83 (which eventually was renumbered as 85[II]), worked as a trailer until 1928, and later became a cottage at Sage's Grove.

The 1901 Brills
(LSE 5000–5009, later 103–112)

The new LSE's most pressing priority in 1901 was to replace some of the weary Sandusky city streetcars just described. This was promptly accomplished with an order to Brill for ten small single-truck cars delivered in February 1902 with Everett-Moore "empire" numbers 5000–5009. These became LSE 103(II) – 112(II) in 1904–1905, taking the old numbers of some of the cars they replaced. By LSE standards they led peaceful lives trudging around Sandusky's streets. Most were last used June 30, 1920, when the new fleet of one-man Birney cars went into service; two, however, including the 111, creaked along on the West Monroe Street line until replaced in 1925.

Ten Brill city streetcars came in 1902 to replace worn-out equipment in Sandusky. Examples are shown here in both their original 5000-series numbering and the 103–112 series adopted in 1904. (Both, John A. Rehor collection)

The 1906 Kuhlman Cars
(LSRR 90–94)

The Lorain Street Railroad's first new equipment under LSE control came in May 1906 in the form of five single-end double-truck pay-as-you-enter wood city cars. Numbered LSRR 90–94, the Kuhlman products had straight sides and a railroad-type monitor roof, giving them an interurbanish look; as originally built they had open rear platforms, later closed. Their lives were spent on the Lorain–Elyria runs, but they were rarely used after the new steel St. Louis cars arrived in 1930. Car 91 burned in March 1931; the others were stored until retired at the end of 1937.

(*Above*) Lorain Street Railroad 92 came from Kuhlman in 1906 after the LSE purchased the line. The big suburban car is at Elyria. (Karel Liebenauer collection)

(*Right*) Open city car 204(II), shown at the Soldiers Home, came from Atlantic City in 1912. (Tom Heinrich collection)

(*Below*) In this case, old open cars never die. The ever-frugal LSE put the former second Nos. 200 and 201 to this kind of work in Sandusky from 1920 to 1938. (W. L. Hay photo)

The 1912 Atlantic City Open Cars
(LSE 200–204[II])

By 1912 the LSE found it necessary to replace the dilapidated single-truck open city cars 201–205, inherited from its Sandusky predecessors. At the same time, more capacity was needed to handle the growing summer crowds. The company frugally went into the used car market and picked up five double-truck single-end 12-bench open cars from the West Jersey & Seashore, a Pennsylvania Railroad subsidiary which, in addition to its steam railroad services, operated streetcar and interurban lines in the Atlantic City area. Their history is unclear, but some sources state that they were built in the 1880s as trailers for a Camden & Atlantic steam dummy line between Atlantic City and Longport. They were motorized in 1893 and eventually rebuilt by Brill.

The Atlantic City opens arrived in May of 1912, in time for the summer season, and were given LSE numbers 200–204(II). From then until 1919 they carried summer riders on the Soldiers Home Belt line in Sandusky — although their use during the war years of 1917 and 1918 is uncertain.

Their mobile life ended when the Birney cars took over Sandusky services on July 1, 1920, but afterward Nos. 200–202 continued to be useful in a stationary status as storage sheds at the Sandusky shops. There they sat until 1938, No. 202 still on its Peckham trucks and the other two on the ground.

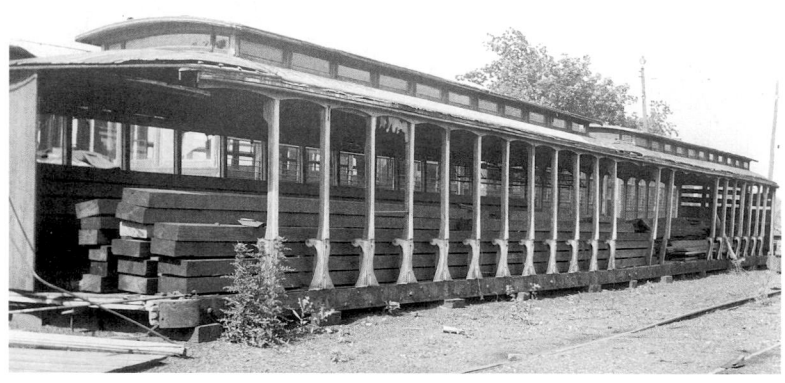

The 1913 Atlantic City Closed Cars
(LSE 118–122)

Having solved its open car problem, the Lake Shore next needed to replace the last survivors of its early closed Sandusky city cars, five veterans now numbered 113–117. Once again it went to the West Jersey & Seashore, which in 1913 was acquiring a new fleet of cars and disposing of older equipment. The LSE picked up five double-truck Brill cars originally dating to 1904–1905, which had been built as part of two separate orders totaling 20 cars numbered WJ&S 6801–6838 (with gaps). Originally single-end, they had been rebuilt as double-end in 1908. The LSE assigned them Nos. 118–122 and put them in service on Sandusky's Soldiers Home Belt line in December 1913 as single-end cars.

There they lasted until the Birney cars arrived in mid-1920. They then went to Lorain, primarily running on the LSE's Colorado and Erie Avenue lines, and also filling in on the Avon Beach & Southern and Lorain Street Railroad local routes when needed. While in Lorain they once again became double-end, and in 1922 were rebuilt for one-man operation; thus modernized most plugged along until replaced again by Birneys in late 1931. Car 120 was burned while in service in December 1929; the other four were dismantled in 1935 and their bodies sent to Sage's Grove to serve as summer cottages.

The 118, another Atlantic City veteran bought in 1913, is at the Soldiers Home some time before 1920. (John A. Rehor collection)

The 1916 Ex–Cleveland Railway Wood Cars (LSRR 73, 86–89)

By 1916 Lorain's steel and shipbuilding industries were booming and the Lorain Street Railroad needed low-cost rush-hour carrying capacity. That year it acquired five used single-end pay-as-you-enter wood cars from the Electric Equipment Company of Philadelphia, which had bought them from the Cleveland Railway in 1915. Four of the group had been Cleveland Railway Nos. 9, 18, 31, and 98; the fifth is unknown. By the time they reached Lorain they had been well worked over. Originally built by Brill in 1901–1902 as 14-bench open cars, they were sent to Kuhlman in 1904 for rebuilding into semi-enclosed cars. Subsequently the Cleveland Railway made them into fully enclosed cars.

The Lorain Street Railroad numbered them 73 and 86–89, and put them to work as tripper cars for the steel mills. They also worked the Oberlin Belt Line after the Lorain Street Railroad took over that route from the Cleveland Southwestern in 1923. Car 73 was gone by 1928, but the other four remained active until the new St. Louis steel cars arrived in 1930.

Lorain Street Railroad's 95–99 group came from Jewett in 1917–18 along with the 170-class interurbans. The 97 is at South Lorain in 1932. (LSE photo, John Keller collection)

The 1917 Jewett Steel Cars (LSRR 95–99)

At the same time that the LSE ordered its 12 big Jewett steel interurbans, its Lorain Street Railroad subsidiary ordered five of what were essentially steel versions of its 1906 Kuhlman-built city cars. And like the interurban cars, they were slow in coming. Ordered December 1, 1916, the first four cars arrived in November 1917 and the last in February 1918. This small fleet held down the basic Lorain–Elyria service until early

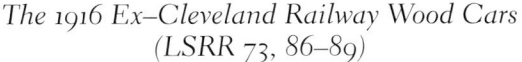

1930; later that year they were converted to one-man cars and continued in tripper service until operations ended May 7, 1938. After retirement their bodies went to Sage's Grove.

The 1920 Birney Cars
(LSE 123–138)

In 1920 the LSE joined the traction industry bandwagon by ordering 16 single-truck Birney cars with the hope of significantly cutting costs on its perennially problematic Sandusky city system. Two orders went to the St. Louis Car Company, the first for six double-ended Birneys (Nos. 123–128) and the second for ten single-end versions (129–138).

The entire group went into Sandusky service July 1, 1920, allowing wholesale retirements of their elderly predecessors. The double-end 123–128 group operated the East Monroe–Tiffin Avenue route, while the single-enders served the Soldiers Home Belt and Depot Belt routes, both of which operated in large loop patterns.

Within six years, however, the mix of single- and double-end cars needed in Sandusky began to change for the worse. In 1926 the Soldiers Home Belt route was temporarily severed for railroad underpass construction, requiring some double-ended cars for the inner Columbus Avenue segment.

It appears that the LSE planned to resume the "belt" routing of the Soldiers Home line after the grade separation work was completed, but the always-weak Milan Road–Hancock Street segment was partially converted to a bus line October 19, 1928, permanently cutting the loop. Now surplus in Sandusky, the single-end Nos. 135–138 were sent to the Oberlin Belt line in Lorain. When the Depot Belt was severed on October 27, 1931, cars 130 and 132 also went to the Oberlin Belt. The four remaining Sandusky single-end Birneys (Nos. 129, 131, 133, and 134) were stored until finally retired in 1938. Several double-enders were similarly shifted to Lorain. Conversion of Sandusky's Tiffin Avenue and East Monroe line to bus in October and November of 1931 sent the 126–128 group east to

Single-end Birney 132 served in both Sandusky and Lorain. Here it is on West Erie Avenue while working Lorain's Oberlin Belt route in the mid-1930s. (John A. Rehor collection)

Lorain for the Colorado–West Erie line. Finally, car 125 also went to Lorain in 1935 after conversion of the remaining Hayes Avenue segment of the Depot Belt line. The twelve operating 1920 Birneys remained running in Sandusky and Lorain until the end in 1938.

The 1925 Baltimore Birneys
(LSE 115–117)

Even before its surplus of single-end Birneys first appeared, the LSE found that it needed three more double-end Birneys for specific situations. For one, car 101, the Sandusky, Norwalk & Southern hand-me-down, had been toiling back and forth on Norwalk's Main Street since 1898 and by 1925 was more than obsolete. At the same time the last two of the two-man 1901 Brill cars in the 103–112 group were still wearily serving Sandusky's West Monroe line. In that year Baltimore's United Railways & Electric Company was trying to rid itself of a large group of single-door Birneys which it had found unsuitable for its own use. Thus in November 1925 UR&E Nos. 4028–4030 migrated to Ohio as the LSE's second 115–117.

Like the Lake Shore's own Birneys, the Brill-built Baltimore cars dated to 1920 and had the same type of motors, but were mounted on Brill 79E1 trucks. It is not known which company regauged the trucks from Baltimore's odd 5-foot 4.5-inch gauge. Car 115 took up long-term residence in Norwalk in December 1925, and all three survived until the end of LSE city services. The 116, in fact, was the very last Lake Shore Electric car in any kind of revenue passenger service when it ceased running on May 30, 1938, in Sandusky.

The 1924 Cleveland Peter Witt Cars
(LSRR 80–84[II])

In 1918 the New York State Railways ordered 75 steel single-end Peter Witt–type city cars from the Cincinnati Car Company for its Rochester Division, but only took delivery of 50.

The other 25 went to the Cleveland Railway as its Nos. 1075–1099. Acquired as a World War I exigency, the Rochester cars turned out to be orphans in Cleveland. With their Taylor trucks, four 25 hp GE 258C motors, and other components, they were mechanically and electrically different from Cleveland's standards — and with their lower-horsepower motors they could not haul trailers, a cardinal sin in Cleveland. Cleveland Railway sold off the group between 1922 and 1924, with five (Nos. 1076, 1077, and 1083–1085) going to

Lorain in June 1924 as the Lorain Street Railroad's second Nos. 80–84. (Since the original No. 83 was still working at this time, it had to be renumbered to second No. 85.)

With their large carrying capacity, the Peter Witts served Lorain well as tripper cars for steel mill and high school services on the Broadway–31st and the Oberlin Belt routes. They lasted until the end of operations in 1938 and were then resold to the Indianapolis Railways, which earlier had bought ten of the same group from Cleveland and liked their performance. As Indianapolis Railways 1057–1061 the former Lorain cars soldiered through World War II, primarily on the East Michigan line, and finally ended active life in November 1947.

Lorain Street Railroad's second 83 was built for Rochester, N.Y., but never got there and instead was delivered to the Cleveland Railway as its 1084. Acquired by the LSRR in 1924, the Peter Witt–style car became Indianapolis Railway 1060 in 1938. It is shown at Sandusky after rebuilding for one-man operation in 1929. (Karel Liebenauer collection)

The 1930 St. Louis Cars
(LSRR 200–209)

In 1929 the LSE ordered ten modern steel one-man city-type cars from the St. Louis Car Company for its Lorain Street Railroad. Though unaffordable for a company which by then

was showing relentlessly increasing deficits, the extravagance was justified by the growing steel mill traffic and large operating and maintenance cost savings. (Aging and battered two-man equipment still made up a large percentage of the Lorain city fleet.) In deference to the company's anemic finances at the time, they were acquired under a car trust-lease arrangement with the builder.

The new fleet arrived in February 1930, numbered LSRR 200–209. The utilitarian-looking single-end cars seated 48 and had front and center doors. They were assigned to Lorain–Elyria service, replacing the wood 90–94 series and steel 95–99 group in base service — and permitting the retirement of many older veterans. In addition, they were occasionally used for summer charters from Lorain to various beach resorts on the LSE; between 1933 and 1937 they were variously observed at Linwood Park and Vermilion, Ruggles Beach, and even Sandusky for a Cedar Point charter. All survived until Lorain's last day, May 7, 1938, and were then taken to Sandusky for temporary storage.

With their bill unpaid, they were returned to the St. Louis Car Company in October 1938. St. Louis rebuilt and resold all ten to the Birmingham (Alabama) Electric Company the following July, and as Birmingham Electric Nos. 521–530 they operated until 1949.

Lorain Street Railroad's ten St. Louis–built Peter Witt–style cars were the LSE's last passenger car purchases. The 208 is at South Lorain in 1933. (LSE photo, John Keller collection)

Freight Equipment

Freight and Baggage Motors (26–49)

When the LSE was born in 1901 it inherited only five of what could truly be called freight motors, four of which were usable. Three single-enders came from the Toledo, Fremont & Norwalk (TF&N Nos. 31–33) and one smaller double-ender, the *Delta*, from the Sandusky & Interurban. A fifth "freight motor," the former Sandusky, Milan & Norwalk No. 5, was originally one of two open-air trailer coaches built by Jewett in 1893 and at some point had been converted to a passenger motor car and then an express motor. It apparently was one rebuilding too many; in 1902 it was listed as worn out and was never used by the LSE.

The three TF&N motors were 1900 Barney & Smith products, essentially identical to its 22 passenger cars in size and equipment — that is, 50-foot 10-inch wood bodies, Barney & Smith "F" trucks, and two 75 hp Westinghouse No. 76 motors. Their principal design difference was an arch roof rather than the railroad-type monitor roofs of the passenger cars. And like their passenger-carrying brethren, they were durable and long-lived. As LSE 31–33, all three survived until the company's demise, and, in fact, Nos. 31 and 33 were on hand well into 1939 helping to dismantle the line. These two motors had been rebuilt for double-end operation in 1927.

A sampling of the LSE's variety of freight motors, both newly built and converted from passenger equipment:

No. 28, shown at Cleveland, was rebuilt from Barney & Smith coach 21 in 1926. (Karel Liebenauer photo)

The 35, one of two 60-foot Jewett–built motors, came in 1918 and was considered the line's fastest. (William Schriber photo)

The *Delta*, built in 1901 by Jewett, was similar to the Sandusky & Interurban's three passenger cars from the same order, the *Alpha*, *Beta*, and *Gamma*. Numbered 28 on the S&I's books, it became the LSE's 39 but lasted only briefly in freight service. In 1907 the LSE converted it to a line car, later renumbered 453, and as such it, too, worked after abandonment, helping to remove the overhead east of Sandusky.

In about 1907 the LSE also converted two other inherited passenger cars to freight motors — its No. 41, originally the Lorain & Cleveland's 1898 Brill combine No. 56, and No. 43, the former S&I *Alpha* (which in the interim had become a combine). No 41 was renumbered 49 in 1929 and although put in storage in 1930, it was not retired until 1938; the 43 was retired in 1928.

In 1916 the LSE ordered two unusually long steel freight motors from Jewett — as it turned out, the only freight motors it would ever buy new from an outside builder and the only ones of this length. First to come was No. 34, some months after the arrival of Jewett-built steel passenger coaches 167–169. This 60-foot-long behemoth closely resembled the three passenger cars and, with four 140 hp motors, was the first of a new fleet of Lake Shore motors capable of hauling trains of trailers. An identical unit, No. 35, was ordered in December 1916 along with the Jewett passenger interurbans 170–181; like the passenger equipment its construction was delayed and it did not arrive until December 5, 1918.

Motor 38 was one of three steel home-builds turned out by Sandusky shops in 1920. (Karel Liebenauer photo)

Wooden Niles coach 145 became motor 41(II) in 1929 during the last burst of freight equipment acquisition. (Karel Lienenauer photo)

By then, however, the Lake Shore apparently had discovered that 60-foot freight motors were impractical, and the program went no further. With typical LSE luck, one of the two was soon lost. On March 7, 1919, No. 34 collided head-on with a new home-built wood freight motor, SF&S 36, south of Berlin Heights and burned; it then donated its salvageable equipment to the home-built freight motor program then under way at Sandusky shop. Survivor No. 35 was primarily assigned to interline runs between Akron and Detroit via the Northern Ohio and Detroit United until that service ceased July 1, 1931. It then worked regular freight service until May 1937 and handled some work duties afterward.

Before World War I the LSE's various freight motors mostly handled Electric Package Agency shipments, milk, baggage, and the like. But as the company edged into the new general freight market in the war's later days it needed new equipment — which at the same time was difficult to obtain quickly. It turned to its own Sandusky shops and inaugurated assembly-line production of new 55-foot-long single-end motors using mostly new components — an unusual procedure for the interurban industry, which typically either bought new freight motors from commercial builders or rebuilt them from existing older equipment. In total, six such motors were turned out between 1918 and 1920, three of them wood and three steel. With the exception of No. 36, all were powered by four 140 hp motors and, along with the steel Jewett motors, were the most powerful on the line. At the same time the company produced its first purpose-built freight trailers.

The first to emerge at Sandusky was wood motor SF&S 36, turned out in October 1918. Short of time and materials, the shop used the only available trucks and equipment, which were from Niles combine SF&S 161, a fire victim at Fremont in April of that year. As just noted, it collided with steel motor No. 34 five months later, but survived after another circuit through the shop.

The SF&S 36 was followed by the in-house construction of five freight trailers, Nos. 460–464, designed to haul new automobiles from the Toledo area. These were mounted on newly built MCB arch-bar trucks and went into service between December 31, 1918, and the end of February, 1919. They were unusual in that, in addition to the usual side doors, they had end doors for loading the automobiles directly from a stub-end high platform or ramp.

In the meantime the LSE had ordered four sets of trucks and motors to equip the remaining cars of its freight motor program, but delivery was slow. By then the wooden body of what was intended to be LSE motor 37 was finished and awaiting its equipment. By an unpleasant coincidence another set of the same type of trucks and motors suddenly became available in March 1919 when steel motor 34 was wrecked and burned. Thus wedded to the defunct No. 34's trucks and motors, the now-completed wood body became second No. 34 rather than its planned No. 37. It departed from the shop May 6, 1919, and was then followed in November by a sixth wooden trailer, No. 470.

At about the same time, the company decided to finish its freight motor program with steel equipment rather than wood, and fabricated three 55-foot-long steel bodies which were otherwise similar to the 60-foot Jewett motors 34 and 35. These became Nos. 38–40. But with the switch of trucks and equipment between the demolished motor No. 34 and its newly built wood replacement, the LSE found itself with four sets of new trucks and motors ordered but only three new bodies for them. The problem was solved by converting the newly completed wood trailer 470 to a motor, giving it the missing number 37. The three new steel motors were eventually completed in 1920, finishing the home-building program.

These new freight motors generally served without major mishaps for their first few years, but the LSE luck eventually caught up with three of them. Motor SF&S 36 derailed at high speed at the notorious Undergrade crossing west of Lorain on March 6, 1926, destroying the car and killing its motorman and conductor. While operating on the Cincinnati & Lake Erie on June 30, 1932, the second 34 collided head-on with lightweight C&LE passenger car 303 north of Middletown, Ohio, killing nine people on the C&LE car, including seven employees. The motor was returned to Sandusky yard where it was finally scrapped in April 1938. Finally, on July 15, 1935, No. 40 was wrecked in a derailment at the Toledo Terminal Railroad grade crossing in Toledo and subsequently stored until it was scrapped in April 1938.

The decade of the 1920s saw a major expansion of LSE freight equipment, this time by rebuilding surplus wood passenger cars as freight motors and buying both new and used trailers. In most cases, the rebuilds kept their original trucks and motors, giving them less horsepower than the earlier home-builds. Five one-time Toledo, Fremont & Norwalk Barney & Smith coaches became freight motors between 1924 and 1926. These were numbered 26–30 to create a compatible series with the original TF&N Barney & Smith freight motors 31–33. Following them in 1929, five Niles passenger coaches (SF&S 141 and 145–148) were rebuilt as freight motors SF&S 41–45. And a sixth Niles car, coach 152(II), was refitted with the trucks and motors from wrecked motor 36 and in 1929 became LSE motor 46. Except for SF&S 45, which was stored after overturning at Woodville on October 4, 1932, all of the various passenger car rebuilds miraculously survived until the end of freight service in 1937 and were officially retired in 1938.

Freight Trailers

The LSE's first freight trailers, the 1919 home-built automobile-carrying cars 460–464, have been mentioned earlier. Beginning in 1919 and continuing through the 1920s, the LSE ordered a total of 45 wood freight trailers from various commercial builders, all of them compatible for interline use in the Midwestern interurban network. First came fifteen 55-foot cars from the Cincinnati Car Company in 1920–21, Nos. 465–479. (The 470 actually was 470 [II] replacing the original home-built 470, which became a freight motor.) These rode on secondhand MCB arch-bar freight trucks from the Wheeling & Lake Erie Railroad. Next were ten from Kuhlman in October 1923, with new MCB trailer trucks; these carried Nos. 480–489 and technically were assigned to the Lorain & Cleveland mortgage. Twenty more trailers (Nos. 700–719) arrived in May 1926, this time American Car & Foundry products.

Typical of LSE's standardized box trailers was the 475, built by Cincinnati Car Co. in 1920. (Karel Liebenauer collection)

Finally, when the Lake Shore bought its four Michigan Electric Railway steel interurban coaches in 1929, it also picked up 14 freight trailers which had been built by Kuhlman in 1924; as LSE 800–813 they went into service in the fall of 1929. The ever-thrifty LSE ran them with revenue loads from Jackson, Michigan, to its own line to save shipping charges —probably the last freight movements on the Michigan Electric Railway and the Detroit United Railway's Jackson line.

The Bonner Railwagons

The LSE's Bonner Railwagon trailer-on-flatcar experiment often has been mentioned and pictured in histories of modern railroad "piggyback" and container transportation, but surprisingly little has been published specifically about the system or its actual operation. Originally designed in the late 1890s by Colonel Joseph C. Bonner of Toledo, it was essentially inspired by the European "transporter" cars used to move standard gauge railroad cars on narrow gauge lines. In its original incarnation, a single horse-drawn wagon was carried on a small two-axle rail car; the wagons were manufactured by Bonner's own company. In this form it was demonstrated on two Toledo suburban electric lines in 1898 and, in early

These two photos illustrate the essentials of the Bonner Railwagon system. *(Top)* The special flatcar (right foreground) is pushed under the semitrailer, which straddles the track on a slightly raised ramp. Note the pedestal-type axle suspension, the key to the Bonner system. *(Bottom)* Three semitrailers loosely attached to the flatcar are slowly pulled away from the ramp (at left), and as they are, they nestle down onto the car's frame. (Both, George Krambles collection)

1899, on the Detroit & Pontiac and the Detroit Citizen's Electric Railway. At both locations the system was a technical success but a commercial failure. The first full-time application was on, of all things, Great Britain's narrow-gauge Isle of Man Tramways & Electric Power Co. (later Manx Electric Railway). This novel operation involved two stone-carrying wagons hauled behind primitive interurban cars. It was inaugurated in September 1899 with Bonner himself present, and is believed to have operated regularly until the wagons were destroyed in a January 1914 wreck.

Sadly for Bonner, that turned out to be his only real sale. He continued to promote the system without success into the 1920s, including an attempt during World War I to sell it to the military as a fast and efficient way of moving materials and supplies. Undismayed by indifference, he refined it for American railroad and highway operations in the late 1920s.

It was quite sophisticated by the standards of that time or even now, allowing low clearances (no higher than a standard freight car) and a simple form of automated loading and unloading from the rail car. It thus permitted all the benefits of both the container and trailer-on-flatcar systems without their disadvantages which most notably were high clearance requirements for TOFC and specialized loading/unloading cranes for containers. The Railwagon rail car was essentially what the railroad industry would later call a "spine car," simply a wide underframe with no deck. The underframes of the special pedestal-type semitrailer bodies rested directly on the car's frame, with their wheels and landing gear straddling the frame and extending below it on each side.

The road-to-rail transfer terminal consisted of a stub track with a pair of raised "runways" set on the outer sides of the rails. The semitrailers were then backed onto the runways and parked, their wheels and landing gear thus straddling the rails. Up to three semitrailers in a group were pushed together on the runway and the rail car was slowly pushed underneath them by a switcher or freight motor. The trailers were loosely attached to the car, and the car was pulled forward. As it moved forward, the trailers would drop down slightly from the end of the runway, so that their bottoms rested on the car frame. The car's trucks had inside bearings in order to clear the trailer wheels and trailers' extended landing gear as the car was moved beneath them at the terminal ramps.

Kuhlman built a single prototype flatcar in July 1929. Numbered LSE 500(II), it was about 55 feet long, designed to carry up to three 18-foot trailers, and had inside bearing trucks as just noted. At the same time, Brill turned out the prototype Railwagon semitrailer, No. 1001. A year later, in August 1930, the trailer manufacturer Fruehauf completed five more semitrailers, Nos. 1002–1006. All were 18-foot ten-ton capacity closed vans with a single set of rear wheels and solid rubber tires, designed for in-city use. A 24-foot van with

dual rear wheels and pneumatic tires, for over-highway services, was also designed for the system but none were built. The single flatcar and six semitrailers constituted the LSE's entire Railwagon fleet. Beginning September 1, 1930, these regularly operated in overnight revenue service between Cleveland and Toledo. The Railwagons were transferred between road and rail at Glendale yard in Toledo and at Beach Park at the Cleveland end — 19 miles west of the city itself.

The company was pleased enough with their performance and potential that in January 1931 Fred Coen formally proposed creating a separate equipment company which would purchase eight 24-foot trailers with pneumatic tires, 55 18-foot trailers with solid rubber tires, and 19 flatcars. This company in turn would lease the cars and trailers to the LSE, Cincinnati & Lake Erie, Eastern Michigan–Toledo, Northern Ohio, and Penn–Ohio as needed — itself a prototype for the railroad industry's Trailer Train Company of three decades later. But clearly that was not to be, and the lone LSE operation with its one rail car and six semitrailers continued for two years and then disappeared into the mist of history. The service ended by December 1932, the result of regulatory problems with operating rights for the trucking service. Three trailers were used in local pickup and delivery work at Cleveland through 1934. By 1935 all of these relics of the grand experiment were in storage, where they mouldered sadly until retired in late 1938.

Nothing further was ever heard of the Bonner system itself after its brief life on the Lake Shore, either. Most likely, the combination of the Depression, the decay of the interurban system, and Bonner's own advanced age ended it for all time. Bonner himself, however, was a tough survivor; he finally died September 28, 1944, at the age of 89.

Work Equipment

Doing the LSE's drudge work was the usual unpretentious assortment of motor and trailer cars, some of them, predictably, of unknown or mixed parentage.

Tantalizingly unknown are the details of three steam locomotives inherited from predecessors in 1901. These had been used in construction and were sold or scrapped soon afterward. Two were owned by the Sandusky & Interurban and were noted merely as weighing 65 tons each. The third came from the Toledo, Fremont & Norwalk and was used for both the TF&N's construction and work on the new LSE line between Huron and Lorain in 1902. According to contemporary newspaper reports, this was a former Lake Shore & Michigan Southern light switcher which came from Jackson, Michigan. During its construction in 1893 the Sandusky, Milan & Norwalk used a tiny 0-4-2 saddletank engine which came secondhand from New York's Manhattan Railway and probably was originally built for the New York Elevated Railroad in the late 1870s. Carrying number 3 on the SM&N, it also occasionally pulled passenger trailers, but apparently disappeared before the LSE was formed.

Initially, the LSE "numbered" its motorized work equipment with letters — "A" through "K" — but beginning in 1911 most were put into the lower 400-series. The exceptions after 1911 were three snow sweepers and a plow, which carried letter designations.

Flat Motors (400–404, 407)

The Lake Shore's all-purpose work motor was essentially a motorized flatcar with a small center cab, a design useful for carrying all manner of materials on its open deck. These were sometimes called "monitors," presumably in honor of the famous Civil War ironclad with its flat deck and single center turret. (Some employees less elegantly called them "outhouses on rafts.") The double-end monitors had standard railroad-type MCB couplers and were truly beasts of burden, hauling work trailers, freight trailers, and standard railroad cars. They also served as freight locomotives for various specialized types of commercial freight

No two of LSE's five 400-series all-purpose flat work motors seemed exactly alike. Typical examples are *(top)* the 400 at Fremont in 1934 (C. E. Helms photo), and *(bottom)* the 401 at Sage's Grove in 1938. (Bruce Triplett photo)

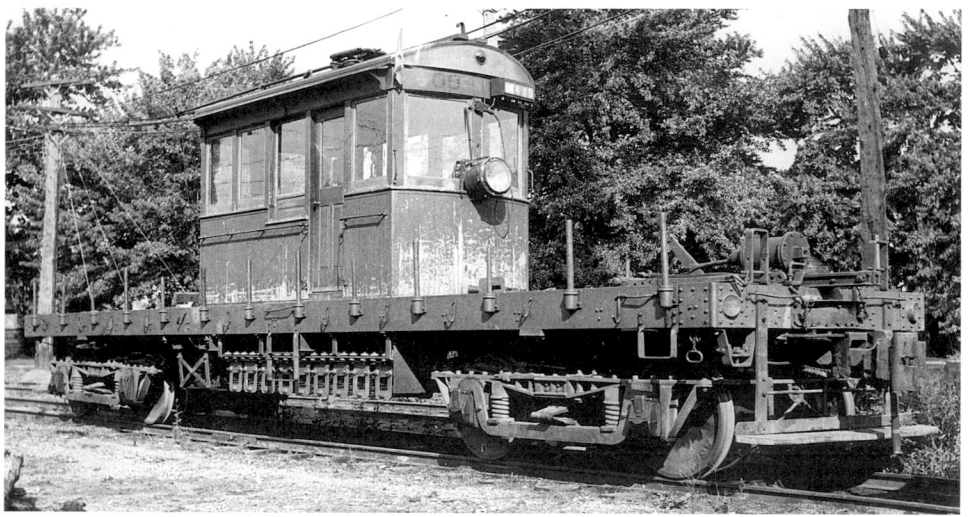

movements, including stone, sand, cinders, and coal for on-line customers. During the sometimes brutal Lake Erie winters they were fitted with snowplows.

The first two were hand-me-downs from LSE predecessors. No. 400 (originally LSE "J") was an 1897 Brill product from the Lorain & Cleveland, but in 1925 was substantially rebuilt with a steel cab, Barney & Smith trucks, and four 75 hp motors. The 401 (ex- "K"), was originally the Toledo, Fremont & Norwalk's *Mary Ann* (also TF&N No. 41), built by Barney & Smith in 1900 and rebuilt with a five-window steel cab in 1927. The 400 lasted into 1940, but the 401 was sold to Ohio Power for switching at the Ballville power plant in 1939.

Between 1908 and 1910 the LSE turned out three additional flat motors, originally "F," "G," and "H," with three-window center cabs and varying trucks and motors from wrecked or obsolete passenger cars. Motor "F," built in 1908, became Lorain Street Railroad 402 in 1914, based at South Lorain carhouse. The "G" of 1909 became 403 in 1914 and put on the Sandusky, Fremont & Southern's books; it worked as a switcher at the Ballville power plant until 1932. The final flat motor, "H" (No. 404 in 1914), appeared in 1910 and worked systemwide. All three lasted until 1938–39.

A more specialized flat motor was No. 407, home-built in 1920. Its four-window cab was offset at one end, and after 1932 it was teamed with crane flat No. 410 as a wrecker. As such the pair survived into 1940 handling the dolorous job of dismantling the line.

Line Cars (102, 120, 451–456)

Included in the LSE's early line car roster were two former single-truck city cars dating to the 1890s, Nos. 102 and 120. The 102 had been Sandusky, Norwalk & Southern No. 15, the original Norwalk city car; the 120 was Lorain & Cleveland's No. 1, a thirdhand veteran from the East Lorain Street Railway. Both worked until 1914.

Passenger motor 59, an 1898 Lorain & Cleveland Brill coach, became the Beach Park line car at an early date and was renumbered 451 in 1914. Its original trucks were replaced by those from 1903 Brill interurban combine 67, a victim of the Fremont carbarn fire October 16, 1906. It was finally retired in 1931, after again switching trucks as noted below.

Nos. 452 and 454 were home-built in 1914 using trucks and motors from retired ex–Lorain & Cleveland Brill passenger cars. The 452 switched trucks and motors with No. 451 (see above) in 1927, receiving Brill 27 A2 trucks and four Westinghouse 76 motors. It was reassigned to wreck duty and as a spare freight motor at Fremont in 1931, where it lasted until retirement in October 1938. No. 454 was put on the Lorain Street Railroad roster and assigned to South Lorain carhouse until the end of service.

Line car 453, originally LSE 39, started life as the Sandusky & Interurban's freight motor *Delta*, Jewett-built in 1901; it became 453 in 1917, originally assigned to Sandusky but moved to Beach Park in 1932.

Last to join LSE's line car fleet were Nos. 455–456, rebuilt in 1931 from 1903 Brill interurban combines 62 and 63. Interestingly, the LSE's more solvent subsidiary, the Lake Erie Power & Light Company, paid for the rebuilding work to relieve its cash-strapped parent. The 455 went to Beach Park, replacing No. 451 which in turn was retired — but within a year it traded places with the 453 and took up residence at Sandusky. The 456 replaced No. 452 for line work at Fremont. The 456 was retired in December 1938 but the 455 lasted until early 1940 after helping to scrap the line.

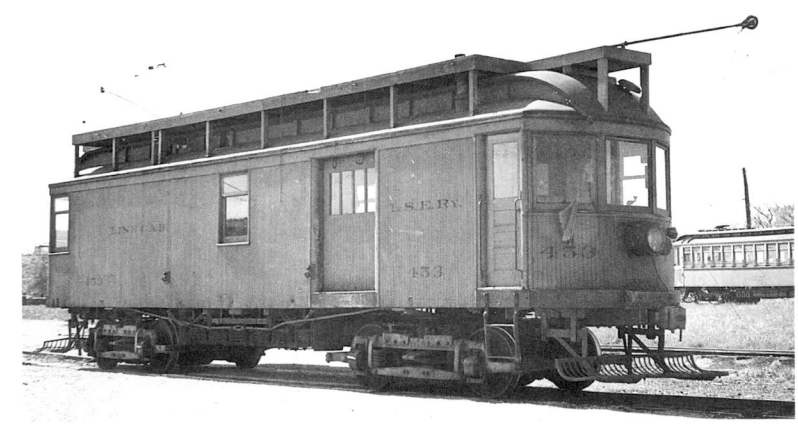

(Top) Line car 452, shown here at Fremont, was one of two 1914 home-builds. (William R. Heller photo)

(Middle) A veteran of pre-LSE days, line car 453 began life in 1901 as the Sandusky & Interurban's sole express motor, the *Delta*. Posed here at Sandusky in 1933, it survived until 1939. (LSE photo, John Keller collection)

(Bottom) In a bit of final irony, line car 456 was home-built in 1931 from Brill Combine 63, one of the fleet that the new LSE bought in 1903 to inaugurate its famous high-speed limited services. Now in altered form it helps dismantle the line in 1938. (Ralph H. Sayles photo)

Snow sweepers were necessary for street trackage in Sandusky and Lorain. The "A" is at South Lorain in 1937. (Bruce Triplett photo)

Two discarded rarities moulder in Sandusky in 1938. Dinky No. 405 switched coal cars at the LSE's Beach Park power house from 1918 to 1925, then worked the Cleveland freight house until the early 1930s. Behind it is freight motor 49, by then the oldest survivor on the line. The 1898 Brill product was originally Lorain & Cleveland Combine 56; it became LSE 41 and was rebuilt as freight motor 41 in 1907. It received its last number in 1929. (Ralph H. Sayles collection)

Snow Sweepers ("A" to "C")

Among the few pieces of new purpose-built work equipment the LSE owned were a pair of McGuire-Cummings single-truck snow sweepers, "A" and "B," delivered in 1904 and equipped with three 50 hp GE 57A motors — the third motor powering the brooms. Company records indicate that these motors were also used to power open cars in the summertime. "A" worked in Lorain and "B" in Fremont. A third sweeper, "C" (II), came secondhand in 1929 from the Michigan Electric Railway and worked in Sandusky from 1930 through the winter of 1937–38. All three sweepers were retired in 1938.

Miscellaneous Work Motors and Trailers

Rounding out the LSE's work roster was a diverse collection of specialized motors and trailers, some only sketchily documented and some of them genuine oddities. What details are known are shown in the roster tabulation, but several pieces of equipment deserve special note.

In 1918 the LSE bought a tiny single-truck electric locomotive from Taunton to switch steam railroad coal cars at the Beach Park power plant. Numbered 405, this 14-foot-long pygmy had a wood cab. After Beach Park's fiery demise on August 23, 1925, it was reassigned to the Cleveland freight house.

Lorain Street Railroad 406 was a heavily rebuilt double-truck wrecker car, rebuilt in 1919 from LSRR passenger car 85, an 1895 American Car Company product from the Lorain Street Railway. It retained its original monitor deck roof, but both of its ends and platforms were removed in the rebuilding, giving it a truncated look. Originally it probably was mounted on Peckham 14A trucks, but around

1918 it traded trucks with car 443 and received Brill 27Es. It worked out of South Lorain until 1938.

The 441 was a tiny single-truck flat motor, completely open with a wooden framework to support its trolley pole; it first showed up in the records in November 1912. Its Brill 21E truck and two Westinghouse No. 3 motors probably came from some old Sandusky city car. Based at Fremont carhouse, it worked as a shop switcher and flanger until the end of service and was scrapped in July 1939.

Motor 444 was the LSE's "high water car," a custom-built locomotive which pulled a trailer to transfer passengers through flood waters — mostly at Fremont, but elsewhere on occasion. Built by the LSE's Fremont shop in 1912, it was a single-truck wood-bodied box motor mounted on a Dupont truck with large 36-inch wheels.

Lorain Street Railroad's work motor 406 was much-rebuilt from an 1895 city streetcar. It is at South Lorain in 1933. (LSE photo, John Keller collection)

An electric motor (or motors) was mounted inside the carbody with a chain drive to the axles. Specific mechanical descriptions differ; according to later LSE records it is shown as having a single 30 hp Lorain C motor. But an article in the March 9, 1913, issue of *Electric Traction Weekly* states that "on the floor in the cab were placed two 25 hp motors, each geared to a countershaft placed parallel to the car axles. On one end of each of these shafts is a cast steel sprocket wheel, while another sprocket wheel was installed on each of the axles. These are connected by a sprocket chain." The unit was geared for a top speed of eight mph. It also contained equipment for heating and lighting its companion "flood train" passenger trailer, former Lorain Street Railroad No. 79. It saw service mostly in the 1913–16 period, but remained on the property until scrapped in April 1938.

A phantom on the Lake Shore's work roster was car 100, a 25-foot single truck wood box motor originally built for the Sandusky, Milan & Norwalk. This shows up on the LSE's 1902 inventory as unnumbered and noted as "worn out," but it somehow survived and was listed in a 1905 roster as No. 100. Subsequently it was listed as being painted in 1912, then vanishes from the record.

At the bottom of the glamour scale was a mixed assortment of flat and specialized trailer cars. These included such unusual cars as steel well-center flatcar 408, built by the company shops in 1923 to haul substation transformers, and flat 409, which was "built" in 1930 from the underframe of steel Jewett interurban No. 175, which had been wrecked and burned in a gasoline truck collision in February 1929.

Numerous other work trailers appear on various rosters, many of them probably secondhand such as wood flatcars Nos. 300–329. Certainly secondhand were steel flats 330-334, built in 1924 for the Toledo, Bowling Green & Southern and bought by the LSE in 1931, possibly for a contemplated freight container operation which never materialized. (One of the LSE's major interline freight connections, the Cincinnati & Lake Erie, had adopted a container system at this time.) Wooden ballast dump cars 500–507 were built by Rogers in 1907 for use building the Sandusky, Fremont & Southern, and were carried on the SF&S books and lettered for that company; in later years they carried stone from a quarry at Castalia. Ballast dump cars 508–511, of unknown origin, first show up in LSE service about 1909. Finally, ten stake-pocket flats, Nos. 600–609, came new from Haskell in 1909. These were fitted with wood sides for gondola use.

While primarily used for company maintenance and construction, several groups of these cars doubled in revenue freight service carrying stone, sand, and cinders to highway and other commercial construction projects — most notably the 500-series ballast cars and 600-series gondola-flatcars.

APPENDIX 1

Equipment Rosters

Roster—Lake Shore Electric Railway Passenger Cars

Car #	Type	Builder	Date	SE/DE	Trucks	Motors	Control	Seats	Weight (lbs)	Length o/a	Gear Ratio	Wheel Diam	Disposition	Remarks
1-12	Pass	B&S	1900	SE	B&S F	4 WH 76 75hp	L4	56	66700	50' 8.5"	24:58	36"		Ex-TF&N 1-12
14-22	Pass	B&S	1900	SE	B&S F	4 WH 76 75hp	L4	56	66700	50' 8.5"	24:58	36"		Ex-TF&N 14-22
23	Pass	B&S	1900	SE	B&S F	4 WH 76 75hp	L4	56	66700	50' 8.5"	24:58	36"		Ex-LSE 8000 1903
24	Pass	B&S	1900	SE	B&S F	4 GE 66 125hp	GE	56	?	50' 8.5"	?	36"	To LSE18 1906	Ex-LSE 18 1903
8000	Pass	B&S	1900	SE	B&S F	4 WH 76 75hp	L4	56	66700	50' 8.5"	24:58	36"	To LSE 23 1903	Ex-TF&N 13

24 had experimental New York subway controls

All B&S cars equipped with toilets and closed rear platforms 1901-1903. From 1901-1903 number 9 had 3 motors.

L4 control replaced by C6 control on 17 cars: 2,3,5-8,10,12,14-21 & 23

Destroyed: 4 in 1902(trucks etc to second 4, then to 162); 9 in 1917 and 11 in 1906(trucks etc to 163)

1, 6, 19, 21 & 22 converted to freight motors respectively 30(1924), 26,27 & 28(1926) and 29(1925)

In 1927, 5 &16 converted to combine; 18 & 23 converted to double end.

Stored: 15(1928); 2,3,5,7,8,10,12,14,16,17,&20(1932). 20 reactivated and converted to DE(1937).

All surviving B&S cars retired 1938 except 15(1939)

Car #	Type	Builder	Date	SE/DE	Trucks	Motors	Control	Seats	Weight (lbs)	Length o/a	Gear Ratio	Wheel Diam	Disposition	Remarks
40	Comb	Brill	1898	SE	Brill 27E	4 GE 57A 50hp	GE K35	34	42000	42'9"	24:61	33"	Destroyed 1903	Trucks etc. to F(402) 1908
41	Comb	Brill	1898	SE	Brill 27E	4 GE 57A 50hp	GE K35	34	42000	42'9"	24:61	33"	To 41 frt 1907	40 &41 were L&C 55&56
42	Comb	Jewett	1893	DE	McGuire 20	2 WH 3 20hp	2 WHD	30	?	38'	?	?	Destroyed 1906	Ex-SM&N 9
43	Comb	Jewett	1900	DE	Peck 14 AXX	4 Lorain 34 50hp	2 Lorain 43	40	59000	42'	?	36"	To 43 Frt 1907	Ex-S&lE 25, Alpha
44	Comb	Jewett	1900	DE	Peck 14 AXX	4 Lorain 34 50hp	2 Lorain 43	40	59000	42'	?	36"	Scrap 1928	Ex-Sl&E 26, Beta
-	Comb	Jewett	1900	DE	Peck 14 AXX	4 Lorain 34 50hp	2 Lorain 43	40	59000	42'	?	36"	Destroyed 1903	Ex-Sl&E 27, Gamma

Trucks etc to LSE 50. Used by LSE but not renumbered.

Car #	Type	Builder	Date	SE/DE	Trucks	Motors	Control	Seats	Weight (lbs)	Length o/a	Gear Ratio	Wheel Diam	Disposition	Remarks
-	Comb	Jewett	1893	DE	McGuire 20	2 WH 3 20hp	2 WHD	30	?	38'	?	?	Scrap 1903	Ex-SM&N 7
-	Pass	Jewett	1893	DE	McGuire 20	2 WH 3 20hp	2 WHD	40	?	38'	?	?	Destroyed 1906	Ex-SM&N 11
-	Pass	Jewett	1893	DE	McGuire 20	2 WH 3 20hp	2 WHD	40	?	38'	?	?	Scrap 1903	Ex-SM&N 12

SM&N 11 last used as shelter at Gibsonburg Junction; SM&N 7,11 & 12 used by LSE but not renumbered

Car #	Type	Builder	Date	SE/DE	Trucks	Motors	Control	Seats	Weight (lbs)	Length o/a	Gear Ratio	Wheel Diam	Disposition	Remarks
50	Pass	Brill	1898	DE	Peck 14 AXX	4 Lorain 34 50hp	2 Lorain 43	42	42000	42'6"	?	36"	Scrap 1930	Ex-L&C 64:to LSRR 1925
51-57	Pass	Brill	1896	SE	Brill 27E	4 GE 57A 50hp	K35GR2	42	42000	42'6"	24:61	33"	See note	Ex-L&C 10-17(one missing)

50 had same trucks & equip as 51-59 1901-1903; then trucks etc transferred to 72. 50 then received trucks etc from Gamma. 50 SE to 1903.

Destroyed:51(?) (trucks etc to "G"[403]1909); 54 1904(trucks etc to 2nd 54-1905) and 57 1902(trucks only to 2nd 57-1903)

Balance to LSRR 1907 and scrap 1931

Car #	Type	Builder	Date	SE/DE	Trucks	Motors	Control	Seats	Weight (lbs)	Length o/a	Gear Ratio	Wheel Diam	Disposition	Remarks
58	Pass	Brill	1898	SE	Brill 27E	4 GE 57A 50hp	K35GR2	42	42000	42'6"	24:61	33"	Scrap1931	Ex-L&C 18: LSRR 1907
59	Pass	Brill	1898	SE	Brill 27E	4 GE 57A 50hp	K35GR2	42	42000	42'6"	24:61	33"	To line car 59 1907	Ex-L&C 19:LSRR 1907
ll 4	Pass	Kuhlman	1902	SE	B&S F	4 WH76 75hp	WH C6	46	46000	47'	?	33"	To 2nd 54 1907	Trks etc from 4;to 162 (1907)
2nd 54	Pass	Kuhlman	1902	SE	Brill 27E	4 GE 57A 50hp	K35GR2	46	46000	47'	?	33"	Scrap 1938	Trks etc from 54. Ex ll 4 1907
2nd 57	Pass	Kuhlman	1902	SE	Brill 27E	4 WH101D 50HP	K35GR2	46	46000	47'	?	33"	Scrap 1938	Trks from 57, new motors

2nd 54 & 2nd 57 stored 1930. Originally built for CSW, rejected and sold to LSE 1903. 3 other cars sold to Rockford (IL) Interurban.

Car #	Type	Builder	Date	SE/DE	Trucks	Motors	Control	Seats	Weight (lbs)	Length o/a	Gear Ratio	Wheel Diam	Disposition	Remarks
60-69	Comb	Brill	1903	SE	Brill 27A2	4WH76 75hp	WH C6	50	52000	52'2"	24:58	36"	See notes	61,64 & 68 to 3 window ends

Destroyed: 60 1925(Trucks etc to 407-1927); 66 1903(trucks etc to 2nd 66-1904); 67 1906(trucks etc to 59-1907).

60-69 built as MU but never so used. 62 & 63 to line cars 455 &456 (1931). 69 to DE 1937. 61,64,65,68 & 69 retired 1938

After 1927, Brill cars OM on Gibsonburg Branch only. 61, 64, & 68 stored 1932

Car #	Type	Builder	Date	DE SE	Trucks	Motors	Control	Seats	Weight (lbs)	Length o/a	Gear Ratio	Wheel Diam	Disposition	Remarks
Roster—Lake Shore Electric Railway Passenger Cars (continued)														
2nd 66	Comb	Kuhlman	1904	SE	Brill 27A2	4WH76 75hp	WH C6	50	52000	52'2"	24:58	36"	Destroyed 1928	Body only new. Trucks etc from 66-To 453 in 1928
70&71	Pass	Stephenson	1904	SE	Peck 40 A	4 GE 57A 50hp	K34	46	62200	45'3"	?	?	Scrap 1930	Burned 1918 and stored
72	Pass	Stephenson	1904	SE	Brill 27E	4 GE 57A 50hp	K35GR2	46	62200	45'3"	?	?	Stored '23 scrap '28	Body only—trucks etc from 50.

70-72 joint order with NOT&L 22-26 (to 1422-1426)

Roster—Lorain Street Railroad Passenger Cars

Car #	Type	Builder	Date	DE SE	Trucks	Motors	Control	Seats	Weight (lbs)	Length o/a	Gear Ratio	Wheel Diam	Disposition	Remarks
73	Pass	Brill	1901	SE	Brill 27F	4 WH49 35HP hp	K 12	?	?	48'	?	?	Scrap 1924	Ex-Cleveland Ry 18 1916
75-79	Pass	Stephenson	1894	SE	Dupont	Trailer	None	?	?	?	?	?	See note	Ex-LSRY12-20 even

75-79 orig. from spliced single truck cars. One Dupont truck to 444 in 1912. Trailers 75-79 scrap: 75-1912,76-1921,77-1922, 78-1923 & 79-1925.
79 to LSE for Hi-water car 1912, returned to LSRR 1916

| 4 cars | Pass | ? | ? | ? | ? | ? | ? | ? | ? | ? | ? | ? | Scrap 1916 | Ex LSRy, no other data |
| 80-85 | Pass | American | 1895 | SE | Peck 14AX | ? | ? | ? | ? | ? | ? | ? | See note | Ex LSRy |

83 to II 85 1924, 85 to 406 1919, 80,81,82 & 84 scrap 1920

| II 85 | Pass | American | 1895 | SE | Peck 14AX | Trailer | none | ? | ? | ? | ? | ? | retired 1928 | To Sages Grove & var museums |
| II 80-II 84 | Pass | Cincinnati | 1918 | SE | Taylor HLB | 4 GE 258C 25hp | K35GR2 | 55 | 39920 | 50' | ? | 26" | OM 1929; sold 1938 | Ex Cleveland Ry 1924 |

ex Cleveland Peter Witt Cars 1076-77,1083-84 & 1095 respectively. Became Indianapolis Rys 1057-1061 respectively. Originally built for Rochester, NY.

| 86-89 | Pass | Brill | 1901 | SE | Brill 27F | 4 WH49 35HP hp | K-12 | ? | ? | 48' | ? | ? | Scrap 1930 | |

All acquired 1916 from Cleveland Rwy. CRynumbers 86(?), 87(9), 88(31) & 89(98). Same type as 73

| 90-94 | Pass | Kuhlman | 1906 | SE | Brill 27F | 4 WH101D 50hp | K35GR2 | 48 | 45000 | 48'6" | ? | 33" | Stored '31;scrap'37 | 91 destroyed 1931 |
| 95-99 | Pass | Jewett | 1917* | SE | Bald 71-18 C | 4 WH514C 35-40hp | K35GR2 | 52 | 38600 | 48'6" | ? | 33" | OM '30, ret 1938 | To Sages Grove |

*car 99-1918

Roster—Lake Shore Electric Railway Passenger Cars

Car #	Type	Builder	Date	DE SE	Trucks	Motors	Control	Seats	Weight (lbs)	Length o/a	Gear Ratio	Wheel Diam	Disposition	Remarks
101	Pass*	Pullman	1898	DE	McGuire	2 WH3 20hp	2 WHD	?	?	21'	?	?	Ret 1925	Ex SN&S 4; ex SM&N 17
102	Pass*	Jewett	1893	DE	McGuire	2 WH3 20hp	2 WHD	?	?	21'	?	?	To line car 102 1902	Ex SM&N 15
103-105	Pass*	?	1891	DE	Brill 7	2 WH3 20hp	2 WHD	?	?	16'	?	?	Ret 1902	Ex PRy 2-6 even
106-107	Pass*	Brill	1892	DE	Brill 13	2 WH3 20hp	2 WHD	?	?	16'	?	?	To 116 &117 '05	Ex PRy 14 &16
108	Pass*	Brill	1892	DE	Brill 7	2 WH3 20hp	2 WHD	?	?	16'	?	?	Ret 1902	Ex PRy 8
109-111	Pass*	?	?	DE	Brill 13	2 Walk 4	?	?	?	16'	?	?	Ret 1902	SSRy 1-24 series
112	Pass*	?	?	DE	Brill 13	1Walk4/1WH3	?	?	?	16'	?	?	Ret 1902	SSRy 1-24 series
113-115	Pass*	?	?	DE	Brill 21	2 WH3 20hp	?	?	?	18'	?	?	Ret 1914	SSRy 1-24 series
116-117	Pass*	Brill	1892	DE	Brill 13	2 WH3 20hp	?	?	?	16'	?	?	Ret 1914	Ex LSE 106-107 (1905)
120	Pass*	?	?	DE	Brill 21	2 GE 800 27hp	2 K-2	?	?	16'	?	?	To line car 120 1903	Ex L&C 1

*cars 101 through first 120 all single truck. 101 in Norwalk city service. 103-105 and 108-112 used in Sandusky city service but not renumbered
106,107, 113-117 used in Sandusky city service but were renumbered. 120 used in Lorain (E. Erie)

| 118-122 | Pass | Brill | 1904-5 | DE | Brill 27G | 2 WH 101B 50hp | K28B | 40 | 36000 | 41' 10" | ? | 33" | See note | Ex WJ&SSRR |

118-122(including second120) purchased 118-119(1913) and 120(II)-122(1914) from West Jersey and Seashore RR, Atlantic City, NJ
Exact WJ&SSRR numbers unknown. Originally cars were SE; converted to DE 1908; to SE on LSE1913-1914 and finally to DE in 1920.
All five cars from Sandusky city to Lorain 1920. All to OM 1922. 120(II) destroyed 1929 rest stored 1931, retired 1935 to Sages Grove

Roster—Lake Shore Electric Railway Passenger Cars (continued)

Car #	Type	Builder	Date	DE/SE	Trucks	Motors	Control	Seats	Weight (lbs)	Length o/a	Gear Ratio	Wheel Diam	Disposition	Remarks
103(II)-112(II)	Pass	Brill	1902	DE	Brill 21E	?	?	?	?	267"	?	?	See note	Single truck
									103(II)-110(II) retired 1920, balance 1925. 105(II) was ex LSE 5007. Remainder were, in order, ex LSE 5000-5006,5008 & 5009(1904-05).					
115(II)-117(II)	Pass	Brill	1920	DE	Brill 79E1	2 WH508A	?	?	28	17700	27' 9.5"	?	26"	Ret 1938	Sandusky city; 115 Norwalk city
					Ex URY&ECo (Baltimore) 4028-4030, acquired by LSE 1925									
123-128	Pass	St Louis	1920	DE	St Louis 7	2 WH508A	2 WH K63 BR	28	17700	27' 9.5"	?	26"	Ret 1938	Sandusky city
129-138	Pass	St Louis	1920	SE	St Louis 7	2 WH508A	WH K63 BR	34	17700	27' 9.5"	?	26"	Ret 1938	Sandusky city
					Transferred to Lorain city service—1929(135-138), 1931(126-128,130 &132), 1935 (125). 129, 131, 133 & 134 stored (1931)									
					115(II)-117(II) & 123-138 are Birney cars-all single truck and one man									
152(II)	Pass	Niles	1907	SE	Bald 84-30-A	4 WH121A 85hp	WH C36 A	52	75000	519"	24:51	38"	To frt motor 46 1929	body only-trucks etc from 152 Trucks etc to 162 1929
141-148	Pass	Niles	1907	SE	Bald 84-30-A	4 WH121A 85hp	WH C36 A	52	75000	519"	24:51	38"	See note	Owned by SFS
149	Pass	Niles	1907	SE	Bald 84-30-A	4 WH121A 85hp	WH C36 B	52	75000	519"	24:51	38"	Ret 1938	
					143 had GE C 36 C controls. 142 &144 destroyed 1915. Trucks etc to SFS 168 & 169 1915									
					To freight 1929:141to 42(II),145 to 41(II),146 to 43(II), 147 to 45 and 148 to 44(II).									
					143 and 149 extended to 60' in 1923—64 passengers and 82700# car weight. Retired 1938.									
					152(II) was built as 140. received trucks etc from 36—summer 1929 only									
150-159	Pass	Niles	1906	SE	Bald 84-30-A	4 WH121A 85hp	WH C36 A	52	75000	519"	24:51	38"	See note	158 had GE C36A motors
					Destroyed: 152(1906), 153(1914), & 154 (1917). 152's trucks etc to 152(II). 153's trucks only to 167 (1915) and 154's trucks and etc to 163 (1918)									
					Retired 1938: 150,151and155-159									
160	Comb	Niles	1907	SE	Bald 84-30-A	4 WH121A 85hp	WH C36 B	46	75000	519"	24:51	38	Ret 1938	Owned by SFS
161	Comb	Niles	1907	SE	Bald 84-30-A	4 WH121A 85hp	C6	46	75000	519"	24:51	38	Destroyed 1918	Trucks etc to SFS 36 1918
162	Comb	Niles	1907	SE	B&S F	4 WH 76 75hp	L4 to C6	46	75000	519"	24:58	38	Ret1938	Owned by SFS
163	Comb	Niles	1907	SE	B&S F	4 WH 76 75hp	L4 to C6	46	75000	519"	24:58	38	Scrap 1931	Wrecked and stored 1930
					162 body only; trucks etc from II 4, final trucks etc from (II)152-1929. 163 body only; trucks etc from 11, final trucks from 154-1918.									
164	Comb	Niles	1907	SE	Bald 84-30-A	4 WH121A 85hp	C6	46	75000	519"	24:51	38	Ret 1938	
					Niles notes: Original weight 73930#, wheels 37.25'. Storm sash added 1908. Large destination signs and train number signs in 1914									
					152 capable of hauling freight trailers—summer of 1929 only (K 64 control). Van Dorn couplers exchanged for MCB (1911)									
165-166	Comb	Jewett	1911	SE	Standard C 80 P	4 GE 205E 100hp	GE C 36 C	60	80000	60'1.5"	24:50	38	166 ret 1938	165 wreck & stored '35; scrap 1938
					Western Ohio had two identical cars (their 198-199) which were pooled with the Lake Shore cars for joint Cleveland-Lima through service (1911-1922).									
					WO 198 was sold to Interstate Public Service(IN)1922 as 149. WO 199 stored 1930 and retired 1932									
167	Pass	Jewett	1915	SE	Bald 84-30-A	4GE 205E 100hp	GE C 36 E	64	86900	60'2"	24:50	38	Ret 1939	Trucks only from 153
168-169	Pass	Jewett	1915	SE	Bald 84-30-A	4 WH121A 85hp	GE C 36 E	64	84000	60'2"	24:51	38	Ret 1939	Trks etc from SFS 142 &144 resp.
					Both cars owned by SFS. 169 burned 1918—rebuilt Jewett1919. 167,168 & 169 steel but with truss rods									
170-172	Pass	Jewett	1917	SE	Bald 84-30-AA	4 WH 557A2 140hp	WH C36 C	64	84900	60'2"	?	38	Ret 1939	
173-181	Pass	Jewett	1918	SE	Bald 84-30-AA	4 WH 557A2 140hp	WH C36 C	64	84900	60'2"	?	38	Ret 1939	
					170, 179 & 180 sold to Des Moines and Central Iowa (1710, 1712 & 1714), converted to combine and truss rods and bell added 1939									
					173 &174 burned 1918 and rebuilt by Jewett 1919. 175 wrecked, burned and stored 1929, ret 1930. Underframe to 409—1930, all others retired 1939.									
182-183	Pass	St Louis	1916	SE	Bald 84-40-AA	4 WH 557A2 140hp	GE C36 C	53/64*	95300	6'15"	?	38	Ret 1938	Ex Mich Ry 851 & 853. to LSE 1929
					182-183 rebuilt from combo to passenger by LSE 1930 &1932 respectively. Though steel cars, both had truss rods. *182 had lounge section and 53 passenger seats.									

Roster—Lake Shore Electric Railway Passenger Cars (continued)

Car #	Type	Builder	Date	DE/SE	Trucks	Motors	Control	Seats/ Cap'y	Weight (lbs)	Length o/a	Gear Ratio	Wheel Diam	Disposition	Remarks
2 cars	Comb	St Louis	1916	SE	Bald 84-40-AA	4 WH 557A5 140hp	?	?	107000	61'5"	?	38	Ret 1938	Ex Mich Ry 849 & 855. To LSE 1929

These two cars were never used or renumbered by LSE

152(II), 141-161,164-183 all equipped for multiple unit operation

Car #	Type	Builder	Date	DE/SE	Trucks	Motors	Control	Seats/ Cap'y	Weight (lbs)	Length o/a	Gear Ratio	Wheel Diam	Disposition	Remarks
200	ST open	?	?	DE	Note	Note	Note	8 bench	?	?	?	?	Ret 1908	Ex L&C Lorain city
201-202	ST open	?	1891	DE	Note	Note	Note	8 bench	?	?	?	?	Ret 1912	ExPRy10 & 20 resp. Sandusky city
203	ST open	?	?	DE	Note	Note	Note	10 bench	?	?	?	?	Ret 1912	ExPRy 18.Sandusky city
204-205*	ST open	?	?	DE	Note	Note	Note	9 bench	?	?	?	?	Ret 1912	Ex SSRy 1-24 series Sandusky cty

* a third car in this group was neither used nor renumbered by LSE and was retired 1902

ST open cars used trucks, motors and controls of closed cars in season.

200(II)-

Car #	Type	Builder	Date	DE/SE	Trucks	Motors	Control	Seats/ Cap'y	Weight (lbs)	Length o/a	Gear Ratio	Wheel Diam	Disposition	Remarks
204(II)	DT open	Rebuilt Brill	1880's	SE	Peckham 14A	note		?	12 bench	?	?	?	?	Ret 1920	Sandusky city

ex WJ&SS(Atlantic City) 6831-6850 series acquired in 1912. DT open cars shared motors with sweepers A and B and :plow C.

200(II) - 201(II) stored 1920-1938 without trucks; 202(II) stored 1920-1938 with trucks

Roster—Lorain Street Railroad Passenger Cars

Car #	Type	Builder	Date	DE/SE	Trucks	Motors	Control	Seats/ Cap'y	Weight (lbs)	Length o/a	Gear Ratio	Wheel Diam	Disposition
200-209	Pass	St Louis	1930	SE	St Louis EIB-64	4 WH 510A 35hp	WH K 75 A	48	35700	41'10.5"	?	26	See note

LSRR 200-209 on a lease-purchase agreement from St Louis car. Returned 1938 to St Louis and rebuilt for service in Birmingham(AL) as their 521-530 series

All LSE and LSRR passenger cars were wood except steel cars II 80-II 84, 95-99, II 115-II 117, 123-138, 167-183 & LSRR 200-209

Roster—Lake Shore Electric Railway—LSE Freight and Work Equipment 1901-1940

Earliest Freight Equipment 1901-1939

Car #	Type	Builder	Date	DE/SE	Trucks	Motors	Control	Seats/ Cap'y	Weight (lbs)	Length o/a	Gear Ratio	Wheel Diam	Disposition	Remarks
31-33	Frt	B&S	1900	SE	B&S F	4 WH 76 75hp	L4 to K64 D	24000	68200	50' 10"	18:64	36"	R 1939	31&33 to DE '27.32 stored '37

31-33 were ex TFN 31-33 respectively—to LSE 1901

Car #	Type	Builder	Date	DE/SE	Trucks	Motors	Control	Seats/ Cap'y	Weight (lbs)	Length o/a	Gear Ratio	Wheel Diam	Disposition	Remarks
39	Frt	Jewett	1901	DE	Peck 14AXX	2 Lorain 34 50hp	2 Lorain 43			42'			Line car 1907	Ex S&I 28, Delta.
41	Frt	Brill	1898	SE	Brill 27E	4 GE57A 50hp	GE K 35	12000	42000	42'9"	24:61	33"	To 49 1929	Ex combine 41, 1907
43	Frt	Jewett	1900	SE	Peck 14AXX	4 Lorain 34 50hp	2 Lorain 43			42'			Scrap 1928	Ex combine 43, 1907
See note	Frt	Jewett	1893	DE	McGuire 20	2 WH3 20hp	WH-D			38'			Scrap 1902	Ex SM&N 5 to LSE '01

Body was to have been 37

Not used or renumbered by LSE

Car #	Type	Builder	Date	DE/SE	Trucks	Motors	Control	Seats/ Cap'y	Weight (lbs)	Length o/a	Gear Ratio	Wheel Diam	Disposition	Remarks
49	Frt	Brill	1898	SE	Brill 27E	4 GE 57A 50hp	GE K 35	12000	42000	42'9"	24:61	33"	R 1938	Stored 1930, ex 41 1929

49 on L&C mortgage

Later Freight Equipment 1916-1940

Car #	Type	Builder	Date	DE/SE	Trucks	Motors	Control	Seats/ Cap'y	Weight (lbs)	Length o/a	Gear Ratio	Wheel Diam	Disposition	Remarks
26-30	Frt	B&S	1900	SE	B&S F	4 WH 76 75hp	K64 D	24000	68200	50' 8.5"	18:64	36"	R 1938	Stored '37

LSE 26-30 were ex LSE 6,19, 21 22 & 1 respectively; 26-28 converted to freight 1926, 29 in 1925, 30 in 1924.

Car #	Type	Builder	Date	DE/SE	Trucks	Motors	Control	Seats/ Cap'y	Weight (lbs)	Length o/a	Gear Ratio	Wheel Diam	Disposition	Remarks
34	Frt	Jewett	1916	SE	Bald 84-30-AA	4 WH557A2 140hp	WH 15 ES	30000	75800	60'2"		37"	Destr 1919	Trucks etc to Il34
34(II)	Frt	LSE	1919	SE	Bald 84-30-AA	4 WH557A2 140hp	WH 15 ES	30000	77000	55'2"		38"	Scrap 1938	Wrecked & stored 1932

Trucks etc from 161. Trucks etc to (II)152

Car #	Type	Builder	Date	DE/SE	Trucks	Motors	Control	Seats/ Cap'y	Weight (lbs)	Length o/a	Gear Ratio	Wheel Diam	Disposition	Remarks
35	Frt	Jewett	1918	SE	Bald 84-30-AA	4 WH557A2 140hp	WH 15 ES	30000	75800	60'2"		37"	R 1938	Stored 1937
36	Frt	LSE	1918	SE	Bald 84-30-A	4 WH 121A 85hp	GE K 64 D	30000	77000	55'2"		38"	Destr 1926	SFS owned
37	Frt	LSE	1919	SE	Bald 87-40-AA	4 WH 557A2 140hp	WH 15 A2	51000	81200	55'2"		37"	R 1939	Rblt fr 470,1920;trucks etc new
38	Frt	LSE	1920	SE	Bald 87-40-AA	4 WH 557A2 140hp	WH 15 A2	48000	84200	55'2"		37"	R 1939	Trucks etc new. Stored 1937
39(II)	Frt	LSE	1920	SE	Bald 87-40-AA	4 WH 557A2 140hp	WH 15 A2	48000	84200	55'2"		37"	R 1938	Trucks etc new. Stored 1937

Car #	Type	Builder	Date	DE SE	Trucks	Motors	Control	Seats/ Cap'y	Weight (lbs)	Length o/a	Gear Ratio	Wheel Diam	Disposition	Remarks
					Later Freight Equipment 1916-1940 (continued)									
40(II)	Frt	LSE	1920	SE	Bald 87-40-AA	4 WH 557A2 140hp	WH 15 A2	48000	84200	55'2"		37"	Scrap 1938	Trks etc new. Wreck & stored '35
					37 followed 38, 39(II), and 40(II) into service.									
1(II)-44(II)	Frt	Niles	1907	SE	Bald 84-30-A	4 WH 121A 85hp	GE K 64 D	30000	73600	519"	15:59	36"	R 1938	Rblt from pass car; stored '37
45	Frt	Niles	1907	SE	Bald 84-30-A	4 WH 121A 85hp	GE K 64 D	30000	73600	519"	15:59	36"	R 1938	Rblt pass car; wreck & sto '32
					41(II)-45 were all SFS owned and were ex SFS 145,141,146,148 &147 renumbered in 1929									
46	Frt	Niles	1907	SE	Bald 84-30-A	4 WH 121A 85hp	GE K 64 D	30000	73600	519"	15:59	36"	R 1938	Rblt from 152(II)'29; stored '37
460-64	Frt	LSE	1919	DE	MCB	Trailer		60000	38500	54'		33"	R 1939	End doors for carrying autos
					460 built 1918; 464 retired 1938									
470	Frt	LSE	1919	DE	MCB	Trailer		60000	40000	55'2"		33"	To 37 1920	Includes 470(II)
465-79	Frt	Cinc	1920	DE	MCB	Trailer		60000	40000	55'		33"	R 1939	
					470(II),472,474,476,478 & 479 retired 1938. Trucks from W&LE.									
480-89	Frt	Kuhlman	1923	DE	MCB	Trailer		60000	40900	551"		33"	R 1939	On L&C mortgage
					482 scrapped in 1939, 483 destroyed 1926 and not on L&C mortgage									
700-19	Frt	ACF	1926	DE	MCB ARA #3AB	Trailer		80000	43400	488"		33"	See note	CERA type
					703 destroyed 1934. 704 retired 1938. 702,716 and 718 retired 1939. Balance scrapped 1939.									
800-13	Frt	Kuhlman	1924	DE	?	Trailer		60000	39000	504"		33"	R 1939	CERA type
					800-813 ex Michigan Rys 1616-1630 series. Aquired by LSE 1929. 807 retired 1940.									
					All freight equipment wood except 34,35,38,39(II),40(II) & 500(II) which were steel.									
500(II)	Flat	Kuhl	1929		Brill	Trailer		60000		54'5"		33"	R 1938	Bonner Railwagon Hauling car
1001	Flat	Brill	1929		Brill			15000	6850	17'2.5"			R 1938	Bonner Pedestal Railwagon
1002-6		Fruehauf	1930					15000	9100	17'2"			R 1938	Bonner Pedestal Railwagon
					1001-1006, 3 stored 1934, 3 stored 1936									
					Work Equipment 1901-1940									
A	Sweeper	McGuire	1904	DE	McGuire	3 GE57A 50hp	2 K35, 1 K10			28'10"			R1938	Lorain city in 1937
B	Sweeper	McGuire	1904	DE	McGuire	3 GE57A 50hp	2 K35, 1 K10			28'10"			R1938	Fremont city in 1937
C(II)	Sweeper	McGuire	?	DE	McGuire	3 GE57A 50hp	2 K35, 1 K10			28'10"			R1938	Sandusky city in 1937
					Acquired from Michigan Railways 1929. Their number 550									
C	Plow	Taunton		DE									R by 1929	Ex SM&N ? 1901
					Shared motors and controls:1902 Inventory —no other information. Sweepers and plow all single truck									
LSRR F	Flat cab	LSE	1908	DE	Brill 27E	4 GE57A 50hp	K35-GR2			34'8"		33"	To 402 1914	3-window center cab monitors
SFS G	Flat cab	LSE	1909	DE	Brill 27E	4 GE57A 50hp	K35-GR2			34'6"		33"	To 403 1914	3-window center cab monitors
H	Flat cab	LSE	1910	DE	B&S F	4 WH 76 75hp	K64 D			41'9"		36"	To 404 1914	3-window center cab monitors
J	Work	Brill	1897	DE	Brill 27E	4 GE57A 50hp	K35			30'			To 400 1911	Ex L&C J 1901
K	Work	B&S	1900	DE	B&S F	4 WH 76 75hp	L4			42'			To 401 1911	Ex TF&N 41-1901
39	Line car	Jewett	1901	DE	Peck 14AXX	4 Lor.34 50hp	Lorain #43			42'			To 453 1917	Ex frt motor-1907
					Assigned Fremont 1907; Sandusky 1914-1917									
59	Line car	Brill	1898	DE	Brill 27A2	4 WH 76 75hp	K35			42'6"			To 451 1914	Trucks etc from 67
					Assigned Beach Park 1907-1914. Ex passenger car-1907									
100	ST Work												Scrap 1914	Ex SM&N ? 1901
					No info except OK in 1902, '05 & '12									
102	ST Line	Jewett	1893	DE	McGuire	2 WH#3 20hp	WH-D						Scrap 1914	From LSE 102 1902
120	ST Const	Jewett		DE	Brill 21E	2GE800 27hp	K2			16' Body			Scrap 1914	From LSE 120 1903
					102 assigned Sandusky 1902-1914; 120 assigned Lorain area 1903-1914									

Car #	Type	Builder	Date	SE	DE	Trucks	Motors	Control	Capacity (lbs)	Weight (lbs)	Length o/a	Gear Ratio	Wheel Diam	Disposition	Remarks
							Work Equipment 1901-1940 (continued)								
300-29	DT Flat				DE	Armour MCB	Trailer		60000	20900	34'7"			See note	Ex TBG&S, Acqu 1931
310-329 weighed 21400 lbs. Scrapped:1938,301,326;1939,303,305,306,308,313,316,317,&327; 1940, 314,319 & 321-323															
Retired by: 1910, 307, 309, 1912, 302, 1913, 300, 1933, 304,310-312,315,318,320,324,325,328 & 329															
330-34	DT Flat		1924		DE	MCB	Trailer		60000	28700	42'7"		31"	Scrap 1939	
330-334 steel. 333 scrapped 1940, Originally for container service but used as work cars.															
400	Flat Cab	Brill	1897		DE	B&S F	4 WH76 75hp	K64 D	63500		40'11"	18:64	36"	R 1940	Ex LSE J 1911
401	Flat Cab	B&S	1900		DE	B&S F	4 WH76 75hp	K64 D	63500		40'11"	18:64	36"	Sold 1939	Ex LSE K1911
400 & 401 rebuilt to steel & center cab (5W) in1925 and1927 resp. 401 to Ballville1939-1953(Ohio Power Co.)															
402	Flat Cab	LSE	1908		DE	Brill 27E	4 GE57A 50hp	K35-GR2			34'8"	18:64	33"	Scrap 1938	LSRR 402, ex LSRR F 1914
403	Flat Cab	LSE	1908		DE	Brill 27E	4 GE57A 50hp	K35-GR2			34'8"	18:64	33"	Scrap 1938	SFS 403 EX SFS G 1914
402 Assigned S. Lorain for work and freight trailer hauling. 403 used at Fremont-Ballville. Center cab (3W), stored 1932															
404	Flat Cab	LSE	1910		DE	B&S F	4 WH76 75hp	K64 D			41'9"	18:64	36"	Scrap 1939	On TFN mort. ctr cab (3W); Ex LSE H in 1914
405	ST Loco	Taunton	1918	DE		McGuire	4 GE57A 50hp	K35-GR2			14'		33"	Scrap 1938	Air brakes
405 assigned to B. P. power house to 1925. Then to Cleveland freight switcher.															
406	DT Work	American	1895	DE		Brill 27E	4 GE57A 50hp	K35-GR2			34'5.5"		33"	R 1938	LSRR 406 ex LSRR 85 1919
Heavily rebuilt															
407	Flat Cab	LSE	1922		DE	Brill 27A2	4 WH76 75hp	K64 D		69500	40'11"	18:64	36"	Scrap 1940	End cab wrecker.
Pulled 410 after 1932. Trucks etc from 60-1927. Earlier trucks etc unknown.															
408	Flat-stl	LSE	1923		DE	MCB	Trailer		40000	34000	36'10"		33"	R 1939	Drop ctr for transformer haul
409	Flat-stl	Jewett	1918		DE	MCB	Trailer		60000	37500	60'2"		33"	R 1939	Ex LSE 175 1930.
From passenger car for container service but used as work car.															
410	DT Flat	LSE	1932		DE	MCB	Trailer		60000		36'10"		33"	Scrap 1940	5-ton elec. crane on flat car
441	ST Loco	LSE			DE	Brill 21E	2 WH 3 30hp	K12			14'4"		33"	Scrap 1939	Shop switcher Fremont car barn
442	Rail bond													R by 1933	ST rail bonder ok 1907
443														R by 1933	Wiring car or sub station no info
444	ST Loco	LSE	1912		DE	Dupont	Lorain C 30hp	K2			21'8"		36"	Scrap 1938	Stored by 1933
High water car at Fremont. Originally pulled 79.															
445														R by 1933	Cement car ok 1914
446	DT Flat	LSE	1916		DE	Armour MCB	Trailer				38'2.5"		33"	Sold 1938	Weed spray car sold to OPS.
6000 gallon tank. ok in 1946															
451	Line car	Brill	1898		DE	Brill 27E	4 GE57A 50hp	K35-GR2		42000	42'6"	18:64	36"	Scrap 1931	Assigned Beach Park 1914-31; Ex LSE 59-1914
452	Line car	LSE	1914		DE	Brill 27A2	4 WH76 75hp	K35-GR2			39'1"	18:64	36"	R 1938	Assigned Freemont 1914-1931
452 became Fremont wrecker in 1931. 451 and 452 switched trucks in 1927. Final truck assignment shown above															
453	Line car	Jewett	1901		DE	Brill 27E	4 WH76 75hp	K35-GR2			42'	24:58	36"	R 1939	Ex LSE 39 1917
453 received trucks & motors from 66(II) in 1928. Orig. had Peckham 14AXX trucks & 4 Lorain 34 motors (50hp). Assigned Sandusky1917-1932; Beach Park 1932-38															
454	Line car	LSE	1914		DE	Brill 27E	4 GE57A 50hp	K35-GR2			39'1"	24:58	36"	R 1938	LSRR. Asgn So. Lorain 1914-38
455-456	Line car	Brill	1903		DE	Brill 27A2	4 WH76 75hp	K35-GR2		74000	52'2"	24:58	36"	R 1938 &40	Ex LSE 62 & 63 1931
455 assigned Beach Park 1931, assigned Sandusky 1932-1938. 456 assigned Fremont 1931-1938															
500-507	Dump	Rogers	1907	DE		ACF			60000	30000	36'10"		33"	See note	Ballast dump car
503(II)	Dump	Rogers	1907	DE		ACF			60000	30000	36'10"		33"	See note	Ballast dump car
All SFS owned. SFS 500 to SFS 503(II) in 1929. Retired by 1929: 501-503 & 507. Scrapped 1938: 504-506 & 503(II).															

Work Equipment 1901-1940 (continued)

Car #	Type	Builder	Date	DE/SE	Trucks	Motors	Control	Seats/Cap'y	Weight (lbs)	Length o/a	Gear Ratio	Wheel Diam	Disposition	Remarks
508-511	Dump			DE	MCB			60000				33"	Scrap 1930	Ballast dump

Second hand, builder unknown. Aquired by LSE 1909

Car #	Type	Builder	Date	DE/SE	Trucks	Motors	Control	Seats/Cap'y	Weight (lbs)	Length o/a	Gear Ratio	Wheel Diam	Disposition	Remarks
600-609	Flat	Haskell	1909	DE	MCB	Trailer		60000		36'11"		33"	See note	See note

Stake pocket flats with sides for gondola use. 600 Scrapped 1938. 601-603 scrapped 1939. Remainder retired before 1933

Fostoria and Fremont Equipment 1909-1932

Car #	Type	Builder	Date	DE/SE	Trucks	Motors	Control	Seats/Cap'y	Weight (lbs)	Length o/a	Gear Ratio	Wheel Diam	Disposition	Remarks
40-41	Comb	Kuhlman	1922	SE	Brill 177E 1	4 GE265 35hp	GE K35	48	32462	45'1	62:21	26"	R 1932	Reversed(to one man)1930

Steel cars identical to Western Ohio Ry 50-57. Both stored LSE Fremont 1932. Out by 1934.

Car #	Type	Builder	Date	DE/SE	Trucks	Motors	Control	Seats/Cap'y	Weight (lbs)	Length o/a	Gear Ratio	Wheel Diam	Disposition	Remarks
241, 245	Comb	B&S	1896	SE	?	?	?	?	?	?	?	?	R 1923	Wrecked and stored 1914
243	Comb	B&S	1896	SE	?	?	?	?	?	?	?	?	R 1923	

241, 243 & 245 built for Columbia and Maryland. Diverted to Union Traction of Indiana. Sold to F&F1911

Car #	Type	Builder	Date	DE/SE	Trucks	Motors	Control	Seats/Cap'y	Weight (lbs)	Length o/a	Gear Ratio	Wheel Diam	Disposition	Remarks
2 cars	DT Open	?	?	?	?	?	?	12 bench	?	?	?	?	R 1915	From Fremont St Ry 1909
50-51	Frt	WO	?	?	Peckham	?	?	?	?	?	?	?	R 1932, 1928	

50 had monitor deck roof and double center doors. 51 had railroad roof and single center door.

Car #	Type	Builder	Date	DE/SE	Trucks	Motors	Control	Seats/Cap'y	Weight (lbs)	Length o/a	Gear Ratio	Wheel Diam	Disposition	Remarks
150	Frt	WO	?	?	Peckham	?	?	-	?	?	?	?	Sold 1932	Ex WO 150

150 had arch roof . To Ohio Power Co. Ballville plant 1932-1953. Scrap 1965

Car #	Type	Builder	Date	DE/SE	Trucks	Motors	Control	Seats/Cap'y	Weight (lbs)	Length o/a	Gear Ratio	Wheel Diam	Disposition	Remarks
159	Frt	WO	?	?	?	?	?	-	?	?	?	?	R 1932	Ex WO 159

Roster— Lake Shore Electric Railway—Predecessor companies

Toledo Fremont & Norwalk

Car #	Type	Builder	Date	DE/SE	Trucks	Motors	Control	Seats	Length o/a	Disposition	Remarks
1-12	Pass.	B&S	1900	SE	B&S	2 WH76 75hp	K-13	60	50'8.5"	To LSE 1-12	
13	Pass.	B&S	1900	SE	B&S	2 WH76 75hp	K-13	60	50'8.5"	To LSE 8000	
14-16,21	Pass.	B&S	1900	SE	B&S	2 WH76 75hp	K-13	60	50'8.5"	To LSE 14-16, 21	
17-20,22	Pass	B&S	1900	SE	B&S	None	None	60	50'8.5"	To LSE 17-20, 22	Not used by T F & N

These cars all had open rear platform, RR roof and no toilet

Car #	Type	Builder	Date	DE/SE	Trucks	Motors	Control	Seats	Length o/a	Disposition	Remarks
31-33	Freight	B&S	1900	SE	B&S	2 WH76 75hp	K-13		50'10"	To LSE 31-33	Arch Roof
41	Work	B&S	1900	DE	B&S		K-13		36'0"	To LSE "K"	

All motor cars had 2 motors on rear truck

Lorain and Cleveland

Car #	Type	Builder	Date	DE/SE	Trucks	Motors	Control	Seats	Length o/a	Disposition	Remarks
1	Pass	?	?	DE	Brill 21	2 GE800 27hp	K-2	?	16' Body	To LSE 120	Ex-E Lorain St Ry (1896)
?	Open	?	?	DE	Peck 70	See note	See note	8 Bench		To LSE 200	Ex-E Lorain St Ry (1896)

These two cars exchanged motors and controls in summer and winter. Car 1 from Northern Electric Ry Co (Chicago) 1896

Car #	Type	Builder	Date	DE/SE	Trucks	Motors	Control	Seats	Length o/a	Disposition	Remarks
64	Pass	Brill	1898	SE	Brill 27E	4 GE57A 50hp	B-9 Magnetic	42	42'6"	To LSE 50	L&C number in CP&E series
10-17	Pass	Brill	1896	SE	Brill 27E	4 GE57A 50hp	B-9 Magnetic	42	42'6"	To LSE 51-57	Only seven cars.
18-19	Pass	Brill	1898	SE	Brill 27E	4 GE57A 50hp	B-9 Magnetic	42	42'6"	To LSE 58-59	
55-56	Combine	Brill	1898	SE	Brill 27E	4 GE57A 50hp	B-9 Magnetic	34	42'9"	To LSE 40-41	L&C number in CP&E series
J	Work	Brill	1897	DE	Brill 27E	4 GE57A 50hp	B-9 Magnetic	-	30'0"	To LSE "J"	

Roster— Lake Shore Electric Railway—Predecessor companies

Sandusky and Inter-Urban

Car #	Type	Builder	Date	SE/DE	Trucks	Motors	Control	Seats	Length o/a	Disposition	Remarks
25-27	Pass	Jewett	1900	DE	Peck14AXX	4 Lorain 34 40hp	Lorain #43	48	42'6"	To LSE 43 & 44	Gamma (27) never got LSE number

These three cars also named respectively Alpha, Beta & Gamma on the S&I

Either 25 or 27 was a combination car with dimensions same as S&I 30

Car #	Type	Builder	Date	SE/DE	Trucks	Motors	Control	Seats	Length o/a	Disposition	Remarks
28	Freight	Jewett	1901	DE	Peck14AXX	4 Lorain 34 40hp	Lorain #43	-	43'0"	To LSE 39	Named Delta on S & I
29	Pass	Jewett	1901	DE	Peck14AXX	4 Lorain 34 40hp	Lorain #43	48	42'6"	Toledo & Western 1901	
30	Combine	Jewett	1901	DE	Peck14AXX	4 Lorain 34 40hp	Lorain #43	40	42'0"	Toledo & Western 1901	
4 cars	ST Pass	?	?	DE	Brill 13	2 Walker#4			16' Body	To LSE 109-112*	
3 cars	ST Pass	?	?	DE	Brill 21	2 Walker#4			16' Body	To LSE 113-115	
3 cars	ST Open	?	?	DE	McGuire	**	**	9-Bench		To LSE 204 & 205	

*These cars were renumbered in the books only, never so painted. All single truck cars originally Sandusky Street Ry 1-24 series

**Open cars used motors and controls of the closed cars in season. Third open car not used by LSE

Sandusky, Norwalk & Southern

Car #	Type	Builder	Date	SE/DE	Trucks	Motors	Control	Seats	Length o/a	Disposition	Remarks
5	Express	Jewett	1893	DE	McGuire 20	2 WH 3 20hp	2 WH D		38'	Not used by LSE	Ex-SM & N
7	Combine	Jewett	1893	DE	McGuire 20	2 WH 3 20hp	2 WH D	30	38'	To LSE not renumber	Ex-SM & N
4	ST Pass	Pullman	1898	DE	McGuire	2 WH 3 20hp	2 WH D			To LSE 101	Ex-SM & N 17
9	Combine	Jewett	1893	DE	McGuire 20	2 WH 3 20hp	2 WH D	30	38'	To LSE 42	Ex-SM & N
11-12	Pass	Jewett	1893	DE	McGuire 20	2 WH 3 20hp	2 WH D	40	38'	To LSE not renumber	12 was SM & N 13
15	ST Pass	Jewett	1893	DE	McGuire	2 WH 3 20hp	2 WH D			To LSE 102	Ex-SM & N
?	ST Work	?	?	DE	?	?	?			To LSE 100	Ex-SM & N
6 cars	ST Pass	?	?	DE	Brill #7	2 WH 3 20hp	2 WH D		16' Body	To LSE 103-108	

Orig. Peoples Railway 2,4,6,8,14 &16. 14 &16 orig. double deck.

LSE 103,104,105, & 108 used by LSE but numbers were "books only"

Car #	Type	Builder	Date	SE/DE	Trucks	Motors	Control	Seats	Length o/a	Disposition	Remarks
2 cars	ST Open	?	?	DE	**	**		8-Bench		To LSE 201-202	Ex-Peoples Ry 10 & 20
1 car	ST Open	?	?	DE	**	**		10-Bench		To LSE 203	Ex-Peoples Ry 18

Open cars shared trucks, motors, and controls with single truck Peoples Ry cars

Car #	Type	Builder	Date	SE/DE	Trucks	Motors	Control	Seats	Length o/a	Disposition	Remarks
	ST Plow	Taunton								To LSE "C"	ex-SM & N

Abbreviations used in these Rosters

Equipment

ACF American Car & Foundry Company
American American Car Company, St Louis, Mo.
B&S The Barney & Smith Car Company, Dayton, Ohio
Bald Baldwin Locomotive Works, Philadelphia, Pa.
Brill The J. G. Brill Company, Philadelphia, Pa
Cincinnati Cincinnati Car Company, Cincinnati, Ohio
Dupont A. B. DuPont, designer
Fruehauf Fruehauf Corporation
GE General Electric Company Schenectady, N.Y.
Haskell Haskell Car Works, Michigan City, In.
Jewett Jewett Car Company, Newark, Ohio
Kuhl G. C. Kuhlman Car Company, Cleveland, Ohio
LSE Lake Shore Electric Railway, Cleveland , Ohio
MCB Master Car Builder
McGuire McGuire-Cummings Manufacturing Company
Niles Niles Car Company, Niles, Ohio
Peck Peckham Truck Company, Kingston, N. Y.
Pullman Pullman Company, Chicago, IL
Rodger Rodger Ballast Car Co.., Chicago, IL
St Louis St Louis Car Company, St Louis, Mo.
Standard Standard Motor Truck Company, New Castle, Pa.
Stephenson John Stephenson Company, Elizabeth, N.J.
Taunton Taunton Locomotive Works, Taunton, Mass.
Taylor Taylor Electric Truck Company, Troy, N. Y.
WH Westinghouse Electric and Manufacturing Co.

Railroads

CERA Central Electric Railway Association
CP&E The Cleveland Painesville & Eastern Railroad Co.
CSW The Cleveland Southwestern Railway & Light Co.
L&C Lorain & Cleveland Railway
LSE Lake Shore Electric Railway Co.
LSRR Lorain Street Railroad
LSRY Lorain Street Railway
Mich Ry Michigan Railway Co.
NOT&L Northern Ohio Traction & Light Co.
OPS Ohio Public Service Co. (Pt. Clinton Division)
PRy Peoples Ry
S&IE Sandusky & Inter-Urban Electric Railway
SFS Sandusky Fremont & Southern Railway
SM&N Sandusky Milan & Norwalk Electric Ry.
SN&S Sandusky Norwalk & Southern Ry
SS Sandusky Street Railway
T&W Toledo & Western Railway Co.
TBG&S Toledo Bowling Green & Southern Traction Co.
TF&N Toledo Fremont & Norwalk Street Ry.
WO Western Ohio Railroad
W&LE Wheeling & Lake Erie Ry (steam)
WJ&SSRR West Jersey & Seashore Railroad Co.

Miscellaneous

SE Single end
DE Double end
OM One Man
MU Multiple Unit

Lake Shore Coach Company Equipment Roster 1925-1939

LSC Number	Previous Owner Year to LSC	Builder	Type	Year Built	Serial Number	Seats	Scrap/Retire or Sold	Remarks
100-101	-	-	-	-	--	-	-	Not accepted by LSC from C-L-S
102	C-L-S 1927	White	50A	?	?	22 pass	R 1938	Bender body
150	C-L-S 1927	White	50A	1924	?	21 pass	R 1928	Traded in for 105
151	C-L-S 1927	White	50A	1924	?	21 pass	SO 1929	Replaced by 106. Sold to LEP&L for truck
152	C-L-S 1927	White	50A	1924	?	21 pass	R 1928	
153	-	-	-	-	?	-	-	Not accepted by LSC from C-L-S
154	C-L-S 1927	White	50A	1924	?	22 pass	SO 1929	Replaced by 107 Sold to LEP&L for truck
155	C-L-S 1927	White	50A	1924	?	22 pass	SO 1929	Replaced by 108 Sold to LEP&L for truck
156	C-L-S 1927	White	50A	1924	?	22 pass	R 1928	Traded in for 103
157	C-L-S 1927	White	50A	1924	?	22 pass	R 1938	Schafter body. Stored 1932-1935
158	C-L-S 1927	White	50A	1924	?	22 pass	R 1928	Traded in for 104
Clydesdale	C-L-S 1927	Clydesdale	?	?	?	?	SO 1928	Sold to LSRR for line truck T25
101(II)	CSW 1931	Studebaker	?	?	?	22 pass	R 1935	Superior body
103	New	White	53	1928	137994	24 pass	OK 1939	Bender body for interurban use.
104	New	White	53	1928	139330	24 pass	OK 1939	Bender body for interurban use.
105	New	White	53	1928	156708	24 pass	OK 1939	Bender body for interurban use.
106-108	New	Yellow Coach	W C 331	1929	130501-3	21 pass	OK 1939	For Sandusky city
109-112	New	Yellow Coach	733	Apr 1938	?	21 pass	OK 1939	For Lorain and Sandusky city
LSCL 120-122	New	Yellow Coach	739	Jan 1938	?	23 pass	OK 1939	Interurban use Ceylon Jct to Clyde
150(II)-158(II)	New	Yellow Coach	742	May 1938	?	?	OK 1939	Interurban use
159	New	Yellow Coach	742	May 1938	?	?	OK 1939	Interurban use
160-162	New	Yellow Coach	742	Sept 1938	110-112	?	OK 1939	Interurban use
LSE B-1 & B-2	New	White	50A	1925	?	?	R 1938	For E. Erie(Lorain)
LSE B-3	2nd hand 1925	White	50A	1922	?	?	R 1938	For E. Erie(Lorain)
LSC 253	CT 1938	White	65	1930	?	21 pass	OK 1939	Leased then bought
LSC 552	CT 1938	White	54	1928	?	33 pass	OK 1939	Bender body. Leased, then bought
LSC 559	CT 1938	White	54	1928	?	33 pass	OK 1939	Bender body. Leased, then bought
CT 254	CT 1938	White	65	1930	?	21 pass	-	Leased 1938 for one week only
CT 551 & 553	CT 1938	White	54	1924	?	33 pass	-	Bender body leased 1938 only

253 returned to Community Traction (Toledo, OH) after purchase and 551 substituted in 1939.

C-L-S	Cleveland Lorain & Sandusky Bus Co.	LSC Lake Shore Coach Co.
CSW	Cleveland Southwestern Bus Co.	LSCL Lake Shore Coach Lines, Inc.
CT	Community Traction Co., Toledo, OH	LSE Owned by Lake Shore Electric
LEP&L	Lake Erie Power & Light Co.	LSRR Lorain Street Railraod

APPENDIX 2

Carbarns, Shops,
Power Houses, and Substations

Carbarns and Shops

Each of the LSE's five predecessors built its own central operating complex consisting of a power house, car shop, and car storage facilities. All of these were taken over by the LSE in 1901, and all but one of them served the railway until its last days. Always economy-minded, the Lake Shore itself never built a new car shop of its own. In 1902 it planned a carhouse on Whittlesey Avenue in Norwalk, and after the Fremont barn was seriously damaged by fire on October 16, 1906, it announced that it would build a large new shop there. Neither materialized, and the company managed to spread various construction and repair functions among the old facilities.

Beginning in 1903, heavy repairs and new construction work were concentrated primarily at Sandusky and secondarily at Fremont; the other carhouses handled only storage, light repairs, and servicing. The five were:

Beach Park
Built by Lorain & Cleveland 1897; located at Stop 65 in Avon Lake. Brick carhouse 65.5´×200´, with 12´×12´ brick oil house. Carhouse included passenger facilities.

Sandusky
Built by Sandusky & Interurban 1899 at southeast corner of Columbus and Perkins Avenues. Originally stone carhouse 120´×200´; later rebuilt and expanded to two sections, 50´×250´ and 100´×125´. Complex also included a 40´×125´ brick storeroom building and, later, a 36´×51´ concrete bus garage.

Fremont
Built by Toledo, Fremont & Norwalk 1900 near southwest corner of E. State and 5th Streets. Three adjoining brick buildings totaling 141´×214´.

South Lorain
Built by Lorain Street Ry. 1894 on northeast corner of 28th and Seneca Streets; expanded later and acquired by LSE in 1906. Brick inspection and maintenance shop 36´×227´ and brick car storage barn 36´×185´, with 20´×40´ brick offices, crew quarters, and waiting room in between.

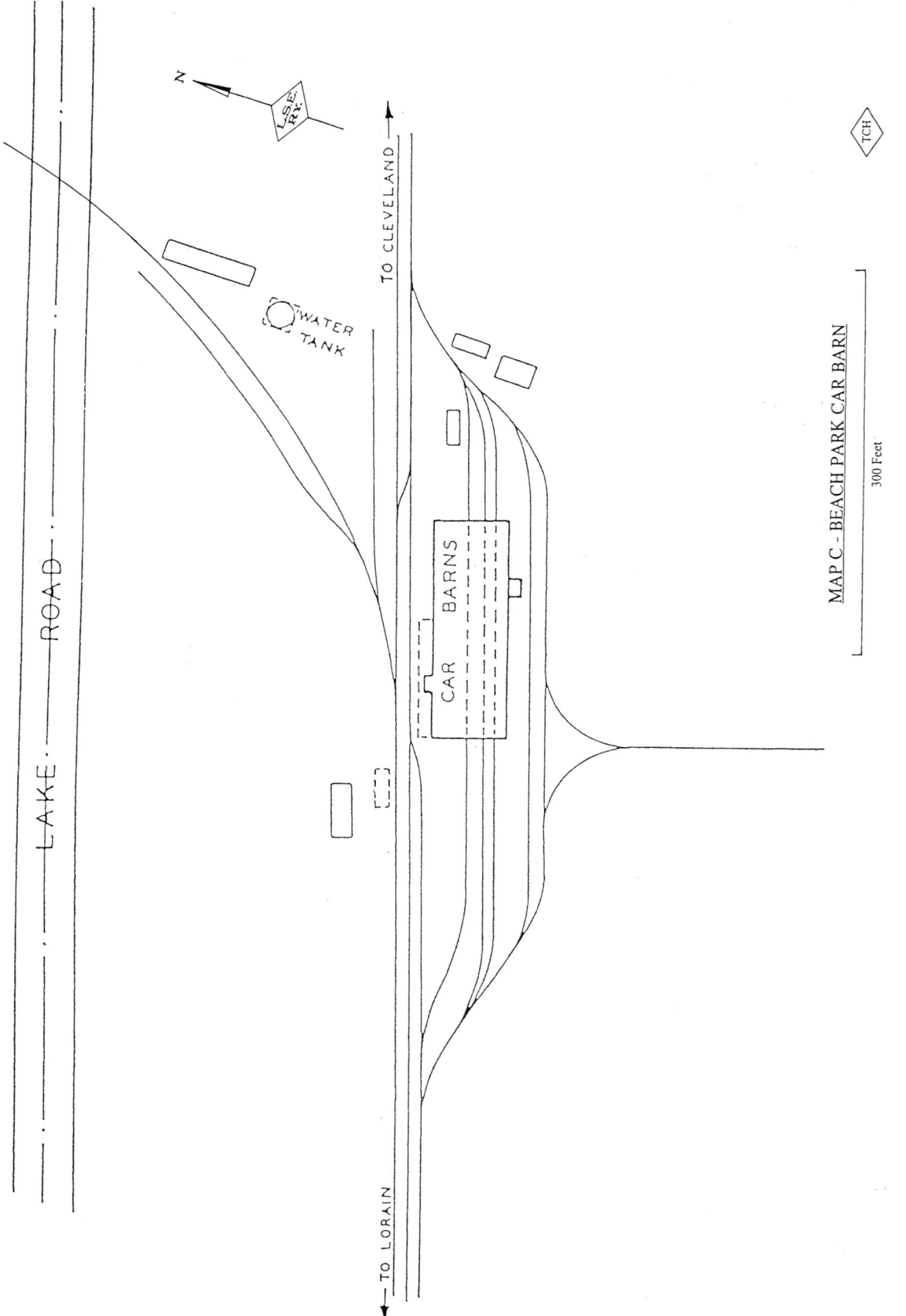

MAP C - BEACH PARK CAR BARN

300 Feet

Beach Park (Tom Heinrich)

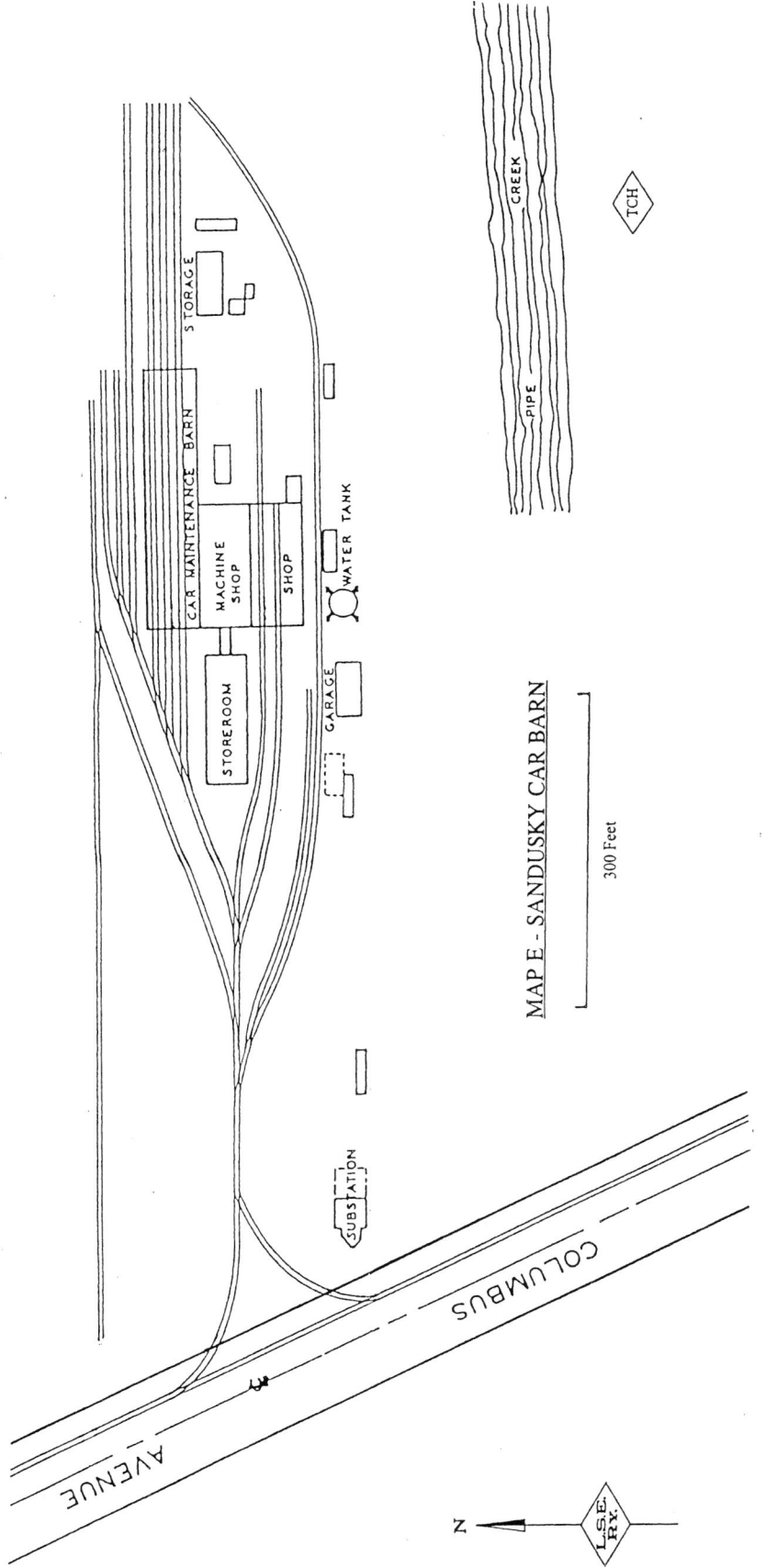

MAP E - SANDUSKY CAR BARN

300 Feet

Sandusky (Tom Heinrich)

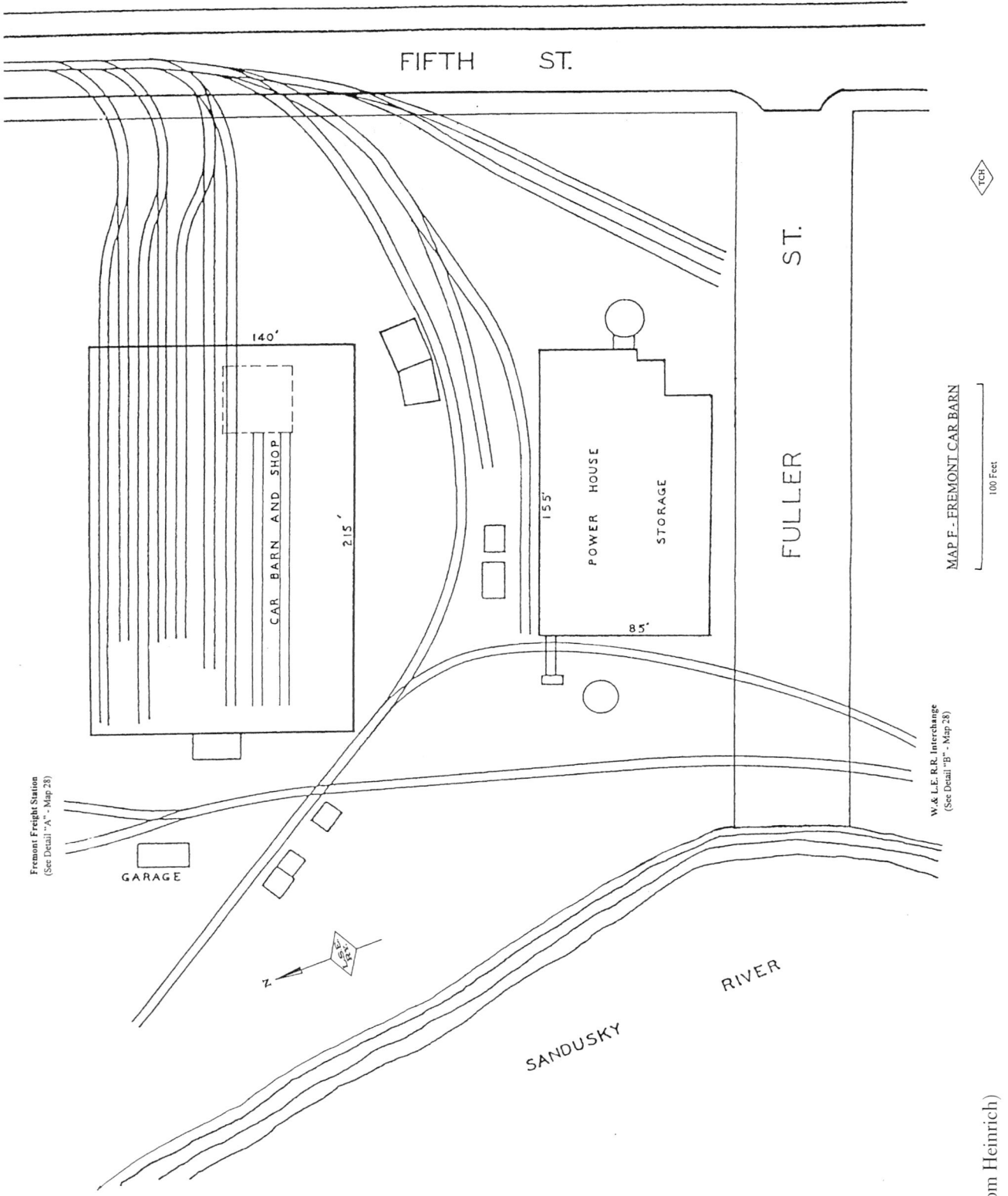

FIFTH ST.

FULLER ST.

140'

215'

CAR BARN AND SHOP

155'

POWER HOUSE

STORAGE

85'

GARAGE

Fremont Freight Station
(See Detail "A" - Map 28)

W.& L.E. R.R. Interchange
(See Detail "B" - Map 28)

SANDUSKY RIVER

N

MAP F - FREMONT CAR BARN

100 Feet

Fremont (Tom Heinrich)

Lorain city operations were based at the 1894 Lorain Street Railroad carhouse on 28th Street at Seneca in South Lorain, shown here in the early 1900s. (John A. Rehor collection)

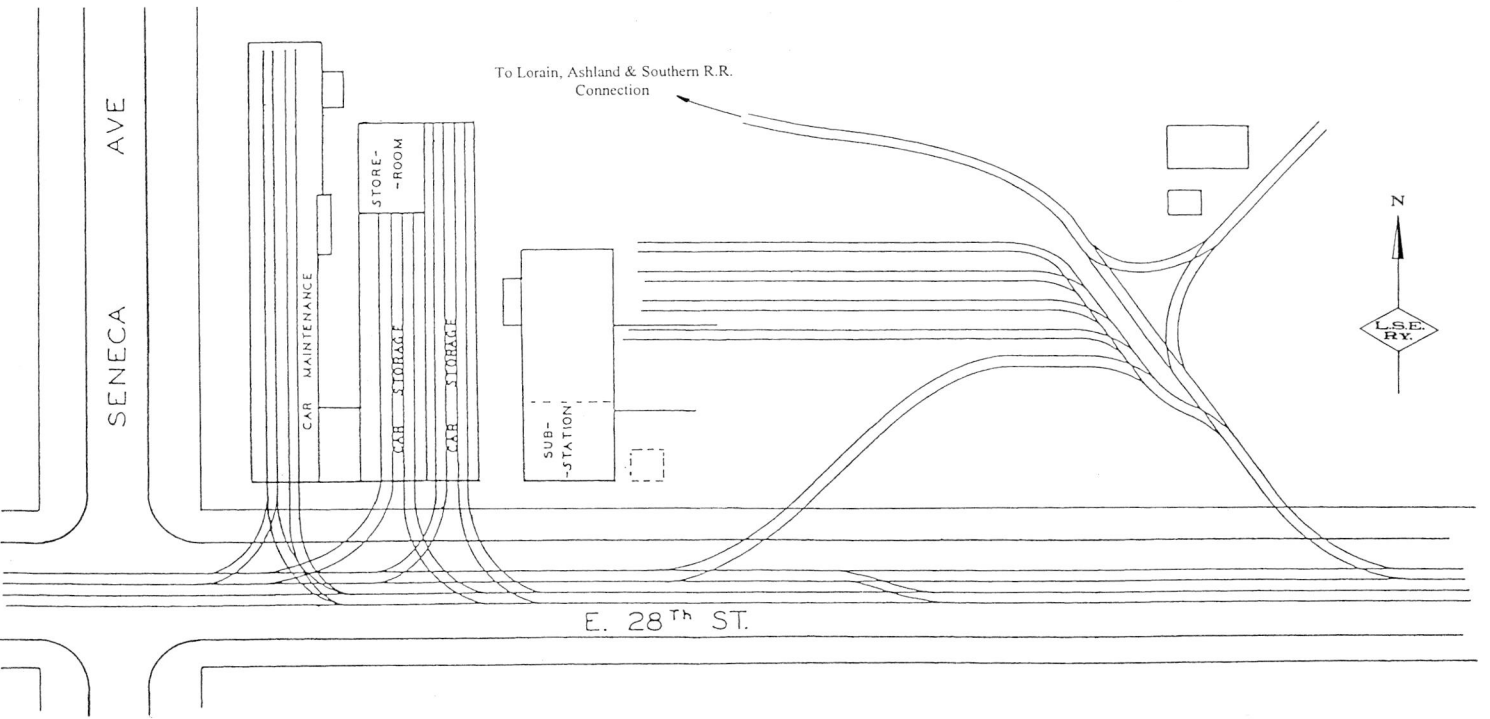

To Lorain, Ashland & Southern R.R. Connection

SENECA AVE

CAR MAINTENANCE

STORE-ROOM

CAR STORAGE

CAR STORAGE

SUB-STATION

E. 28TH ST.

N

L.S.E. RY.

MAP D - SOUTH LORAIN CAR BARN
Lorain Street Railroad

200 Feet

TCH

South Lorain (Tom Heinrich)

The Sandusky, Milan &
Norwalk built its carhouse
and power house in the
Huron River valley just
north of Milan and adjacent
to the Wheeling & Lake
Erie's Huron branch. This
view looks north in 1893.
(H. C. Morrison photo)

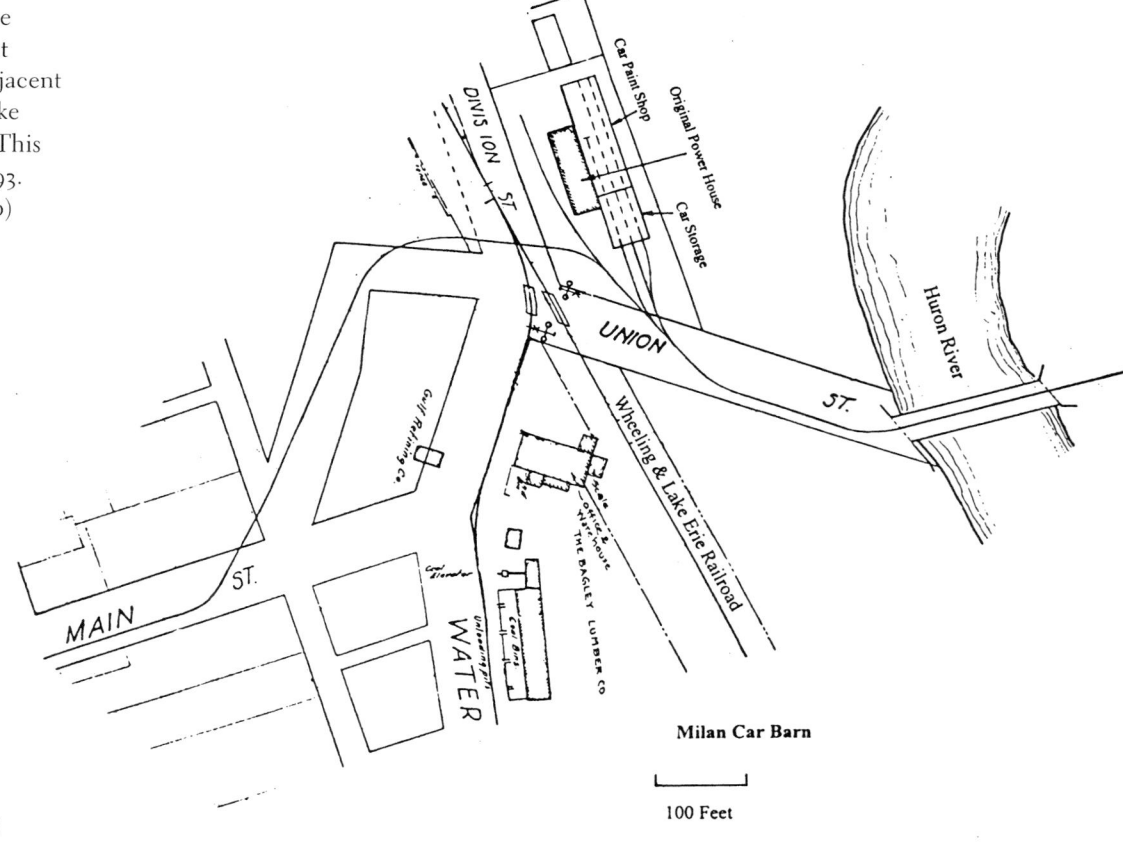

Milan (Tom Heinrich)

Milan

Built by Sandusky, Milan & Norwalk 1893 at northwest corner of Sandusky Road and Division Street. Frame carhouse 38´×200´. Used as carbarn and paint shop until September 31, 1921, then as paint shop only until March 1, 1927.

Early Carhouses

During the late nineteenth century, four LSE predecessors had carhouses which were abandoned before the LSE's formation. These were:

Sandusky Street Ry.: SE corner Hayes Ave. and N. Depot St. (1883–1899)
People's Ry.: 60´×100´ brick carhouse at Lawrence and W. Market Sts. (1889–1901)
East Lorain Street Ry.: Wood shed at SE corner E. Erie and Root Rd. (1896–1898)
Lorain Street Ry.: Horse car barn, Broadway at 21st St. (c. 1887–1894)

Power Houses

The Lake Shore Electric's predecessors followed the contemporary practice of building their own steam-operated power houses because most commercial plants of the time were of limited capacity. As technology improved and commercial generating capacity substantially increased, these plants became uneconomic and technologically obsolete, and were phased out in favor of cheaper purchased power. The LSE inherited four such plants, each located near or adjacent to that predecessor's carhouse. Two were shut down soon after acquisition and their loads transferred to Fremont and Beach Park; those in turn were replaced by commercial power in 1916 and 1925 respectively.

Beach Park

Built by Lorain & Cleveland 1897. Original output 625 volts DC; equipment consisted of two 400 kw Siemens-Halske generators connected to Cooper Corliss engines and four 300 hp Stirling boilers with Murphy stokers. Addition built 1906–1907 and plant converted to output of 16,500-volt 25-cycle AC; old generators replaced with Westinghouse turbo-alternator, Parsons turbine, and 3000 hp Babcock & Wilcox boilers. Destroyed in explosion and fire August 23, 1925, and replaced by 60-cycle purchased power from CEI Avon Lake plant.

Fremont

Built by Toledo, Fremont & Norwalk 1900. Output 390 volts AC stepped up to 15,000 volts 25-cycle AC. Original equipment: four 500 kw Westinghouse AC generators connected to four 800 hp Westinghouse enclosed-type engines, with five 300 hp Babcock & Wilcox boilers with Roney stokers. A 2000 hp Westinghouse Parsons turbine added 1906. This power house also supplied power for the TF&F Toledo extension in 1906 and Fostoria & Fremont Ry. in 1911. Last used December 31, 1916; replaced by 60-cycle purchased power from Ballville plant.

Sandusky

Built by Sandusky & Interurban 1899. Output 575 volts DC; equipment consisted of two 400 kw Siemens-Halske generators directly connected to two Russell Corliss engines, with four 300 hp hand-fired Babcock & Wilcox boilers. Closed 1904.

The Lorain & Cleveland's 1897 lakeside power house at Beach Park in Avon Lake supplied power to the LSE's eastern lines until it was destroyed in 1925. It is shown here in its original form in 1902; in 1906–1907 a large addition was built and a second stack added. (Gilbert Hodges photo, John A. Rehor collection)

The Toledo, Fremont & Norwalk's large and modern (for its time) power house on Fremont's east side fed the line's western half until it was replaced by commercial power in late 1916. This 1926 view faces north. (Ralph Sayles collection)

Milan

Built by Sandusky, Milan & Norwalk. Output 525 volts DC; equipment consisted of two 100 kw 4-pole Westinghouse belted generators driven by two McIntosh & Seymour tandem compound engines, with two 150 hp hand-fired Babcock & Wilcox boilers. Last used 1903.

Early Power Houses

Data is sketchy on how LSE's predecessors obtained their power. The People's Railway in Sandusky did generate its own power from a plant at its Lawrence St. carbarn, last used March 27, 1901. At South Lorain, the Lorain Street Ry.'s original 1894 power house consisted of four straight-line engines belted to GE generators and a Buckeye tandem compound engine direct-connected to a Siemens-Haskell generator of 210 rpm. Closing date unknown.

Substations

Originally only the ex-TF&N section of the LSE had substations, fed by the Fremont power house. Others were added systemwide beginning in 1902. The LSE's train operation required substations of greater capacity than the typical interurban railway which operated single cars on hourly headways. Where many lines used 300-kilowatt rotary converters spaced about ten miles apart or more, by the 1920s the LSE had substations averaging every 8.4 miles apart. Some were equipped with two 500 kw converters, some with one 500 kw, while others had two 300 kw machines. The relatively busy 19-mile double-track section between Rocky River and Lorain had four substations, counting the one at North Lorain which had one 100 kw converter and also fed downtown Lorain—an average of one substation each 4.75 miles.

Over the years substations were added and/or locations were changed. Beginning in the early 1920s, some automatic substations were built. As the LSE got into commercial power sales, it also built some substations strictly for non-rail use, which are not included in this listing. Several substation buildings included passenger ticket offices and waiting rooms, and these are noted.

LSE's substation locations were (going west from Cleveland):

Cleveland–Norwalk–Toledo Main Line

Dover Bay, Stop 13 at SW corner of Clague Rd., Bay Village (manual, 1907–38)

Stop 49, SW corner Jaycox Rd., Avon Lake (automatic, 1925–38)

Stop 95, west of Root Rd., Lorain (automatic, 1925–38)

North Lorain, in Ohio Public Service building, First & Hamilton Sts. (manual)

Water Works, north side of Lake Rd. at Lorain west city limit (automatic, c. 1920–25; afterward used only for commercial power)

Vermilion, Liberty & Exchange Sts., with ticket office (manual, 1903–38)

Ceylon Junction (manual, 1901–1903; equipment from Hayes substation; later equipment used only for commercial power)

Berlin Heights, south side of W. Main St., with ticket office (manual, 1903–38; rebuilt after two fires, 6/17/13 and 3/23/19)

Monroeville, at B&O crossing, with ticket office; built by TF&N (manual, 1900–38)

Bellevue, off E. Main St. east of Nickel Plate Road tracks (manual, 1902–38)

Mussers, Stop 225 (manual, 1902–25)

Clyde, Stop 235½; built by TF&N (manual, 1900–38; not always used)

Fremont, in power house; built by TF&N (manual, 1900–38)

Hessville, Stop 288, west of Long Rd.; built by TF&N; with ticket office (manual, 1900–38)

Genoa, SW corner Main & Jefferson Sts.; built by TF&N (manual, 1900–38)

Hayes, Stop 336A; built by TF&N (manual 1900–38; equipment to Ceylon Jct. 1901 but replaced; burned 11/19/23 and rebuilt 1925)

Ceylon Junction–Sandusky–Fremont Line

Huron, on cutoff line between Main and William Sts., with ticket office (1917–38)

Sandusky, originally in shop building; separate building built 1923 (manual, 1899–1938)

Castalia (SF&S), at corner Depot & Norwalk Sts. (semi-automatic, 1926–38; equipment from Whitmore)

Whitmore (SF&S), Stop 443½, east of Pickeral Rd. (manual, 1907–26; equipment to Castalia)

Brugger Road (SF&S), Stop 447 (automatic, 1926–38; equipment from CP&E)

Branches

Milan, Main St. south of Church (1903–28)

South Lorain (LSRR), in former power house at 28th and Seneca (manual; later semi-automatic, 1894–1938)

BIBLIOGRAPHY

Most material for this book was drawn from official documents in various collections noted in the Acknowledgments section, contemporary newspaper reports, and personal interviews. But the following publications were useful in many ways:

Books and Monographs

Blower, James M. *Northern Ohio Traction Revisited.* Akron, Ohio: James M. Blower, 1970.

————, and Robert S. Korach. *The N.O.T.&L. Story* (CERA Bulletin 109). Chicago, Ill.: Central Electric Railfans' Association, 1966.

Brashares, Jeffrey R. *The Cleveland, Southwestern & Columbus Railway Company.* Ohio Interurban Memories, Inc., no address or date shown.

————. *The Story of the Mansfield Transit System.* No publisher or date shown.

Christiansen, Harry. *New Lake Shore Electric.* Lakewood, Ohio: Trolley Lore, 1978.

————. *Northern Ohio's Interurbans and Rapid Transit Railways.* Cleveland, Ohio: Transit Data, Inc., 1965.

————. *Ride the Red Devils along Ohio Trolley Trails.* Euclid, Ohio: Transit House, Inc., 1971.

————. *Trolley Trails through Cleveland and Northern Ohio* (3 volumes). Lakewood, Ohio: Trolley Lore, 1975. (Shown also as published by the Western Reserve Historical Society, Cleveland, Ohio.)

Everett, Glenn D. *The Streetcars and Interurbans of Old Sandusky.* Rutland, Vt.: Academy Books, 1988.

Francis, David W., and Diana D. Francis. *Cedar Point: The Queen of American Watering Places.* Fairview Park, Ohio: Amusement Park Books, Inc., 1995.

Hague, Wilbur E., and Kirk F. Hise. *The Detroit, Monroe & Toledo Short Line Railway.* Forty Fort, Pa.: Harold E. Cox, 1986.

Hilton, George W. *The Toledo, Port Clinton and Lakeside Railway.* Chicago, Ill.: Electric Railway Historical Society, 1964.

————, and John F. Due. *The Electric Interurban Railways in America.* Stanford, Calif.: Stanford University Press, 1960.

Keenan, Jack. *Cincinnati & Lake Erie Railroad: Ohio's Great Interurban System.* San Mateo, Calif.: Golden West Books, 1974.

Moody's Public Utilities Manual, various issues 1925–1935.

Morrison, R.G. *The Sandusky, Milan and Norwalk Electric Railway.* Cleveland, Ohio: self-published, 1963.

Rose, William Ganson. *Cleveland: The Making of a City.* Cleveland, Ohio, and New York, N.Y.: The World Publishing Co., 1950.

Ryan, James A. *The Town of Milan.* Sandusky, Ohio: James A. Ryan, 1928.

Schramm, Jack E., William H. Henning, and Richard R. Andrews. *When Eastern Michigan Rode the Rails: Book 4, Detroit to Wyandotte, Monroe and Toledo. . . .* Polo, Ill.: Transportation Trails, 1994.

Wilcox, Max E. *The Cleveland Southwestern & Columbus Railway Story* (including the Sandusky, Norwalk & Mansfield). No publisher or date shown.

Magazine Articles

"Analysis of the Operation of an Interurban Railway" (Lorain & Cleveland). *Street Railway Journal,* May 1899.

Hess, Robert T. "Lake Shore Electric's Beach Park Power Plant." *Traction & Models,* May 1965.

"Historical Interurban Electric Roads." *Electric Railway Journal,* October 2, 1909.

Keenan, Jack. "Electric Street Railways of Lima: The Formative Years." *Allen County* [Ohio] *Reporter,* Lima, Ohio, 1992.

Korach, Robert S. "Lake Shore Coach." *Motor Coach Age,* April–June, 1997.

"Lake Shore System." *Motor Coach Age,* September 1970.

Miller, Carol Poh. "The Rocky River Bridge: Triumph in Concrete." *IA: The Journal of the Society for Industrial Archeology,* Vol 2, No. 1, 1976.

"The Cleveland and Lorain Railway." *Electrical Engineer,* September 15, 1898.

Periodicals and Newspapers

Bellevue [Ohio] *Gazette, Cleveland Leader,* Cleveland *Plain Dealer, Cleveland Press, Electric Railway Journal, Electric Traction Weekly, Fremont Daily News, Genoa* [Ohio] *Gazette, Lorain* [Ohio] *Herald, Lorain Journal, Lorain Times, Norwalk* [Ohio] *Weekly Reflector, Daily Reflector,* and *Reflector-Herald, Official Guide of the Railways* (various specific titles, 1893–1938), *Sandusky* [Ohio] *Register, Sandusky Star-Journal, Street Railway Journal.*

Selected Major Internal Documents

Joint Agreement for the Consolidation . . . forming the Lake Shore Electric Railway, September 25, 1901.

Circuit Court of the United States for the Northern District of Ohio–Eastern Division, Case No. 6306: Valentine Clark Co. vs. Lake Shore Electric Railway: Inventory of Property, March 27, 1902.

Hodges, Gilbert. Report on the Lake Shore Electric Railway; Gilbert Hodges, Consulting Engineer, Boston, August 1902.

Carpenter, F.D., and J.D. McDonel. Prospectus for The Fostoria–Fremont Railway Line . . . Lima, Ohio, February 8, 1910.

Ohio Inspection Bureau: Report on the Lake Shore Electric Railway, Sandusky, Fremont & Southern Railway, and Lake Erie Power & Light Company, October 1927.

United States District Court for the Northern District of Ohio–Eastern Division, Case No. 4586: Ohio Utilities Finance Co. et al., vs. Lake Shore Electric Railway Company et al., Inventory of Physical Property of the Lake Shore Electric Railway, January 20, 1933.

INDEX

HERBERT H. HARWOOD, JR., has carried on concurrent careers as a railroad historian, writer, photographer, and working railroader. A history graduate of Princeton University, he received his M.B.A. from Columbia University and then spent 30 years in various management positions at the Chesapeake & Ohio and Baltimore & Ohio railroads and their successor, CSX Transportation. He has also authored 11 books on railroad and electric railway history plus numerous articles, and has contributed photos to various other books and articles.

A native of Cleveland, Ohio, ROBERT S. KORACH has had a lifelong fascination with the transportation business and particularly with urban transit and the long-departed interurbans—an interest stimulated by his contacts with the Lake Shore Electric as a child. It led him to a career in the transit business which, after graduation from the University of Wisconsin with a B.S. in Economics, included management positions with the Cleveland Transit System, PATCO's Lindenwold (N.J.) high-speed line (where he was Assistant General Manager), and the Massachusetts Bay Transportation Authority. He retired in 1988 as Assistant General Manager for Operations at the Los Angeles transit system. Korach is past president of the Association of Railway Museums and in 1995 was elected to the American Public Transit Association's Hall of Fame.